Joseph Chamberlain

Joseph Chamberlain

International Statesman, National Leader, Local Icon

Edited by

Ian Cawood
Newman University, UK

Chris Upton
Newman University, UK

JOSEPH CHAMBERLAIN: INTERNATIONAL STATESMAN, NATIONAL LEADER, LOCAL ICON

First published 2016 by
PALGRAVE MACMILLAN

The authors have asserted their rights to be identified as the authors of this work in accordance with the Copyright, Designs and Patents Act 1988.

Palgrave Macmillan in the UK is an imprint of Macmillan Publishers Limited, registered in England, company number 785998, of Houndmills, Basingstoke, Hampshire RG21 6XS.

Palgrave Macmillan in the US is a division of Nature America, Inc., One New York Plaza, Suite 4500 New York, NY 10004–1562.

Palgrave Macmillan is the global academic imprint of the above companies and has companies and representatives throughout the world.

Hardback ISBN: 978–1–137–52884–1
E-PUB ISBN: 978–1–137–52886–5
E-PDF ISBN: 978–1–137–52885–8
DOI: 10.1057/9781137528858

Distribution in the UK, Europe and the rest of the world is by Palgrave Macmillan®, a division of Macmillan Publishers Limited, registered in England, company number 785998, of Houndmills, Basingstoke, Hampshire RG21 6XS.

Library of Congress Cataloging-in-Publication Data
Names: Cawood, Ian, editor, author. | Upton, Christopher, editor, author.
Title: Joseph Chamberlain: international statesman, national leader, local icon / Ian Cawood, Newman University, UK, Chris Upton, Newman University, UK.
Description: New York, NY: Palgrave Macmillan, 2016. | Includes bibliographical references and index.
Identifiers: LCCN 2015035445| ISBN 9781137528841 (hardback) | ISBN 9781137528865 (epub) | ISBN 9781137528858 (epdf)
Subjects: LCSH: Chamberlain, Joseph, 1836–1914. | Statesmen–Great Britain–Biography. | Great Britain–Politics and government–1837–1901. | Great Britain–Politics and government–1901–1936.
Classification: LCC DA565.C4 J67 2016 | DDC 941.08092–dc23
LC record available at http://lccn.loc.gov/2015035445

A catalogue record for this book is available from the Library of Congress.

A catalogue record for the book is available from the British Library.

Typeset by MPS Limited, Chennai, India.

For Chris, who died in the final stages of this project and whose good humour and immense local knowledge made organising the conference and editing this volume together a pleasure and a privilege

Contents

List of Illustrations

Foreword

Birmingham has good reason to thank 'Joe' Chamberlain for the work of his municipal years, but two political parties, the Liberals and the Conservatives, each had good reason to wish he had never darkened their doors.

Joe Chamberlain was a Unitarian. His early life was steeped in the values of this small but hugely influential denomination, which nurtured pioneering scientists, great literary figures and successful entrepreneurs. He was related to the Martineau family, and he imbibed the liberal Christian theology of the Unitarians. He happily made common cause in later years with the Carrs Lane Congregationalists who had the nationally recognised leadership of R.W. Dale. He taught slum children in Sunday school; he promised £200 a year if one of his sons would become a Unitarian Minister. But the *Dictionary of National Biography* makes an interesting comment about the family's business in London. As cordwainers, they made shoes, and soldiers had to be shod. They appreciated the blessings of a belligerent state. One can only speculate as to how far this background made it easier for him to be a Liberal Imperialist than others from a nonconformist background. Chamberlain remained a regular chapel-goer until his 40s, but the tragic death of two of his wives hit him hard. He never left the Unitarian movement, and was a generous supporter of Birmingham's newly built Unitarian Church of the Messiah, even if his attendance became less frequent.

Being a Liberal was part of Chamberlain's upbringing. Being a radical was an outworking of his social concern, itself a product of Unitarian social thought. The fullest statement of his social priorities was in his 1885 'Unauthorised programme'. Although these were causes he was later to pursue at a national level, such as workmen's compensation, he saw the enormous scope to improve the lot of so many of his fellow citizens in Birmingham, a city that had burst into economic life without any inheritance of public facilities from an earlier age. As councillor and mayor, he used city power and the profits of the municipal water undertaking to make Birmingham a habitable city. He was the original pavement politician – a term by which Liberals are derided but of which he would have been proud. Indeed, at the end of his Birmingham civic career he said that he could 'sing his nunc dimittis' and go in peace, because Birmingham had been 'parked, paved, assized, marketed, gas-and-watered and improved'.[1]

I should make clear that Chamberlain was not, in the conventional sense, a Radical Liberal: he was not sufficiently concerned about the dangers of concentrated state or civic power. He was much more interventionist than John Bright. But he gave a new generation of Liberals in cities across Britain an example and an agenda of municipal improvement which has never since been absent from the Liberals or the Liberal Democrats. Late twentieth-century radical Liberals developed it into a doctrine of community politics.

Chamberlain's success depended on a high level of political organisation. He organised to promote elementary education through the National Education League. This evolved into the National Liberal Federation, the direct predecessor of the Liberal Party's modern national structure. The organisational genius was Francis Schnadhorst – a Carrs Lane Congregationalist – who organised the Birmingham Liberal Association and the National Liberal Federation, which itself remained based in Birmingham. This was Chamberlain's machine, the Birmingham part of which he was later to take with him when he went, as the nonconformists might say, in search of foreign gods by leading the Liberal Unionists. His fame spread far and wide, and his entry into national politics, late though it was, had been expected. He looked young for his years, and clearly had 'presence'. I will rely on one witness to this, Beatrice Webb:

> As he rose slowly and stood silently before his people, his whole face and form seemed transformed. The crowd became wild with enthusiasm. At the first sound of his voice they became as one man. Into the tones of his voice he threw the warmth and feeling which were lacking in his words, and every thought, every feeling ... was reflected in the face of the crowd. It might have been a woman listening to the words of her lover.[2]

He looked as if he would go far.

Chamberlain's national political achievements, although creditable in some respects, were dogged by failure and cannot be compared with the scale, innovation and drive of his civic career in Birmingham. His national career was dominated by his belief in and commitment to the Empire, and its capacity to develop economically to the benefit of the UK and the colonies themselves. But that enthusiasm, as well as diverting him away from the cardinal Liberal principle of free trade, also embroiled him in morally ambiguous colonial issues such as those which led to the Boer War. And it drew from him the ludicrous charge that 'A vote for the Liberals is a vote for the Boers.'[3] Campbell-Bannerman said this was 'plumbing the depths of infamy and party malice'.[4] Chamberlain continued to promote social reforms, mostly without success, and greatly imperilled the Liberal cause by his careless use of language. His famous talk of the better-off owing a 'ransom' to the poor threatened to scare off middle-class Liberal voters and wealthy Liberal families. 'What ransom will property pay for the security it enjoys?' was a phrase which was used heavily against him.[5] And he broke with his nonconformist allies in his failure to block the Balfour Education Act, which they hated – in many areas it led to nonconformists refusing to pay their rates, and motivated them to back the Liberals in 1906. Interestingly Chamberlain's influence in Birmingham was still noticeable even in that Liberal landslide, as Unionists held on to all the Birmingham seats.

To have split one party, taking a large number of its MPs and a whole region of its organisation with you, is bad enough. To split two parties suggests unmanageability. This is what Chamberlain did when, unable to accept Gladstone's Home Rule plans and to recognise the aspirations of the majority in Ireland, he joined with the Marques of Hartington in forming the Liberal Unionists. Step by step they moved from temporary independence to a full transfer to what became the Conservative and Unionist Party. But that was not the end of Chamberlain's divisiveness. Opposed as he was to free trade, preferring preferential tariffs for the Empire, he proceeded to split the Conservatives on that issue. It was a battle strangely predictive of the current internal Tory battle over Europe. He lost on both counts. Home Rule eventually came; imperial preference was trounced even in the Conservative party, which now proclaims free trade with only a few dissenters.

So what was Chamberlain's impact on the Liberal Party? With his municipal liberalism and his pavement politics, Chamberlain contributed a powerful and persisting strand to modern Liberalism. With his encouragement and leadership of Birmingham's Liberal political organisation, he helped create the modern election-fighting structures of the Liberal Party, and other parties followed suit. But he produced a deeply damaging split over Home Rule which cost the party many seats and many people. He greatly weakened Liberalism in Birmingham compared with many other cities. He provided, for some middle-class Liberals, a stepping stone to Conservatism at a time when a direct switch from Liberal to Tory would have seemed too disloyal to many. He broke with the fundamental Liberal principle of free trade. Since that also split the Tories, I will leave them to shed the tears on that account. Joseph Chamberlain is more happily remembered not as a national figure, but as the civic leader who made Birmingham a modern city. The university clock tower still known affectionately as 'Joe' looks out over a city which owes him a lot.

Lord Alan Beith, former MP for Berwick-upon-Tweed

Notes

1. Letter from Joseph Chamberlain to Jesse Collings, 6 June 1876, Joseph Chamberlain Papers, Cadbury Research Library, University of Birmingham, JC5/16/54.
2. N. MacKenzie and J. MacKenzie (eds), *The Diary of Beatrice Webb, Vol. 1: 1873–1892* (Cambridge, MA: Harvard University Press, 1983), entry for 16 March 1884, p. 108.
3. The phrase was first used by J.L. Wanklyn in the contest for the constituency of Central Bradford, but it became the unofficial Unionist election slogan. D.C. Somervell, *British Politics since 1900* (London: Andrew Dakers, 1950), p. 12.
4. Herbert Asquith, rather more vigorously, described Chamberlain's behaviour in the election as 'the manners of a cad and tongue of a bargee'. Asquith to Herbert Gladstone, 7 October 1900, Herbert Gladstone Papers, British Library, Add. MSS 45989 f. 427.
5. Speech to the Birmingham Artisans' Association, 5 January 1885, reported in *The Times*, 6 January 1885.

Acknowledgements

The papers in this collection arise from the Joseph Chamberlain Centenary conference held at Newman University, Birmingham and the Library of Birmingham on 4 and 5 July 2014. This conference was held with the financial and organisational assistance of several bodies and individuals whom I would like to take this opportunity to thank: Birmingham City Council, in particular, Councillor John Cotton, the leader of the Council, Sir Albert Bore, and Councillor Phil Davis provided generous support, including valuable discounted rates of venue hire. The research committee of Newman University, in particular, Professor Yahya Nakeeb, Professor Peter Childs, Dr Noelle Plack and John Howard supported the conference enthusiastically from the start. The Liberal Democrat History Group, the Conservative History Group and the Labour History Group provided invaluable publicity and contacts and assisted in facilitating the contribution of Sir Alan Beith, Lord Carrington, Michael Meadowcroft, Greg Clark and Gisela Stuart to the conference. Duncan Brack, editor of the *Journal of Liberal History*, Lord Lexden and Stephen Parkinson of the *Conservative History Journal*, Gisela Stuart, editor of *The House Magazine* and Sarah Probert of the *Birmingham Post* are all owed a debt of thanks for promoting the conference expertly. Mike Gibbs and the editorial team of the journal *History West Midlands* did significant work in promoting the conference by producing a special edition of the journal on the life and career of Chamberlain as well as a professional documentary film, *Joseph Chamberlain: An Icon of Birmingham*, which was premiered on the second day of the conference. *History West Midlands* was also responsible for commissioning the premiere of the *Fanfare for Birmingham*, written by Charlotte Bray and performed by the Birmingham Contemporary Music Group at the start of the second day of the conference. I was particularly thankful for the generous assistance of those who acted as chairs for the panels at the conference: Professor Vernon Bogdanor, Professor Stuart Ball, Professor Peter Childs and Dr Malcolm Dick. I am also grateful for the support of the conference's sponsor, Severn Trent Water and to Kevin Griffiths for having arranged this. Graham CopeKoga of the *History and Policy* briefing organisation recorded the whole conference, which has proved very helpful in preparing this volume.

I am very grateful to all the delegates who gave papers at the conference including those for which there was not enough space to include in this collection. Graham Goodlad, Naomi Lloyd-Jones, Andrew Reekes, Henrietta Lockhart of the Birmingham Museums Trust, Matthew Schofield, Martin Killeeen, Pete Bounous and Stephen Roberts all contributed excellent papers which helped to make the conference such a success.

The staff of the wonderful new Library of Birmingham, in particular, Rachel MacGregor and Fiona Tait of the Archives and Heritage Service and the conference team at the Studio Theatre, made the second day of the conference particularly successful. Many thanks are also due to the work of the staff of Newman University, especially the conference administrator, Emma Board, my students who generously gave their time to act as conference support staff and the marketing team, in particular Andrea Dalglish, Liz Laidlaw, Colin Harris, Hayley Barry and Roger Simmonds. The conference dinner at Highbury Hall added a wonderful dimension to the conference experience and I am very grateful for the professionalism and care with which the civic catering team, led by Claire Cadby, entertained delegates.

I am also grateful to the support of Clare Mence of Palgrave Macmillan and her successors Emily Russell and Angharad Bishop, in the commissioning and production of this volume. Edited collections are ticklish things to coordinate and they have allowed a virgin editor considerable liberties.

Finally, the conference could not have succeeded without the unparalleled expertise of Professor Peter Marsh, the world's leading Chamberlain scholar who acted as the calm centre to the conference, benignly smiling as academics, enthusiasts and politicians constantly quoted his words and tried to meet his high standards.

Notes on Contributors

Lord Alan Beith is a member of the Liberal History Group and former member of Parliament for Berwick-upon-Tweed. He was the longest-serving Liberal Democrat MP and was deputy leader of the Liberal Democrat party between 1992 and 2003.

Oliver Betts is an early career researcher at the University of York where he gained his PhD on working-class homes in urban communities, 1870–1918.

Tom Brooking is professor of history at the University of Otago, New Zealand. His most recent major books are *Making a New Land: Environmental Histories of New Zealand* (2013), edited with Eric Pawson; *Unpacking the Kists: The Scots in New Zealand* (2013), co-authored with Brad Patterson and Jim McAloon; and a monograph on the life of Richard John Seddon entitled *Richard Seddon: King of God's Own* (2014).

Ian Cawood is head of history and reader in modern history at Newman University. He is author of *The Liberal Unionist Party 1886–1912: A History* (2012), a number of scholarly articles on Victorian political culture and is a reviewer for journals such as the *Times Literary Supplement* and *English Historical Review*.

James Dixon is a retired chartered accountant, great-great-grandson of George Dixon and author of *Out of Birmingham: George Dixon (1820–98) – 'Father of Free Education'* (2013).

Jackie Grobler is senior lecturer in history and heritage and cultural tourism at the University of Pretoria, South Africa. His many publications include *The War Reporter. The Anglo–Boer War through the eyes of the Burghers* (2004) and *Decisive Clash: A Short History of Black Protest Politics in South Africa, 1875–1976* (1988).

Peter Marsh is emeritus professor of history at Syracuse University and honorary professor of history at the University of Birmingham. His publications include *The Discipline of Popular Government* (1978), *Joseph Chamberlain: Entrepreneur in Politics* (1994) and *The Chamberlain Litany* (2010).

T.G. Otte is professor of diplomatic and international history at the University of East Anglia. He is the author of *The Foreign Office Mind: The Making of British Foreign Policy 1865–1914* (2011) and co-editor of *By-elections in Victorian and Edwardian Politics, 1832–1914* (2013).

Roland Quinault is a senior research fellow at the Institute of Historical Research, University of London and a former honorary secretary of the Royal Historical Society. He is the author of *British Prime Ministers and Democracy, from Disraeli to Blair* (2011) and co-editor of *William Gladstone: New Studies and Perspectives* (2012).

Eleanor Tench is a postgraduate research student at the University of Plymouth currently writing a thesis on the career of Leonard Courtney.

Chris Upton is reader in public history at Newman University, author of *A History of Birmingham* (1993), *A History of Wolverhampton* (1998), *A History of Lichfield* (2001), *Living Back to Back* (2005) and is a regular columnist for the *Birmingham Post*.

Andy Vail is a postgraduate research student in the Centre for War Studies at the University of Birmingham studying the history of Christianity.

Introduction
Did Joseph Chamberlain Really 'Make the Weather'?

Peter Marsh

Looking back in the next generation, Winston Churchill recalled Joseph Chamberlain as 'incomparably the most live, sparkling, insurgent, compulsive figure in British affairs' at the end of the nineteenth century. He was 'the one', said Churchill, 'who made the weather'.[1] Joseph Chamberlain was then Colonial Secretary, in effect chief minister of the British Empire. He gave voice to the imperialist sentiments that surged through Britain and parts of the British Empire as he widened its already global reach. Over the previous dozen years he had prevented Ireland from receiving a generous measure of Home Rule, a threat as he saw it to the cohesion of the United Kingdom. Meanwhile he set the pace of national debate on social reform, attempting to apply the low-cost principles of his scheme of workmen's compensation for industrial accidents to the more important but more expensive subject of old-age pensions.[2]

But, by the time he died on the eve of the First World War, Chamberlain's accomplishments were already receding. His initiatives had been either repudiated by the electorate or superseded by his political opponents. Only in the local arena where forty years earlier he made his debut as mayor of Birmingham did his achievement prove substantially enduring. Even there the essential preconditions for his achievement were to be eroded through the rest of the twentieth century. Yet remarkably in the opening yeas of the twenty-first century the leaders of all the main British parties turned for national inspiration to the model of city governance that he had set in Victorian Birmingham.

There are also less substantial ways in which Joseph Chamberlain left an enduring impression on British public life and political culture. He introduced the forms of organisation that all British political parties adopted and adapted for their varied purposes. He widened British

1

assumptions about the social responsibilities of local and national government. But on the whole his impact was as much disruptive as formative. He retains the distinction of having split both of the main British political parties of his day.

All of Chamberlain's achievements in political life, his failures as well as his successes, arose from the experience and understanding he derived in his initial career in business as a metal manufacturer. He was the first industrialist to push his way into the front ranks of British politics. He was thus an intruder among the British governing elite. And he had a religion to match. He was a proud Dissenter, hostile to the Established Church of England. Even within the ranks of nonconformity he adhered as a Unitarian to one of its smallest and most unorthodox denominations; and his Unitarianism was insistently rationalist rather than romantic and thus out of tune with the predominantly evangelical character of English Protestantism. His religious perspective sharpened his perception of the social consequences of the transformation in Birmingham industry that he was helping to bring about.

Chamberlain has been a much-studied figure by a range of historians, from his earliest authorised biography. The first three volumes of this exhaustive and hagiographic account appeared in the 1930s, written by Chamberlain's close associate, the former editor of the *Observer*, J.L. Garvin.[3] After Garvin's death and the post-war decline in interest in the Chamberlain dynasty and the British Empire, however, it took until the 1960s for the final volumes to appear, written in a much less polished manner by Julian Amery, son of Chamberlain's acolyte, Leo.[4] All subsequent post-war biographies have focused on Chamberlain's personal limitations with varying degrees of success, with only Richard Jay's study of 1981 offering a fresh perspective on the context of the politics of the period.[5] My own approach in my 1994 biography was to reconsider Chamberlain as the progenitor of a new breed of businessmen in politics, middle-class and non-Anglican, who opened the doors for others, most notably David Lloyd George, who nearly joined the Liberal Unionist cause himself in 1886.[6] It illustrated that, by the 1990s, we needed to take a wider view of the first age of mass politics than had hitherto been the case.

The recent growth of the 'New Political History' with its focus on postmodernist concerns such as language and identity has, unsurprisingly, shied away from biography, perhaps with good reason. Studies of particular crisis moments in Chamberlain's career, the political causes he espoused and the reactions of the newly enlarged electorate have proved that there is much in Chamberlain's life that biography has hitherto failed to examine.[7] Recent studies of Gladstone's career based on successful conferences have demonstrated that a multi-author collection, such as this volume, can offer a fuller picture than a single scholar, who, after years in the Chamberlain archive, can lose his or her sense of perspective, in much the same way that Vincent Cronin famously did in his study of Napoleon.[8]

Born into a prosperous family of shoe manufacturers in London, Joseph Chamberlain was sent to Birmingham at the age of 18 to look after the large investment that his father had made in the wood-screw manufacturing business of his brother-in-law, John Sutton Nettlefold. Over the next 17 years, four men, the Nettlefold and Chamberlain fathers and sons, turned themselves, as young Joseph boasted, into the 'Screw Kings'. They built themselves a monopoly in the manufacture of metal screws and wire fasteners, first throughout Britain, then into a dominating presence in the global market. Beginning as bookkeeper, Joseph Chamberlain took charge of marketing and sales, and proceeded to establish the discounting arrangements and percentage scales that were to dominate the industry worldwide for another century. Meanwhile Joseph Nettlefold, an engineer by training, oversaw the construction of large factories equipped with the most advanced machinery for mass production of all sorts of screws and fasteners from steel wire.

Great though this industrial accomplishment was, it was perhaps less remarkable than Chamberlain's insight into the social and political consequences of the industry he was building up. Scrutinising the production costs of the material that it used and the labour that it employed, he observed that while he and his partners were amassing great profits, they were widening the economic and social distance between themselves and their workforce. Mass production in large factories was a comparatively new phenomenon in Birmingham. Manchester was famous for its great textile mills, but they had given rise to social turbulence, whereas Birmingham had been characterised by small metalworking shops where masters and men toiled more peaceably side by side.

The factory-based mass production that Nettlefold and Chamberlain introduced at their main mill in Smethwick provided work for the rapidly growing population that came to Birmingham in search of employment. But Joseph Chamberlain was the first industrialist to point out the threat that this large factory-based production posed to the well-being of the town. When the British Association convened in Birmingham in 1866, he warned them that a revolution ... is taking place in the principal hardware trades, and ... is assimilating the town to the great seats of manufacturing in the North and depriving it of its special characteristic, viz., the number of its small manufactures, which has hitherto materially influenced its social and commercial prosperity as well as its politics.[9]

Chamberlain did not yet know how to deal with the social danger he recognised. But in the year that he issued this warning, one of the leading nonconformist ministers of Birmingham, George Dawson, declared in opening the town's first public library that this library was

the first fruits of a clear understanding that a great town exists to discharge towards the people of that town the duties that a great nation exists to discharge towards the people of that nation ... that a great town is a solemn organism through which should flow, and in which should be shaped, all the highest, loftiest and truest ends of man's intellectual and moral nature.[10]

This unorthodox message assigned to the town council much of the moral responsibility hitherto claimed by the churches and particularly by the Church of England. Dawson's message appealed to Chamberlain who was similarly unorthodox in religion and welcomed the opportunity to challenge the pretensions of the Established Church. Chamberlain first stepped into public life as chairman of the executive committee of the National Education League founded in Birmingham to wrest elementary education from the control of the Church of England, whose efforts had proven woefully unequal to the need.

But it was in the civic arena, on the Birmingham town council, that Chamberlain best put into practice Dawson's teaching of what became known as the 'Civic Gospel'. Elected to the town council from a ward in its densely populated heart, Chamberlain's understanding of the Civic Gospel was broadened, another insight he gained as finance manager for the family business. Through detailed examination of the hourly rates of pay and productivity at its main factory in Smethwick, he had discovered that the amount the men and women in his employ could produce increased when their hours of labour were decreased from the customary 11 or 12 to 10. This lesson was driven home during the Franco–Prussian War when German forces lay siege to Paris, in the process cutting Nettlefold and Chamberlain's leading French competitor off from its customers. Seizing the opportunity to capture these customers, Nettlefold and Chamberlain pushed production at Smethwick to full throttle, sometimes right through the night. But under this pressure the rate of productivity of the workers at Smethwick markedly declined. This experience showed Chamberlain how industrial capital and labour could work together for their mutual benefit. Nettlefold and Chamberlain reduced the working day at their main mill to nine hours, though still for a six-day week, with provision for two hours of overtime at higher rates of pay. The immediate effect of the change was to increase the labour costs of the firm by 16.5 per cent, but in subsequent years this percentage fell. In other words the productivity and also the pay and conditions of labour at the firm were further improved.

His industrial fortune secure, Chamberlain was ready to shift his focus from business to politics and concentrate on putting the Civic Gospel into practice. But first he had another political lesson to learn. The Liberal education reformers of Birmingham were so confident of their electoral support that they nominated candidates for all 15 positions on the school board that the Education Act of 1870 empowered the town to elect. But in order to protect minority interests in the town, the Act gave each elector as many votes as there were seats to be filled. The Roman Catholics took advantage of this provision by instructing their 3000 electors to cast all of their votes for the priest the church put up for election; and he duly came head of the poll with 35,000 votes. Eight Conservative churchmen stood for election, just enough to give them control if all eight won – which they did by collecting two votes from each of their supporters. The far more numerous Liberal electors divided their 15 votes a piece among the 15 Liberal candidates, with the result that only six were elected, Chamberlain near the bottom of the successful six.

The Liberals learned from this painful lesson. In the next local elections for the town council as well as the school board, they organised their supporters to concentrate their electoral power on the election of a winning majority. And the winning majority on the town council promptly elected Chamberlain to be mayor. He knew what he wanted to achieve in the governance of the town and how to go about it. But the earlier electoral setback also taught him the prior importance of tight organisation and mobilisation of his support, a lesson that through all the shifts and changes of his subsequent political career he never forgot.

What did Chamberlain accomplish is his eventually nearly three years as mayor? As in industry so in civic government, he recognised that nothing could be accomplished without the requisite financial resources. Chamberlain began by asking the town council to authorise negotiations for a municipal takeover of the local gas companies.

His main object was not municipal control of the gas supply so much as a large increase in the town's financial base for further civic undertakings. Even so, pursuing Dawson's line of thought, he elevated municipal control of the gas supply to a matter of principal: 'all monopolies which are sustained in any way by the State', he insisted, 'ought to be in the hands of the representatives of the people ... to whom their profits should go'.[11] He warned the council that his proposal would increase the debt of the town fivefold; but he assured them from his industrial experience that municipal consolidation of the gas companies would yield the town an annual profit of at least £15,000 rising to £50,000 within 14 years – a prediction which proved to be a great underestimate.

To secure approval of his proposal, Chamberlain had to win over first the town council, then the ratepayers and finally the committees of inquiry that the two Houses of Parliament set up. He made his case with such speed, verbal power and command of detail that he transformed the office of mayor. Its previous holders had treated it as a disabling honour that required them to preside impartially over the deliberations of the council, like Speakers of the House of Commons. Chamberlain behaved from the outset as prime minister. He could not have achieved what he did if he had behaved in any other way.

Once he had secured a greatly increased financial base for the town, he addressed its most acute social need: clean water. The local water company was an ably conducted enterprise and the prices it charged were reasonable. But naturally it provided better service where customers paid up and where costs were low: hence the inner city suffered. The need for repairs there and the costs of collection were high. The denizens of the central slums had to choose between drawing water from open wells scarcely distinguishable from sewers and stealing it from the company's taps. Their choice was between disease and prison, and often they suffered both. The only alternative to a municipal takeover of the company was to close the wells; but to do so would increase the commercial worth of the company by enforcing its monopoly and give it 24,000 more houses to serve. The ease with which Chamberlain secured approval of this proposal from the council, the ratepayers and Parliament, though it trampled on private interests, testified to the stature that he had achieved as mayor.

He pushed on after re-election for a third term. Keeping his eye on the crowded centre of the town, he proposed its extensive redevelopment in two reciprocal ways, to clean up the slums and in doing so to turn the area into the commercial heart of the Midlands. In defending the scheme, he sharpened the moral thrust of the Civic Gospel, preaching a secular religion according to which social conditions were the source of sin and legislation the basis for salvation. He blamed 'the dank, dark, dreary, filthy courts and alleys' of the town centre rather than the people who lived in them for their criminal behaviour. 'Yes, it is legally their fault, and when they steal we send them to gaol, and when they commit murder we hang them. But', he argued,

> it is no more the fault of these people that they are vicious and intemperate than it is their fault that they are stunted, deformed, debilitated, and diseased. The one is due to the physical atmosphere – the moral atmosphere as necessarily and surely produces the other. Let us remove the conditions, and we may hope to see disease and crime removed.[12]

And indeed the mortality rates in the town soon markedly improved.

Even so, the reality of his proposals did not match this rhetoric. His improvement scheme was more entrepreneurial than socially reforming in character. It did more for the business and professional interests of the town than for the denizens of the slums. And in contrast to his takeover of gas and water which increased the debt but not the rates levied by the town, his new improvement scheme increased the rates as well as the debt. Ultimately the financial dividend from the investment would be enormous, but it would not be reaped until most people then living in Birmingham were dead. Meanwhile little was done to rehouse the people dispossessed in the eradication of the slums. There was, nevertheless, a marked improvement in the centre of the town, and business certainly boomed along what was now named Corporation Street. Many of the Italianate shops, offices and law courts that line its sides stand today as an enduring embodiment of Chamberlain's Civic Gospel – as do the towering schools built in his day that still distinguish the skyline of Birmingham, and the grand Council House that he opened in the town centre as he left local for national politics. He also gave rise among friend and foe in Birmingham to one of the liveliest political cultures in the country.

Three things had proved indispensable in achieving what he did as mayor. One was his building up of the financial and economic resources of the town. Another was his imperious leadership. But equally important was the cooperation he secured between the local and the national government, in particular with the Home Secretary, Richard Cross. It was an unlikely partnership: Chamberlain the rapidly rising Radical and the Home Secretary in Disraeli's Conservative ministry. But Cross was happy to cooperate with the municipal reform movement in Britain's major provincial cities which Gladstone's preceding Liberal ministry had neglected. Moreover, the Conservatives' approach to finance was less austere than Gladstone's, and they proved willing to grant these cities the economic powers they needed to improve the health of the public on their crowded streets. The centrepiece of the cooperation between Cross and the leading provincial cities was the Artisans' and Labourers' Dwellings Act of 1875. Basing the legislation on an initiative from Glasgow, Cross welcomed Chamberlain's advice in shaping its terms, recognising with a refreshing modesty that has long since disappeared that these cities understood their needs better than Westminster could.

Chamberlain's improvement scheme for Birmingham and the legislation of Richard Cross that made it possible marked an early step in a process that raised the share of local authorities in all forms of governmental expenditure from over 30 per cent in the early 1870s to over 50 per cent by 1905. Led by Birmingham and Glasgow, Britain's provincial cities rode on this wave to a height of power from which thereafter the central government at Westminster, regardless of party, relentlessly deprived them.

The way in which Chamberlain put the Civic Gospel into practice and enhanced the powers and prestige of local government in Birmingham advanced his own ambitions. His performance as mayor attracted admiring attention nationwide and in so doing highlighted the significance of the Radical agenda which he was developing for the country as a whole in the pages of the *Fortnightly Review*. Eager to make his mark on the national stage, in 1876 he pushed one of the MPs for Birmingham, George Dixon, into early, reluctant retirement and replaced him. With similar assertiveness four years later Chamberlain secured a seat in Gladstone's Cabinet as President of the Board of Trade. He had given up the mayoralty upon election to Parliament but remained on the town council until he was appointed to the Cabinet. He had accomplished so much as mayor that he wondered in a reflective moment whether he could accomplish as much at Westminster as he had in Birmingham. He was right to wonder.

He was to discover in the national arena to his repeated dismay that Britain did not have a pervasively national economy but was made up of a host of regional economies with often clashing interests. His accomplishments as mayor of Birmingham were based upon his intimate understanding of its industrial economy. But he had not been closely involved in other economic regions of the country. Though his business experience at Nettlefold and Chamberlain had extended to banking – he had helped to turn Lloyds from a private into a public bank – and more broadly to global marketing, he tended to regard the industrial economy of Birmingham as normative. And impatient to accomplish what he had in mind, he had little inclination to reconcile differing standpoints.

These shortcomings became painfully apparent in his handling of the most serious industrial scandal that confronted him at the Board of Trade. Over the previous 12 years a staggering total of 36,000 merchant sailors had died at sea, one out of every six who signed on. Over-insurance lay at the root of the problem. Through over-insurance, the ship owners on the east coast profited egregiously when their ships went down. Some large shipping firms on the west coast, particularly in Liverpool, refused to follow this practice, and they sympathised with Chamberlain in deploring it. But he neglected to secure their cooperation in drafting his bill. The inflammatory language with which he then presented the national casualty figures and insurance abuses to the public turned this lack of cooperation into injury by seeming to accuse the whole industry of callous inhumanity. He stirred up such a storm of resentful opposition that the Cabinet deferred proceedings on his bill until they secured the great expansion of the working-class franchise which Chamberlain agreed was more important. Nothing more was accomplished on merchant shipping until the third Reform bill was enacted, whereupon the Liberals lost office.

The enlarged electorate and redrawing of the electoral map into single-member constituencies transformed the political landscape in uncharted ways. The transformation encouraged Chamberlain to initiate debate about extending to the country as a whole his Civic Gospel about using the powers of government to promote cooperation between labour and capital. But as in his campaign over merchant shipping, the emotive force of his speeches proved more alarming than persuasive. The new political landscape also enhanced the ability of the Irish Nationalists led by Charles Stewart Parnell to demand a substantial measure of self-government for their island. British politicians thus entered the new electoral terrain facing two unsettling issues, one about extending the powers of government for social purposes, the other about rival nationalisms, issues that pulled in different directions. The results of the general election at the end of 1885 intensified the confusion. The Liberals made headway in agricultural constituencies, previously Conservative strongholds. The Conservatives made headway in suburban constituencies, previously Liberal strongholds. And Irish Nationalists emerged holding the balance of power.

British party politics underwent a wrenching realignment over the next 15 months with consequences that endured for 20 years. Gladstone precipitated the realignment by proposing to give Ireland electoral autonomy with its own legislature and removal of its representatives from the House of Commons. That was too much for Chamberlain who wished to strengthen, not weaken, the legislative power of the United Kingdom. His opposition to Gladstone's bill for Irish Home Rule made Chamberlain of pivotal importance in the ensuing crisis, though at searing political and personal cost. He had to fight for his political life, and many of his close friends and allies turned against him. The way in which he rode the political waves over the next decade, however, led young Churchill to exclaim that Chamberlain was the man who made the weather.

Chamberlain rode two waves that appealed to the Conservatives who were his otherwise uneasy allies in the fight to preserve the union with Ireland. His defence of the union resonated with the sentiments of imperialism which were swelling in Conservative breasts, sentiments that Chamberlain was coming to share but from which Gladstone and his disciples recoiled. This imperial accord between Chamberlain and the Conservatives led him to hark back to his first experience of cooperation with Conservatives. As mayor of Birmingham he had worked well with the Conservative Home Secretary over the improvement scheme for the town centre. Now once again in cooperation with the Conservatives, Chamberlain fashioned a solution to the problem of workmen's compensation for industrial accidents. Conservatives admired the way in which his solution fostered cooperation between capital and labour, unlike the solution favoured by the Liberals which pitted the trade unions against the owners of industry.

There was, nevertheless, a crucial difference between the Workmen's Compensation Act that Chamberlain and his Conservative colleagues saw onto the statute books and his implementation of the Civic Gospel in Birmingham. He had based his practice there on widening the economic resources at the town's command. The Workmen's Compensation Act, by contrast, minimised the cost of the measure to the Treasury and the consumer by relying upon insurance taken out by the employer, an economy that appealed to Conservatives otherwise repelled by costly social reforms. Chamberlain tried but failed to devise a similar, essentially self-funding scheme for old-age pensions.

But the wave that he rode to make the weather in the final decade of the nineteenth century had less to do with social reform than with imperialism. Offered his choice of office when Lord Salisbury formed a ministry in coalition with the Liberal Unionists, Chamberlain made the astute but at the time surprising choice of the Colonial Office, hitherto one of the lesser Secretaries of State. Chamberlain used the position to become in effect the first minister of the British Empire. He extended the already global reach of the Empire, particularly in Africa.

But here again he pushed too far. By supporting the confrontational stance of the British High Commissioner in South Africa, Alfred Milner, against the equally confrontational President of the South African Republic, Paul Kruger, Chamberlain bore responsibility for the Boer War at the end of the nineteenth century, a war that taxed the military and financial resources of the British Empire almost to breaking point. Though Britain ultimately won, the war shook British confidence in the imperial mission that Chamberlain had come to embody.

Concerned about the soaring financial cost of Britain's imperial responsibilities, Chamberlain found an imperial response to the problem. The Canadian prime minister, Sir Wilfrid Laurier, attempted to foster trade with the mother country through a preferential tariff. Though Laurier's attempt proved immediately ineffective, it appealed to Chamberlain in several ways. In addition to strengthening the bonds between Great Britain and its major colonies, an imperial tariff could protect British industries with which Chamberlain remained familiar, particularly in Birmingham, against stiffening competition from Germany and the United States. It could also raise revenue to fund the further social reforms he had in mind.

But such a departure from tariff neutrality violated the canons of free trade to which Britain had been devoted for the past half century after the repeal of the Corn Laws reduced the cost of living, most emotively the price of the working man's daily bread. When Chamberlain found himself unable to persuade the Cabinet to initiate this momentous departure in governmental policy, he resigned and launched a nation-wide campaign to build popular and party support for the cause. He threw all his organisational and oratorical resources into this campaign and in doing so whipped up a political storm more furious than any since the repeal of the Corn Laws in the 1840s.

As had happened back then, this campaign split the Conservative party along with its Liberal Unionist allies, and it drove them from power for a generation. The next general election which came in 1906 exposed the severe geographical limits to Chamberlain's appeal. While he secured undiminished support from Birmingham, everywhere else the Conservative and Unionist alliance went down to crushing defeat. And though the alliance extended its support substantially in the ensuing general elections, they left Irish Nationalists holding the balance of power as in 1885, enabling the Liberals to remain in office. Chamberlain's campaign for Tariff Reform and imperial preference had failed repeatedly to win commanding national support. It also wore him out. After a three-day rally in Birmingham to celebrate his seventieth birthday and the fortieth anniversary of his election to Parliament, he suffered a stroke that left him angrily paralysed for a further eight years. He died on the eve of the First World War.

At first glance he seemed to have left little mark beyond the confines of Birmingham upon the political landscape. His brand of economic imperialism had been repeatedly rejected by the electorate. Irish Home Rule, which he fought so hard to prevent, was enacted within weeks of his death, though its implementation awaited the conclusion of the war. His Liberal opponents had discovered in graduated taxation of the rich a means to fund old-age pensions and other popular social reforms without violating the principles of free trade.

Even these Liberal accomplishments paid tribute to Chamberlain's achievement in pushing the social expectations of government in Britain beyond the narrow confines of Gladstonian finance. The organisational model which he had set up in the 1870s through the National Federation of Liberal Associations had been adopted by both of the major British parties. The spirit of imperialism that he had done so much to foster prevailed now in one form or other across the political spectrum. And though the model of city government that he had established in Birmingham was to be undermined through the rest of the twentieth century by the absorption of political and economic power by national government (away from local government), all the major British parties would turn back to it for inspiration in the twenty-first century. Though by the time he died Joseph Chamberlain no longer made the weather, he certainly left currents in the air that continued to circulate in the political atmosphere.

Notes

1. W.S. Churchill, *Great Contemporaries* (London: Thomas Butterworth, 1937), p. 57.
2. Most recently examined in P. Readman, 'The 1895 General Election and Political Change in Late Victorian England', *Historical Journal*, 42 (1999), pp. 467–93, at pp. 473–81; M. Pugh, 'Working-class Experience and State Social Welfare, 1908–1914: Old Age Pensions Reconsidered', *Historical Journal*, 45 (2002), pp. 775–96.

3. J.L. Garvin, *The Life of Joseph Chamberlain*, vols 1–3 (London: Macmillan, 1932–34).
4. J. Amery, *The Life of Joseph Chamberlain*, vol. 4 (London: Macmillan, 1951); J. Amery, *The Life of Joseph Chamberlain*, vols 5 and 6 (London: Macmillan, 1969).
5. R. Jay, *Joseph Chamberlain: A Political Life* (Oxford: Clarendon, 1981). See also P. Fraser, *Joseph Chamberlain: Racialism and Empire, 1868–1914* (London: A.S. Barnes, 1967); H. Browne, *Joseph Chamberlain: Radical and Imperialist* (London: Longman, 1974); D. Judd, *Radical Joe: A Life of Joseph Chamberlain* (London: Hamish Hamilton, 1977); E. Powell, *Joseph Chamberlain* (London: Thames and Hudson, 1977); T.L. Crosby, *Joseph Chamberlain: A Most Radical Imperialist* (London: I.B. Tauris, 2011).
6. P. Marsh, *Joseph Chamberlain: Entrepreneur In Politics* (New Haven, CT: Yale University Press, 1994); K.O. Morgan, 'The Liberal Unionists in Wales', in K.O. Morgan (ed.), *Modern Wales: Politics, Places and People* (Cardiff: University of Wales Press, 1995).
7. J.M. Lawrence, 'Class and Gender in the Making of Urban Toryism, 1880–1914', *English Historical Review*, 108 (1993), pp. 629–52; P.A. Readman, 'The Conservative Party, Patriotism and British Politics: The Case of the General Election of 1900', *Journal of British Studies*, 40 (2001), pp. 107–45; I. Cawood, 'Joseph Chamberlain, the Conservative Party and the Leamington Spa Candidature Dispute of 1895', *Historical Research*, 79.206 (2006), pp. 554–77; J. Thompson, '"Pictorial Lies?" – Posters and Politics in Britain c.1880–1914', *Past and Present*, 197 (2007), pp. 177–210.
8 M.E. Daly and K.T. Hoppen (eds), *Gladstone: Ireland and Beyond* (Dublin: Four Courts, 2011); R. Windscheffel, R. Swift and R. Quinault, *William Gladstone: New Studies and Perspectives* (Aldershot: Ashgate, 2012).
9. J. Chamberlain, 'Manufacture of Iron Wood Screws', in S. Timmins (ed.), *The Resources, Products, and Industrial History of Birmingham and the Midland Hardware District* (London: Robert Hardwicke, 1866), pp. 604–9.
10. G. Dawson, Inaugural Address at the Opening of the Free Reference Library, 26 October 1866, published by the Borough of Birmingham (1866).
11. Quoted in J.T. Bunce, *History of the Corporation of Birmingham*, vol. 2 (Birmingham: Cornish Brothers, 1885), p. 347.
12. Chamberlain to the town council, *Birmingham Daily Post*, 12 October 1875.

Part I
International Statesman

1

'Intimately dependent on foreign policy': Joseph Chamberlain and Foreign Policy

T.G. Otte

To examine the role of foreign affairs in Joseph Chamberlain's political career may appear whimsical, quixotic even, like so much else in it. After all, beyond his position as a Cabinet minister, he had no official involvement in foreign policy. Yet, it is no eccentric exercise. Unlike so many other senior politicians of the period, Chamberlain had clear views on Britain's external relations. For the most part, as the Earl of Kimberley noted in 1893, ministers 'know and care nothing about foreign affairs'.[1] Not so Joseph Chamberlain. And, again unlike many of his colleagues, he had real influence on foreign policy-making. Indeed, it is impossible to make sense of Chamberlain as a political figure without giving some consideration to his views on Britain's external relations.

This is more easily asserted in the abstract than demonstrated conclusively. To do so, moreover, is not without conceptual or methodological problems. As Chamberlain's hands were not placed on the levers of the Foreign Office machinery, his views on foreign policy cannot be gauged by his political actions. The historian has to rely on private comments and public speeches instead, all of which were conditioned by the prevailing contemporary political winds. Frequently, they reflected Chamberlain's frustrations with a particular course chosen. More often still, they were shaped by his calculations of personal or party political advantage. The historian, then, needs to be on guard more than might be the case with other political figures of the period.

Foreign policy nevertheless was crucial to defining Chamberlain's position in government. It helped, more especially, to shape the dynamic within the Unionist coalition after 1895, stimulated his own thinking on imperial and external matters, and determined to some degree the parameters within which he could operate. To appreciate

17

this, however, some thought needs to be given to the earlier phases of Chamberlain's career. This chapter, then, like ancient Gaul, falls into three parts. After some reflections on Chamberlain's political style and early forays into the field of Britain's external relations, his position in the Unionist fold will be examined before distilling his general views on foreign policy and dealing more especially with his views on Britain's so-called 'isolation'.

It has become something of a truism to suggest that Chamberlain was the first modern politician in Britain. He accepted the idea of 'party', and he was the pioneer of a British version of machine politics. But beyond the quotidian concerns of the business of politics, his modernity also rested on his global conception of Britain as an imperial power.

'Party' also mattered in this context. Unlike most Tories and many Whigs, Chamberlain embraced 'democracy' as a necessary stage in humanity's ineluctable progress, and he welcomed it. Unlike most Radicals, however, he had grasped that the advent of the age of the masses had altered the nature of politics, and that it made different demands of political leaders. While he advocated democratic reforms, he understood that democracy needed to be tamed so as to harness it to progressive purposes. This was the principal function of party organisation. It was an engine of power. Sustained by the idealist and material support of activists, in whose hands control of the party ultimately lay, it was geared towards constructive purposes. In sharp contrast to such arch high-Tories as Lord Salisbury, Chamberlain believed in the invigorating power of democracy, not least also with regard to Britain's international position. As he explained to A.J. Balfour in 1886, he considered

> a democratic government ... the strongest government from a military and imperial point of view in the world, for it has the people behind it. Our misfortune is that we live under a system originally contrived to check the action of Kings and Ministers, and which meddles far too much with the Executive of the country. The problem is to give the democracy the whole power, but to induce them to do no more in the way of using it than to decide on the general principles which they wish to see carried out. My radicalism at all events desires to see established a strong government and an Imperial government.[2]

There was, of course, tactical diplomatic advantage to be gained from domestic support, as Chamberlain explained to his confederate, the Birmingham Congregationalist minister, Dr R.W. Dale, at the height of the Pendjeh crisis in the previous spring: 'The great security for peace lies in impressing the Russians with the conviction that they cannot do as they like and that English opinion is united. Otherwise, the experience of the Crimean War will be repeated.'[3]

But beyond such practical considerations, Chamberlain's comments are revealing on several counts. In the first instance, they are suggestive of his belief that the new political arrangements required leadership of a different type: '[P]art of my democratic creed is that if a scheme is truly absurd ... people can be made to understand its absurdity.'[4] It meant that political leaders had to educate the electorate. There was nothing especially novel about this. The educative impulse, after all, was rooted in the Liberal tradition, and had become deeply entrenched, certainly since Midlothian days. Chamberlain himself was shaped by his own Unitarian background, with its emphasis on rational exposition and scientific progress, and his youthful days as a Sunday School teacher at the Church of the Messiah in Birmingham's Broad Street.[5] Ministers, he observed to Gladstone, 'cannot move much quicker or much in advance of those behind them, and English public opinion has to be educated quite as much as or more than English statesmen'.[6]

This conviction shaped Chamberlain's thinking about political organisation. If party was an engine of power, it was also a vehicle for conveying to the public a programme of political action:

> the platform has become one of the most powerful and indispensable instruments of Government ... A new public duty and personal labour has thus come into existence, which devolves to a great extent ... on those members of a Government who may be considered especially to represent the majority who are appealed to.[7]

This was the essence of Chamberlain's political credo. Party and platform were to secure majorities; majorities mattered because they could be converted into positive action; and both reinforced the importance of leadership. Chamberlain's determination to prevail was legendary already in his lifetime. Indeed, much of the force of his public persona rested on that very reputation. He was also not overly fastidious in the choice of his means or associates. His precise role in the murky doings preceding the divorce cases that damaged beyond repair the political careers of his fellow-Radical Sir Charles Dilke and Charles Parnell, the Irish leader, may never be established beyond reasonable doubt. Nor may the whiff of corruption ever be fully dispersed that clung to government contracts during the Boer War for Kynochs, the

Birmingham-based cordite manufacturers, one of the three 'giants' of this industry, in which company his younger brother Arthur held a directorship.[8] But there can be no doubt that Chamberlain thought of himself, and presented himself, as a man of action. As mayor of Birmingham he crushed municipal opposition – those on the receiving end called him 'the Napoleon of Birmingham';[9] he elbowed one of the sitting MPs for the Midlands capital out of the way in 1876;[10] he barged his way into the Cabinet in 1880; and, five years later, he threw down his 'unauthorised' gauntlet in challenge to Gladstone and the bulk of the Liberal party. There was, indeed, as Chamberlain himself perceived, something of *'a Radical Autoritaire'* in his political make-up: 'a Radical must be "autoritaire" if his radicalism was to serve any purpose'.[11]

Directed towards practical ends, Chamberlain's approach to politics was entirely rational, if confrontational and direct. He was suspicious of sophistries and subtleties, just as he was impatient with the compromises and concessions inherent in life at Westminster. Parliament existed to facilitate political action. For that reason he was wary also of Gladstone's attempts to launch ideological crusades to mobilise Radical sentiments ultimately to preserve Whig dominance over the Liberal party. It was a form of inverted Whiggery on Chamberlain's part. Party organisation and reform programmes were the means to heave men like him into the saddle, hence also his enthusiastic support for the 1884–45 franchise reforms. Here, indeed, is one of the many ironies of Chamberlain's career. For a man who emphasised leadership, loyalty and discipline as much as he, his record is one of division and destruction; and in the 20 years after 1885 he left behind him a long trail of political debris. And for all his own aggressive political style, he was remarkably thin-skinned. Salisbury confessed never to have come across 'so sensitive a public man ... I never met anyone before who was disturbed by articles in the *Standard*.'[12] Still, Chamberlain's political craft rested on the ability to identify and to exploit dividing lines. Politics was the art of defeating the opponent, whether by means of persuasion or by forcing him into a minority position.

The Gladstone acolyte and senior Treasury official, E.W. Hamilton, was not far of the mark when he reflected that Chamberlain 'was not born, bred or educated in the ways which alone secure the necessary tact and behaviour of a real gentleman'.[13] As for Chamberlain himself, he was not much given to introspection, nor did he harbour any doubt that he was a real leader. There was, he noted in 1885, a dearth of people like him: 'the rank and file are all right, but there is an awful lack of generals, and even non-commissioned officers'.[14] It is ironic that Chamberlain, who shared many of the instinctive nonconformist suspicions of the armed forces, resorted to such military language. But if anything, personality and political craft were fused into one here. Although there is no shortage of contemporary evidence testifying to his personal charm, he rarely troubled himself to deploy it to conciliate opponents or to placate reluctant colleagues. In the charmed circles of London Society the 'born and bred gentlemen', the Tory magnates and the Whig cousinhood had all the advantages, much to Chamberlain's intense frustration. He had little to rely upon but his own abilities, and the battering ram of the caucus organisation. Courting popular support was therefore necessary more especially also to advance his own programme. And here his regional stronghold, his midlands 'duchy', allowed him increased leverage elsewhere: 'the local was, in fact, a national success'.[15] The converse of this was the need for Chamberlain constantly to keep himself in the public eye, using his charismatic appeal to impress upon the electorate his reputation as a leader. That he won the affection of the public, or of large parts of it at any rate, cannot be doubted. Just as 'Pam', 'Dizzy' or the 'G.O.M.' had captured contemporary public imagination, so 'Joe' (or more often at the time 'Joey') could only mean one man and one programme, combined in one public persona, carefully fashioned by Chamberlain himself. In a similar manner, 'Highbury', his *rus in urbe* Venetian Gothic mansion at Moor Green, then on the outskirts of Birmingham, was a useful short-hand, much like Hatfield, Hawarden or Hughenden. His public appearance reinforced this effect, as a contemporary commentator observed: '[The orchid] became almost as much a personal feature as his nose or his eyeglass! In fact, it but needed the combination of these three to make a likeness of him which millions would recognise at a glance for "Joey", the man and his programme.'[16]

Chamberlain's abrasive oratorical style in part reflected this reality; in part, it reflected the hostility he encountered. His rhetoric was direct and devoid of any overt emotional appeal. His carefully chosen words threw everything into sharp relief, clear and hard, but without generating much warmth, rather like the sun on a bright winter's day, even though his speeches were invariably adorned with uplifting poetic allusions. As H.H. Asquith observed in paying tribute to Chamberlain the parliamentarian, '[i]f he kept ... closer to the ground, he rarely digressed, and he never lost his way'. But his style also included the liberal use of such devices as 'raillery, sarcasm, invective, but more perhaps – so at least it seems to me – than any orator of our time, he gave the impression of complete and serene command both of his material and of himself'.[17] According to J.A. Spender, no friend of Chamberlain's but a sound judge of political performance, his style was 'lucid and business-like in its exposition, short and sharp in its attack, unerring in its aim'. Chamberlain gave the impression of 'a man who knew exactly what he meant to say, and could reduce the most stubborn and complicated material to a sequence of definite propositions'. His style of delivery was part of his charismatic appeal:

> One felt the charm of the clear low voice and of that expressive lack of expression in the face, which yielded only a faint smile or slight curl of the lip, as the trenchant sentence drew to its extremely pointed conclusion. The sting was always in the tail of Mr Chamberlain's sentences.[18]

The combined effect of organisation, programme and charismatic personality strengthened Chamberlain's position in politics, principally because it reinforced the conviction of others, fearful of his negative powers, that it was better to appease than to lose him. And this, too, defined the political space within which Chamberlain operated in the field of foreign and imperial policy.

Chamberlain's views on Britain's external relations were 'far from being fully formed when he first entered public life',[19] and historians should be wary of attributing to him any adamantine imperial and foreign policy schemes or intellectual breadth and subtlety, none of which he possessed. But he was not without views on Britain's place in the world and the necessary means to defend it. There is, indeed, an interesting parallel here with his thoughts on commerce, his first Cabinet portfolio. When Chamberlain took charge of the Board of Trade, Sir Thomas Farrer, the department's permanent secretary, evinced surprise at his new master's ignorance 'of all economic questions'. Yet he acknowledged 'his adroitness in assimilating and reproducing arguments which he did not understand'.[20] Chamberlain showed a similar ability in imbibing and developing further ideas about international politics. His mind was, indeed, as a later twentieth-century Birmingham MP noted, 'as capricious as it was fertile'.[21]

Predictably, perhaps, Chamberlain's first forays into foreign affairs were couched in his native political tongue, that of militant dissent and with a distinct Midlothian inflection. But his views were distinct from mainstream radicalism in that they contained an imperial nucleus, mingled with revulsion at Disraeli's flashy appeal to the vulgar patriotism of the music halls. The Suez Canal coup, Chamberlain noted, was 'a clever thing'. Whether it was right 'that we should have a finger in the Egyptian pie' he left open: 'But we have got it and that is the point of view from which the purchase ought to be regarded.'[22] His criticism of the Beaconsfield government's handling of the great Eastern crisis gives a flavour of his views, which combined Gladstonian sentiments with a harder-edged appreciation of international realities. Any settlement leaving significant sections of Balkan Christians under 'Turkish misrule' could only ever be 'a hollow truce'. Further insurrection was certain to erupt, and lead to intervention by one or more of the Great Powers 'with all its consequent risk and danger'. Britain's imperial interests, he intoned, required a rapprochement with Russia; and he attributed the rise in Anglo–Russian tensions to the 'want of frankness' in Britain's diplomacy since 1875. British interests in the Eastern Mediterranean required 'the good government and the welfare of the Christian inhabitants of Turkey'. More importantly, they also included

> more cordial and friendly relations between the two great countries of Russia and England. If this Eastern Question were once satisfactorily settled, he did not see any reason why England and Russia should be alienated from one another. So far as our interests in the Indian Empire were concerned, the responsibility we had in reference to India might be glorious, but it could not be profitable. It was not a responsibility that any other nation need covet. We might yet, he thought, look for cooperation from Russia instead of jealousy in carrying on a work which was the most onerous and responsible any nation ever undertook.[23]

When Disraeli and Salisbury returned from the Berlin Congress, seemingly having secured 'peace with honour', Chamberlain's verdict was damning. The treaty itself was 'only an armistice, and not a permanent settlement', and official policy, especially under Salisbury's hapless predecessor, the dithering Earl of Derby, had been 'misty and shadowy'. There was a glimmer of Chamberlain's caustic temperament, too. The government, it seemed, was convinced that it could 'educe order out of chaos [in Turkey] – by a stroke of the pen, and by virtue, forsooth, of that increasing wisdom which ... the Sultan had been showing from month to month'. In reality, however, British policy was reduced to attempt such a feat 'by the stroke of a harlequin's wand'. This was predictable opposition point-scoring. Underpinning his critique, however, was a deeper recognition of the need for a strategic conception of foreign policy. It was necessary, he concluded, 'to ascertain where the vital interests of England really lay, and where her real defence properly began, and to wait till those interests were menaced, instead of rushing to meet a danger which possibly had no existence'.[24]

Just as there was an imperial dimension to his private business dealings (he was one of the original subscribers of the Royal Niger Company in 1882), so his political views were infused with 'a vague imperialism'.[25] Liberals, too, had 'imperial instincts', he noted, 'but ... we desire that these should be directed to worthy objects, and not used as the Prime Minister [Disraeli] is doing, for ignoble party purposes'.[26]

The need for a carefully calibrated strategic approach informed Chamberlain's criticism of Disraeli's hawkish colonial secretary, Sir Michael Hicks Beach, and the even more bellicose High Commissioner for South Africa, Sir Bartle Frere, who had plunged Britain into a war with the Zulu kingdom. But here, too, shone through his determination to preserve the Empire. A 'comparatively uncivilized power', he suggested, might coexist with the British Empire, albeit only on the basis of Britain's supremacy. Asserting regional dominance was one thing, but there were pitfalls: 'where is this policy to stop?' If taken to its logical conclusion, 'we shall have shortly the whole burden of responsibility of the government of South Africa on our hands'. The British Empire could bear no strong country in its neighbourhood, 'but there was no occasion of recklessly forcing on a war before it became necessary'.[27] It was almost a premonition of Chamberlain's later involvement in South African complications.

His vague imperialism was tempered by concerns about the need for government to be held accountable by Parliament for its imperial policy. During a Commons debate on yet another of the Tories' little wars, that with Afghanistan, he tabled a motion censuring the government for its failure to obtain 'the consent of the nation, through its representatives ... before war was declared', and for omitting to publish the necessary papers 'which would have enabled a correct opinion to be formed as to its justice and necessity'.[28]

South Africa remained much to the fore of Chamberlain's thinking after the general election of 1880. With the Colonial Secretary sitting in the House of Lords, the newly minted President of the Board of Trade was now also the government's spokesman on matters relating to the Cape Colony and the Transvaal. He was too consummate a party politician not to use the opportunity to attack the previous administration's record and that of Frere, now recalled from Cape Town. The High Commissioner had 'had been found guilty of leading this country into an unjust and unnecessary war without the authority or sanction of the Government at home', he averred. At the same time, however, his annexation of the Transvaal had altered the situation on the ground: 'whatever they might think of the original act of annexation, they could not safely or wisely abandon the territory'.[29] That, of course, was precisely what the Gladstone administration ultimately decided to do, and Chamberlain fell in with this new line. In parliament, he justified retrocession with a mixture of realpolitik calculations and an appeal to Liberal instincts. As to the British Empire, he asserted, the 'strength of the giant was there, but it would have been tyrannous to employ it'. Retention would serve neither justice nor would it safeguard British imperial interests.[30]

Chamberlain's imperialism grew more pronounced during the second Gladstone administration. At the Cabinet discussions on Egypt in 1882, he 'stirred them [ministers] up to action', and was 'almost the greatest jingo'.[31] Having established a British military presence on the banks of the Nile, and soon finding it impossible to withdraw, Chamberlain was ready to accept the consequences. Following Gordon's Khartoum disaster there was no alternative but to seek to destroy the Mahdi and his regime in the Sudan. Not to do so would be a sign of weakness: 'We must show these fierce fanatics that we are strong, as they respect nothing but physical force.'[32]

Inevitably perhaps, given the strength of the imperial sentiments evinced by Chamberlain in the mid-1880s, historians have speculated as to the influence on him of J.R. Seeley's contemporaneous *Expansion of England*. That the work of Gladstone's choice for the Regius chair at Cambridge left some impression on Chamberlain seems beyond doubt, though it is difficult to establish the extent to which it stimulated his own imperialism.[33] Whatever the precise influence of Seeley's work, it found a ready recipient for its message in Chamberlain.[34] In a similar vein, his response to Gladstone's Home Rule scheme was shaped by concerns for the political cohesion of the Empire. Chamberlain was not opposed, in principle, to some degree of devolution of powers to a Dublin-based administration, provided it was 'consistent with the integrity of the Empire and the supremacy of Parliament'. Fears for imperial cohesion were an important factor. 'Where, in all of this, is the integrity of the Empire?', he asked during the Home Rule debate in April 1886.[35] This should not diminish Chamberlain's own inconsistency on Ireland; nor should it disguise the fact that 'The Empire in danger' was the most potent slogan to unite all shades of opposition to Gladstone, as he understood only too well.[36]

The years in the political wilderness after 1886 were nevertheless important to the further development of Chamberlain's views on

Britain's international position. His gradual drifting into Salisbury's embrace played a significant role in this. But it was not so much a matter of Chamberlain being forced into positions which were inconsistent with his earlier politics;[37] nor was it, as yet, primarily a question of his searching for a new platform to extend his authority beyond the small number of anti-Gladstonian Liberals to include the Conservatives, in Beatrice Webb's trenchant phrase, 'the ladder up which Joe climbs into a Conservative government waving aloft his banner of shoddy reforms'.[38] Rather the emerging Unionist alliance established the broader parameters within which his thinking evolved, and within which he could operate. No doubt, the events of 1886 were as much as a watershed in Chamberlain's career as they were a geological shift in the political landscape of Britain. But elements of the old were to be found among the new. His well-established concerns with social reforms became enmeshed with his imperialism. Both, in fact, were constituent elements of his political programme, as will be discussed below.

As for the Unionist alliance, this was the result of two parallel and mutually reinforcing processes. There was the move of the Hartingtonians and Chamberlainites away from the Liberal camp after the failed attempt, in 1887, to reunite the Liberal Unionists with Gladstone under the umbrella of the old party.[39] But equally important were Salisbury's skilful coalition-building and management. These were part of his domestic statecraft. If he had earlier maligned Chamberlain to 'a Sicilian brigand' or dismissed him as 'an inveterate cockney', he was shrewd enough to appreciate now his utility in keeping the Liberals divided.[40] Complain as he might that he had 'to mak[e] bricks without straw', Salisbury, in fact, led a de facto coalition, even if there was no formal coalition ministry.[41] Without a majority of its own, the government had to give some of its measures a certain Liberal appearance, as Salisbury repeatedly impressed upon his followers.[42] Indeed, the legislative programme up to 1892 contained various measures which were designed to appeal to Radical Unionists.

Meanwhile, unity among the anti-Home Rulers was essential to lock Gladstone out of office; and on his return to Britain in 1888 Chamberlain announced to the Unionists that he was 'glad to be able once more to take my part amongst you'.[43] He readily conceded that 'more progress [had been] made with the practical application of my political programme' with the Tories than had been possible with Gladstone: 'I am bound to bear this in mind in my future speeches.'[44] It helped to narrow the gap between the two Unionist groupings, as Chamberlain indicated to Balfour in 1892. He wished, if possible, 'to unite with us [Conservatives], and sit with us, under the common denomination of a national party'. To safeguard his own position, however, he required certain political guarantees to enable him 'to appeal to a substantive programme of social legislation'.[45]

For his part, Salisbury used the most powerful weapon in a prime minister's armoury to ease Chamberlain's progress into the Conservative camp: patronage. In August 1887, he offered Chamberlain, embattled now, embarrassed and embittered, the position of Chief Commissioner, a grand title for a temporary position at Washington to act as Canadian representative in negotiations to settle an ongoing dispute about fishing rights off Newfoundland. Such an appointment was not without precedent. In 1880, Gladstone had made the Whig outlier, G.J. Goschen, ambassador at Constantinople in an effort to keep him in the Liberal fold.[46] Now Salisbury hoped to use a diplomatic posting in order to widen the chasm between Chamberlain and his old party. And he had shrewdly judged both the man and the problem.

The fisheries controversy was a somewhat involved, but ultimately lower-league, political problem. Yet Chamberlain turned it into a notable success, with lasting consequences on three counts. In the first place, he secured a treaty acceptable to all sides, though part of it was repudiated by the Americans within a year of its conclusion. London was satisfied because the settlement was one further small step in the direction of Anglo–American reconciliation. Canadian and US interests, meanwhile, were safeguarded by a reciprocal arrangement which granted US fishing vessels entry into Canadian waters in return for an exemption for Canadian fish from US import tariffs.[47] In the second place, as so many among the Victorian social and political elite, Chamberlain, twice-widowed already, won the hand of 'a pretty puritan maid'.[48] His marriage to Mary Endicott, daughter of Grover Cleveland's Secretary of War and influential Massachusetts politician, not only gave him greater stability in his domestic arrangements, it also forged new ties with the East coast establishment.[49]

Lastly, and perhaps most significantly, there was Chamberlain's speech to the Toronto Board of Trade during his visit to Canada at the turn of 1887/8. He appreciated the importance of trade and tariffs in Canadian politics. If he were a Canadian, he reflected in private, he would favour a 'commercial union' with the United States as preferable for the dominion. However, this would ultimately mean political independence from the mother country.[50] In part to counter this tendency, he developed for the first time in the Toronto speech his own thoughts on imperial federation; and he sketched out what would become the *basso continuo* accompaniment to his future pronouncement on the subject, the notion of racial bonds between the various branches of the English-speaking world. The Anglo-Saxon race, he argued, 'that proud, persistent, self-asserting and resolute stock', was destined to become 'the predominant force in the future history and civilization of the world'. A common past and culture, but also commercial interests would draw the Anglophone nations together. As for the Empire, he reflected, that

> the burdens are vast ... but we will not lessen them by cowardly surrender ... or a mean betrayal of the interests entrusted to our care. Relief must be found in widening the foundations of the great Confederation, and not in cutting away the outposts ... The interest of true democracy is not towards anarchy or the disintegration of Empire, but rather the uniting together of kindred races with similar objects ... It may yet be that the federation of Canada may be the lamp lighting our path to the federation of the British Empire.[51]

To an extent there was little that was innovative in Chamberlain's arguments. Canada had been held up as a role model by the advocates of a federal solution to the Home Rule problem before.[52] Closer and more formal ties between the different parts of the Empire, meanwhile, were a prominent topic in the political discourse of the 1880s. Earlier in 1887, the first conference of colonial premiers had taken place in London, convened at the prompting of the Imperial Federation League, a lobby group established by Seeley and his fellow historian, J.A. Froude, and drawing on broad, cross-party support. Even Salisbury had made his obeisances to the idea of federation, albeit based on a variation of the German model. Time was not yet ripe for an imperial *Zollverein*; but the Empire might establish a *Kriegsverein*, a 'union for purposes of mutual defence' that would allow for the 'the drawing closer and closer and closer of those bonds ... created by a common origin, a common history, and a common allegiance'.[53]

Whatever the Toronto speech may have lacked in originality, it marked the transition of Joseph Chamberlain to an imperial radical, who conceived of the solutions to Britain's domestic and external problems in a geopolitical context. In the years following his fisheries 'peace with honour', his public utterances were more frequently laced with appeals to patriotic sentiment. Claiming the mantle of patriotism was not new for Chamberlain. Prior to the Liberal split, he had presented social reform measures as true patriotism.[54] Now the tone became more consciously Beaconsfieldian, a consequence of both the emphasis on imperial integrity in the Unionist platform and of the G.O.M.'s political longevity. His speeches also more frequently now contained appeals to be ready to make sacrifices for the larger cause of Britain's imperial greatness, honour and prosperity:

> It is true, as was so well said by the poet [Matthew Arnold] ... that 'the weary Titan staggers under the too vast orb of his fate.' But if we honour our obligations ... the honour and credit will be proportional to the sacrifices that we may make, and nothing is to be gained by an abandonment of those duties which will be as fatal to our material prosperity as they will be discreditable and derogatory to our national character and our national honour.[55]

Chamberlain's efforts in this direction culminated in his rectoral address at Glasgow University, his great paean to patriotism. It was, he averred, 'that greatest of civic virtues, and most important element of national character'. It reflected 'the pursuit of commercial interests, the defence of common independence, and the love of common liberties', and was strengthened by a sense of a shared past and traditions. More importantly – and this made for the distinctive quality of Chamberlainite patriotism – he linked such sentiments to his earlier politics. Patriotism, he argued, had become 'a democratic passion, and ha[d] ceased to be a privileged distinction'. It involved personal sacrifice, and so set it apart from jingoism:

> Is it contended ... that we have not the strength to sustain the burden of Empire? We are richer, more numerous, and in every way more powerful than our ancestors ... We have the firm assurance of the loyalty and affection of the sons of Britain across the sea and of their readiness to play their part in the common defence. We do not lack efficient instruments for our great purpose ... [W]here the British flag floats – Englishmen, Scotsmen and Irishmen are to-day fronting every danger and every hardship ... They ask from us that their sacrifices shall not be in vain.[56]

Chamberlain's notion of patriotism evolved from the earlier, vaguer imperialism during his years in the political wilderness. As a leitmotif of his public utterances it was aimed at cementing his position within the wider Unionist camp. And yet there was a social reform aspect to his patriotic platform that ought not to be overlooked.

By 1895, Chamberlain's transition to the Conservatives was complete. Ironically, there were greater constraints on him now than had been the case before 1892. In vain did he strive to keep alive the spirit of 'Radical Joe' with his 'Memorandum of a Programme for Social Reform' in the run-up to the 1895 election.[57] If anything, the scope of the government's legislation fell well short of Chamberlain's expectations. In many ways it bore a decidedly Tory aspect, for instance, in its prioritising of agricultural interests. But, for now, he was anxious not to rock the coalition boat.

Chamberlain's new departmental remit, moreover, meant that his formidable energy was focused on external problems. His surprise choice of the Colonial Office, in preference to any of the senior domestic departments, begs the question whether, as Salisbury hoped, he had 'put [his] philosophy in the lumber-room for the moment, as Pitt did his views on reform'.[58] For once, Salisbury had misjudged his Radical partner. Chamberlain's transformation from 'Radical Joe' to 'Imperial Joe' was not a Damascene conversion; it was rather an evolution from the reforming priorities he had espoused earlier. It was radicalism projected onto a larger plane. The Midlands manufacturer, the practitioner of municipal socialism who had articulated nonconformist grievances, appreciated the constraints and the opportunities which the Unionist alliance presented. His coalition with the Cavendishes and Cecils, the class that neither toiled nor spun, was dictated by the logic of post-1886 politics. But it also made an ambitious social reform programme all but impossible now. Such matters, Salisbury let him know, 'would require much care & consideration'.[59] There was no doubt that if, as the Tory leader reasoned with characteristic pith, Chamberlain 'means to shape his political life on the Birmingham view of church & squire, those two authorities will in the long run refuse to take him for their leader'.[60]

The Empire now offered the solution to the social ills that 'Brummagem Joe' had sought to heal by means of slum clearances and municipal collectivism. Progress and prosperity at home depended on weaning the country off its lazy laissez-faire habits, and on developing and reorganising the Empire along more efficient lines. It entailed the need for a firm foreign policy, guided by a clear strategic appreciation of Britain's global position:

> If you read history you will find that the expansion of the Empire and the growth of our commerce are intimately dependent upon foreign policy which has been pursued since the times of Queen Elizabeth down to the present day ... [B]y the enterprise, the courage,

and the resolution of our ancestors there has been built up this world-wide dominion and we have been given that commanding position without which these small islands would be unable to support the crowded population even for a single week.[61]

Frequently, he exhorted his audiences to be on guard against threats from abroad. The 'age of peace' had not come, he warned. On the contrary, 'the nations [were] armed and arming', and international politics had become more fiercely competitive.[62] But it also meant that the development of the Empire was indispensable to a programme of domestic reforms. Chamberlain thus fused the notion of Empire with radical collectivism. State action in the furtherance of the larger cause of Empire was to solve the complex social problems at home and Britain's relative economic decline. This consideration explains his reverting to the idea of imperial federation, a theme which he developed in the later 1890s. Such a project, he expounded, ought to be approached from a trading angle: 'a true Zollverein' would guarantee free trade inside the Empire, and so protect its prosperity.[63] Intriguingly, in light of his later Tariff Reform campaign, Chamberlain thought it necessary then to perform a series of intellectual contortions to demonstrate that a commercial union would constitute 'the greatest advance that free trade has ever made since it was first advocated by Mr Cobden'. Over time, its creation would necessitate parallel political structures, not least for defensive purposes, 'for imperial defence is only another name for the protection of imperial commerce'. Thus, gradually 'a real federation of the Empire' would emerge, generating wealth and prosperity for its constituent parts.[64]

Chamberlain's vision of the Empire as an organic union, to be secured by advancing along the two converging lines of commerce and defence, had undoubted popular appeal.[65] However compelling the case appeared in the abstract, Salisbury was not altogether wrong in thinking 'that Chamberlain's interest in the colonies [was] entirely theoretic'.[66] Perhaps, as Chamberlain opined at the 1897 colonial conference, 'the idea of federation [was] in the air' in Britain; and, no doubt, he held it firmly in his gaze. But he looked at the scheme through a rose-tinted eyeglass. His appeal to the colonial premiers for imperial burden-sharing testified to this. For the scheme of a commercial union, as the first step towards eventual federation, ran counter to the economic interests of most of the settler colonies. In Canada more especially, questions of commerce and politics were closely entwined, so much so that trade and tariffs were the handmaidens of politics.[67] Politics and tariffs were symbiotic; and high tariffs were a symbol of Canadian identity, as the protectionist Tories' trouncing of Sir Wilfrid Laurier's free-trading Liberals in 1891 underscored. True, Laurier won in 1896, but high tariffs remained a fact of Canadian politics, the introduction of a lower tariff ('preference') for British-made imports notwithstanding. For Canada, the Empire offered protection against external challenges; its economic integration, however, threatened to swamp the country with British goods.[68]

Just as Chamberlain, when Mayor of Birmingham, had shown scant regard for his opponents, so he had no real comprehension of the interests of the colonies. The difference, of course, was that he was not now dealing with backwards borough-mongers, but premiers of self-governing colonies. True, his imperial schemes were geared towards practical ends, but the interests they served were principally metropolitan ones rather than those of the imperial periphery. This lack of subtlety also characterised Chamberlain's approach to foreign policy, and this had practical consequences.

The divisions between Chamberlain and Salisbury in matters of foreign policy have frequently attracted scholarly attention. What has tended to be ignored, however, is the quite different conceptualisations of foreign policy which informed their politics. That public opinion mattered also in external affairs both acknowledged, Salisbury reluctantly, Chamberlain enthusiastically. 'Public opinion is a very good guide', he observed to the Prime Minister at the end of 1897 when problems in East Asia complicated great power politics.[69] The implications were clear. Ministers had to educate, mobilise and lead the public in international matters. This was not novel as such, perhaps. Past politicians of very different stripes, from Canning to Palmerston and Disraeli, had played to the gallery at home to harness public opinion for their own purposes. But in the context of the Chamberlain–Salisbury relationship, it reflected the former's quite different background and experience. Here was a middle-class machine politician in tune with, and adept at, 'mass politics'. But leadership also implied the need for an active policy. The Unionist government, he noted during the 1895 general election, ought to pursue 'a strong policy at home and abroad'.[70] Failure in this respect would lead to problems at home. 'We shall be sharply questioned when Parliament meets', he prognosticated during the Far Eastern crisis: '& if we do absolutely nothing before then I fear the effect of our self-effacement'.[71] As the crisis wore on, and Cabinet divisions threatened to relegate Britain to the role of a bystander, Chamberlain warned that 'our prestige will be gone and our trade will follow. I would not give a year's life to the Government under such conditions'.[72]

Chamberlain had an acute sense of the fiercer competition among the great powers in the 1890s. Imperial federation was, in part, meant to buffer Britain against external threats: 'the league of kindred nations, this federation of Greater Britain, will not only provide for its own security, but will be a potent factor in maintaining the peace of the world'.[73] In the more immediate future, Chamberlain was determined that 'we can[not] be left behind' in the race for influence overseas. Inactivity would merely encourage 'further tail-twisting on the part of our dear friends & allies in the Concert of Europe'.[74]

Such notions were to some extent rooted in Chamberlain's business background, but they owed even more to the then dominant intellectual currents. The accent on the imperial theme resonated with a public sensitised to it by politicians like Disraeli but also by intellectuals such as Seeley or Froude. Above all, his views reflected the kind of Social Darwinism which had gained currency in public discourse, with its emphasis on international competition and the rise and fall of nations. 'The days are for great empires and not for little states', he impressed upon a Chamberlainite meeting in his Midlands 'duchy' in 1902: 'The question for this generation is whether we are to be numbered among the great empires or the little states.'[75] Such notions provided the context to Chamberlain's advocacy of a 'new course'. Here, too, one could 'not have omelette without breaking eggs'.[76] The traditional tools of British foreign policy were no longer suitable to the task of safeguarding the country's national interests. Old diplomacy had run its course, and 'the mysteries and reticencies of the diplomacy of 50 years ago' had to be replaced by a new approach to foreign policy.[77]

In the context of the Cabinet divisions on foreign affairs in the first half of 1898, this speech, the 'long spoon speech', was a direct attack on Salisbury, who appeared to epitomise the failings of traditional diplomacy. But it also reflected Chamberlain's quite different conceptualisation of foreign policy. While underpinned by Social Darwinian notions, its corollary was that kind of racialism to which many late Victorians were prone. Chamberlain viewed international politics through the prism of race, and he was imbued with a sense of Anglo-Saxon racial superiority. The 'traditions of the proud-spirited race', he reminded an audience in Philadelphia in 1888, left it 'surely destined in the near future to outstrip all others'. Although he tended to emphasise 'the unbroken amity' between the two countries as the best guarantee of peace,[78] in the late 1890s his exhortations of Anglo-Saxonism were often tinged with belligerence: 'even war itself would be cheaply purchased if in a great and noble cause the Stars and Stripes and the Union Jack should wave together ... over an Anglo-Saxon alliance'.[79]

Linked to the notion of a special transatlantic bond was the idea that the kindred Germanic nations were Britain's natural allies in Europe. Chamberlain's advocacy of an Anglo–American–German combination left little room for doubt on that score:

> I may point out to you that at bottom the main character of the Teutonic race differs very slightly from the character of the Anglo-Saxon ... and if the union between England and America is a powerful factor in the cause of peace, a new Triple Alliance between the Teutonic race and the two potent branches of the Anglo-Saxon race, will be a still more potent influence in the future of the world.[80]

Indeed, the fellow-Protestant German *Kaiserreich*, more modern and more advanced in some respects than Britain, had obvious attractions for the Unitarian Chamberlain, as it had for many Radicals of the period.[81]

The imperial idea was the intellectual force that lent meaning to Chamberlain's political manoeuvres after 1895. Whatever his precise role in the origins of the second Boer War, for him the Empire was an end in itself, not merely an instrument of policy.[82] But 'Empire' as an organising political idea also provided the relevant context to his evident and mounting frustration with official foreign policy.[83] Here one encounters another of the many paradoxes of Chamberlain's career. His adhesion to the Unionist alliance, as seen earlier, had curtailed the scope for any ambitious social reform programme. Yet, his official influence had never been greater. Salisbury was ready to go far in appeasing the de facto leader of the Liberal Unionists. In the government he occupied a position resembling that of a 'co-premier',[84] while a system of dual control by Chamberlain and Balfour kept the Unionists together in Parliament. For his part, Chamberlain was reluctant to strain relations with the Tory leader. Ultimately, he knew that he had to resort to threats of resignation to get his way or accept being outvoted.

The peculiar nature of Chamberlain's position in the Unionist coalition explains the mixture of clandestine manoeuvrings and scarcely concealed public attacks on Salisbury, which characterised his attempts to influence foreign policy decision-making. True, in the early months of the Unionist coalition, he pressed on Salisbury a madcap scheme for an Anglo–American alliance to intervene in the Armenian Question.[85]

But in public he praised the Premier's 'firm hand ... at the helm'.[86] Two years into the administration, however, relations between the two men had reached their nadir. The Colonial Secretary took umbrage at being kept in ignorance of Salisbury's negotiations with the Portuguese on a railway connection from Delagoa Bay to South Africa.[87] Worse, Salisbury's attempts to divert French expansionism to West Africa were 'most discouraging'. It was a policy of 'give away everything and get nothing', he observed to his parliamentary under-secretary, who happened to be the Prime Minister's son-in-law: 'I am more than sorry to differ from him, but I cannot stand it. I would rather give up office than allow French methods to triumph. We shall pay for it sooner or later & I cannot be party to such a surrender.'[88]

It was no secret in London circles that Chamberlain was 'very sick with our present head of the F[oreign] O[ffice] whom he considers past work'.[89] Salisbury's appeasement of France in Africa was a source of constant frustration for Chamberlain, soon aggravated by events in East Asia: 'He [Chamberlain] talked of China and West Africa, and of France and Russia with an amplitude of view and phrase that would have astonished Birmingham ten years ago .... [W]e are at the parting of the way, and ... we must stand fast for imperial expansion.'[90] In Cabinet and in private, Chamberlain advocated a firm policy to contain Russia in Asia, and threw the idea of an Anglo–American–Japanese combination into the debate, with the aim of forcing Russia to accept that 'no exclusive rights [were] to be allowed' to any foreign power in China.[91] Indeed, he was ready to deploy naval pressure to evict Russia from its recently acquired Port Arthur naval base: 'If we do not do something and that quickly we shall have a bad quarter of an hour when Parliament meets.'[92]

Such demands proved too strong for the Cabinet, reluctant as yet openly to challenge Salisbury in foreign affairs. This provides the context to Chamberlain's involvement in the clandestine alliance talks with the German ambassador in April 1898. There was something of the hyena about Chamberlain. He sensed that Salisbury had been weakened by internal and public criticism of his handling of foreign affairs, and this created further space for him. In 1896, the notion of isolation, brought into circulation by a senior Canadian Conservative, was an indication of British strength: 'She stands secure in her own resources, in the firm resolution of her people ... and in the abundant loyalty ... of the Empire.'[93] The country's position two years later was rather different, and there can be no doubting the attraction for many Tories of Chamberlain's programme of a firm policy coupled to an alliance with a major power. It was not a case of Liberal Unionist preferences foisted on an, as always unwitting, Tory party.[94] At Westminster senior Tory backbenchers called for 'a bold, big line, and a clear line ... [T]he time for our "splendid isolation" is gone ... [I]f the Government ... would make an alliance with Germany that really would make for peace for a very long period.'[95] Junior ministers were beginning to look beyond the current leader in the hope of 'form[ing] a "caucus" with a Cabinet & I trust [we] will do some real big work for the Empire'.[96]

This palpable sense of dissatisfaction among the political class and in the country with Salisbury and his policy created additional room for manoeuvre for Chamberlain. It also provided the vital stimulus for his abortive alliance offer in 1898. As recent scholarship has shown, Chamberlain initiated the talks with the German ambassador. His objective was some form of Anglo–German alliance: 'it should be of a defensive character based upon mutual understanding on the policy in China & elsewhere'.[97] The scheme was misjudged. Once again, the rose-tinted eyeglass was firmly screwed in, and Chamberlain misread German interests. If he thought that the 'establishment of a friendly understanding between Germany & G[rea]t Britain [was] desirable in the interests of both countries', Berlin concluded that it had better wait in order to drive up the price for an alliance.[98] Even so, the ultimate success or failure is less significant here than the fact that Chamberlain's initiative was condoned by Balfour and supported by a growing number of ministers, critical of Salisbury, and aided by influential figures from the City of London.

Chamberlain's ability to tap into such discontent lent greater political potency to his idea of a 'new course'. He remained 'a strong partisan of the alliance under present circumstances'.[99] But he could only force a change if he was able to harness public opinion to his crusade against 'isolation'. That was the purpose of the 'long spoon' speech, in which he presented himself as a popular tribune, calling for a 'new course'. It included the customary plea for an alliance 'with our kinsmen across the Atlantic'. Significantly, it was an undisguised attack on Salisbury's supposed 'policy of isolation', and concluded with a call for an alliance with 'some great military power [i.e. Germany] as ... in the Crimean War'.[100] His attempt to stir public opinion, however, failed; his *éloquence vigoreuse et brutale* kindled no enthusiasm for a fresh departure in foreign policy.[101] Salisbury's deft handling of the Anglo–French Fashoda crisis in the autumn undermined Chamberlain's case for a new course, and so contained him further.

The inverse correlation between the perception of Britain's growing external problems and Chamberlain's ability to influence the foreign policy debate within the government is crucial to any understanding of the internal dynamics of the Unionist coalition. It explains also why his conversation with the German chancellor, Prince Bülow, at Windsor in the autumn of 1899 did not yield any practical results; nor did his public affirmation of the need for an Anglo–German combination within days of the interview move matters forward. Chamberlain confessed himself to be 'disappointed in [Bülow's] own utterances which so far as England is concerned appear ... to be limited to *le plus stricte necessaire'*.[102] But if he was disappointed, then this was nothing but the interest he had to pay on his own illusions. As one of his Cabinet colleagues observed of the Leicester speech, it had been 'somewhat injudiciously made': 'How few really first-class speakers there are who are good diplomatists. They cannot help exaggerating, or painting in too rosy colours, the probable results of their efforts.'[103]

Matters changed when East Asian problems reared their head again in the summer of 1900. Chamberlain joined an informal Cabinet committee, established to supervise British policy in China; and it was Chamberlain's memorandum of 10 September that broke the impasse between Salisbury's inactivity and the clamour of senior Cabinet ministers for a new departure in foreign policy. The memorandum was an exposé of the anti-isolationists' case. The rose-tinted eyeglass, however, remained firmly in place. Against an inherently expansionist and hostile Russia, only a combination with Germany offered any prospect of success, Chamberlain argued. He projected his strategy onto a vast geopolitical canvas. In China and elsewhere, Britain and Germany shared the same interests, and an Anglo–German compact would be 'a guarantee of our safety'. It was in Britain's interest 'that Germany should throw herself across the path of Russia', he asserted. Very likely it was, though why Germany should sacrifice itself in such a manner for Britain, Chamberlain chose not to explain. The memorandum is remarkable on two counts. In the first place, it indicated a more offensive strategic purpose – the active containment of Russia. And furthermore, it underlined Chamberlain's infinite capacity for inconsistency. In 1898, he had toyed with various international combinations to uphold the 'open door' principle in China. Now he proposed, in effect, shutting the door to all but British commerce in the lucrative Yangtze basin.[104]

To some extent this line of argument foreshadowed some of Chamberlain's later protectionism, with its emphasis on securing certain, specially protected, spheres of interest in East Asia. The concerted push by Chamberlain and the anti-isolationists for talks with Berlin paved the way for the Anglo–German China agreement of October 1900. Chamberlain welcomed its conclusion: '& I think that events are slowly tending to draw us closer together & to separate Germany from Russia'.[105] In this he was swiftly proved wrong when the anticipated German support did not materialise during the Manchurian crisis in the spring of 1901 and a second round of clandestine alliance talks, this time at the initiative of Baron Eckardstein, the counsellor at the German embassy in London, fizzled out and ended in public recriminations with Bülow.[106]

Ironically, at just the moment when Chamberlain's standing in the public reached its zenith, his actual influence on policy-making was more limited. The decision to don 'khaki' in the general election campaign and drape the Unionist platform in the Union Jack was Chamberlain's; and so was the Unionist victory. Yet success at the ballot box did not translate into 'Joe's mandate'. If anything, the Cecilian reconstruction of the Cabinet in November 1900 curtailed his influence further.[107] In yet another twist of irony, Chamberlain was rendered *hors de combat* by a cab accident when the government was reconstituted again in July 1902. To add insult to injury, his horse had slipped as the hansom cab passed underneath the Canadian Arch, a vast, temporary ceremonial archway across Whitehall, erected by the Canadian government to mark the coronation of Edward VII.[108] The Empire remained a slippery platform for Chamberlain to the end. While he was laid up at Charing Cross Hospital, the Cecils moved with unusual speed but characteristic ruthlessness. Salisbury resigned the premiership and his nephew Arthur Balfour was installed at 10 Downing Street.

Chamberlain's eventual exit from the Unionist administration falls outside the remit of this chapter. Historians have accepted the argument of a link between the 1902 Education Bill and the Tariff Reform campaign ever since the free-trading Tory Lord George Hamilton first made the connection in his memoirs.[109] Staying would have meant 'los[ing] Birmingham & the Birmingham influence', as Chamberlain himself understood, and thus political impotence.[110] The setback of 1902 no doubt persuaded Chamberlain to embark on his latest crusade to salvage his embattled position in British politics. But Tariff Reform did not materialise out of nothing. As seen earlier, he had been a consistent advocate of a more efficient and strategic reconfiguration of the Empire. His alliance initiatives had failed, and now 'Joe's War' in South Africa had swallowed up any surplus revenue that would otherwise have helped to finance the social welfare programmes to which he remained committed. The Empire, Chamberlain argued as the war drew to a close,

> is being attacked on all sides; in our isolation we must look to ourselves. [...] We must draw closer our internal relations ... If by adherence to old shibboleths, we are to lose opportunities of closer union ... we shall deserve the disasters which will infallibly come upon us.[111]

Protectionism, then, was to generate the revenues needed and thus reverse Britain's relative economic decline, the spectre of which had haunted Chamberlain since the beginning of the previous decade: 'I am a jingo', he complained to Devonshire', '& I never can get any real support from you or anyone else in the Cabinet.'[112]

It is not necessary here to re-examine Chamberlain's iconoclastic challenge to the free trade orthodoxy. Two points are worth making, however. First, Chamberlain's protectionist crusade had a foreign policy dimension in that it was motivated in part also by his earlier failure to bring about a 'new course': 'the tremendous issue is whether the great Empire of ours is to stand together, one free nation, against all the world, or whether it is to fall apart ... losing sight of the common weal, and losing also all the advantages which union alone can give'.[113]

An oblique comment by Lord Lansdowne, who had secured the alliance with Japan in 1902, underscores this connection. The pact bore the appearance of a break with 'our old policy of isolation', he observed. In reality, it eschewed European commitments; and it was expected to curb additional naval expenditure. The Anglo–Japanese alliance, then, undermined the rationale for the radical break with current foreign policy which Chamberlain had advocated.[114] Second, the Unionist coalition was not strong enough to contain such a dynamic force as Joseph Chamberlain. But equally, Chamberlain failed to develop a populist mass appeal within an essentially Conservative framework. Indeed, in his failure he also drove the Unionist alliance to the brink of destruction.

Perhaps it is true that 'all political lives, unless they are cut off in midstream at a happy juncture, end in failure'.[115] Chamberlain's career certainly offers sufficient supporting evidence for this contention. But this is to miss the importance of foreign policy for Chamberlain's career at its zenith. It is true, in terms of basic tradecraft, that Chamberlain's approach to foreign policy left much to be desired. It showed all the hallmarks of a man who tends to think in terms of grand projects and single solutions to complex problems. He never lost the habit of viewing foreign policy problems through a rose-tinted eyeglass. And he never appreciated that the principal problem in foreign affairs was that they required dealing with foreigners, who, quite properly, considered international problems in light of their own experiences and interests. His own protestations to the contrary notwithstanding, Chamberlain tended to rush things. He sought to hothouse his geopolitical schemes, just as he did his orchids at Highbury. Like those exotic plants, his political schemes were often hybridised. Unlike them, they won him no prizes.

Whatever Chamberlain's shortcomings, questions of foreign policy shaped the dynamic in the Unionist camp and established the political space within which he operated. His ability to tap into a powerful current in Tory and wider Unionist thinking on foreign and imperial matters elevated his position in the coalition. His failure to secure a 'new course', ultimately, propelled him into the political wilderness and tested the Unionist model of mass politics to destruction.

Notes

1. Kimberley to Ripon (private), 6 November 1893, Ripon MSS, British Library, Add. MSS 43526; see also N.S. Johnson, 'The Role of the Cabinet in the Making of Foreign Policy, 1885–1895' (D.Phil. thesis, Oxford, 1970).
2. As 'Boswellized' by Balfour, Balfour to Salisbury, 24 March 1886, Balfour MSS, BL, Add. MSS 49688; also in A.J. Balfour, *Chapters of Autobiography*, ed. by B.E.C. Dugdale (London: Cassell, 1930), pp. 220–1.
3. Chamberlain to Dale, 30 March 1885, as quoted in J.L. Garvin *The Life of Joseph Chamberlain*, vol. 1 (London: Macmillan, 1932), p. 569; see also A.W.W. Dale, *The Life of R.W. Dale of Birmingham* (London: Hodder and Stoughton, 1898), pp. 445–6.
4. Balfour to Salisbury, 24 March 1886, Balfour MSS, BL, Add. MSS 49688.
5. D.W. Bebbington, *The Nonconformist Conscience: Chapel and Politics, 1870–1914* (London: Harper Collins, 1982), pp. 4–5.
6. Chamberlain to Gladstone (private), 17 April 1882, in J. Chamberlain, *A Political Memoir, 1880–1892*, ed. C.H.D. Howard (London: Batchworth, 1953), p. 35.
7. Chamberlain to Gladstone, 7 February 1885, ibid., p. 116.
8. For some thoughts on these matters see P.T. Marsh, *Joseph Chamberlain: Entrepreneur in Politics* (New Haven, CT: Yale University Press, 1994), pp. 199–201, 308–10, 499–503. For Lloyd George's allegations of war-profiteering see *Parliamentary Debates* (4) lxxxviii (10 December 1900), cols 397–409; for some further thoughts on the background see R.C. Trebilcock, 'A "Special Relationship" – Government, Re-armament and the Cordite Firms', *Economic History Review*, 19.2 (1966), pp. 364–79.

9. Anon., *The Life of Joseph Chamberlain* (London: George Newnes, s.a. [1914]), p. 23.
10. For some of the difficulties encountered en route to the Commons see P.T. Marsh, '"A Working Man's Representative": Joseph Chamberlain and the 1874 Election in Sheffield', in J.M.W. Bean (ed.), *The Political Culture of Modern Britain: Studies in Memory of Stephen Koss* (London: Hamilton, 1987), pp. 56–74.
11. Summarised in Austen Chamberlain to Mary (stepmother), 5 May 1907, in A. Chamberlain, *Politics from the Inside: An Epistolary Chronicle, 1906–1914* (London: Cassell, 2nd ed., 1936), 81. For some reflections on the extent, nature and significance of the Chamberlain family correspondence see P.T. Marsh, *The Chamberlain Litany: Letters within a Governing Family from Empire to Appeasement* (London: Haus, 2010), pp. xi–xiii.
12. Salisbury to Selborne (private), 20 April 1895, Selborne MSS, Bodleian Library, Oxford, Ms Selborne 5. The Tory-supporting *Standard* was strongly influenced by Salisbury; see S. Koss, *The Rise and Fall of the Political Press in Britain Vol. 1: The Nineteenth Century* (London: Hamilton, 1981), pp. 300–3.
13. Hamilton diary, 1 December 1899, Hamilton MSS, BL, Add. MSS 48675. Such comments, from both sides of the political divide, were legion. Disraeli referred to him as 'Chamberlain the Cheesemonger', to Lady Bradford, 20 August 1880, in W.F. Monypenny and G.E. Buckle, *The Life of Benjamin Disraeli, Earl of Beaconsfield Vol. 6* (London: John Murray, 1920), p. 588. Asquith attributed to him 'the manner of a cad and the tongue of a bargee', to H. Gladstone, 7 October 1900, H. Gladstone MSS, BL, Add. MSS 45989.
14. Chamberlain to Labouchere, 30 October 1885, as quoted in A. Thorold, *The Life of Henry Labouchere* (London: Constable, 1913), p. 240.
15. M.C. Hurst, *Joseph Chamberlain and West Midlands Politics, 1886–1895* (Oxford: Dugdale Society, 1962), p. 9; for the undiminished electoral strength of Chamberlainite Radical Unionism see also H. Pelling, *Social Geography of British Elections, 1885–1910* (London: Macmillan, 1967), pp. 181–2.
16. Anon., *Life of Chamberlain*, p. 25; for Highbury see P. Ballard, *'Rus in urbe': Joseph Chamberlain's Gardens at Highbury, Moor Green, Birmingham, 1876–1914* (Birmingham: Birmingham Museum and Art Gallery, 1987), pp. 2–3 (originally in *Garden History*, 14.1 (1986), pp. 61–76).
17. *Parliamentary Debates* (5) lxiv (6 July 1914), cols 847–8. Enoch Powell also noted the 'form of ironically humorous invective' which Chamberlain had perfected; J.E. Powell, *Joseph Chamberlain* (London: Weidenfeld and Nicholson, 1977), p. 18.
18. J.A. Spender, 'Mr Chamberlain as a Radical: The Unauthorized Programme', in [A.] Viscount Milner, J.A. Spender, Sir H. Lucy, J.R. Macdonald, H. Cox and L.S. Amery, *Life of Joseph Chamberlain* (London: Associated Newspapers, 1914), pp. 104–5.
19. Sir C. Petrie, *The Chamberlain Tradition* (London: Right Book Club, 1938), p. 89.
20. Sir A. West, *Contemporary Portraits* (London: Thomas Nelson and Sons, 1920), pp. 68–9. At the Board of Trade Chamberlain toyed with the notion of merging parts of it with the Foreign Office to supervise foreign commerce; see min. Dilke, 23 November 1882, Gladstone MSS, BL, Add. MSS 44149.

21. R. Hattersley, *The Edwardians* (London: Little, Brown, 2004), p. 106.
22. Chamberlain to Morley, 27 November and 19 December 1875, Garvin, *Life of Chamberlain*, vol. 1, p. 223.
23. *Parliamentary Debates* (3) ccxxxvii (4 February 1878), cols 997, 998–9.
24. Ibid. ccxlii (1 August 1878), cols 911 and 914.
25. See the pertinent comment by A.N. Porter, *The Origins of the South African War: Joseph Chamberlain and the Diplomacy of Imperialism, 1895–99* (Manchester University Press, 1980), p. 35.
26. Chamberlain to W.T. Stead, 10 August 1878, ibid.
27. *Parliamentary Debates* (3) cclxliv (27 March 1879), cols 1910, 1913 and 1914.
28. Ibid. cclxiii (6 December 1878), col. 177.
29. Ibid. cclvi (31 August 1880), cols 909 and 908.
30. Ibid. cclxiii (25 July 1881), cols 1825 and 1831.
31. Quotes from Dilke diary, 15 June 1882, Dilke MSS, BL, Add. MSS 43925, and Granville to Spencer, 22 June 1882, Lord E. Fitzmaurice, *Life of the Second Earl Granville Vol. 2* (London: Longmans, Green & Co., 1905), p. 265.
32. Chamberlain to Morley, 15 February 1885, Chamberlain MSS, Birmingham University Library, JC 5/54/612.
33. For some thoughts see T. Crosby, *Joseph Chamberlain: A Most Radical Imperialist* (London: I.B. Tauris, 2011), pp. 43–4. Seeley's move to Cambridge seems to have motivated Chamberlain to send his eldest son there; see Powell, *Chamberlain*, p. 52. Seeley's presidential address to the Midlands Institute in 1887 is said to have inspired Chamberlain's plans for a civic university in Birmingham; Sonnenschein to Seeley, 19 October 1892, Seeley MSS, Senate House Library, University of London, MS 903/1B/20; see D. Wormell, *Sir John Robert Seeley and the Uses of History* (Cambridge University Press, 1980), p. 62.
34. Chamberlain acknowledged the influence of Seeley and also of J.A. Froude later; see Chamberlain speech at Royal Colonial Institute, 31 March 1897, 'Mr Chamberlain on the Colonies', *The Times*, 1 April 1897.
35. *Parliamentary Debates* (3) ccciv (9 April 1886), cols 1185 and 1196.
36. Chamberlain to Gladstone, 19 December 1885, Garvin, *Life of Chamberlain*, vol. 2, p. 143; see also R. Jay, *Joseph Chamberlain: A Political Study* (Oxford: Clarendon, 1981), p. 128. The 'integrity of the Empire' would become a recurring theme in Chamberlain's speeches; see his addresses at Edinburgh and Dingwall, 15 and 16 April 1887, *The Times*, 16 and 18 April 1887. It was a far cry from his 1885 tour of the Highlands; see E.A. Cameron, '"A far cry to London": Joseph Chamberlain in Inverness, September 1885', *Innes Review* 57.1 (2006), pp. 36–53.
37. R.V. Holt, *The Unitarian Contribution to Social Progress in England* (London: Allen and Unwin, 1938), pp. 144, 210; implicit also in D. Judd, *Radical Joe: A Life of Joseph Chamberlain* (London: Hamilton, 1977), pp. 162–3.
38. As quoted in Hurst, *West Midlands Politics*, p. 70; for this line of argument see also Crosby, *Chamberlain*, pp. 81–8.
39. M. Hurst, *Joseph Chamberlain and Liberal Reunion: The Round Table Conference 1887* (London: Routledge, 1967); Marsh, *Joseph Chamberlain*, pp. 255–80.
40. 'Mr Chamberlain in Wiltshire', *The Times*, 15 October 1885. Stafford Northcote compared him to Jack Cade, the leader of riotous peasants during Henry IV's reign; 'Mr Chamberlain in Lambeth', ibid., 25 September 1885.

41. Salisbury to Austin (private), 29 July 1886, Austin MSS, Bristol University Library, DM668/Austin; see also P.W. Clayden, *England under the Coalition: The Political History of Great Britain and Ireland from the General Election of 1885 to May 1892* (London: T.F. Unwin, 1892), pp. 56–60, 106–7.
42. *Annual Register 1888* (London, 1889), 5. For pertinent comments on this see P.T. Marsh, *The Discipline of Popular Government: Lord Salisbury's Domestic Statecraft, 1881–1902* (Hassocks: Harvester, 1978), pp. 126–37.
43. Chamberlain to Wolmer, 13 Mar. 1888, Chamberlain MSS, JC 5/74/1; and to Lansdowne, 10 Feb. 1888, Lansdowne MSS, BL, Lans (5) 20.
44. Chamberlain to Dale, 1 May 1890, as quoted in Judd, *Radical Joe*, p. 173.
45. Balfour to Salisbury, 24 July 1892, Balfour MSS, Add. MSS 49690; also in B.E.C. Dugdale, *Arthur James Balfour, First Earl Balfour Vol. 1*(London: Hutchinson, 1936), p. 211, but misdated and with minor errors.
46. Goschen to Granville (personal), 2 July 1880, Granville MSS, National Archives, Kew, PRO 30/29/188.
47. Marsh, *Joseph Chamberlain*, 281–99; for the 1877 Halifax Award and the fisheries question see C.C. Tansill, *Canadian–American Relations, 1875–1911* (New Haven, CT: Yale University Press, 1943), pp. 23–5. For a contemporary account see Sir W. Maycock, *With Mr Chamberlain in the United States and America, 1887–88* (London: Chatto & Windus, 1914).
48. Lord Salisbury's encomium, A. Roberts, *Salisbury: Victorian Titan* (London: Weidenfeld and Nicholson, 1999), p. 600.
49. Marsh, *Joseph Chamberlain*, pp. 298–9.
50. Chamberlain to Lansdowne, 10 Nov. 1887, Lansdowne MSS, BL, Lans (5) 20.
51. Chamberlain Toronto speech, 30 Dec. 1887, Maycock, *With Mr Chamberlain*, pp. 102–12. Chamberlain also emphasised the idea of an Anglo–American racial bond in public speeches in America; see his speech at Philadelphia on 29 Feb. 1888, *The Times*, 2 March 1888; for some further thoughts see D.C. Watt, 'America and the British Foreign Policy-Making Elite, from Joseph Chamberlain to Antony Eden', *Review of Politics* 25.1 (1963), pp. 6–7.
52. Chamberlain himself had toyed with the idea of a federal solution of sorts; see to Morley, 21 Dec. 1885, Garvin, *Life of Chamberlain*, vol. 2, pp. 147–8, but soon concluded that this would be tantamount to the wholesale destruction of the constitution; see anon. [J. Chamberlain], 'A Radical View of the Irish Crisis', *Fortnightly Review* (February 1886).
53. 'The Colonial Conference', *The Times*, 5 April 1887; see also T.G. Otte, '"We are part of the community of Europe": The Tories, Empire and Foreign Policy, 1874–1914', in J. Black (ed.), *The Tory World: Deep History and the Tory Theme in British Foreign Policy, 1679–2014* (Farnham: Ashgate, 2015), pp. 216–18; for some of the background see also Wormell, *Seeley*, pp. 154–8; C.A. Bodelsen, *Studies in Mid-Victorian Imperialism* (Copenhagen and London: Gyldendalske, 1924), p. 205; W.H. Dunn, *James Anthony Froude: A Biography, 1818–1894 Vol. 2* (Oxford: Clarendon, 1963), pp. 351–60.
54. See his speech to the London and Counties Liberal Union in Lambeth, 24 Sept. 1885, *The Times*, 25 September 1885.
55. Chamberlain speech at Cannon Street Hotel, 'Mr Chamberlain on British Interests in Africa', *The Times*, 15 May 1888.
56. J. Chamberlain, *Patriotism: Address Delivered to the Students of the University of Glasgow on November 3rd, 1897, on the Occasion of His Installation as Lord*

Rector (London: Constable, 1897), pp. 10, 15, 28, 47–8, 59–60. The lecture is somewhat baroque in its rich adornments of tags from Bacon, Dr Johnson, de Tocqueville, Shakespeare, Bolingbroke, 'Junius', Horace, Carlyle and Molière.
57. Chamberlain to Wolmer, 12 October 1894, Selborne MSS, MS Selborne 8; P. Fraser, *Joseph Chamberlain: Radicalism and Empire, 1868–1914* (London: Cassell, 1966), pp. 149–54. There were bumps in the road; I. Cawood, 'Joseph Chamberlain, the Conservative Party and the Leamington Spa Dispute of 1895', *Historical Research*, 79.206 (2006), pp. 554–77.
58. Salisbury to Selborne (private), 13 April 1895, Selborne MSS, MS Selborne 5.
59. Wolmer to Chamberlain, 15 October 1894, Chamberlain MSS, JC 5/74/24; Chamberlain to Salisbury, 15 Nov. 1894, Garvin, *Life of Chamberlain*, vol. 2, p. 617.
60. Salisbury to Selborne, 13 April 1895, Selborne MSS, Ms Selborne 5 – this in response to Chamberlain's letter on Welsh disestablishment, but its application was general; for the background see P.M.H. Bell, *Disestablishment in Ireland and Wales* (London: SPCK, 1969).
61. Chamberlain speech to Liverpool Working Men's Conservative Association, 5 Sep. 1894, 'Mr Chamberlain in Liverpool', *The Times*, 6 September 1894.
62. 'Mr Chamberlain at Durham', ibid., 17 October 1894.
63. Chamberlain speech to Canada Club, Albion Tavern, Aldgate Street, 25 March 1896, 'Mr Chamberlain on Imperial Federation', ibid., 26 March 1896; see also A.S. Thompson, *Imperial Britain: The Empire in British Politics, c. 1880–1932* (London: Longman, 2000), pp. 17–18.
64. Chamberlain speech at the Congress of the Chambers of Commerce of the Empire, 9 June 1896, 'Congress of Chambers of Commerce of the Empire', *The Times*, 10 June 1896; see also S.H. Zebel, 'Joseph Chamberlain and the Genesis of Tariff Reform', *Journal of British Studies*, 7.1 (1967), pp. 139–41.
65. For some thoughts see T.G. Otte, '"The Swing of the Pendulum at Home": By-elections and Foreign Policy, 1865–1914', in T.G. Otte and P. Readman (eds), *By-elections in British Politics, 1832–1914* (Woodbridge: Boydell and Brewer, 2013), pp. 142–6.
66. Salisbury to Selborne (private), 30 June 1895, Selborne MSS, MS Selborne 5; see also P. Fraser, 'The Liberal Unionist Alliance: Chamberlain, Hartington and the Conservatives, 1886–1904', *English Historical Review*, 78.4 (1962), pp. 62–78.
67. B. Forster, *A Conjunction of Interests: Business, Politics and Tariffs, 1825–1879* (University of Toronto Press, 1986) offers the best discussion of this.
68. For a detailed discussion see M. Hart, *A Trading Nation* (Vancouver: University of British Columbia Press, 2002); also Jay, *Chamberlain*, pp. 210–11.
69. Chamberlain to Salisbury (private), 29 December 1897, Salisbury MSS, Hatfield House, 3M/E/Chamberlain (1896–97); Garvin, *Life of Chamberlain Vol. 3*, p. 249.
70. Chamberlain to Selborne, 3 July 1895, Selborne MSS, Ms Selborne 8.
71. Chamberlain to Salisbury (private), 29 December 1897, Salisbury MSS, Hatfield House, 3M/E/Chamberlain (1896–97); T.G. Otte, *The China Question: Great Power Rivalry and British Isolation, 1894–1905* (Oxford University Press, 2007), p. 100.
72. Chamberlain to Balfour (secret), 3 February 1898, Chamberlain MSS, Birmingham University Library, JC 5/5/70; see T.G. Otte, '"Avenge England's Dishonour": By-elections, Parliament and the Politics of Foreign Policy in 1898', *English Historical Review*, 121.491 (2006), pp. 397–400.

73. Chamberlain speech at Queenslander banquet, Whitehall, 21 January 1896, 'Mr Chamberlain on Colonial Loyalty', *The Times*, 22 January 1896.
74. Chamberlain to Salisbury (private), 31 December 1897, Salisbury MSS, 3M/E/ Chamberlain (1896–97).
75. 'Mr Chamberlain in Birmingham', *The Times*, 17 May 1902.
76. Chamberlain speech at the annual dinner of the Royal Colonial Institute, 31 March 1896, 'Mr Chamberlain on the Colonies', *The Times*, 1 April 1896.
77. Chamberlain speech to the Liberal Unionist Executive, 12 May 1898, *The Times*, 14 May 1898; see also M. Crouzet, 'Joseph Chamberlain', in P. Renouvin (ed.), *Les Politiques d'Expansion Impérialiste* (Paris: Presses Universitaires de France, 1949), pp. 164–5.
78. Chamberlain speech at the Union League Club, Philadelphia, 29 February 1888, 'Mr Chamberlain', *The Times*, 2 March 1888. The notion of an Anglo–American alliance was popular among Radicals; see S. Maccoby, *English Radicalism, Vol. 5: 1886–1914* (London: Routledge, 1953), pp. 260–1.
79. Chamberlain speech at Birmingham Liberal Unionist meeting, 12 May 1898, *The Times*, 14 May 1898; see also S. Anderson, *Race and Rapprochement: Anglo-Saxonism and Anglo-American Relations, 1895–1904* (London and Toronto: Fairleigh Dickinson University Press, 1981), pp. 149–51.
80. Chamberlain speech in Leicester, *The Times*, 1 December 1899; for some of the background see W. Mock, 'The Function of "Race" in Imperialist Ideologies: The Example of Joseph Chamberlain', in P.M. Kennedy and A.J. Nicholls (eds), *Nationalist and Racialist Movements in Britain and Germany before the First World War* (London: Macmillan, 1981), pp. 190–203.
81. There is an interesting parallel with Lloyd George; see K.O. Morgan, 'Lloyd George and Germany', *Historical Journal*, 39.4 (1996), pp. 755–66.
82. J. Butler, *The Liberal Party and the Jameson Raid* (Oxford: Clarendon, 1968), p. 289.
83. A misnomer, if ever there was one; see T.G. Otte, '"Floating Downstream"? Lord Salisbury and British Foreign Policy, 1878–1902', in T.G. Otte (ed.), *The Makers of British Foreign Policy: From Pitt to Thatcher* (Basingstoke and New York: Palgrave, 2002), pp. 98–127.
84. Hurst, *West Midlands Politics*, p. 10; the phrase was Garvin's: Garvin, *Life of Chamberlain*, vol. 3, p. 7.
85. Chamberlain to Salisbury (private), 24 December 1895, Salisbury MSS, 3M/E/Chamberlain (1887–95); and reply (private), 30 December 1895, Chamberlain MSS, JC 5/67/36.
86. Chamberlain speech at the Constitutional Club, 22 April 1896, 'Mr Chamberlain on the Political Situation', *The Times*, 23 April 1896.
87. Memo. Chamberlain, 'Delagoa Bay', 24 November 1897, Selborne MSS, Ms Selborne 8.
88. Chamberlain to Selborne (secret), 1 December 1897, ibid.; see also memo. Chamberlain, 'Niger Negotiations', 24 January 1898, CAB 37/46/10. For some of the background see R.V. Kubicek, *The Administration of Imperialism: Joseph Chamberlain at the Colonial Office* (Durham, NC: Duke University Press, 1969), pp. 68–91, and R.E. Dumett, 'Joseph Chamberlain, Imperial Finance and Railway Policy in British West Africa in the Late Nineteenth Century', *English Historical Review*, 90.355 (1975), pp. 304–6.

89. Rumbold to Rumbold sen., 26 Aug. 1898, Rumbold MSS, Bod., MS Rumbold dep. 10; see also Lady F. Balfour, *Ne Obleviscaris*, vol. 2 (London, Hodder and Stoughton, 1930), p. 270.

90. Esher diary, 29 January 1898, M.V. Brett (ed.), *Journals and Letters of Reginald, Viscount Esher*, vol. 1 (London: Nicholson and Watson, 1934), pp. 201–1.

91. Chamberlain to James (secret), 11 January 1898, James of Hereford MSS, Hereford County Record Office, M45/936. Chamberlain's version is confirmed by Devonshire, to James, 11 January 1898, M45/936. Fortunately for the historian, Salisbury's private secretary had forgotten to invite James to the Cabinet meeting; Lord Askwith, *Lord James of Hereford* (London: Ernest Benn, 1930), pp. 254–6.

92. Chamberlain to Balfour (private), 3 February 1898, Chamberlain MSS, JC 5/5/70.

93. 'Mr Chamberlain on Colonial Loyalty', *The Times*, 22 January 1896.

94. See Alan Sykes's ingenious interpretation of Tariff Reform, in *Tariff Reform in British Politics, 1903–1914* (Oxford University Press, 1979), pp. 285–94.

95. Lord Charles Beresford (Conservative, York City), *Parliamentary Debates* (4) lvi (5 April 1898), cols 234–6; for a detailed discussion see Otte, 'Avenge England's Dishonour', pp. 404–6.

96. Brodrick to Selborne (private), 16 August 1898, Selborne MSS, MS Selborne 2.

97. Memo. Chamberlain, 29 March 1898, Chamberlain MSS, JC 7/2/2A/3; also in Garvin, *Chamberlain Vol. 3*, pp. 259–60, but with minor deviations from the original; for a reinterpretation of the alliance talks see Otte, *China Question*, pp. 142–54.

98. Memo. Chamberlain, 23 July 1898, Chamberlain MSS, JC 7/2/2A/10.

99. Chamberlain to Salisbury (private), 2 May 1898, Chamberlain MSS, JC 11/30/118; memo. Chamberlain, 3 May 1898, JC 7/2/2A/8.

100. 'Mr Chamberlain in Birmingham', *The Times*, 14 May 1898.

101. Geoffray to Hanotaux (no. 293), 17 May 1898, Ministère des Affaires Etrangères (ed.), *Documents Diplomatiques Français*, 1st ser., vol. 14 (Paris: Imprimerie Nationale, 1946), no. 193; Otte, *China Question*, pp. 158–9.

102. Chamberlain to Lascelles (private), 12 December 1899, Chamberlain MSS, JC 7/2/2A/36; Chamberlain speech at Leicester, 30 November 1899, *The Times*, 1 Dec. 1899.

103. Hamilton to Curzon (private), 1 December 1899, Hamilton MSS, British Library Oriental and India Office Collection, MSS Eur. C.126/1.

104. Memo. Chamberlain, 'The Chinese Problem', 10 September 1900, CAB 37/53/56; see also Marsh, *Chamberlain*, pp. 495–6; Otte, *China Question*, pp. 205–7.

105. Chamberlain to Balfour (private), 21 October 1900, Whittinghame Muniment MSS, National Archive of Scotland, Edinburgh, GD 433/2/39.

106. Otte, *China Question*, pp. 237–77; 290–1.

107. J. Cornford, 'The Parliamentary Foundations of the "Hôtel Cecil"', in R. Robins (ed.), *Ideas and Institutions of Victorian Britain: Essays in Honour of George Kitson Clarke* (London: G. Bell and Sons, 1967), pp. 268–311; P. Readman, 'The Conservative Party, Patriotism and British Politics', *Journal of British Studies*, 40.1 (2001), pp. 107–45.

108. 'Accident to Mr Chamberlain', *The Times*, 8 July 1902.

109. Lord G. Hamilton, *Parliamentary Reminiscences and Reflections, 1886–1906* (London: John Murray, 1922), p. 315; and S. Koss, *Nonconformity in Modern British Politics* (London: Batsford, 1975), pp. 55–62.

110. See the early ruminations in Chamberlain to Selborne, 7 Nov. 1901, Selborne MSS, MS Selborne 9; also R.A. Rempel, *Unionists Divided: Arthur Balfour, Joseph Chamberlain and Unionist Free Traders* (Newton Abbott: David & Charles, 1972), pp. 28–30.

111. Chamberlain speech at Birmingham, 16 May 1902, *The Times*, 17 May 1902; see also E.H.H. Green, *The Crisis of Conservatism: The Politics, Economics and Ideology of the British Conservative Party, 1880–1914* (London: Routledge, 1996), pp. 73–6.

112. Chamberlain to Devonshire, 22 September 1902, Chamberlain MSS, JC 11/11/10.

113. Chamberlain speech to his West Birmingham constituents, 15 May 1903, J. Chamberlain, *Imperial Union and Tariff Reform: Speeches Delivered from May 15 to Nov. 4, 1903* (London: G. Richards, 1903), p. 4; see also B. Semmel, *Imperialism and Social Reform: English Social-Political Thought, 1895–1914* (London: Allen & Unwin, 1960), pp. 83–97.

114. Lansdowne to Curzon (private), 16 February 1902, Curzon MSS, BLOIOC, MSS Eur. F.111/151; Otte, *China Question*, pp. 305–6.

115. Powell, *Chamberlain*, p. 151.

2
Joseph Chamberlain's Reputation in South Africa

Jackie Grobler

Joseph Chamberlain served as British Secretary of State for Colonies for eight years (1895–1903). Southern African affairs dominated his activities throughout this period. He was the only Colonial Secretary who ever visited South Africa. His policies had a massive impact on the subcontinent and contributed to the outbreak of the Anglo–Boer War in 1899. As a result he is mentioned, if not extensively discussed, in all books focusing on Anglo–South African relations in the period. This is the case both in contemporary books written in Chamberlain's lifetime and also in historical works published in the course of the next century. In some books, such as Garvin and Amery's *The Life of Joseph Chamberlain*, he is portrayed as a heroic figure.[1] On the other hand, cartoonists on the European continent at the time of the Anglo–Boer War portrayed him as a butcher in reaction to his spirited defence of the concentration camp policy of British military authorities in South Africa.[2] The distinguished South African historian Hermann Giliomee recently described Chamberlain as a conspirator.[3] At the centenary of Chamberlain's death it is opportune to revisit his activities and impact, especially with regard to South Africa. It is the specific objective of this chapter to highlight the dissonant reputation that this controversial historical figure gained in South Africa, both in his lifetime and also in South African historical tradition.

As spokesperson of the Liberal party on southern African affairs, Chamberlain could find no justification for the annexation of the South African Republic (Transvaal) in 1877. Even before the outbreak of the Anglo–Transvaal War of 1880–81, he encouraged the Prime Minister, W.E. Gladstone, to withdraw from the region.[4] As President of the Board of Trade in the Gladstone Cabinet from 1880, he was in favour of the restitution of Transvaal's independence after the war, despite the

British defeat in the battle of Majuba Hill. However, in the course of the next decade Chamberlain developed a strong belief in imperialism. He became a staunch supporter of the view that if Britain intended to uphold its status as a world power, it would be essential not only to extend the Empire but also to organise it more efficiently. By the mid-1890s, he believed that this could be achieved through imperial federation, but that the federation of Australia and of South Africa would have to precede that.[5]

When Chamberlain became Secretary for Colonies in the Unionist Government of Lord Salisbury in mid-1895, southern African issues subsequently dominated the activities of his department. Chamberlain in this regard did not hesitate to take strong action. In August 1895 he instituted an inquiry into the behaviour of Boer commandoes in the previous year's campaigns against black communities in the north-east of the South African Republic.[6] At that time it became notable that Chamberlain seemed more than willing to accept anti-Boer newspaper reports from South Africa without questioning their truthfulness, while at the same time revealing a critical attitude towards pro-Boer press reporting in and about South Africa. The British historian, Andrew Porter, ascribes Chamberlain's posture in this regard to his urge to create positive public publicity for his policies.[7]

In November 1895 Chamberlain intervened on behalf of the government of the Cape Colony in the dispute over railway tariffs between that self-governing colony and the South African Republic by sending a strongly worded protest note to President Kruger after the latter had closed the drifts across the Vaal River to ox-wagon traffic. The crisis only ended when Kruger backed down and reopened the trade route into his Republic.[8] Chamberlain's actions during the drifts dispute made him more or less popular with one section of the Afrikaner community of South Africa. These were the so-called "Bondsmen" of the Cape Colony, all members of the *Afrikaner Bond* (League) under their leader Jan Hendrik Hofmeyr, who remained loyal to both Britain and Chamberlain throughout the Anglo–Boer War (1899–1902). Hofmeyr had little love for President Paul Kruger, which probably explains his willingness to cooperate with the prime minister of the Cape Colony, Cecil John Rhodes (up to the Jameson Raid), and with Chamberlain, and why he supported him for most of the duration of his term as Colonial Secretary. Chamberlain furthermore endeared himself to the Bondsmen soon after he became Colonial Secretary when he allowed the Cape Colony to take over British Bechuanaland.[9] The main point was that Chamberlain, Rhodes and the Bondsmen shared in the general indignation against the Kruger government. An undetermined percentage of the so-called Uitlanders in the South African Republic, as well as Rhodes, who was the most prominent mining magnate in Southern Africa, were dissatisfied with the situation in the Republic and decided by the end of 1895 that it was opportune to bring about change by direct intervention. Chamberlain became involved in intrigues driven by Rhodes within six weeks of becoming Colonial Secretary. He was aware of Rhodes's role in fomenting a revolutionary movement against the Kruger government in Johannesburg and of Rhodes's determination to support the uprising that he hoped to bring about militarily. Indeed, by the end of 1895 he had become an accessory to the plot. When Rhodes requested the transfer of a strip of land in Bechuanaland Protectorate bordering on the South African Republic, which he could use to launch an invasion into the Republic, to his Chartered Company, Chamberlain approved, even though he gave less land than Rhodes had asked for.[10] The invasion was led by Leander Starr Jameson, who acted on his own initiative, and soon encountered obstacles. Chamberlain publicly repudiated Jameson's activities on 30 December 1895, even before his final failure. He did not believe that Jameson would be able to overthrow the Kruger government on his own.[11] The raid ended in failure with Jameson being captured by the burghers of the South African Republic, but it nevertheless had far-reaching consequences. President Kruger and his Executive Council decided to hand over Jameson and his companions to the British government in order that they might be punished by their own courts according to their own laws. When Chamberlain was informed of this decision, he immediately telegraphed Kruger to thank him for his magnanimous act. A British court eventually found Jameson guilty of the contravention of the Foreign Enlistment Act of 1870 and sentenced him to 15 months' imprisonment. He was, however, released after only a few months on medical parole. His accomplices were also released before the expiration of their sentences.[12] Kruger's terse commentary on Jameson's early release was that this constituted an ironic reflection on the gratitude shown by England for his magnanimity. He added that the fact that Jameson was released from prison on account of illness, but recovered his health immediately afterwards, confirmed that Chamberlain was nothing but his accomplice.[13]

In the aftermath of the failure of the Jameson Raid, Chamberlain invited Kruger to London for discussions. He furthermore proposed that a sort of Home Rule or self-government should be granted to Johannesburg and added that he was not prepared to consider any amendments to Article 4 of the Convention of London of 1884, which placed restrictions on the foreign relations of the South African Republic. Kruger's conclusion was that Chamberlain believed that it was the Republic, and not Great Britain, that had to make amends. In this respect Kruger pointed out that it was Chamberlain's resistance to the granting of Home Rule to Ireland which caused him to resign from Gladstone's Cabinet, and now he proposed the very same deal for Johannesburg. Kruger was also dissatisfied because Chamberlain allowed this communiqué to be published in London before he despatched it to Pretoria. Consequently Kruger's government replied to Chamberlain that it was undesirable and inadvisable to give previous publicity to views which the British Government thought fit to adopt towards the Republic, adding that the Republic could not permit any interference in its internal affairs. Chamberlain soon answered that if his proposal was not acceptable, he would not insist upon it. Kruger thereupon telegraphed the conditions upon which he would be willing to go to London. These included, in the first place, the substitution of the London Convention by a treaty of peace, commerce and amity. Chamberlain refused this condition. He continued to mention grievances that had to be removed, that it was of the highest importance to Britain to remain the paramount power in South Africa and that, even if the London Convention was replaced by another, Article 4 of that treaty had to be included in a new agreement. Kruger now decided that it would make no sense to journey to England and Chamberlain withdrew his invitation.[14] This was the first of a series of instances in which Chamberlain demanded strict adherence to Article 4 of the London Convention. Jan Kemp, who made a name for himself as a Republican general during the Anglo–Boer War of 1899–1902, probably reflected the united opinion of the whole Transvaal government of those years when he later wrote that Chamberlain seemed to have been possessed by Article 4.[15]

When it had become clear to Chamberlain by April 1896 that Kruger would not visit London, the Colonial Secretary took steps to strengthen the British garrison in South Africa and to send troops to the borders of the South African Republic. There were even rumours circulating that Chamberlain considered issuing an ultimatum to the Republic.[16] However, his own officials, the British High Commissioner in South Africa and the governments of the Cape and Natal, convinced him that it was still possible to reach a diplomatic solution.[17] It was at this time that Chamberlain voiced the premonition that would subsequently come back to haunt him when he warned that

A war in South Africa would be one of the most serious wars that could possibly be waged. It would be in the nature of a civil war. It would be a long war, and ... it would leave behind it the embers of a strife which I believe generations would be hardly long enough to extinguish.[18]

The British House of Commons had meanwhile appointed a Parliamentary Commission of Inquiry (later nicknamed the Commission of No-Inquiry), of which Chamberlain was a member, to investigate the Jameson Raid. The Commission did, in one of its sessions, come very close to exposing Chamberlain's complicity. The latter immediately intervened to repudiate insinuations that he knew about the plot by the following declaration: 'I never had, any knowledge, or, until, I think it was the day before the actual raid took place, the slightest suspicion of anything in the nature of a hostile or armed invasion of the Transvaal.' Chamberlain's biographer Peter Marsh very generously comments that 'only the touch of ambiguity in the last eight words of this assertion saved it from being an outright lie'.[19] Jan Smuts, who was a junior lawyer in Johannesburg at that time, reacted as follows to what he regarded as Chamberlain's manipulation of the commission: 'My opinion is that Chamberlain is determined to drive things to extremes: "to wipe off old scores" as they say. Who knows what doctrines friend Rhodes has preached to him.'[20] That belief contributed to Smuts's growing concern, as the inquiry progressed, about the line of questioning followed by Chamberlain:

When I saw how Mr Chamberlain – in those leading questions and that spirit of partisan animosity which have been deeply pondered by every thinking man in South Africa – continually referred to the maintenance of England's rights in South Africa *even by force*, I thought of the same phrase as it was bandied about the floor of the Houses of Parliament in the years immediately preceding the War with the American Colonies.[21]

Smuts categorically condemned Chamberlain. In 1897 he wrote in an unpublished article that Chamberlain's policies had in his first two years as Secretary for Colonies done untold harm to South Africa. Smuts added that it was difficult to gauge Chamberlain's motives because of his changes of opinion as a politician in the past. It was even possible that South Africa was a mere pawn in Chamberlain's political games in Britain itself.[22] This view was widely shared. President Kruger's special envoy to Europe in the years immediately preceding the Anglo–Boer War, Willem Leyds, regarded Chamberlain as an ambitious person who was striving to become British prime minster and would do whatever he felt was necessary to place himself in centre stage.[23]

The British commission of inquiry into the Jameson Raid reported in July 1897 that neither the Secretary for Colonies, nor any official of his department, had received any information that could have made them aware of the plot.[24] This finding was immediately rejected by a number of prominent South Africans, including President Kruger, who believed that there was overwhelming evidence to indicate that Chamberlain had known all about the matter all along.[25] In July 1897 the British Lower House debated the report on the Jameson Raid. Rhodes was severely criticised in the report, but in his speech Chamberlain vigorously defended him. Kruger's reaction to Chamberlain's declaration in the House that Rhodes was a man of honour was that Chamberlain publicly defended Rhodes 'because he feared least the latter should make statements which would be anything but pleasant hearing for the Colonial Secretary. This, at least, was the view taken of the matter in the Republic.'[26] Decades later, the noted South African historian Burridge Spies agreed with Kruger that it is possible that Chamberlain spoke under the threat that Rhodes's friends would expose him if he did not defend the former Cape prime minister. What is certain is that many, especially Afrikaners in South Africa, were appalled by Chamberlain's stance.[27]

With his apparent complicity in the Jameson Raid and his defence of Rhodes, Chamberlain's reputation as an honourable person with impeccable integrity was permanently shattered in the eyes of many in South Africa, including both Afrikaners and prominent South Africans of English descent. Thus Kemp remarked that if Chamberlain's statement that Rhodes was honourable really reflected what he regarded as honourable, it explains the series of political misdemeanours he later committed in the Transvaal.[28] The venerated Cape politician, John X. Merriman, who initially admired the Colonial Secretary, turned into a firm critic after the Raid. He predicted early in 1896 that Chamberlain would have South Africa 'in a blaze before the year is out'. Mrs J. Merriman commented on Chamberlain's defence of Rhodes that he was obviously "betwattled" by him.[29] Two sons of Sir John Molteno, who was the first prime minister of the Cape Colony, seem to have admired Chamberlain initially, but turned into critics in the wake of the Raid. Thus Percy Molteno referred to Chamberlain's suggestion about Home Rule for the Witwatersrand as a 'foolish proposition', while John Tennant Molteno indicated that he could not trust Chamberlain since the latter edited correspondence to the Cape Colony to protect Rhodes and that Chamberlain's defence of Rhodes in the House of Commons was disgraceful.[30] Chief Justice J.G. Kotzé of the South African Republic, who was a fierce critic of Kruger, observed that Chamberlain had by his defence of Rhodes conceded that the British Empire 'had been gained by fraud and treachery'.[31] Even J.W. Sauer, who was a prominent member of the Afrikaner Bond, wrote that 'The fair-minded people have lost all confidence in Chamberlain because of his attitude in the Committee of Enquiry.'[32] W.P. Schreiner, who became the prime minister of the Cape Colony in 1898, spoke of 'the *insult* of the whole affair [the Raid] from beginning to end, culminating with Mr. Chamberlain's ... cynical defence of Rhodes's honour'.[33] On the other hand, however, Chamberlain certainly had supporters in southern Africa. Thus the South African League, which emerged as a direct result of the Jameson Raid and of which Rhodes became the president, supported the Secretary for Colonies' policies in the subcontinent.[34]

In January 1897 Chamberlain took the fateful decision to appoint Sir Alfred Milner as Governor of the Cape Colony and High Commissioner of South Africa. Kruger's terse comment was that Chamberlain 'had found the man he wanted for his dealings with the South African Republic'. The President was convinced that Chamberlain appointed Milner 'only with a view of driving matters in South Africa to extremes' and that Milner was a 'tool' in Chamberlain's hand that would fulfil his mission 'faithfully'.[35] Kemp shared that opinion.[36] Chamberlain and Milner initially agreed that it would be wise to remain aloof as long as British treaty rights were not seriously threatened by the Kruger government. Spies notes that Chamberlain was obviously aware that there was at that stage very limited public or Cabinet support for action against Kruger.[37] In Kruger's opinion that was why Chamberlain began sending an uninterrupted series of dispatches, which he kept up until the war broke up, 'which had no other object than to embitter the British people against the Republic and to make them believe that the Republic was constantly sinning against England'.[38]

Early in 1897 Chamberlain alleged in a dispatch that the South African Republic had contravened Article 4 of the London Convention inter alia by concluding a treaty with Portugal without acquiring the approval of the British government. Kruger's government answered that under the terms of the Convention, they did not have to acquire approval until the treaty was finally settled. The Republic added that, in view of the difference of interpretation as to this issue, it would be advisable to seek the opinion of an impartial arbitrator. Chamberlain replied that since Britain was the suzerain of the South African Republic, he could not consent to refer a difference to arbitration. Kruger found Chamberlain's sudden raking up of the claim to suzerainty, which was part of the Convention of Pretoria of 1881 but left out of the Convention of London of 1884, as nothing but vexatious to the highest degree. Kruger believed that when it was pointed out to Chamberlain that his predecessor, Lord Derby, had specifically omitted the concept of suzerainty from the 1884 treaty, Chamberlain would concede that he was wrong, but that did not happen. As a result Kruger was forced to conclude that Chamberlain was a victim of what he called 'English inso-lence' in continuing to keep up his nonsensical argument and main-taining that suzerainty still existed.[39] Kruger was expressing the view of many Republican or Boer leaders as well as burghers of that period. Thus President Steyn of the Orange Free State also had nothing but contempt for Chamberlain's claim to suzerainty. In a letter to his wife he referred to suzerainty as a vague word with a vague meaning and therefore very useful to the Colonial Secretary, since in terms of that concept all sorts of demands could be made.[40] In September 1899 Smuts told Sir William Conyngham Greene, the British agent in Pretoria, that nothing had upset the government and the burghers of the South African Republic as much as Chamberlain's persistent assertion of the suzerainty. As far as Smuts was concerned, suzerainty was 'pure nonsense' and moreover in conflict with historical facts and the Convention of 1884.[41]

The so-called 'Edgar incident' further contributed to Chamberlain's negative reputation in South Africa. Kruger specifically mentioned the way in which the Colonial Secretary reacted to this minor though tragic affair as an example of his duplicity. The details of this incident are of little importance and can be briefly stated: on the night of 18 December 1898 Edgar, a British subject living in Johannesburg, assaulted Foster, another British subject, so badly that the latter died a few days later. When the police attempted to arrest Edgar, he resisted and assaulted a policeman, Jones, who then shot him. Edgar died on the spot. When Chamberlain was informed about this incident, he publicly attempted to defend Edgar's actions. Kruger reacted angrily: 'can malevolence go further that this? And ought not a minister to be ashamed thus to vio-late the truth in an official dispatch?'[42] What is even more astonishing, when one reads of this history today, is that, not only did Chamberlain attempt to defend the actions of a murderer, but that a British Cabinet minister involved himself in the details of a fatal confrontation between two mineworkers in a distant country. Truth seems to have been of limited consequence to him. He was clearly on the lookout for a stick with which to hit out at Kruger and his Republic.

By the end of 1898, Milner concluded that British supremacy in South Africa could, in the long term, only be ensured either by drastic changes in the South African Republic or by war. He began sending Chamberlain lengthy despatches in an attempt to convince him to accept his proposals for British intervention. The last significant attempt to avoid war was the conference that took place in Bloemfontein, the capital of the Republic of the Orange Free State, from 31 May to 6 June 1899 between Kruger and Milner in an attempt to resolve differences. It ended in failure. Chamberlain's telegram to Milner requesting him not to break off negotiations, reached the High Commissioner after he had already done so.[43] Milner kept pressing for intervention, but Chamberlain and the British Cabinet felt that another conference should be convened, this time in Cape Town. On 27 July 1899, the South African Republic was, on Milner's insistence, informed that a joint inquiry on the issue of the granting of the franchise to Uitlanders in the South African Republic should precede the conference. Chamberlain was by that time busy inciting the British public by denouncing Kruger and demanding the right to interfere in the domestic affairs of the Republic. Percy Molteno commented that 'Chamberlain is behaving in a most dangerous manner, and throwing South Africa into confusion and possibly a war'.[44] John X. Merriman believed that Chamberlain was 'creating a position that will enable him to use force. If it was anyone else one would call such action treacherous in the extreme.'[45] Milner and Chamberlain agreed that an ultimatum should be issued in the event of a rejection by Kruger of a joint inquiry. The South African Republic was not prepared to accept a joint inquiry. Thus attempts to reach a peaceful solution ended.[46] The British Government drew up an ultimatum and Chamberlain decided to have it handed to the Kruger Government on 11 October 1899. In the meantime his government despatched 10,000 additional troops to South Africa. On 9 October 1899 the Kruger government, supported by the Republic of the Orange Free State, handed an ultimatum to the British agent in Pretoria. With the rejection by the British Government of that ultimatum two days later, the Anglo–Boer War began.[47] Merriman commented that 'Milner and Chamberlain in two years by their rampant Imperialism and their neurotic desire for notoriety have put the clock back for twenty-five years.'[48]

South African historians such as J.S. Marais,[49] F.A. van Jaarsveld,[50] Fransjohan Pretorius[51] and Hermann Giliomee[52] are in agreement that Chamberlain must shoulder a large share of the responsibility for the outbreak of the Anglo–Boer War. Spies believes it was Milner who convinced Chamberlain that war was necessary to protect British supremacy in South Africa. Chamberlain in turn convinced the British Government of this necessity.[53] Jan Smuts's condemnation of Chamberlain's South African policy was so wide-ranging that it seems as if there is only one statement of the Secretary for Colonies with which he was in agreement. That was Chamberlain's declaration at the end of 1899 in the House of Commons, that the war arose from mistakes and misunderstandings. Smuts added that these mistakes and misunderstandings were morally indefensible.[54] The historian can only wonder if Chamberlain and Smuts had the same mistakes and misunderstandings in mind.

Chamberlain's optimistic belief that the Boers would quickly be defeated was soon proved wrong. He was often in a hurry to advise the Minister of War and the generals in South Africa on tactics that should be followed. Thus, in December 1899, after the disastrous British losses on the battlefield during the so-called 'Black Week', he proposed that a British force should be sent through the Orange Free State to emulate General Sherman's notorious march through Georgia in the American Civil War. To the South African historian, Helen Bradford, this request serves as an indication that Chamberlain considered retribution through devastation long before the guerrilla phase of the war.[55] Chamberlain remained the target of severe criticism in the House of Commons throughout the course of the war. Many South Africans, including especially the Boer leadership, were shocked by the wartime parliamentary statements of the Colonial Secretary. Percy Molteno referred to 'that barking demagogue Chamberlain'.[56] J.W. Sauer, who met with Chamberlain early in 1901, reported that the Colonial Secretary did not seem to have any real conception of the situation as it existed in South Africa. Later in 1901 he wrote: 'I see that Chamberlain has said that the Boers shoot women from behind hedges. Why is an application not made to some proper court for a curator over the fellow?'[57] Kemp rejected with contempt Chamberlain's statement that 'never in the history of war has war been carried out with so much humanity on the part of the officers and of the soldiers concerned as in the present war'. Kemp's explanation was that Chamberlain was one of the accused, and his opinion should be seen against that background.[58]

Chamberlain was condemned for his public statements regarding the concentration camps both in Britain and in South Africa, especially when he attempted to defend the institution of the camps as a necessity, despite the fact that mortality in all the camps together ended on the catastrophic figure of more than 20 per cent of the camp inhabitants. Boer leaders were astonished by Chamberlain's white-washing of the camp system when he declared that 'as regards the formation of those concentration camps, I do not hesitate to say that it was a policy of humanity ... a humanity absolutely unprecedented in the history of war'. Kemp, to mention one example, regarded the camps as the ultimate in inhuman treatment and the Leader of the Opposition in Britain, Campbell-Bannerman, was driven by Emily Hobhouse's reports on conditions in the camps, to refer to them as 'methods of barbarism'.[59]

A further series of statements made by Chamberlain during the course of the war contributed to his reputation in South Africa as a person whose word could not be trusted. Smuts claimed in a letter to the anti-war campaigner and leading journalist, W.T. Stead, in January 1902 that Chamberlain had malicious or at least wrongful motives when he officially declared in the House of Commons that the policy of farm-burning had been discontinued at the very moment when almost every farm in the two Republics was being torched and destroyed under directions of Lord Kitchener.[60] Kemp was even more outspoken. He called Chamberlain a 'plutocratic barbarian' in reaction to the latter's statement in the British parliament that the burning of farmhouses was not important from an economic standpoint, since 'a farmhouse in the Transvaal is little better than, if so good as, a labourer's cottage in this country, and accordingly the pecuniary damage done is really not so very great'.[61] The negative feelings towards Chamberlain that were revealed by Boer generals such as Smuts and Kemp seem to have been shared by the rank-and-file burghers who were fighting for their independence. John X. Merriman observed that 'they nourish towards Chamberlain and Milner a detestation that has almost obliterated their dislike of Rhodes'.[62] An unimportant but nevertheless amusing incident in a prisoner of war camp for captured burghers in Bermuda underlines these feelings. The burghers were warned that they would be shot should they enter the coastal waters surrounding the Bermuda islands. Some prisoners-of-war decided to test the resolve of their guards by secretly constructing a small wooden boat and placing a doll dressed in old clothing on board. Just before launching it one moonlit night on a favourable wind, they painted the name Chamberlain in red letters on the side of the boat. Everything went according to plan and Chamberlain drifted past a British guard post. A sentry shouted 'Halt! Halt! Come back!' Chamberlain ignored him. Soldiers keenly opened fire. A rowing boat was even launched to pursue Chamberlain, who kept drifting away. The next morning the prisoners-of-war could not keep themselves from asking the sentries, 'why did you fire on Chamberlain? He is English after all!'[63]

After peace was concluded, in the period when Milner attempted to bring about the suspension of the constitution of the Cape Colony, the leaders of the Afrikaner Bond re-established their personal rapport with Chamberlain.[64] The latter's refusal to allow Milner to suspend the constitution certainly played a role in this rapprochement. In September 1902 Chamberlain met a Boer delegation consisting of Generals Louis Botha, Christiaan de Wet and Koos de la Rey in London for a lengthy interview on various issues which were causing dissatisfaction, especially in the ranks of the so-called old burgher population of the former Boer republics. Chamberlain in effect rejected all their requests. He explained to the delegation that he was not prepared to replace the stipulations of a peace agreement reached at Vereeniging with new ones. He also rejected their claim that the compensation of three million pounds was inadequate.[65] To the Boers the outcome of the interview was not satisfactory. Botha's next step was to have an article published in the British media on 1 November 1902 in which he pointed out that it was the duty of the British government to assist the Boers to find a way out of the misery caused by material want. Five days later Botha sat in the gallery in the House of Commons when Chamberlain announced that he intended visiting South Africa to see for himself if enough money had been granted to cover the cost of reconstruction. To Botha, it seemed as if his final appeal was not in vain.[66]

Chamberlain felt that it would be useful to visit South Africa personally in order to inform himself on the true state of affairs. He was accompanied by his wife, who made extensive notes of their experiences. They visited numerous centres, both urban and rural, starting in Durban in the last week of December 1902 and ending in Cape Town two months later. In almost all instances they were heartily welcomed by the imperialist section of the population. Indeed, the visit served as signal for a fresh outburst of jingoism. The Chamberlains had to attend several receptions and the Colonial Secretary frequently had to address audiences. He received memorials from a variety of interest groups, including British South Africans, Boers who supported Britain in the latter stages of the Anglo–Boer War (the so-called hands-uppers and joiners or National Scouts), Boers who fought to the end and with whom the peace treaty was negotiated (the so-called 'bitter-enders') as well as black South Africans.[67]

Chamberlain made it clear from the outset that 'I come in a spirit of conciliation and also in a spirit of firmness', but he quickly added that 'the British flag is, and will be paramount in South Africa'. According to G.D. Scholtz, a nationalist newspaper editor and author of numerous books on South African history, Chamberlain meant that British authority was now once and for all firmly established across the whole of South Africa and that Afrikaners should abandon their dream of remaining a separate people with their own identity and ideals, since their future was entrenched in that of the British Empire.[68] When it became known that Chamberlain would be visiting the Transvaal, a provisional committee of prominent burghers of the capital city, Pretoria, and surrounding areas held a number of meetings in December 1902 in order to discuss how they could most profitably exploit Chamberlain's visit to advance the interests of the Afrikaner population.[69] A contemporary newspaper reported that, even before meeting any delegation of former Republicans, Chamberlain ascribed the complaints of the Afrikaners about certain stipulations in the peace treaty of May 1902 to their inheritance of certain characteristics from their Dutch ancestors, namely to give little but to demand a lot. His advice was that the Afrikaners had to learn to trust the British, who will not disappoint them.[70] Writing under the pseudonym 'Old Boer' from Heidelberg in the Transvaal, an Afrikaner explained their attitude towards Chamberlain's recommendation to trust the Milner regime. It made him think of a coloured agter-ryer (servant) of the Boer general, Alberts, who in the heat of battle during the Anglo–Boer War decided to abandon the horses that were entrusted to him and to flee for his life. The general shouted to him: 'Klaas, why are you afraid? Don't you have any faith?' 'Yes, my master', he answered, 'you will trust, and keep trusting till you are a goner, and what then?' 'Old Boer' was suggesting that the Afrikaners were expected to trust and to keep trusting Milner and Chamberlain until they were goners as well.[71]

On 8 January Chamberlain had a meeting with prominent Afrikaners, including Botha, Smuts and De la Rey. A memorial drawn up by Smuts was read out by him and handed to Chamberlain.[72] Smuts served as the spokesperson of the deputation. Hancock points out that, if any evidence is needed of Smuts's antagonistic feelings towards Chamberlain, it should be noted that at this meeting Smuts refused to transact his part of the business in English, which he commanded excellently since he was a graduate of the University of Cambridge, but used Dutch which was translated into English by an interpreter.[73] The Colonial Secretary nevertheless made full use of the opportunity presented to him to impress his own adverse opinion of the Afrikaner community in his answer to the deputation.[74] He expressed his displeasure that the deputation insisted on changes to the stipulations of the peace treaty. His impression was that, even though the Afrikaners 'are most excellent people at bargaining they fail to recognize that when a bargain is once made it should be stuck to'. He added that the stipulations of the peace treaty 'are the charter of the Boer people'. This would be carried out. There could be no amnesty for the Cape rebels, since that was not part of the bargain. To their request for assistance to resettle Boer families in the rural areas, Chamberlain replied by accusing them of ingratitude for the compensation already given to them; and to the leaders' request for trust and cooperation, Chamberlain replied that they would have to prove it – by assisting Britain to find the legendary 'Kruger millions'.[75] According to the historian J.A. Wiid, Chamberlain's objective probably was to impress on Afrikaners who were struggling to survive economically that their exiled leaders in Europe had huge fortunes at their disposal, which they did not have. Botha immediately retaliated by asking the Colonial Secretary if any mention was made in the peace treaty of that money. Chamberlain had to concede that there was no mention of it, thus ending official British enquiries into the 'Kruger millions' which never existed.[76] The Boer leaders were disgusted by Chamberlain's answer to their memorandum. Kemp's interpretation was that the Secretary of Colonies had used the opportunity to deliberately insult those leaders and their followers. Nevertheless, at the request of Botha and as a gesture of goodwill, the deputation shouted three hurrahs to Chamberlain at the end of the meeting.[77]

From Pretoria Chamberlain proceeded to Johannesburg where he was a guest of Milner for three weeks and did not meet with members of the Afrikaner community. From Johannesburg he proceeded to Potchefstroom, Lichtenburg, Mafeking and Kimberley before travelling to Bloemfontein, the capital of the former Republic of the Orange Free State.[78] When it became known that Chamberlain would be visiting Bloemfontein, four groups of inhabitants, of which three claimed to represent Afrikaners, approached him with memorials. The first consisted of Piet de Wet (the wartime leader of the National Scouts in the last phase of the Anglo–Boer War and brother of the well-known Christiaan de Wet) and other former Scouts. The second mainly consisted of former 'hands-uppers', who complained that they had not all received compensation for items that had been commandeered from them during the war. Third, members of the black community of the Orange River Colony applied for opportunities to discuss their grievances with Chamberlain.[79] Finally Christiaan de Wet and other bitterenders of the Anglo–Boer War intended to discuss with Chamberlain issues such as their complaints with regard to the way in which Milner was spending the £3 million compensation money which was promised in clause 10 of the Treaty of Vereeniging.[80] This was an issue which caused endless dissatisfaction to the bitter-enders in the Orange River Colony. The interpretation of the bitter-enders was that the 'free grant' of £3 million was exclusively intended to resettle the burghers who were still in the veld as well as the prisoners-of-war who had to be brought back to South Africa. Milner on the other hand ruled (and subsequently convinced Chamberlain) that the money was to be used as a resettlement fund for all the former burghers in the newly established colony, including the 'hands-uppers' and the joiners (or National Scouts). The former Orange Free State generals, Christiaan de Wet and Barry Hertzog, regarded Milner's stance as fraudulent. De Wet's standpoint was that the 'hands-uppers' and joiners had no part in the peace negotiations and that the British were in effect rewarding them for their treason by giving them compensation from the £3 million fund.[81] Not surprisingly, De Wet hoped that Chamberlain's visit would provide him with an opportunity for the Boers to obtain redress from what they regarded as unjust actions by Milner.

From the Orange Free State Chamberlain proceeded to the Cape Colony where he first visited a number of towns and gave numerous speeches.[82] Cape Town was the last stop of his tour of South Africa. There again he met prominent members of the Afrikaner community who expressed their support, but used the opportunity to air complaints as well. Thus Jan Hendrik Hofmeyr of the Afrikaner Bond attempted to make Chamberlain aware of the fact that the colonial Afrikaners, even though loyal to Britain (with the exception, of course, of the Cape rebels), nurtured real grievances and pointed out examples of the victimisation of Afrikaners.[83] Chamberlain's true feelings about the information provided to him by Hofmeyr is not known, but the fact that he specifically warned the Cape Premier, Sir Gordon Sprigg, against the re-enfranchisement of the Cape rebels, reflects a real lack of empathy with the feelings of the Afrikaner community.

Chamberlain's visit to South Africa between December 1902 and February 1903 is best remembered for the inability of the two main protagonists, namely Chamberlain and his support team on the one side and the spokesmen of the bitter-ender Republican burghers of the Anglo–Boer War on the other, to reach any form of understanding on the post-war dispensation. Indeed, Smuts afterwards wrote that 'Mr Chamberlain's visit to South Africa has been a dismal failure and has left matters worse than he found them.' In many instances, according to Smuts, the visit produced acrimony rather than healing.[84] Smuts was not alone in his criticism. From the Cape Colony John X. Merriman wrote to John Bryce in England in August 1903 that 'the ridiculous visit of Chamberlain, though it did less harm than some of us expected, did no good ... Not one single act emanated from him that justified his absurd plea of being a pacificator.'[85] Scholtz argues that of all the insults that Afrikaners had to endure in the months following on from the conclusion of peace at the end of May 1902, Chamberlain's visit was the most painful. It was as if the Colonial Secretary, who was, in conjunction with Milner, responsible for the outbreak of the war, was now following the example of a Roman general who would, after having scored a magnificent victory on the battlefield, undertake a victory parade through the streets of Rome. Chamberlain's parade was through South Africa, with the objective of gloriously forcing British supremacy down the throats of Afrikaners.[86]

Why did Smuts, Merriman and Scholtz regard the visit as a failure? The immediate post-war years were the era of British supremacy in South Africa. Chamberlain simply could not (or refused to) develop any form of empathy with the wishes and needs of his former foes. Indeed, he preferred to castigate them for their presumption when they requested amnesty for the Cape rebels. He blamed them for the damage caused by the war, since they kept fighting after their Republics had been annexed. And he accused them of ingratitude, since they did not thank Britain for the relief of distress in the former Republics. Little came of Chamberlain's vision of the new South Africa, since ultimately the bitter-enders refused to become part of the purely British 'new nation' which he had in mind. Indeed, his South African visit, which on the surface seemed to have been a crowning glory in his distinguished career, probably had more negative than positive results.

Chamberlain resigned as State Secretary for Colonies in September 1903. That was also the end of his involvement with South Africa. Subsequently nothing of significance occurred with regard to his relationship with South Africa. Neither did his reputation in South Africa change. In Afrikaner circles he remained the apostle of aggressive imperialism. Indeed, his supporters seemed to fall silent very soon after his political demise while the circle of his critics, especially in South African historiography, seemed to grow across language and racial barriers. Chamberlain is not fondly remembered in this country. The blame for this state of affairs lies largely on his own shoulders.

Notes

1. J.L. Garvin and J. Amery, *The Life of Joseph Chamberlain*, 6 volumes (London: Macmillan, 1932–68).
2. M.C.E. van Schoor, *Spotprente van die Anglo–Boereoorlog* (Cape Town: Tafelberg, 1981), pp. 49, 84.
3. H. Giliomee, *The Afrikaners: Biography of a People* (Cape Town: Tafelberg, 2003), p. 242.
4. P.T. Marsh, *Joseph Chamberlain: Entrepreneur in Politics* (New Haven and London: Yale University Press, 1994), p. 156.
5. S.B. Spies, 'Chamberlain, Joseph', in D.W. Krüger and C.J. Beyers (eds), *Suid-Afrikaanse Biografiese Woordeboek*, part III (Cape Town: Tafelberg Publishers for the Human Sciences Research, 1977), p. 144.
6. Ibid.
7. A.N. Porter, *The Origins of the South African War, Joseph Chamberlain and the Diplomacy of Imperialism, 1895–99* (Manchester University Press, 1980), p. 63.
8. Spies, 'Chamberlain, Joseph', p. 144.
9. T.R.H. Davenport, *The Afrikaner Bond, The History of a South African Political Party, 1880–1911* (Oxford University Press, 1966), pp. 161–2.
10. Spies, 'Chamberlain, Joseph', p. 144; Marsh, *Joseph Chamberlain*, pp. 378–81.
11. Spies, 'Chamberlain, Joseph', p. 144; Marsh, *Joseph Chamberlain*, p. 383.
12. T.R.H. Davenport, 'Jameson, Sir Leander Starr', in Krüger and Beyers (eds), *Suid-Afrikaanse Biografiese Woordeboek*, part III, p. 451.
13. S.J.P. Kruger, *The Memoirs of Paul Kruger, Four Times President of the South African Republic, Told by Himself* (London: T. Fisher Unwin, 1902), pp. 271–3, 279.
14. Ibid., pp. 275–7.
15. J.C.G. Kemp, *Vir Vryheid en vir Reg* (Cape Town: Nasionale Pers, 1941), p. 83.
16. Porter, *The Origins of the South African War*, p. 105.
17. Spies, 'Chamberlain, Joseph', pp. 144–5.
18. Quoted in Marsh, *Joseph Chamberlain*, p. 390.
19. Ibid., p. 401.
20. W.K. Hancock and J. van der Poel (eds), *Selections from the Smuts Papers, Volume I: June 1886–May 1902* (Cambridge University Press, 1966), document 41, p. 152.
21. Ibid., document 43, pp. 155–8.
22. Ibid., document 43, pp. 178ff.
23. L.E. van Niekerk, *Kruger se Regterhand, 'n Biografie van dr W.J. Leyds* (Pretoria: J.L. van Schaik, 1985), p. 144.
24. Spies, 'Chamberlain, Joseph', p. 144.
25. Kruger, *The Memoirs of Paul Kruger*, pp. 257–9.
26. Ibid., pp. 278–9.
27. Spies, 'Chamberlain, Joseph', p. 145.
28. Kemp, *Vir Vryheid en vir Reg*, p. 80.

29. P. Lewsen (ed.), *Selections from the Correspondence of John X. Merriman 1890–1898* (Cape Town: The Van Riebeeck Society), no. 44, 1963, pp. 48, 103, 209n and 229. The word 'betwattle' can probably be taken to mean 'robbed of common sense'.
30. V. Solomon (ed.), *Selections from the Correspondence of Percy Alport Molteno 1892–1914* (Cape Town: The Van Riebeeck Society), second series no. 12, 1981, pp. 11, 14, 57.
31. Ibid., p. 29.
32. Ibid., p. 52.
33. Ibid., p. 60.
34. B. Williams, *Cecil Rhodes* (New York: Greenwood Press, 1968 reprint), pp. 318–19.
35. Kruger, *The Memoirs of Paul Kruger*, pp. 289–90.
36. Kemp, *Vir Vryheid en vir Reg*, p. 92.
37. Spies, 'Chamberlain, Joseph', p. 145.
38. Kruger, *The Memoirs of Paul Kruger*, pp. 279–80.
39. Ibid., pp. 280–3.
40. M.T. Steyn, *'n Bittereinder aan die Woord, Geskrifte en Toesprake van Marthinus Theunis Steyn*, edited and annotated by M.C.E. van Schoor (Bloemfontein: Oorlogsmuseum van die Boererepublieke, 1997), p. 20.
41. Hancock and Van der Poel (eds), *Smuts Papers, Volume I*, document 121, pp. 285–8.
42. Kruger, *The Memoirs of Paul Kruger*, pp. 302–3.
43. Spies, 'Chamberlain, Joseph', p. 145.
44. Solomon (ed.), *Correspondence of Percy Alport Molteno*, p. 95.
45. Lewsen (ed.), *Correspondence of John X. Merriman*, p. 72.
46. Spies, 'Chamberlain, Joseph', p. 145.
47. Ibid., p. 145.
48. Lewsen (ed.), *Correspondence of John X. Merriman*, p. 85.
49. J.S. Marais, *The Fall of Kruger's Republic* (Oxford University Press, 1961), p. 69.
50. F.A. van Jaarsveld, *Van Van Riebeck tot P.W. Botha, 'n Inleiding tot die Geskiedenis van die Republiek van Suid-Afrika* (Johannesburg: Perskor, 1982), pp. 228–32.
51. F. Pretorius, *Die Anglo–Boereoorlog 1899–1902* (Kaapstad: Struik Uitgewers, 1998), pp. 9–13.
52. H. Giliomee, 'Afrikaner Nationalism, 1875–1899', in F. Pretorius (ed.), *A History of South Africa, from the Distant Past to the Present Day* (Pretoria: Protea Book House, 2014), p. 236.
53. Spies, 'Chamberlain, Joseph', p. 145.
54. Hancock and Van der Poel (eds), *Smuts Papers, Volume I*, document 169, p. 480.
55. H. Bradford, 'The Defiance of the *Bittereinder* Women', in B. Nasson and A. Grundlingh (eds), *The War at Home: Women and Families in the Anglo–Boer War* (Cape Town: Tafelberg, 2013), p. 48.
56. Solomon (ed.), *Correspondence of Percy Alport Molteno*, p. 144.
57. Ibid., pp. 175, 189.
58. J.C.G. Kemp, *Die Pad van die Veroweraar* (Kaapstad Nasionale Pers, 1942), p. 27.
59. Ibid., p. 41; J. Wilson, *C.B.: A Life of Sir Henry Campbell-Bannerman* (London: Constable, 1973), p. 349.

60. Hancock and Van der Poel (eds), *Smuts Papers, Volume I*, document 169, p. 465.
61. Kemp, *Die Pad van die Veroweraar*, p. 27.
62. Lewsen (ed.), *Correspondence of John X. Merriman*, p. 112.
63. Buurman, *Oorlogswolke oor die Republieke, Die herinneringe van 'n Boere-offisier* (Johannesburg: Voortrekkerpers Beperk, 1944), pp. 209–11.
64. Davenport, *The Afrikaner Bond*, p. 236.
65. Spies, 'Chamberlain, Joseph', p. 146.
66. F.V. Engelenburg, *General Louis Botha* (London: George G. Harrap & Co., 1929), pp. 106–10.
67. W.K. Hancock and J. van der Poel (eds), *Selections from the Smuts Papers, Volume II, June 1902–May 1910* (Cambridge University Press, 1966), document 204, p. 58; Spies, 'Chamberlain, Joseph', p. 146; Engelenburg, *Botha*, p. 113.
68. G.D. Scholtz, *Die Ontwikkeling van die Politieke Denke van die Afrikaner, Deel V, 1899–1910* (Johannesburg: Perskor-Uitgewery, 1978), p. 262.
69. Ibid.
70. *The Star*, 1 July 1903, quoted in P.M.B. Schutte, 'Die verhouding tussen Boer en Brit in Transvaal, 1902–1910' (MA dissertation, University of Pretoria, 1979), p. 61.
71. "Ou Boer" vanuit Heidelberg, *De Volkstem*, 11 September 1904, quoted in ibid., pp. 61–2.
72. Scholtz, *Die Ontwikkeling van die Politieke Denke*, p. 262.
73. W.K. Hancock, *Smuts, The Sanguine Years 1870 – 1919* (Cambridge University Press, 1962), p. 193.
74. Scholtz, *Die Ontwikkeling van die Politieke Denke*, p. 263.
75. Kemp, *Die Pad van die Veroweraar*, pp. 91–2.
76. J.A. Wiid, 'Weeropbou (1902–1910)', in A.J.H. van der Walt, J.A. Wiid and A.L. Geyer (eds), *Geskiedenis van Suid-Afrika*, vol. 1 (Cape Town: Nasionale Boekhandel Beperk, 1951), p. 628; Engelenburg, *Botha*, p. 116.
77. Scholtz, *Die Ontwikkeling van die Politieke Denke*, p. 264.
78. Ibid., p. 265.
79. Ibid.
80. M.C.E. van Schoor, *Christiaan Rudolph de Wet, Krygsman en volksman* (Pretoria: Protea Boekhuis, 2007), p. 222.
81. Ibid., p. 221.
82. Davenport, *The Afrikaner Bond*, p. 242.
83. Ibid., p. 243.
84. Hancock, *Smuts, The Sanguine Years 1870–1919*, pp. 192–3.
85. Lewsen (ed.), *Correspondence of John X. Merriman*, pp. 384–5.
86. Scholtz, Die Ontwikkeling van die Politieke Denke, pp. 261–2.

3

'King Joe' and 'King Dick': Joseph Chamberlain and Richard Seddon

Tom Brooking

The large cache of letters held in the Seddon Papers in the Alexander Turnbull Library, Wellington, makes it clear that the Premier of New Zealand and the Secretary of State for the Colonies, Joseph Chamberlain, became close friends as well as allies in the cause of closer Imperial unity between 1897 and Seddon's death in 1906.[1] At first glance this friendship between the wealthy and privileged Chamberlain and the self-made mechanical engineer, storekeeper, publican and autodidact populist from St Helens and Kumara, Richard John Seddon, makes little sense. Indeed, it is hard to imagine two men who were more different. Seddon's corpulent, pear-shaped body which signified success in the late nineteenth-century world because it suggested a man who had never gone hungry, contrasted with Chamberlain's more svelte shape. Chamberlain was also a clean-shaven dandy with his monocle, cravats, yellow jackets and orchids in his lapel, whereas, despite his penchant for classy, dark coats and white carnations, the bearded Seddon could hardly be described as either sartorial or fashionably dressed.[2] His own former Minister of Labour turned historian, William Pember Reeves, rather described him as

> noteworthy for a fine chest girth and an equal measure of self-confidence ... His head made one think of iron wedges, stone axes and things meant to split and fracture. And the pallor of the face was lit by two alert blue eyes and by a peculiarly pleasant – nay, sweet smile playing round a well-shaped mouth. He looked as though he might be handy with his fists, as indeed he could be. Most things about him appeared big, vigorous, restless: you thought him a man made for drums and tramplings.[3]

Reeves quite misleadingly reinforced the idea that Seddon was poorly educated, rough and coarse, by reporting to the British press in 1900 that his former leader came from the 'humblest ranks of mechanical workers' even though he was a fully qualified mechanical engineer who came from the top of the skilled trades.[4] A little earlier the Fabian socialist, Beatrice Webb, who visited New Zealand in 1898, reinforced such an impression by judging Seddon to be 'a gross, illiterate but forceful man, more like a trade union official in such an industry as steel-melting, than an M.P.'[5] Seddon's clearly identifiable if rather soft Lancastrian accent attracted derisive comment, especially from New Zealand politicians and journalist who grew up in the south of England (a clear majority in fact).[6] Their condemnations reveal much more about their aural intolerance and snobbery than they do about Seddon, but such complaint added to the sense that Seddon was a 'rough diamond' and very different from an extremely wealthy, smooth industrialist and local worthy like Chamberlain who made it into the highest circle of British politics.[7]

Seddon also grew up in a 'popular Liberal' household rather than a 'high Liberal' one because his school teacher parents befriended the editor of the local *St Helens Weekly News and General Advertiser* (and the *St Helens Newspaper* from 1862) that espoused classic popular Liberal causes such as support for Garibaldi's unification of Italy and relentless advocacy of self-reliance via such mechanisms as penny savings banks, free libraries, mechanics' institutes and literary societies.[8] Young Richard Seddon went on to espouse many of the tenets of what Eugenio Biagini and Patrick Joyce have described as 'popular Liberalism', including open hostility to privilege and monopoly, a willingness to use the state to reduce inequality, and unrelenting advocacy of universal manhood suffrage and finding gradualist, constitutional solutions to resolving problems such as poverty.[9] Like Chamberlain, Seddon always considered himself to be a 'radical' kind of Liberal.[10] Seddon also became a classic autodidact by reading popular Liberal texts to build upon the education he had received as a mechanical engineer. He shared a passionate love of Dickens with Chamberlain (and many other politicians throughout the English-speaking world).[11]

Once in Parliament Seddon pursued a somewhat different trajectory from Chamberlain by supporting Home Rule for Ireland (partly to win the support of Irish gold miners who migrated to the west coast of New Zealand) and trade unions, and he never changed sides, despite a brief flirtation with acting as an independent.[12] Indeed, from 1890 he became a very loyal party man who as Premier from 1893 brought badly needed unity to the extraordinarily diverse and broad-based New Zealand Liberal party, partly by utilising organisational strategies pioneered by Chamberlain.[13] Potentially Seddon and Chamberlain should have been adversaries because Seddon's idolised William Ewart Gladstone and openly modelled his populist style on Gladstone's switch to mass meetings and intensive contact with the public during the later part of his career.[14] Seddon even visited the by now ancient 'People's William' when he attended Queen Victoria's Diamond Jubilee in 1897 and rated this meeting the highlight of his visit.[15] Such adulation, however, did not seem to worry Chamberlain particularly. This was partly because Seddon and Chamberlain, despite their obvious differences in wealth, were not as socially different as they first appear. Chamberlain was neither aristocrat nor grandee but came from the upper middle classes, while Seddon was decidedly lower middle class in that both his parents were school teachers and his paternal grandfather was a reasonably substantial tenant farmer.[16] Although he left school at 12 and flunked Latin whereas Chamberlain left at 16 from the rather superior University College School and became fluent in French, Seddon did gain his full mechanical engineer's certificate.[17] As a result he ended up being not especially different from many of the skilled tradesmen Chamberlain dealt with in Birmingham. Chamberlain was no rhetorician but rather a plain and prosaic speaker; like 'a cheese monger', sneered Disraeli.[18] Critics made even worse comments on Seddon's lack of oratorical skills, but both were effective communicators whose unadorned speaking has arguably better stood the test of time than the flowery rhetoric of supposed 'orators' of particular eras.[19]

They differed in their religious background, however, in that while Chamberlain came from a family of Unitarians and later claimed to be an atheist, Seddon remained an active broad-church Anglican his entire life. Seddon did, though, have links to the chapel with which Chamberlain was also familiar through his mother who, unusually, was a Scottish Methodist of the primitive variety. Jane Seddon taught at the Primitive Methodist Sunday School in St Helens that her son visited in 1897. Yet again the two men shared more in common in terms of their social background than surface appearance suggested.[20]

Seddon and Chamberlain were similar too in that both men were devoted to their wives (one in Seddon's case and three in Chamberlain's). Unlike the aristocracy neither man had any truck with mistresses or boyfriends. Later the third Mrs Chamberlain (Mary Endicott, the daughter of a high-ranking Democrat politician from Washington, D.C.)

became quite friendly with the rather more homely Australian Louisa Jane Seddon and her daughters who visited London, continuing to correspond with the third Mrs Chamberlain.[21]

Like Chamberlain, Seddon came from somewhere outside the metropolis in being the Member for the House of Representatives (hereafter MHR) for the West Coast rather than Wellington, Canterbury or Auckland. He had no links to older landed elites in provinces such as Canterbury, Otago and Hawke's Bay, or even business and industrial elites in Auckland, Christchurch and Dunedin.[22] Both were 'outsiders' in this sense. Furthermore, despite their different views of Gladstone and the Irish question, the two men held similar views on several key internal policies as well as imperial policy, particularly in relation to public education, workmen's compensation, old-age pensions and public housing. Seddon shared Chamberlain's enthusiasm for providing greater access to education although he concentrated his efforts on making secondary education available to all children of ability no matter where they lived or who their parents were through reforms he piloted through Parliament in 1903. All New Zealand children received 'compulsory, free, and secular' primary school education from 1877 (at least in theory) and Anglican schools did not provide the staunch opposition to reform as Chamberlain experienced in England. A separate Catholic school system did emerge from that time, however, and Seddon spent his career carefully navigating a path between opposing denominationalism while accepting the Catholic school system given that Irish immigrants were heavily over-represented in his West Coast electorate. Chamberlain's enthusiasm for technical education and opening access to tertiary education also seemed to influence Seddon, who had something of a reputation for being opposed to higher education. On his return to New Zealand after Victoria's jubilee, the Premier surprised his critics and opponents by dropping his former opposition to a university in the capital and helped to establish Victoria University of Wellington, just as Chamberlain made mighty efforts to develop the University of Birmingham. Seddon went on to establish technical secondary schools as part of his 1903 reforms, several of which were named after him. Seddon also introduced superannuation for primary teachers and improved their salaries and conditions. After the 1902 visit to London, he became a staunch supporter of the notion that Imperial College should be established to help Britain close the growing gap with Germany and the USA by operating as a specialised university of advanced technology and applied science within the University of London system.[23]

Seddon paid close attention to Chamberlain's views on old-age pensions as well as those of the Geoffrey Drage, Canon William Lewery Blackley, General William Booth of the Salvation Army, and the Governments of Germany and Denmark, as he set about devising a scheme for New Zealand from 1896. His scheme differed from Chamberlain's 1892 proposals mainly in that it was not contributory and did not directly involve the Friendly Societies and lodges, and, more importantly, that he succeeded in introducing it in 1898 despite a mighty stonewall by the parliamentary opposition. Once he got the Bill through both Houses and passed into law, Seddon did not have to move it past a Royal Commission chaired by a super-wealthy magnate such as Lord Rothschild. Otherwise, despite being slightly more generous at seven shillings per week or £18 per year rather than five shillings per week or £13 per year, this taxpayer-funded scheme was miserly and prescribed by all kinds of conditions such as length of residence in the Colony and limited to the 'deserving poor' of 65 years and over. Yet, as Seddon claimed, although not universal, it was the most generous pension anywhere in the world in 1898 even if, inevitably, it was not as generous as Lloyd George's national insurance introduced in 1911. Seddon certainly talked about the pension to Chamberlain along with several public audiences when he attended the coronation of Edward VII in 1902. By then Chamberlain had lost any chance of persuading either the Conservative party or the Treasury to accept such a message, partly because of the huge costs involved in upgrading the navy and fighting the Boer War.

Seddon increased New Zealand's pension to £26 per year in 1905, moved applicants out of open court into 'chambers' and eased conditions for the Māori, but tightened the property qualifications. He also wanted to augment it with voluntary superannuation but died before he could implement such a scheme. Given that he remained a Liberal rather than joining the Conservatives, Seddon always had more chance of passing such progressive legislation into law, especially as New Zealand trade unions seemed less concerned than their British counterparts about the age of eligibility being 65 rather than 60.[24] Seddon learnt from the Colony's experience with old-age pensions that most New Zealanders wanted the security of owning their homes. In 1897 he talked to Chamberlain about council housing and requested more information in 1902. But he resolutely refused to countenance building large apartment blocks and remained reluctant about making these houses available for purchase. Land was still abundant in Britain's farthest-flung colony and the New Zealand dream included owning a stand-alone house on its own piece of land fronted by a hedge with a flower garden in the front and a vegetable garden out the back. So, when Seddon introduced New Zealand's first state housing programme in 1905 (municipal authorities simply lacked the capital resources to undertake Birmingham-style house-building programmes), he insisted that each new house should be free standing and designed by architects. Most were built on the edge of spreading suburbs and, although attractive, the rents proved too high and the houses too remote to win popularity.[25] Even the Labour government elected in 1935 failed to address the provision of housing for the very poor by only building one set of large, multi-story apartments. The country still struggles to countenance Chamberlain's solutions. As a result, in 2015 its biggest city, Auckland, contains some of the most expensive real estate in the world.

Chamberlain and Seddon also consulted each other over the matter of workers' compensation. New Zealand had introduced one of the first schemes in the Empire in 1891 but the Brunner mine disaster of 1896, which caused the deaths of 65 miners and boys, revealed the early New Zealand scheme to be totally inadequate. Seddon did not reveal this when asked for his advice by both Chamberlain and Arthur Balfour when he visited Westminster in 1897, but he drew upon the British example in framing a new accident compensation scheme between 1897 and its final introduction in 1900. The Workers' Compensation Act of 1900 had to demonstrate an advance beyond the Imperial legislation to satisfy Seddon's supporters within the Labour movement. Consequently, he relied less on New Zealand's moderately wealthy employers and stepped up the state's responsibility by routing compensation payments through the Government Life Insurance Department, established by Sir Julius Vogel much earlier in 1869. The first claim also went to miners' families rather than to debenture holders of coal-mining companies. New Zealand's arbitration court, set up by William Pember Reeves in 1894 to resolve industrial disputes, assumed responsibility for sorting out complicated cases. Seddon's solution was, therefore, far more statist and less reliant on the deep pockets of big business than its British equivalent, even if it did little to improve inspection of mine safety.[26]

Any search of late nineteenth-century New Zealand newspapers reveals plenty of interest in and discussion of Chamberlain's loyal ally and sometime parliamentary secretary, Jesse Collings, and his 'three acres and a cow' solution to unemployment, but the hard-nosed practical farmer, John McKenzie, as Minister of Lands rather concentrated on making available to settlers viable farms of 320–640 acres for mixed stock and crop farming and a minimum of 50 acres for dairying.[27] Seddon supported this pragmatic land redistribution programme wholeheartedly.[28] There was some interest among groups like the Knights of Labour and Liberal Associations in workmen's allotments, orchards and gardens on the edge of the main centres, but only small numbers took advantage of government efforts in the late 1890s to make such sections available to working men.[29]

Chamberlain talked a lot about industrial arbitration and conciliation and always argued that employers and employees should work cooperatively together. Opposition from both unions and employers, as well as from within the Tory party, ensured that he failed to progress let alone introduce such a system. In contrast, New Zealand's weaker unions supported its introduction and Reeves obliged by introducing compulsory industrial arbitration and conciliation in New Zealand based around an arbitration court overseen by a judge. Seddon consolidated this 1894 system, staunchly defended Reeves's reforms and always insisted it should be 'compulsory', but failed to stop it becoming voluntary in 1905 during one of his rare absences from Parliament.[30]

The area where Chamberlain and Seddon had most in common, however, was in relation to Imperial policy, even if there is little mention of that alliance in any of the major biographies of Chamberlain.[31] Chamberlain and Seddon already had a reasonably positive relationship before they met personally. The Secretary of State for the Colonies supported the colonial Premier in 1895 and 1896 against the Governor (Robert Boyle, the Earl of Glasgow) in his appointment of supporters to New Zealand's Upper House known as the Legislative Council, as had his predecessor, the Marquess of Ripon, in 1893 and 1894.[32] Seddon proved to be a most useful ally for Chamberlain's 'radical' objective of encouraging greater imperial unity through changed constitutional arrangements and the introduction of imperial preference, especially given that there was very little support for such ideas either in Britain or elsewhere in the Empire. Chamberlain wanted to introduce 'imperial preference', or a quid pro quo in which the colonies would receive privileged access to the British market in return for removing tariffs on British-manufactured goods, rather like the German 'Zollverein'. He also talked of establishing a 'Great Council of Empire' to strengthen links between Britain and its colonies. Such a possibility suited Seddon and the tiny colony he led with a population of only 743,000 (including 42,564 Māori) in 1896 because it would provide more direct access to the levers of power at a high level within the Empire. If New Zealand could be represented on some kind of Imperial Council in London it would be much easier to punch well above its weight. Equally, Imperial preference would guarantee New Zealand greater access to the lucrative British market for its yellow butter, fatty meat and greasy wool.

Unfortunately for both Chamberlain and Seddon, the major pressure group advocating such schemes, the Imperial Federation League, had ceased operation in 1893.[33] Furthermore, the 'parliamentary' federation model involving the setting up of some sort of Imperial Council at Westminster had lost out by the early 1890s to the more modest 'extra-parliamentary' model, or an advisory council working through informal networks. The much grander 'supra-parliamentary' alternative advocated by the historian J.R. Seeley, which envisioned the creation of an English-speaking union including the USA and potentially a new world government, had also gained more popularity by 1897 than the imperial parliamentary model.[34] Despite New Zealand trying to prove it was the most loyal of the self-governing colonies by contributing the most troops for South Africa on a per capita basis and the Premier's stellar performance at the Victoria's jubilee, Seddon and Chamberlain achieved little in the way of advancing Imperial unity.[35]

Seddon caught the eye of the English press when he claimed that Macaulay had got it wrong when he wrote that it would be a New Zealander one day sitting on 'a broken arch of London bridge while he sketched the ruins of St Paul's'. According to Seddon, 'little the historian knew of the New Zealander! If the Empire was to fall, the New Zealanders would fall too.'[36] He also undertook a punishing schedule of speeches all around Britain as well as in London to promote Imperial unity and built relations with several leading grandees, sending them pairs of Paradise Ducks and collections of native plants.[37] Some papers soon treated Seddon as kind of oracle while *Punch* had a field day. Yet, despite raising his own personal profile as well as that of the colony he represented through his energetic efforts, he, along with Chamberlain, failed to make much advance in securing either an Imperial Council or Imperial preference.

On 4 June 1897 he held a press interview at which he advocated the establishment of an imperial council so that 'colonial delegates would be heard in regard to all matters affecting colonial interests'. He thereby aligned himself with Chamberlain's 'parliamentary' model of imperial federation. The problem was that the only self-governing colony that supported Chamberlain was even tinier Tasmania, led by Sir W. Edwin Braddon. Most other delegates were hostile, especially the premiers of free trade, New South Wales and protectionist Victoria. George Reid of New South Wales and George Turner of Victoria could, therefore, see no reason for a change in the status quo. The suave Sir Wilfrid Laurier of Canada, despite his emphasis upon the importance of strengthening sentimental ties, could see no way of reducing tariffs if Canada hoped to build its manufacturing capacity. Seddon countered that 'the way to encourage inter-Empire trade was for the Government to subsidise the steamers and so reduce the freights, and thus prevent foreigners underselling British goods owing to their receiving state subsidies'. He also suggested that branches of the Imperial League be established in the colonies to promote closer relations.[38]

At a more formal meeting between the premiers and Chamberlain on 24 to 25 June, it seemed that Seddon had failed to convince anyone of the need for closer Imperial relations. Sir John Forrest of Western Australia and C.C. Kingston of South Australia joined Reid and Turner in arguing against change because Australians were the equals of Britons, although they pledged support in terms of supplying troops to help with imperial defence. After embarrassing Seddon concerning New Zealand's modest contribution to naval defence of the region, they left it to New Zealand's leader to come up with concrete proposals on how to increase trade within the Empire and how to organise more regular meetings. The Australian state premiers also resented the fact that as the leader of a single political entity, Seddon tended to be treated as a full prime minister rather than a lowly premier.[39] Imperial federation remained a distant dream, with the formal conferences producing nothing more than a vague set of good intentions.

Seddon and Braddon dissented from the resolution that 'the present political relations between the United Kingdom and the self-governing Colonies are generally satisfactory under the existing condition of things'. On the other hand, Seddon and Chamberlain managed to pass a resolution to hold 'periodical conferences of representatives of the Colonies and Great Britain for the discussion of matters of common interest'; arguably an aim that opened the way for development from Empire to Commonwealth.[40] A third resolution also proclaimed, 'it is desirable, whenever and wherever practicable, to group together under a federal union those colonies which are geographically isolated'.[41] Such good intentions, while constituting a step forward, fell well short of what Seddon wanted, and their vagueness was typical of the whole 'Greater Britain' project.

Reid, an old-fashioned free-trade Liberal, who was as large and noisy as Seddon, would repeat his arguments against Seddon's vision of closer relationships, as well as complaints concerning New Zealand's failure to pay its fair share of the costs of the Australian naval squadron, at other banquets and gatherings.[42] Reid also vied with Seddon in claiming that their respective colonies were more loyal to the Empire. The only thing the Australians, excepting Braddon, could agree on with Seddon was the need to keep Asians out of their jurisdictions. Seddon joined the others in making this clear to Chamberlain on 8 July when, with the exception of Queensland, they refused to sign the 1894 Anglo–Japanese Treaty of Commerce and Navigation.[43]

During his time in London in 1897, Seddon established a lifelong friendship with Chamberlain, describing him as a man of 'great ability, great earnestness and discernment'.[44] Chamberlain's quip about his 'booming eloquence' only added to his prestige with the majority of the electorate back home.[45] Even so, Seddon had to be content with what he called getting 'within measurable distance of an understanding' and only made very modest claims concerning closer relations within the Empire when talking to Australian journalists on the way home.[46] He made it clear that he had not 'pledged' New Zealand to anything, but hoped for closer relations within the Empire with the assistance of the very able Chamberlain and Lord Rosebery.[47]

Seddon's enthusiastic support of the Boer War from 1899 ensured that New Zealand earned the reputation of being the most loyal self-governing colony in the Empire and assisted Chamberlain in continuing the war despite significant opposition from within Britain. Huge crowds bade farewell to each of the earlier contingents, and communities chipped in by supplying troopers with their horses. Volunteer numbers rose to 17,000 by July 1901 from all sectors of New Zealand society (even though 6500 actually served) and school cadet corps increased spectacularly. Even women formed corps in small towns such as Dannevirke, Temuka and Te Awamutu, the latter group naming themselves 'Amazons'. Daughters of Wellington's élite families, including May Seddon, regularly practised drill.[48] This euphoria, which waned a little by 1901 as casualty rates rose and the bungling British failed to secure decisive victories, certainly helped explain Seddon's big electoral victory in 1899.

Thereafter, Seddon kept sending contingents with widespread public backing. Some New Zealand newspapers began to complain about agreeing to send another 1000 men with the eighth contingent in December 1901, in response to both Colonial Office pressure and provocation by the German paper *Vossische Zeitung* and the so-called 'Anglophobe' press of continental Europe. Parliament largely backed the action, despite supposed growing war-weariness among the public.[49] The *Observer* and *Nelson Evening Mail* worried about the disruption to the labour force, and the *Evening Post* had earlier wondered about overstrain of the colony's limited manpower resources and criticised the Premier's 'note of boastfulness'.[50] All agreed, nevertheless, that Seddon's patriotic response reflected the views of the 'vast majority' of New Zealanders, rather than the Premier's pursuit of 'imperial distinction for himself'. They also applauded Seddon's condemnation of pro-Boers in Britain for prolonging the war, and congratulated him for acting while Australia dithered.[51] Volunteering also seemed enthusiastic, with 4000 men offering their services.[52] Yet again, public opinion seemed to follow Seddon's intuitive and decisive actions.[53] Significantly, *the New Zealand Observer* also detected the strong New Zealand interest in this commitment that won much praise from British newspapers when its editorial proclaimed, '[o]ur future happiness and prosperity depend absolutely upon the pre-eminence of the British nation'.[54]

Throughout the course of the war the Premier continued to show a keen interest in the welfare of the troops and, after initial reluctance, came to play a key part in sending nurses to support New Zealand's soldiers, and teachers to help Boer children adjust to the new order.[55] He sent constant telegrams and letters, usually of an extreme congratulatory kind, but sometimes of a rather critical tone, to key players. Seddon congratulated Lords Roberts and Kitchener on various victories, wished Roberts a happy birthday, and glowed in descriptions of the New Zealand troops as 'grand fellows' and 'splendid' contingents who had 'distinguished themselves'.[56] He also sent copies of New Zealand legislation that had helped settle troops on land acquired from Māori 'rebels' after the New Zealand wars, and requested that Roberts find a position on his staff for his son, Dick junior.[57] On the other hand, he asked Kitchener that one Colonel White be removed from command of New Zealanders because the colonials disliked him. In reply, Kitchener promised to look in to the matter and stated that he aimed to improve the training of New Zealand officers in technical areas such as drill, ordinance and supply transport.[58]

The Liberal party's mouthpiece, *the New Zealand Times*, sometimes criticised British bungling, both in terms of strategy and the failure to organise adequate medical services.[59] Once hostilities commenced, however, initial editorial caution and publication of letters critical of New Zealand's involvement soon gave way to unquestioning support of New Zealand's patriotic efforts.[60] The Boers were routinely condemned as an 'insolent', 'arrogant' and 'treacherous' people, who opposed the abolition of slavery and denied blacks their political rights. The British, in contrast, were fighting for '[f]reedom, justice and equality'.[61] The government paper did, however, report and support Agent-General

William Pember Reeves's criticisms of English military shortcomings as sent to Seddon in April 1900, especially regarding over-reliance on close-formation fighting and 'guesswork', as well as inadequate medical services; criticisms roundly condemned as unpatriotic by the opposition press. Significantly, Seddon supported Reeves in sending official telegrams on such matters and, unpalatable as they were, actively released them to the press to break the monopoly of the New Zealand Press Association.[62]

Even before leaving for South Africa, Seddon caused alarm in both Australia and Britain by agreeing with the Māori parliamentarian, Wi Pere, at a meeting at Papawai in early April 1902, that 5000 Maori would soon end the fighting in South Africa. Instead of treating the Boers with 'kid gloves', Seddon argued that Māori 'turned loose under Maori leaders ... untrammelled by the orders which, in his opinion, were a drawback to the forces operating in South Africa' would soon end the war, especially if they were given 'instructions to put down the Boers at all costs'.[63] *The Times* reported this speech as suggesting that Seddon would have 6000 mounted Māori soldiers ready for action within six months.[64] In March, and before he left in early April when bidding farewell to the tenth contingent, he caused further embarrassment to the British government by insisting on unconditional surrender and condemning soft British treatment of the Boer generals as 'mistaken leniency' and 'a sign of weakness'.[65]

Seddon set off for Sydney, South Africa and London on 14 April with another large family grouping for company.[66] In Sydney some newspapers complained about Seddon's dangerous suggestions regarding setting Māori soldiers loose in South Africa, but he was, nevertheless, fêted at a banquet held at the Hotel Australia. In reply to the Premier of New South Wales, Sir John See, Seddon claimed that his statements regarding a Māori contingent had been exaggerated by the metaphor associated with Māori oratory and insisted that the British flag must fly over Fiji, whoever controlled those islands.[67] Once he arrived in Durban on 17 May, Seddon charged through South Africa with all the subtlety of a rhinoceros. He lectured Milner that the peace must involve unconditional surrender, and then instructed the architect of the new South Africa on how it should be governed and recommended that land settlement laws similar to those of New Zealand be implemented. He also told Kitchener how he should fight and end the war, and his telegraph en route to Vereeniging published in *The Times* that 'the South Island Battalion Tenth Contingent better hurry up or it will be too late' caused consternation because it suggested that the war was about to end.[68]

His blunt speeches, advocacy of both unconditional surrender and the importation of New Zealand stock, gained attention in the Cape as well as Johannesburg, Pretoria, Kimberley and Bloemfontein because, as the Christchurch based Press put it, he could not stop electioneering.[69] *The Times*, rather, suggested that the locals enjoyed the 'bluntness and directness' in their first encounter with a truly democratic leader.[70] In contrast, some South African papers like the *Johannesburg Star* (reprinted with relish by the *Press*) demanded that someone should shut the mouth of this New Zealand 'larrikin'.[71] As General Ian Hamilton later remarked, 'Personally, I shall never forget the dramatic appearance of your self [*sic*], and the ladies of the family, on the South African veldt at the close of those warlike operations, in which the New Zealanders rendered such admirable service to the Empire.'[72]

Seddon's enthusiastic support of the Boer War won some small concessions from Chamberlain in that he agreed to the colony's annexation of the Cook Islands in 1901, mainly because they held little economic or strategic value. But Chamberlain remained resolute concerning British control of Fiji and Tonga as against administration from New Zealand and thwarted New Zealand's attempts to wrest control of Western Samoa from Germany.[73] Seddon clearly proved in the most compelling manner that New Zealand was the most loyal self-governing colony before he left for the coronation of Edward VII in 1902. Yet, as even he conceded, the proof of his belief that New Zealand would make tangible gains from supporting Britain to prevent its waning as a world power would soon be tested in London at what he called 'the Councils of Empire'.[74]

Given his higher profile than in 1897 and recognition of his ardent support for the Boer War, the prospects of advancing imperial unity seemed bright when Seddon and family set off for the coronation in April 1902. Yet, despite his enthusiastic speech-making at the staggered meetings of the Imperial Conference, he achieved little in terms of tangible advance. New Zealand had asked for preferential tariffs, or the granting of rebates on manufactured goods carried in British-owned ships; the establishment of an Imperial reserve force in each of the self-governing colonies; strengthening of the Australasian naval squadron; the right for lawyers and administrators from Canada, Australia and New Zealand to participate in the building of a new South Africa; the establishment of subsidised mail services between Australia, New Zealand, Canada and Britain; and the holding of triennial conferences between the Secretary of State for the Colonies and premiers and prime ministers of the self-governing colonies.

Canada and Australia did not share New Zealand's enthusiasm for many of these objectives and only agreed to unsatisfactory compromises. Triennial conferences proved too difficult and conferences at four-year intervals were substituted. The colonies would also be consulted over the negotiation of treaties with foreign powers so far as confidentiality allowed, so that the colonies would 'be in a better position' to 'give adhesion to such treaties'. Australia increased its contribution towards the cost of improving the Australasian naval squadron from £50,000 to £200,000, while New Zealand lifted its contribution to £40,000. More cadet positions would be made available in the British Navy for young men from the self-governing colonies. Preferential trade proved more difficult to implement because of the hostility of Laurier of Canada and the Australians, forcing Seddon and Chamberlain to drop the notion of a Zollverein in which free trade operated between mother country and colonies. Canada, though, agreed to maintain its existing preference of 33.333 per cent and would further reduce duties in favour of the United Kingdom, while raising duties against foreign imports. New Zealand offered a 10 per cent reduction of the existing duty on British-manufactured goods. Seddon, following the Canadian lead, also agreed to increase duties against foreign imports. In contrast, Australia would have nothing to do with preferential tariffs although the conference passed a vague resolution that it 'is desirable that as far as practicable the products of the Empire should be preferred to the products of foreign countries'. The meeting also called for a review of mail subsidies. Cables should, thereafter, be purchased on equitable terms and the Conference recommended that postage on newspapers and periodicals should be reduced. Delegates agreed to open up the Transvaal and the Orange River Colony to colonial lawyers and administrators. New Zealand promised to pay £1500 to erect the Queen Victoria memorial against Canada's £30,000, although Australia had not yet decided on the size of their contribution.[75] Little wonder, then, that Seddon complained that the Finance Bill before the British Parliament did not mention preferential trade,[76] or that he continued to advocate in speeches as he toured around the country for closer economic relations within the Empire, aided by freight subsidies, to close the gap on Germany and the USA.[77] As he put it to the New Vagabond Club at a reception chaired by Sir Arthur Conan Doyle,

> They [New Zealand] did not desire to interfere with fiscal arrangements, but, as between kindred, to give the Motherland's manufactures

preference, leaving her to grant anything in return in her own way, if she was able, and without agreement or causing dissension'.[78]

Seddon seemed reasonably content with compromises and modest achievements upon his return home. It has been suggested that his prominent role on the imperial stage enabled him to enhance his hold over his fiefdom in New Zealand despite his lack of tangible achievement because 'Seddon, in his crude way, gave his people a sense of importance.'[79] It is hard to dispute this judgment, given that Seddon's attendance at the coronation further increased his popularity in New Zealand in that he actually continued to work away with Reeves at bringing the Empire closer together to compensate for New Zealand's decision to go it alone from federated Australia. What Seddon was trying to do was secure New Zealand a more reliable living through locking in supply of a guaranteed market. As he told a gathering of New Zealanders in London in late July, when they presented him with a model of a New Zealand soldier who served in the Boer War,

> Sir Wilfrid Laurier had claimed for Canada that she would be the granary and the baker of the Empire, and Sir Edmund Barton had claimed for Australia that she would be the Empire's butcher; but in New Zealand they had not all their eggs in one basket, and they could claim a combination of the three, especially as the dairyman was not included, and in that respect he thought New Zealand was unsurpassed in the whole world, while in respect to their beef, it was the nearest approach to, and he was not sure that it did not surpass, the juicy roast beef of old England. [Laughter and cheers][80]

He repeated this view rather more succinctly to a meeting of the New Vagabond Club when he stated, 'if Canada and Australia were the granary and the butcher of the Empire, New Zealand would supply the butter and cheese'.[81] Whether such claims are labelled 'better Britonism' or imperialism with nationalist intent, raising New Zealand's profile with the British public helped entrench the notion that New Zealand's meat was superior to that of Australia and Argentina, while its butter was superior to that of Australia or Canada. His mighty efforts, continually supported by Reeves, helped build the 'protein industry' dependent on the British market, supplemented by fatty yellow butter produced by cows raised on grass and greasy wool shorn from cross-bred sheep.[82] In short, Seddon attempted to bring advantage to New Zealand by claiming that its farming outputs would also benefit Britain and the Empire as a whole; an aim achieved by the 1920s, by which time New Zealand came to outstrip Canada as Britain's main supplier of cheese, and Denmark as its chief supplier of butter.[83]

On his return from London, Seddon realised that the rest of the Empire was lukewarm about closer relations and, Chamberlain aside, generally hostile to preferential trade. All little New Zealand could do was attempt to change the minds of larger nations, improve shipping services, distribute New Zealand agricultural exports more efficiently and work towards some kind of reciprocal relationship with individual Australian states and, potentially, South Africa and Canada. Later, he also came to the conclusion that New Zealand had to step up its diplomatic representation in London given the growing importance of that market, especially as he had failed to establish either an imperial council or regular meetings of the Empire's leaders. One strategy was to strengthen his relationship with Ottawa, especially in relation to gaining access to the trans-Canadian cable to enable news to be sent via the Pacific cable so that the two colonies would 'be less in the dark about each other's doings'. Seddon hoped that this service would be free, but failed to secure the higher degree of cooperation for which he longed.[84]

When he introduced his Preferential and Reciprocal Trade Bill at the start of the 1903 session, Seddon hoped that it would synchronise with Chamberlain's promotion of preferential trade in the British Parliament, so protecting access to the British market and increasing access to the Australian and Canadian markets. The Governor, in opening Parliament, mentioned 'fiscal changes', recommended that New Zealand follow the Canadian example and suggested that ways needed to be found of controlling 'trusts and combines'.[85] Before these good intentions could be acted upon, however, Chamberlain upset Seddon's plans by resigning from Cabinet in September to promote his scheme outside Parliament because his own party was split over protection and Prime Minister Balfour largely opposed it.[86]

Publicly, Seddon expressed 'great regret' before easily passing a resolution through Parliament in appreciation of 'the distinguished patriotic services rendered to the Empire' by Chamberlain. Seddon made it clear in doing so that he rated his ally as far and away the greatest Secretary of State for the Colonies. Only left-wingers, Harry Bedford of Dunedin and Harry Ell of Christchurch, voted against the expression of sympathy, while George-ite and member for Inangahua, Patrick Joseph O'Regan, wrote scathingly to Reeves about the 'exaggerated valuation' of Chamberlain.[87] The maverick George Fisher of Wellington and the Wairarapa conservative W.C. Buchanan quibbled over the wording.

John Duthie, a conservative from Wellington City, also wondered if such an action was constitutionally possible given that Britain and New Zealand were two different political entities.[88] Privately, though, Seddon was splenetic with rage at losing the champion of preferential trade from a position of power. He wrote in a much blunter manner than usual to Chamberlain, blaming the debacle on 'little Englanders'. He went on, oblivious to the need for diplomatic nicety:

Our countrymen are slow to think and move, and have worshipped so long at the Cobden phantom that to effect a change requires strenuous efforts – earthquakes as well as arguments; and the fool's paradise now inhabited assisted for the moment by temporary prosperity, makes them revile their best friend. Fancy working men of England turning on Joseph Chamberlain after he passed 'the Workers' Compensation for Accidents Act'.

He lamented the fact that New Zealand had 'lost a sincere friend', and claimed that so long as politicians allowed the 'old country' to be 'the dumping ground for foreign manufactured goods', unemployment would remain high and capital would be 'unremunerative'.[89]

While Seddon anticipated the criticisms of single-taxers such as Bedford, Ell, O'Regan and George Fowlds (all of whom as disciples of Henry George wanted only one tax on land and no other forms of duty),[90] the problem remained of deciding which items should have a tariff raised against them. Farmers, for example, despite wanting a guaranteed and expanded market for their produce in Britain, opposed increased duties on wire and fertiliser, essential items that came mainly from Germany.[91] Unsurprisingly, both MHRs opposed to the measure and the opposition press took issue with many of the items targeted for increased duties, such as US-manufactured boots, candles, tinned fish and porcelain, and accused Seddon of inconsistency.[92] Seddon retorted that unless the Empire expanded preferential trade it faced 'inevitable dismemberment'.[93] He took some solace, though, from the support of Tom Mackenzie who had only recently returned from London where he had sold frozen meat, butter and wool on behalf of New Zealand farmer cooperatives.[94]

Having lost the major champion of preferential trade to the vagaries of British politics, over which he had no control whatsoever, Seddon's problems were compounded by Australian intransigence towards the idea, even if the Canadians seemed a little more sympathetic.[95] Australia's prosperity had been based either on quite high tariffs as

in the case of Victoria, or largely untrammelled free trade as in New
South Wales. Prime Minister of the new Commonwealth Government,
Edward Barton, would have nothing to do with preferential or reciprocal trade. Seddon hoped that Barton's defeat or retirement would
improve matters,[96] but meantime he had to rely on Canadian good will,
where manufacturers sensed that a new market might emerge for their
products in distant New Zealand.[97] Some pro-Liberal papers such as the
Wanganui Herald worried that giant open territories such as Siberia and
Argentina would also push New Zealand out of unprotected markets.[98]
Seddon responded to their fears by continuing to negotiate reciprocal
trade agreements with Australian states such as South Australia, as well
as the Commonwealth, until his death in 1906.[99]

Despite the loss of the key imperial champion, Seddon rammed the
Bill through the House in late November with what every conservative
newspaper considered indecent haste.[100] Notwithstanding the hostility
of both the remnant of the opposition and the left of the Liberal party,
it passed comfortably, but without change in Britain and elsewhere
in the Empire, achieved little. Reeves, meanwhile, despite his personal
sympathy to free trade in Britain, continued to work away to have an
imperial council established in London so that New Zealand could
secure stronger guarantees concerning its market share, as well as having a more direct say in the operation of the Royal Navy and imperial
defence.[101] All that happened, however, was the appointment of a
committee dominated by British bureaucrats that fell well short of any
kind of meaningful colonial representation. Reeves disassociated himself from such an ineffective entity and instead continued to advocate
the formation of an imperial council with its own secretariat, before
Sir Joseph Ward, Seddon's replacement as premier finally secured the
compromise of an imperial secretariat operating inside the Colonial
Office in 1907.[102]

The proposal to elevate the Agent-General to High Commissioner,
made in 1904, raised the salary to £2000 (£400 more than that of the
Premier), lifted the expenses allowance to £250 per annum and set
the appointment on a three-year basis. It received much opposition
on the grounds that such an office was unnecessary and presumptu-
ous for such a small country, which did not need representation at a
federal level like big Australia or Canada.[103] Seddon wrote to Reeves
about blocking Chinese labour from entering South Africa, but did
not consult him over the change. Rumours also flew once again that
the Premier wanted the job.[104] As in 1897, there is no hard evidence
of this desire other than that Seddon obviously enjoyed his time in

London and thought he could achieve much there. His worsening health in 1904 also encouraged speculation, but Tregear and regular correspondent and critic of Seddon, Frank Waldegrave, told Reeves otherwise. Tregear even wrote that 'King Richard ... said to me "So long as I can hold on to the control of affairs in New Zealand I shall do so; and when I give that up I shall not be able to take the High Commissionership or anything else."'[105] Other Liberal party correspondents with Reeves also suggested that Seddon resolutely refused to be '"shunted" off to London'.[106]

Seddon rather viewed the matter as putting New Zealand on a par with the Canadians, who already had an ambassador, and the Australians, and had made legislative provision for such an appointment. As he said in introducing the Bill, New Zealand needed 'to keep in touch with the leading men of the Mother Country' and

unless we kept abreast of what other colonies have done and are doing we should be left behind in the race ... if we did not consider ourselves important other people would judge us by our own standard ... When other colonies so improved the status of their Agent-Generals, why should New Zealand refuse to do likewise? ... his [the ambassador's] office would be practically a branch in London of the New Zealand Treasury.[107]

The new High Commissioner was also charged with reviving assisted migration to New Zealand, and significant numbers of British migrants began to arrive in New Zealand for the first time since 1878.[108]

Seddon's determination to put the colony's London representative on the same level as those of Australia and Canada, along with his increasing use of the title of Prime Minister, thereby asserted New Zealand's self-governing status in anticipation of the introduction of dominion status in 1907. Once embarked upon pursuing the policy of keeping up with the larger self-governing colonies, Seddon committed New Zealand to seeking dominion status, even if he never spelt out the point and left it to Ward to promote the idea at the 1907 Imperial Conference. Whereas William Ferguson Massey as leader of the opposition considered dominion status absurd,[109] Seddon, as a nationalistic imperialist, wanted it in recognition of the advances made under the Liberal government that had propelled New Zealand beyond the status of a mere colony.[110]

Seddon and Chamberlain corresponded intermittently but at length after 1903 until Seddon's death and then Louisa and her daughters wrote after Chamberlain suffered his stroke in 1907.[111] Chamberlain wrote eloquently on Seddon's death to High Commissioner Reeves:

> On the various occasions on which I had the pleasure of meeting him, I formed the highest opinion of his ability, courage and devotion to the interests of New Zealand, while I had the full opportunity of recognising his far-seeing appreciation of the privileges and responsibilities of the Empire in which he so earnestly desired that New Zealand should take her appropriate place.[112]

Seddon and Chamberlain's unlikely friendship and alliance was, therefore, a marriage of convenience that brought advantage to both men although Chamberlain's earlier 'popular Liberal' initiatives made it easier for Seddon to align with him. At times they also differed in that Seddon, as a champion of the people, refused to have Chamberlain secure him a knighthood.[113] But more often Seddon's nationalistic version of imperialism meshed with Chamberlain's broader vision because stronger imperial union benefited somewhere small like New Zealand much more than other, larger self-governing colonies. As John Darwin puts it, Seddon's consistent and frequently theatrical efforts aimed to make New Zealand into a 'partner' in Empire and a 'member of the management committee of the British world system'.[114] Chamberlain's political failure within the Unionist parties meant that the alliance did not win as many advantages as Seddon hoped, but his alignment with Chamberlain, nevertheless, secured a much higher profile for New Zealand within the conduct of Imperial business than the small size and relative economic unimportance of New Zealand justified.

Notes

1. 'Correspondence with Joseph Chamberlain', Folder 12, Folder Ms 1619, Seddon Papers (hereafter SP), Alexander Turnbull Library, Wellington, New Zealand.
2. On Chamberlain's appearance see D. Judd, *Radical Joe: A Life of Joseph Chamberlain* (London: Hamish Hamilton, 1977), p. 67; R. Jay, *Joseph Chamberlain: A Political Study* (Oxford University Press, 1981), p. 10; P. Marsh, *Joseph Chamberlain: Entrepreneur in Politics* (New Haven and London: Yale University Press, 1994), p. 1.
3. W.P. Reeves, *The Long White Cloud: Aotearoa* (London: Horace Marshall and Sons, 1898), p. 295.
4. Reeves writing to the *Daily Express*, 8 May 1900. This article is full of factual errors, including the claim that Seddon was 45 years old when he was approaching 55 and that he left school at 10 years of age rather than 12. Reeves–Seddon Correspondence, Folder 2, Ms1619, SP.

5. Sidney Webb at least acknowledged Seddon's courageous and energetic determination to act as 'the servant' of 'the common people'. D. Hamer (ed.), *The Webbs in New Zealand* (Wellington: Price Milburn for University of Victoria Press, 1974), p. 38.
6. See J. Phillips and T. Hearn, *Settlers: New Zealand Immigrants from England, Ireland and Scotland 1800–1945* (Auckland University Press, 2008), pp. 68–106 on the origins of British migrants to New Zealand and the dominance of London and the southern counties.
7. Judd, *Radical Joe*, p. xiv; Jay, *A Political Study*, pp. 11, 323 and 334; Marsh, *Entrepreneur in Politics*, p. xi.
8. See *St Helens Weekly News and General Advertiser*, 29 September 1860, on Garibaldi; 6 October, 1860, p. 4, on penny savings banks: 'the artisan must be penny wise if he desires respect, contentment, or prosperity, for his wife and family'; 10 November 1860, on 'the dignity of labour'; 17 November 1860, on 'ragged schools'; 19 January, 1861, on mechanics' institutes.
9. On 'Popular Liberalism', see E. Biagini, *Liberty, Retrenchment and Reform: Popular Liberalism in the Age of Gladstone, 1860–1880* (Cambridge University Press,1992); and P. Joyce, *Visions of the People: Industrial England and the Question of Class, 1848–1914* (Cambridge University Press, 1991).
10. T. Brooking, *Richard Seddon King of God's Own: The Life and Times of New Zealand's Longest Serving Prime Minister* (Auckland: Penguin, 2014), pp. 50, 56; Judd, *Radical Joe*, pp. 63–4, 73, 77–8, 103–4; Jay, *A Political Study*, pp. 29–30, 32, 36–7, 40, 42, 75, 90–1, 112, 116–19, 121–3 and 135–7; Marsh, *Entrepreneur in Politics*, pp. 69–70, 176–9, 192, 196, 213–14, 223 and 258.
11. Brooking, *King of God's Own*, p. 24.
12. Ibid., *passim* and pp. 59 and 82 on his brief flirtations with independence.
13. Ibid., *King of God's Own*, pp. 277–82.
14. M. Barker, *Gladstone and Radicalism: The Reconstruction of Liberal Policy in Britain 1885–1894* (Brighton: Harvester Press, 1977), pp. 92–6, 117–38 and 197–9; Biagini, *Liberty, Retrenchment and Reform*, passim; L. Jenkins, *Gladstone* (Basingstoke: Macmillan, 1995), pp. 230–53; H.G.C. Matthew, *Gladstone 1875–1898* (Oxford: Clarendon Press, 1995), *passim* and especially pp. 392–3.
15. Brooking, *King of God's Own*, pp. 296–7.
16. Ibid., pp. 9–15 on Seddon's family background. On Chamberlain's family background see Judd, *Radical Joe*, pp. 1–34; Jay, *A Political Study*, pp. 1–10; Marsh, *Entrepreneur in Politics*, pp. 1–28.
17. On Chamberlain's education see Jay, *A Political Study*, p. 2; Judd, *Radical Joe*, pp. 4–9; Marsh, *Entrepreneur in Politics*, pp. 7–8. Seddon's Board of Trade Certificate in Mechanical Engineering and membership of the Amalgamated Society of Engineers, Machinists, Millwrights, Smiths and Pattern Makers can be found in 'Letters from Organisations', Folder 44/1, SP.
18. Jay, *A Political Study*, p. 9.
19. Brooking, '"Playing 'em like a Piana": Richard John Seddon and the Mastery of Public Performance', *Journal of New Zealand Studies*, 15 (2013), pp. 50–62.
20. On Chamberlain and religion see Jay, *A Political Study*, pp. 1–2, and 7; Judd, *Radical Joe*, pp. 2–4, 9, 22–3, 25, 32, 103, 145, 167 and 174; Marsh, *Entrepreneur in Politics*, pp. 3, 6–7 and 14. On Seddon's mother's Primitive

Methodism see Brooking, *King of God's Own*, pp. 13–14; on his Anglicanism *passim* and especially p. 15.

21. For example Mary Chamberlain wrote on 14 July 1902 wishing Louisa a quick recovery from her influenza; Mary Chamberlain on 15 November 1907 thanked Mary Stuart Seddon for her inquiries into Joseph's health after his stroke and remembered R.J. Seddon's 'fine qualities', Folder 12, SP.

22. See D. Hamer, *The New Zealand Liberals: The Years of Power, 1891–1912* (Auckland University Press, 1988), pp. 80–1 on this point.

23. Brooking, *King of God's Own*, pp. 176–8.

24. Ibid., pp. 161–3 and 168–75. On Chamberlain's 1891/2 proposals, trade union opposition and indifference and the scuppering of Old Age Pensions by the Rothschild committee, see Jay, *A Political Study*, pp. 174, 177–8 and 251–2; Judd, *Radical Joe*, pp. 3, 178 and 224; Marsh, *Entrepreneur in Politics*, pp. 338, 346, 351, 370, 397–8 and 441–2.

25. Brooking, *King of God's Own*, pp. 385–8; and B. Schrader, *We Call It Home: A History of State Housing in New Zealand* (Auckland: Reed, 2005), on Labour's state housing schemes and that of subsequent governments. On Chamberlain and municipal housing see Judd, *Radical Joe*, pp. 64–6; Jay, *A Political Study*, pp. 25–7; and Marsh, *Entrepreneur in Politics*, pp. 92–102.

26. Brooking, *King of God's Own*, pp. 292–4 and 258–65. On Chamberlain and workmens' compensation for industrial accidents like coal-mining disasters see Judd, *Radical Joe*, p. 212; Jay, *A Political Study*, pp. 176–7, 251 and 311; Marsh, *Entrepreneur in Politics*, pp. 70, 328, 339, 341, 346–7, 352–3, 357, 398, 459, 541 and 640.

27. T. Brooking, *Lands for the People? The Highland Clearances and the Colonisation of New Zealand. A Biography of John McKenzie* (Dunedin: University of Otago Press, 1996), pp. 93 and 97–130. On Chamberlain, Jesse Collings and 'three acres and a cow' see Judd, *Radical Joe*, pp. 117, 123 and 135–6; Jay, *A Political Study*, pp. 72, 76, 99, 131 and 165; Marsh, *Entrepreneur in Politics*, pp. 164, 213 and 222.

28. Brooking, *King of God's Own*, pp. 143–6.

29. Brooking, *Lands for the People?*, pp. 129 and 256–9.

30. Brooking, *King of God's Own*, pp. 146–50 and 268–72. On Chamberlain and industrial conciliation and arbitration see Marsh, *Entrepreneur in Politics*, pp. 60, 63, 328, 341, 356 and 358.

31. Seddon receives little mention in any of the three major biographies, with only Marsh referencing Lilliputian New Zealand (rather than Seddon) more than once: *Entrepreneur in Politics*, pp. 473, 477, 491, 516, 525, 531, 534 (direct reference to Seddon), 550, 591, 598, 641 and 651 and 655 on the period after Seddon's death – while Judd references New Zealand once pre-Seddon: *Radical Joe*, p. 208.

32. Brooking, *King of God's Own*, pp. 142–3 and 154.

33. D. Bell, *The Idea of Greater Britain: Empire and the Future of the World Order, 1860–1900* (New York: Princeton University Press, 2007), pp. 6, and 56–8 on the Imperial Zollerein.

34. Bell, *Greater Britain*, pp. 14–15 building on the earlier work of G. Martin, 'Empire Federation and Imperial Parliamentary Union, 1820–1870', *Historical Journal*, 15 (1973), pp. 65–93; and M. Burgess, *The British Tradition of Federalism* (Leicester University Press, 1990), pp. 6–70.

35. New Zealand sent 6500 soldiers as against 16,600 from Australia and 8400 from Canada, which on a population basis worked out at 1:123 against Australia's 1:229 and Canada's 1:631. Brooking, *King of God's Own*, p. 335.
36. *St Helens Newspaper*, 15 June 1897; *Pall Mall Gazette*, 5 June, 1897, *The Empire*, 5 June 1897, *Newcastle Chronicle*, 7 June, 1897, and *Nottingham Guardian*, 7 June 1897, in 'Misc Correspondence mainly related to the London Trip', Folder 42, SP.
37. Recipients included Lady Jenny Churchill who reported that only one duck had survived the journey, and Chamberlain who sent his pair to the Birmingham zoo. Duchess of Marlborough to Seddon, 18 July 1903; Chamberlain to Seddon, 18 June 1903 in 'Letters of R.J. Seddon', 40/2 (1903), National Archives, Wellington; Brooking, *King of God's Own*, pp. 292–7.
38. *St Helens Newspaper*, 15 June 1897.
39. K. Sinclair, *Imperial Federation: A Study of New Zealand Policy and Opinion, 1880–1914* (London: Athlone Press, 1955), pp. 28–30.
40. Sinclair, *Imperial Federation*, pp. 29–30; C8596, 'Proceedings of a Conference between the Secretary of State for the Colonies and the Premiers of the Self-Governing Colonies, at the Colonial Office, London, June and July 1897'. The full text is contained in the Conference Report, CO 885/6/30, National Archives, Kew.
41. 'Proceedings of a Conference between the Secretary of State for the Colonies and the Premiers of the Self-Governing Colonies', p. 15.
42. *Evening Post*, 12 July 1897. On Reid see W.G. McGinn, 'George Reid', in G. Serle (ed.), *The Australian Dictionary of Biography*, vol. 11 (Melbourne: Melbourne University Press, 1988), pp. 347–54.
43. *Otago Witness*, 15 July 1897.
44. *Evening Post*, 9 September 1897.
45. *Evening Post*, 10 September 1897.
46. *Evening Post*, 7 August 1897; 2 September 1897; 9 September 1897.
47. *Evening Post*, 9 September 1897.
48. J. Crawford w. E. Ellis, *To Fight for the Empire: An Illustrated History of New Zealand and the South African War, 1899–1902* (Auckland: Reed/Historical Branch of the Department of Internal Affairs, 1999), pp. 31–9; C. McGeorge, 'The Social and Geographical Composition of New Zealand Contingents', in J. Crawford and I. McGibbon (eds), *One Flag, One Queen, One Tongue: New Zealand, the British Empire and the South African War, 1899–1902* (Auckland University Press, 2003), pp. 100–18; and J. Phillips, *A Man's Country? The Image of the Pakeha Male – A History* (Auckland: Penguin, 1987), p. 146.
49. Crawford and Ellis, *To Fight for Empire*, pp. 84–5; *Otago Witness*, 18 December 1901; 18 December 1901; *Evening Post*, 16 December 1901.
50. *Evening Post*, 20 May 1901; 14 December 1901; 16 December 1901; *Observer*, 21 December 1901; *Nelson Evening Mail*, 15 December 1901.
51. *Observer*, 21 December 1901.
52. *Otago Witness*, 25 December 1910; Crawford and Ellis, *To Fight for Empire*, p. 84.
53. *New Zealand Freelance*, 21 December 1901.
54. *Observer*, 21 December 1901.
55. On the nurses, see E. Ellis, 'New Zealand Women and the War', in Crawford and McGibbon (eds), *One Flag, One Queen, One Tongue*, pp.

128–33; A. Rogers, *While You're Away: New Zealand Nurses at War* (Auckland University Press, 2003), pp. 12–31. *NZ Times*, 21 October 1899, advocated sending nurses from the commencement of hostilities in October 1899. Seddon can take some credit in that he had the Governor inform the Secretary of State for the Colonies that the people of New Zealand wanted to send nurses to South Africa: Ranfurly to Chamberlain, 17 January 1900, 'Governor's Outwards Registers, 1897–1901', CO 361/15. Initially, they were supported by public subscription, but received imperial support from the end of 1900. Eventually, after Governor Ranfurly, at the urging of the New Zealand Government, intervened on their behalf, they received imperial pensions: Ranfurly to Chamberlain, 27 April 1902, CO 209/264. On the 20 teachers who worked in the refugee/concentration camps in 1902, see Ellis, 'New Zealand Women and the War', pp. 140–8, and E. Ellis *Teachers for South Africa: New Zealand Women and the South African War Concentration Camps* (Paekakariki: Hanorah Press, 2010); Ranfurly to Chamberlain, 17 March 1902, CO 209/264.

56. Undated Seddon telegrams to Roberts on the defeat of Cronje and the victory in the Transvaal; Roberts to Ranfurly, 22 July 1900, on 'grand fellows': 'Correspondence with Lord Roberts', Folder 14, SP; Kitchener to Seddon, 29 March 1901, on 'splendid' contingents and New Zealand troops 'distinguishing themselves': 'Seddon and the Boer War', Folder 15, SP.

57. Seddon to Roberts, 7 September 1900, 'Correspondence with Lord Roberts', Folder 14, SP.

58. Kitchener to Seddon, 28 March 1902, 'Seddon and the Boer War', Folder 15, SP.

59. For example, a *NZ Times* editorial at the end of the war of 1 June 1902 analysed British 'bungles' at the battle of Spion Kop, an acknowledgement of difficulty noted in the naming of holes on older New Zealand golf courses.

60. 'PP' made these rather extraordinary predictions: *NZ Times*, 30 September 1899. 'Looking for Blood' also suggested that New Zealand should not send any troops until the British Parliament granted the vote to all its citizens: *NZ Times*, 2 October 1899. An article published on 6 October warned of the cost of the war: *NZ Times*, 6 October 1899.

61. *NZ Times*, 12 October 1899, on insolence; *NZ Times*, 6 October 1899, on pro-slavery; *NZ Times*, 2 April 1900, editorial on the sending of the fifth contingent and 'Freedom'.

62. *NZ Times*, 14 April 1900; K. Sinclair, *William Pember Reeves: New Zealand Fabian* (Oxford: Clarendon Press, 1965), pp. 281–5.

63. *Evening Post*, 5 April 1902.

64. *The Times*, 8 April 1902; 10 April 1902.

65. *Evening Post*, 20 March 1902; 11 April 1902; *The Times*, 12 April 1902.

66. *Evening Post*, 14 April 1902; *The Times*, 15 April 1902.

67. *Evening Post*, 21 April 1902; 22 April 1902; *Otago Witness*, 23 April 1902; *The Times*, 21 April 1902; K. Henry, 'Sir John See', in Serle (ed.), *Australian Dictionary of Biography*, vol. 11, pp. 560–2.

68. *The Times*, 24 May 1902; confirmed by the publication of a telegram from Seddon to Ward: *Evening Post*, 23 May 1902.

69. *Press*, 1 July 1902.

70. *The Times*, 28 May 1902.

71. *Press*, 8 July 1902.

72. Hamilton to Seddon, 29 October 1905, 'Seddon and the Boer War', Folder 15, SP.
73. Brooking, *King of God's Own*, pp. 286–9 and 306–13.
74. *Evening Post*, 17 February 1902.
75. 'Papers Relating to a Conference between the Secretary of State for the Colonies and the Prime Ministers of Self-Governing Colonies; June to August, 1902' [Cd. 1299], House of Commons Parliamentary Papers Online; Seddon interview on his return home: *Evening Post*, 25 October 1902.
76. *Evening Post*, 28 June 1902; *Otago Witness*, 2 July 1902.
77. For example, he told the North Staffordshire Chamber of Commerce at Stoke that subsidies should be paid to steamers carrying British goods: *Evening Post*, 25 June 1902.
78. *Otago Witness*, 23 July 1902.
79. Sinclair, *Imperial Federation*.
80. *The Times*, 22 July 1902.
81. *Evening Post*, 19 July 1902.
82. James Belich uses the phrase 'protein industry', which as critics pointed out, refers only to meat. J. Belich, *Paradise Reforged: A History of the New Zealanders from the 1880s to the Year 2000* (Auckland: Penguin, 2001), pp. 54–68.
83. Ibid., p. 66.
84. Memos of Sandford Fleming to Seddon, 4 and 5 November 1903, and Seddon's reply, 'Miscellaneous Papers Relating to Australia and Canada', Folder 22, SP.
85. *New Zealand Parliamentary Debates* (hereafter *NZPD*), 1903, vol. 123, pp. 7–8.
86. P. Marsh, 'Joseph Chamberlain', in C.G. Matthew and B. Harrison (eds), *Oxford Dictionary of National Biography*, vol. 10 (Oxford University Press, 2004), pp. 932–3.
87. O'Regan to Reeves, 23 October 1904, in which he also expressed opposition to both the High Commissionership and Seddon's 'spread-eagleism': 'Letters from Men of Mark', vol. III, qMS, P Ree (1680), Alexander Turnbull Library, Wellington.
88. *NZPD*, 1903, vol. 125: Fisher, p. 641; Buchanan, pp. 646–8; Duthie, pp. 641–2; vote, p. 651, which passed by 50 votes to 2.
89. Seddon to Chamberlain, 30 September 1903, 'Correspondence with Joseph Chamberlain', Folder 12, SP.
90. *NZPD*, 1903, vol. 137: Bedford, pp. 736–42; Ell, pp. 750–2; Fowlds, pp. 753–5.
91. Massey, Tom Mackenzie and John McLachlan of Ashburton all mentioned this problem in their speeches. *NZPD*, 1903, vol. 127: Massey, pp. 725–9; T. Mackenzie, pp. 761–6; McLachlan, p. 785; as did an editorial in the *Evening Post*, 18 November 1903.
92. For example, Massey, *NZPD*, 1903, vol. 127, pp. 725–9: *Evening Post*, 18 November 1903.
93. *NZPD*, 1903, vol. 127, pp. 832–3.
94. *Otago Witness*, 25 November 1903; Brooking, 'Sir Thomas Mackenzie', in C. Orange (ed.), *Dictionary of New Zealand Biography*, vol. 3 (Auckland/Wellington: Auckland University Press/Department of Internal Affairs), 1996, p. 333.
95. *Evening Post*, 7 November 1903; *Christchurch Star*, 24 November 1903.

96. Seddon to Chamberlain, 30 November 1903, 'Correspondence with Joseph Chamberlain', Folder 12, SP.
97. *Christchurch Star*, 24 November 1903.
98. *Wanganui Herald*, 20 November 1903.
99. 'Reciprocal Tariff and Preferential Trade' contains letters from Cabinet, negotiations with the South Australian Chamber of Commerce and a schedule of items from May 1906, Folder 21, SP. Further information is contained in Australian newspapers held in the Mitchell Library, Sydney: for example, *Sydney Daily Telegraph*, 29 May 1906; 30 May 1906; 9 June 1906; *Melbourne Argus*, 24 May 1906; *Adelaide Advertiser*, 29 May 1906.
100. *Evening Post*, 20 November 1903; *Otago Witness*, 25 November 1903. It passed by 54 votes to 16.
101. Sinclair, *Imperial Federation*, pp. 32–3.
102. Ibid., pp. 34–8;Sinclair, *Reeves*, pp. 294–301; M. Bassett, *Sir Joseph Ward: A Political Biography* (Auckland University Press, 1993), pp. 152–3.
103. *NZPD*, 1904, vol. 128, pp. 525–69: Massey, esp. pp. 530–2; *Evening Post*, 3 November 1904; 4 November 1904.
104. Sinclair, *Reeves*, pp. 303–4. On 'Chinese labour' and preferential trade, see Seddon to Reeves, 3 February 1903, 'Letters from Men of Mark', vol. 3, qMS, P Ree (1680), ATL. On rumours of Seddon's desire to create such a sinecure for himself, see *Evening Post*, 3 November 1904; 4 November 1904. For a particularly sarcastic imaginary report of the excitement generated in London concerning Reeves's appointment, in which delirious massed crowds awaited the announcement with breathless anticipation, see *Evening Post*, 17 June 1905.
105. Tregear to Reeves, 23 January 1905; Waldegrave to Reeves, 10 August 1904, said that the ill Seddon 'will not take' the High Commissionership even if pressed: 'Letters from Men of Mark', vols 1 and 3, qMS, P Ree (1680), ATL, cited in R. Dalziel, *Origins of New Zealand Diplomacy: The Agent-General in London, 1870–1905* (Wellington: Victoria University Press/Price Milburn, 1975), p. 168.
106. Sinclair, *Reeves*, p. 303.
107. *NZPD*, 1904, vol. 128, p. 826; *Evening Post*, 3 November 1904.
108. M. Harper, '"Everything is English": Expectations, Experiences and Impacts of English Migrants to New Zealand, 1840–1970', in L. Fraser and A. McCarthy (eds), *Far from 'Home': The English in New Zealand* (Dunedin: University of Otago Press, 2012), p. 83.
109. *NZPD*, 1907, vol. 139, p. 375.
110. Bassett, *Ward*, pp. 150–5; K. Sinclair, *A Destiny Apart: New Zealand's Search for National Identity* (Wellington: Allen and Unwin/Port Nicholson Press, 1986), p. 179.
111. Chamberlain to Seddon, 12 November 1903; Seddon to Chamberlain 2 December 1903; Chamberlain to Seddon, 7 January 1904; Seddon to Chamberlain, 28 February 1905; and the 1907 letters with Mary E. Chamberlain already discussed. Correspondence with Joseph Chamberlain, Folder 12, SP.
112. *Manchester Guardian*, 13 June 1906.

113. Chamberlain to Seddon, 5 May 1900, in which Chamberlain was sorry that Seddon was unable to receive any 'titular distinction' in recognition of his great services' but understood 'the causes which prevent you from allowing your name to be submitted.' 'Correspondence with Joseph Chamberlain', Folder 12, SP.

114. J. Darwin, *The Empire Project: The Rise and Fall of the British World System, 1830–1970* (Cambridge University Press, 2009), p. 76.

Part II
National Leader

4
Chamberlain and Gladstone: An Overview of Their Relationship

Roland Quinault

William Gladstone had a profound influence on Joseph Chamberlain's career. He was the leading figure in the Liberal party when Chamberlain rose to national prominence in the late 1870s and early 1880s. But the subsequent rupture in their political association had major consequences for both men and for the nation. Although the immediate cause of their divergence was Gladstone's support for Irish Home Rule, it has been widely believed that other issues, including personal animosity, also contributed to the split. Lloyd George, for example, claimed, retrospectively, that Gladstone treated Chamberlain like a dog and hated and humiliated him.[1]

Most of the relevant historiography also asserts that Chamberlain and Gladstone had little in common and less liking for each other. In the 1930s, Chamberlain's official biographer, J.L. Garvin, stressed the political and personal differences between the two men. He claimed, for example, that 'the Radical leader's new type was partly incomprehensible by the old Prime Minister'.[2] In 1953 C.H.D. Howard, the editor of Chamberlain's political memoir on the years 1880–92, described it as 'an indictment of Gladstone'.[3] Philip Magnus claimed that 'in his heart Gladstone did not believe in Chamberlain's integrity and he never liked or understood him'.[4] In 1978 Richard Shannon observed that there was a latent conflict between the aim and outlook of Chamberlain and Gladstone long before 1886 – a view that I later endorsed.[5] In 1981 Richard Jay concluded that Chamberlain was never 'Gladstone's lieutenant', for although the Liberal leader tolerated a few radicals, he sought the continuation of Whig rule.[6] In 1994 Peter Marsh observed that Chamberlain was driven out of the Liberal party 'less by his convictions than by Gladstone'.[7] However, a close examination of their relationship reveals that it was, in some respects, much more positive than has hitherto been alleged.

Chamberlain welcomed Gladstone's accession to the premiership after the Liberal victory at the 1868 general election. As a nonconformist, he strongly supported Gladstone's decision to disestablish the Church of Ireland.[8] Like other Birmingham Liberals, Chamberlain also wanted educational reform. He played a leading role in the National Education League, which campaigned for a universal and un-sectarian system of elementary education paid for by local rates and government grants. But Forster's 1870 Education Bill was a dire disappointment to Chamberlain and the League because it created a dual system of provision, which benefited denominational education, particularly by the Church of England in rural areas. In March 1870 Chamberlain was a leading member of a League delegation that waited on Gladstone to protest against the Education Bill. He listed the grievances of the nonconformists about the Bill to Gladstone, who, in reply, paid particular attention to Chamberlain and stressed the common ground between them.[9]

As enacted, the 1870 Education Bill was a defeat for the National Education League and a cause of internal disunion in the Liberal party, which contributed to the defeat of Gladstone's Liberal government at the 1874 general election. But Chamberlain made a distinction between what he termed 'a Liberal Government passing Tory measures' and the prime minister. At Birmingham, in 1872, he declared, 'let Mr Gladstone, abandoning false friends, return to his true self and we will return to him'.[10] That reunion occurred after the defeat and resignation of Gladstone in 1874 and his subsequent retirement from the party leadership. In 1876 Chamberlain was returned as one of the three MPs for Birmingham and he then adopted a positive attitude towards Gladstone. He told Charles Dilke, his radical friend and ally, that Gladstone 'is our best card' and that if he were to return to the leadership for a few years he would probably do much for them and 'pave the way for more'.[11] In May 1877, Chamberlain praised Gladstone's 'magnificent' speech in Parliament, condemning the Turkish atrocities in Bulgaria.[12] He invited Gladstone to speak at Birmingham and to stay with him and see something of the city.[13] Gladstone agreed, dismissing Granville's reservations on the grounds that Birmingham could pioneer an improved electoral organisation, which would lead to greater unity of party action. He observed, 'the vital principle of the Liberal party ... is action, and ... nothing but action will ever make it worthy of the name of a party'.[14] That was a sentiment close to Chamberlain's heart.

When Gladstone arrived in Birmingham, he received, as Chamberlain had predicted, an almost royal reception from both trade unionists and middle-class Liberals. At a mass meeting in Bingley Hall, he spoke mainly on the Eastern Question but he also praised Birmingham for instituting the principle of popular electoral organisation, a reference to the Liberal caucus and the nascent National Liberal Association.[15] Gladstone described Birmingham as the national centre of municipal life, to which he attached supreme importance. He called the Radicals 'men in earnest', a phrase that Chamberlain later borrowed from Gladstone in his article on the Liberal caucus.[16] Chamberlain, in reply, praised Gladstone for putting his convictions before the demands of party discipline.[17] There is no evidence to support Garvin's claim that Gladstone remained 'inwardly aloof' and that there was no affinity between the two men.[18] Gladstone concluded that Chamberlain was 'a man worth watching', who was 'expecting to play an historical part and probably destined to it'.[19]

At Westminster, in 1878, Chamberlain regarded Gladstone as erratic but as the only possible leader apart from Hartington.[20] He followed his lead on the Eastern Question and on 'what form our opposition may reasonably take'.[21] Like Gladstone, he opposed the Afghan war, criticised the Zulu war and denounced what he termed the 'new imperialism' of the Conservative government.[22] When Gladstone opposed a resolution on the Zulu war sponsored by Chamberlain, the latter immediately agreed to drop the issue.[23] At that time, Chamberlain was not out of sympathy with Gladstone's international policy, contrary to what has been alleged by some historians.[24]

In 1880 Gladstone included Chamberlain in his new Cabinet as President of the Board of Trade. Garvin claimed that Gladstone considered Chamberlain's appointment an 'irksome and extreme concession to the spirit of the age'.[25] The Premier, however, told Chamberlain that he was seeking 'the selection of the fittest'. While he acknowledged Chamberlain's advanced views, he stated that 'there can be no practical impediment on this score to your acceptance of my proposal'.[26] Gladstone later wrote that because Chamberlain was a man 'of Cabinet calibre', he did not hesitate to offer him a place even though he was prepared to serve in a junior post.[27] His decision was a striking act of confidence in Chamberlain, who had been an MP for only four years and had no prior experience of central government office. Gladstone, by contrast, had become President of the Board of Trade only after 11 years as an MP and several posts as a junior minister. The Prime Minister did not regret his faith in Chamberlain. When he reshuffled the Cabinet, in December 1882, he kept Chamberlain at the Board of Trade, 'a place he fills extremely well'.[28]

In retrospect, Chamberlain observed that Gladstone, in the early 1880s, was often more Liberal than the majority of his Cabinet colleagues and that on those occasions the Prime Minister could only count on the support of Bright and himself.[29] That alignment was evident when Gladstone asked Chamberlain to answer for the government on South African questions in the Commons as the Secretary of State for the Colonies was in the Lords. While Chamberlain regretted the first Anglo–Boer war, he supported the Cabinet's decision to arrange an armistice, which led to the Convention of Pretoria.[30]

On domestic issues, Chamberlain often strained at the leash but he usually heeded his master's voice and he was always respectful towards the Prime Minister. In late 1880 he threatened to resign if the Habeas Corpus Act was suspended in Ireland but on the grounds that the case for coercion was not capable of the 'clearest demonstration' that the Premier had publicly stated must precede action. He told Gladstone that he was 'a leader whom I have been proud to follow and in whose genius and love of judicious freedom I have the most implicit confidence'. He ended his letter, 'with profound respect and most sincere thanks for all your kindness to me'.[31] In 1884 likewise, Chamberlain threatened to resign if his merchant shipping Bill was rejected by Parliament but he placed himself at the Premier's disposition and thanked him for his kindness on every occasion.[32] That did not stop him from satirising Gladstone's tendency to casuistry in doggerel verse written during a Cabinet meeting on 17 May 1884:

> Here lies Mr G, who has left us repining,
> While he is, no doubt, still engaged in refining
> And explaining distinctions to Peter and Paul,
> Who faintly protest that distinctions so small
> Were never submitted to saints to perplex them,
> Until the Prime Minister came up to vex them.[33]

The issue of parliamentary reform produced both tensions and alignments between the two men. When Chamberlain publicly called for a new Reform Bill in 1883 before that was Cabinet policy, Gladstone advised him that such independent declarations should be made as rarely and as reluctantly as possible.[34] Chamberlain accepted that doctrine[35] but continued to make outspoken statements, advocating, for example, large concessions to the Egyptian nationalists. So Gladstone asked him to rein in his 'strong conviction, masculine understanding and great power of clear expression as far as his conscience would allow'.[36] But when the Queen complained about Chamberlain's support for manhood suffrage, Gladstone observed that while he did not agree with him on that issue, Chamberlain had the right to hold and declare that opinion.[37] He advised Chamberlain to declare that franchise reform would not undermine the monarchy, which he duly did in his next speech.[38] After the introduction of the 1884 Reform Bill, Gladstone told Chamberlain, 'in the matter of the franchise my views, within the walls of the Cabinet, have approximated to yours more than to some other shades'.[39]

Their attitude to the House of Lords also had something in common. Chamberlain told the Premier that he was opposed to a hereditary House of Lords, particularly if it opposed a Reform Bill. Gladstone replied, 'it is my misfortune to have a very considerable degree of concurrence with your estimate of the legislative performances of the House of Lords', though he was loath to curb its power.[40] Chamberlain's attack on the House of Lords, when it rejected the Reform Bill, angered the Queen. She told the Premier that Chamberlain was the most dangerous member of the Cabinet and 'one to whom she fears Mr Gladstone is inclined to listen far more than to those who hold moderate opinions'.[41] Three months later, she asked Gladstone to separate his name from Chamberlain, 'with which unfortunately it is too often, wrongly no doubt, connected'.[42] Gladstone, however, praised Joe for the skill and moderation of his remarks about the proposed compromise on reform.[43] When the Reform Bill passed through the House of Lords, at the end of 1884, Chamberlain wrote to the Premier, 'I should like to add my expression of my sense of the magnitude of your latest triumphs, and the resolution with which you have surmounted all the obstacles which might have daunted anyone less courageous.'[44]

A week later, however, Chamberlain, in a speech to workingmen, controversially asked what ransom property would pay for the security that it enjoyed. Gladstone's secretary, Edward Hamilton, observed, 'Mr G. is annoyed by Chamberlain's latest speeches; but he does not know what he can do after what he has done to no purpose so often before.'[45] Once again, however, the Premier resorted to flattery, attributing Chamberlain's behaviour to his 'abundant store of energy and vigorous period of life'.[46] Chamberlain replied that he would have been happy to cancel any part of his speeches that Gladstone disapproved of, more readily because the Premier made allowances for 'the more advanced section of a mixed government'. He continued,

It may well be that I should best serve the cause I have espoused, and at the same time relieve you from some of the anxieties of the situation by resuming an independent position. I can only say that if I am left to decide this question I should be chiefly guided by my desire to do whatever you may think best for the Government and least likely to add to your cares.[47]

Gladstone thanked Chamberlain for 'the kind and friendly terms towards myself' but warned him that if ministers were allowed to open up questions not in immediate reach, that would lead to a wide field of disagreement. Instead he wanted ministers to concentrate on passing the Redistribution of Seats Bill, to which, he observed, Chamberlain and Dilke had so largely contributed.[48] The former accepted the general justice and expediency of Gladstone's propositions but observed that 'reform is not an end in itself but only the means to an end'. He wanted legislation to lessen the tax burden on the working classes and to multiply the number of small land holdings.[49] He did not, however, push Gladstone to accept such reforms.

Chamberlain's desire not to antagonise Gladstone was also evident with regard to Irish policy. In May 1885 he told the Premier that his hesitation about Irish policy proceeded from 'a deep sense of obligation both personal and public – to yourself which seemed to me to demand the greatest possible sacrifice of private opinions to meet any wishes you might express'. Like Gladstone, he believed that the government now had a final chance of settling the Irish difficulty: the greatest problem of the moment.[50] He proposed a Central Board for Irish local government, which was warmly supported by Gladstone as 'the only hope for Ireland'. But the scheme was rejected by the Whig ministers and a small majority of the Cabinet.[51] Chamberlain thought of resigning but stayed on in the hope of a compromise and a dilution of the duration and terms of the new Irish Crimes Bill. He was, however, strongly opposed to the decision of Gladstone and Spencer to introduce an Irish Land Purchase Bill without any accompanying reform of Irish local government. Consequently he informed Gladstone that he had no alternative but to resign.[52] Gladstone was surprised and concerned by Chamberlain's decision.[53] However, Chamberlain told the Premier that he felt deep regret at being 'the involuntary cause of adding to your great anxieties'.[54] Moreover he did not actually carry out his threat until the whole government resigned several weeks later.

Chamberlain, now free from the restraints of collective Cabinet responsibility, called for the next Parliament to concede to Ireland 'the right to govern itself in the matter of its purely domestic business' and for the wholesale reform of the Dublin Castle administration.[55] Similarly, Gladstone had previously told the Queen that the Dublin Castle administration was 'an enormous mischief of which he was most anxious to get rid'.[56] Chamberlain told Dilke, 'on the greatest issue between us and the Whigs, Mr G. is on our side' because he would adopt their plan of local government and devolution.[57] He assured Gladstone that he wanted him to continue as the party's leader and that he would avoid adopting any position in opposition to him.[58] He wanted Gladstone to lead the party to victory at the forthcoming general election, in order to avoid divisions in the party.[59]

In September 1885 Gladstone told Chamberlain that he would like to explain to him, in conversation, his personal views and intentions, particularly relating to Ireland.[60] Soon afterwards, Chamberlain paid a brief visit to Gladstone's country home, at Hawarden, in North Wales. Gladstone recorded 'three hours of stiff conversation' with his guest.[61] He reported that Chamberlain was 'a good man to talk to, not only from his force and clearness, but because he ... does not ... make unnecessary difficulties, or endeavour to maintain pedantically the uniformity and consistency of his argument throughout'. Gladstone concluded that 'he and I are pretty well agreed' though not on the important question of whether Parnell would be satisfied with a County Government Bill.[62] At that stage, Gladstone had not committed himself to support Home Rule or indeed to continue as leader of the Liberal party. When he confided that he proposed to hand over the leadership to Hartington, after the general election, Chamberlain protested that it was much easier for Hartington and himself to yield to Gladstone than to each other.[63] His stance hardly justified Garvin's claim that Chamberlain now regarded himself as the man of destiny and Gladstone as a man of the past.[64] Gladstone, more accurately, described Chamberlain as 'the most active and efficient representative of what may be termed the left wing of the Liberal Party'.[65]

In October 1885, Gladstone read *The Radical Programme*, a collection of reform proposals by various radicals with a preface by Chamberlain, who had coordinated the project. They formed the basis for what became known as 'the unauthorised programme' at the 1885 general election. Chamberlain campaigned for the disestablishment of the Church of England and other reforms, including the provision of smallholdings for agricultural labourers. Gladstone, however, opposed disestablishment in England and predicted to Chamberlain that 'Ireland may shoulder aside everything else.'[66] His growing preoccupation with Ireland may have been partly encouraged by his private desire to throw 'Chamberlainism into the far future'.[67] But electoral developments convinced Gladstone that greater autonomy should be granted to Ireland.

At the 1885 general election, Parnell called on Irish voters in Britain to support the Tory candidates. That led Gladstone to believe that Salisbury's government was contemplating some form of Home Rule for Ireland, which the Liberals could then support. In Ireland, moreover, 86 Home Rule MPs were elected, most with massive majorities, whereas all the Liberal candidates were defeated. Although the Liberals won a majority of the seats in Britain, they lacked a secure majority without the support of the Irish Nationalists. All these developments put pressure on Gladstone to reach an accommodation with Parnell. On 16 December 1885, Gladstone's intention to prepare a scheme of Home Rule – the 'Hawarden Kite' – was leaked to the press. At that stage, however, he had neither formulated a definite proposal nor secured the approval of his senior colleagues. That may explain why he erroneously told Chamberlain, on 18 December, that on Ireland 'we are very much in accord'.[68]

When the new Parliament met, in January 1885, Salisbury's minority ministry ended its unofficial alliance with the Irish Nationalists, opposed Home Rule and introduced a new coercion Bill. That briefly reunited the Liberal party and Gladstone then supported an amendment introduced by Chamberlain's faithful lieutenant, Jesse Collings, which led to the defeat and resignation of the Tory government at the end of January 1886. Gladstone then formed his third ministry.

In Gladstone's new government, Chamberlain became President of the Local Government Board: a low-status post in the Cabinet, which has been regarded as a snub by the Premier.[69] The post, however, was acceptable to Chamberlain as he was a champion of local government reform and he declined to return to the Board of Trade or to take control of one of the great spending or military departments.[70] His call for property to pay a 'ransom' for the security it enjoyed had scared the wealthy and spoilt his chance of becoming Chancellor of the Exchequer.[71] Although it was rumoured that Chamberlain wanted to be the Irish Chief Secretary, he had 'the greatest horror' of that post and believed that it would have destroyed him.[72] Chamberlain did ask for the Colonial Office but that post was earmarked for Granville, who was demoted from the Foreign Office. Dilke later claimed that when Chamberlain requested the Colonial Office, Gladstone replied, 'Oh, a Secretary of State.' However, Chamberlain did not include that comment in his subsequent political memoir, which was written after his estrangement from Gladstone.

It has been alleged that Gladstone also slighted Chamberlain by his treatment of Jesse Collings, who became parliamentary secretary to Chamberlain at the Local Government Board. Gladstone proposed to reduce the salary of Collings by £300 as part of his campaign to reduce government expenditure. Chamberlain later claimed that the Premier only dropped that demand after the strenuous intervention of Harcourt.[73] But Gladstone told Chamberlain, 'If I cannot convince you and him [Collings], I shall give in.'[74] When Collings was unseated on petition, Gladstone wrote to him to express his regret.[75] The incident did not reveal any personal animus against Chamberlain by the Premier.

Although Chamberlain joined Gladstone's third ministry, he reserved to himself complete freedom of action once the Premier's Irish scheme had matured. He made it clear to Gladstone that he was against an Irish Parliament as opposed to reform of Irish local government, land and education.[76] Hamilton doubted that Gladstone was right to appoint him on such terms. The Premier privately observed that 'Chamberlain was wanting in straightforwardness' and 'not to be trusted'.[77] That was an unprecedented criticism by Gladstone of Chamberlain's personal character and it reflected their growing political divergence. Nevertheless Gladstone was still anxious to keep Chamberlain on side, if possible, and he asked him to draft a long exposition of his ideas about Ireland, which was then circulated to the Cabinet.[78]

In his re-election address as a new minister, Chamberlain declared that the Irish should have more control of their own domestic business providing the supremacy of the Crown and the integrity of the Empire were uncompromised.[79] That seemed acceptable to Gladstone, who told Chamberlain that he had 'steered among the rocks and shoals with much ability'.[80] Some weeks later, however, Gladstone's proposals for an Irish Land Purchase Bill, as a prelude to Home Rule, were unacceptable to Chamberlain. He complained that the land-purchase scheme would involve an enormous and unprecedented transfer of credit from British taxpayers to Irish landlords – for whom he felt little sympathy. He believed, moreover, that since 'the new elective authority' in Ireland would be largely representative of the Irish tenant farmers, it would soon repudiate repayments of the loan to the British government. Consequently Chamberlain tendered his resignation from the government.[81] The Premier, however, asked him to delay resigning as his Irish proposals were still far from definitive.[82]

Chamberlain agreed to stay on but at a Cabinet meeting, on 26 March, he resigned, along with George Trevelyan, when the Premier unveiled his plans for an Irish Parliament with extended powers and no Irish representation at Westminster. Gladstone wrote in his diary: 'C. & T. split from us. I went to work immediately to supply their places.'[83] Chamberlain later claimed that he had not intended to resign but that the Premier had driven him out. Edward Hamilton observed, 'Mr G. is not in a humour to make a compromise ... He has been tried too long and hard by Chamberlain.'[84] Even so, Gladstone bade Chamberlain a fond farewell: 'I have yielded to the inevitable, with profound regret ... your great powers could ill be dispensed with even in easy times. I shall rejoice ... to see them turned to the honour and advantage of the country.'[85]

After his resignation, Chamberlain avoided personal attacks on Gladstone. He praised the Premier's preliminary speech on the Home Rule Bill as 'magnificent' and described his own resignation as the most painful act of his public life because he had separated from 'one whom I have followed and honoured for so many years'. Although the two men disagreed over the scope of Chamberlain's resignation statement, neither accused the other of acting in bad faith.[86] Gladstone told Chamberlain, 'I am most desirous to avoid anything like personal controversy between us, which I do not think would be edifying to the world.'[87] He wanted to be conciliatory and not to aggravate any breach in the party.[88] When Chamberlain criticised the Irish Land Purchase Bill, he dealt with Gladstone's interruptions in a deferential manner.[89] He also acknowledged that there had been some welcome modifications to the Bill.[90] In a speech to the Birmingham Liberal Association, Chamberlain suggested that his opposition to the Home Rule Bill would be removed if Irish representation at Westminster was retained.[91]

Nevertheless Chamberlain's prominence in the opposition to Home Rule ensured that he bore the brunt of criticism from those who accused the unionist Liberals of disloyalty to Gladstone. He complained that although he had shown nothing but respect for Gladstone and belief in his absolute sincerity, the supporters of the Prime Minister were more bitter against him than anyone else.[92] Gladstone did not accuse Chamberlain of any personal animus against him but did complain that he had 'tried me rather hard'.[93] He declined, moreover, to try to win over Chamberlain because that would require concessions, which would split the Cabinet.[94] He told John Morley, 'I cannot write kootoo-ing [*sic*] letters to Chamberlain & I doubt as to their effect.'[95] In any case, Gladstone observed, early in May 1886, that 'Chamberlainism is rather in the dust, Hartingtonism is on its high horse.'[96] Certainly most Liberal Unionist MPs were Whigs who followed Hartington and at that stage it was far from certain that many Radical MPs or their constituents would follow Chamberlain in opposing Home Rule.[97] But on 31 May, Gladstone recorded in his diary, 'great dismay in our camp', when Chamberlain persuaded his acolytes to follow the example of John Bright and vote against the second reading of the Home Rule Bill.[98] 'This ensures its defeat', Gladstone told the Queen, and he described Chamberlain as 'the most wakeful and persistent' of all the opponents of the Bill.[99]

In his speech on the second reading of the Home Rule Bill, Chamberlain acknowledged that 'the British democracy has a passionate devotion to the Prime Minister – a devotion earned and deserved by fifty years of public service'. He then stated that although 'every personal and political interest would lead me to cast my lot with the Prime Minister', he was not 'base enough to serve my personal ambition by betraying my country'.[100] In other words, Chamberlain's break with Gladstone was based on policy differences, not on personal grounds.

At the 1886 general election, fought solely on the Home Rule issue, Chamberlain and his Liberal Unionist colleagues in Birmingham retained their seats, thanks partly to their electoral alliance with the Conservatives. Nevertheless the defeat of the Gladstonian Liberals at that election and the creation of a Conservative government, rather than a coalition with the Liberal Unionists, appeared to create a more favourable climate for Liberal reunion. Gladstone noted that Chamberlain was always declaring his anxiety for an accommodation but added that declarations had to be matched by acts.[101] At the start of 1887, he gave his blessing to talks with Chamberlain and Trevelyan with a view to a possible *modus vivendi* between the Gladstonian and Unionist Liberals.

Gladstone did not take part in the round-table negotiations but he privately praised Chamberlain's character and talents.[102] Chamberlain, by contrast, privately blamed Gladstone's political behaviour on his old age and allegedly claimed that the Liberal party could be reunited under his own leadership.[103] But when the two men met informally, at the Devonshire Club, Gladstone recorded, 'Much conversation with C – who was very friendly.'[104] A few days later, however, Chamberlain wrote a letter to *The Baptist*, in which he complained that the British people went without much-needed legislation because the Irish were disloyal. Chamberlain's prioritisation of the needs of the British, rather than the Irish, angered the Gladstonians, who suspended the talks.[105]

Chamberlain expressed regret to Gladstone that 'the opportunity from which I had hoped so much was suffered to pass away'.[106] But the two men then met for a private discussion at Dollis Hill, after which Gladstone wrote, 'ambiguous result but some ground made'.[107] He recorded that Chamberlain had plenty of qualms about the Unionist government's coercion policy and foresaw that the bulk of Radical Liberal Unionists would be defeated at the next general election. Chamberlain also predicted that the Hartington wing would join the Tories, which he never could.[108] The decision of Salisbury's government to reintroduce coercion, in the form of Balfour's 1887 Crimes Act, put Chamberlain in a difficult position, as he had been a strong critic of coercion in the past. Although he supported the measure, he feared that its unpopularity with both Irish Nationalists and British Radicals would ensure that Gladstone was prepared to make only minimal concessions to the Liberal Unionists.[109]

After 1887 neither man tried to bridge the political gulf between them. When Gladstone spoke at Birmingham in 1888, he made no direct reference to Chamberlain but he castigated 'the Liberal anti-Liberals', who had made 'a Tory minority into a Unionist majority' and whose fate would be 'speedy extinction'.[110] That prediction was partly borne out at the 1892 general election, when the Liberal Unionists lost over a third of their seats in the Commons, although Chamberlain and his followers retained their seats in and around Birmingham. In Parliament, Gladstone criticised Chamberlain for failing to secure the remedial legislation for Ireland that he had promised in 1886.[111] On his part, Chamberlain remained firmly loyal to the unionist alliance with the Conservatives and resolutely opposed to Home Rule.

Nevertheless both men retained a good personal opinion of each other. In 1887 Gladstone told John Morley that Chamberlain exhibited 'more energy, suppleness and brains generally' than the rest of the Liberal Unionists.[112] He told Dilke that, since the split, Chamberlain had shown 'even greater speaking and debating talents than he had shown before'.[113] In 1888 Gladstone voted for Chamberlain's admission to Grillions Club – a venue for men with opposing views – and was surprised that he was blackballed.[114] Chamberlain, on his part, strongly denied John Morley's assertion that he was animated by personal dislike of Gladstone.[115] Even so, after reviewing the events of 1885, he described it as 'a record of unexampled duplicity, concealment and even actual falsehood on the part of the G.O.M.'[116] While there is little evidence to support that view of Gladstone's conduct before the 1885 general election, his clandestine commitment to Home Rule in

December 1885 was somewhat underhand. Even John Morley, who was a leading supporter of Home Rule, concluded that 'the machinations of December 1885' were 'the most absolutely indefensible thing in Mr. Gladstone's career'.[117] During Gladstone's fourth and final ministry, from 1892 to 1894, Chamberlain remained respectful towards him. He perceptively predicted that the Liberals would keep Gladstone as premier as long as they could because he was the figurehead that they all supported.[118] Chamberlain was visibly moved when the maiden speech of his son, Austen, was described by Gladstone as 'dear and refreshing to a father's heart'.[119] When Gladstone finally retired, in 1894, Chamberlain praised him as 'the greatest parliamentary orator and statesman of our time'. He stressed that although they had differed on policy, he had never questioned Gladstone's transcendent abilities or personal worth.[120] A few months later, the two men and their wives met at Dollis Hill, when Gladstone remarked that Chamberlain had always been very kind to him.[121] He told others that Chamberlain was 'the most remarkable man of his generation'.[122]

The positive aspect of the relationship between Gladstone and Chamberlain needs more emphasis than it has received. Each admired the other even after their rupture over Home Rule. Chamberlain's stance was based on genuine respect but also on gratitude. For Gladstone was quick to identify Chamberlain as an outstanding politician and he retained that opinion thereafter. Gladstone also played a key role in advancing Chamberlain's career by swiftly promoting him to the Cabinet in 1880. During his second ministry, Gladstone sometimes regarded Chamberlain as a loose cannon on issues such as parliamentary reform, but he always displayed a desire to reach an accommodation with him.

Until 1886, Chamberlain's periodic threats to resign reflected not a lack of confidence in Gladstone personally but disagreement with collective Cabinet policy. Like other leading politicians at that time, such as Harcourt and Lord Randolph Churchill, Chamberlain used the threat of resignation as a tactic to advance his political objectives. He was also a demanding Cabinet colleague during his later career as a Unionist minister and he resigned from Balfour's Cabinet in 1903.

Philip Magnus claimed that Gladstone could have kept Chamberlain loyal if he had acknowledged his claim to the party leadership, while Peter Marsh has observed that Gladstone's longevity denied Chamberlain the Liberal leadership.[123] But even if Gladstone had retired in 1885, the leadership would have reverted to Hartington. Chamberlain lacked sufficient support in the parliamentary Liberal party and, unlike all the premiers since the Duke of Wellington, he had not served either as Chancellor of the Exchequer or as a Secretary of State. The Queen, moreover, would have been most reluctant to ask Chamberlain to form a government, given her objections to his radical policies and brief flirtation with republicanism.

It was not personality or personal ambition but policy that led to the rupture between Gladstone and Chamberlain. Although Chamberlain's support for radical domestic reform in Britain strained their relationship, it was his opposition to Gladstone's radical Irish policy that created the impasse between them. In the later 1870s and early 1880s, both men were advocates of extended local government in Ireland.[124] But Chamberlain was, at the same time, an opponent of Home Rule in the form of an Irish Parliament. He wrote in 1884, 'I can never consent to regard Ireland as a separate people with the inherent rights of an absolutely independent community.'[125] Gladstone, by contrast, concluded that the Irish people, as represented by the great majority of their MPs, had a justified right to a parliament of their own. Henceforth he was committed to what he called 'the speedy concession to Ireland of what she most justly deserves'.[126] Richard Jay claimed that Chamberlain broke with Gladstone, not over the principle of Home Rule, but over matters of detail and timing that could have been compromised.[127] In reality though, the policy gulf between them on Ireland was too wide to be bridged.

In 1903 Chamberlain told Winston Churchill, 'I bear no malice for political opposition.' He continued, 'you can attack a policy without imputing all sorts of crimes to its author. Mr Gladstone was a good model in this respect & in all the Home Rule controversy he almost entirely avoided personal attack.'[128] Gladstone was a model for Chamberlain in other respects as well. Although Chamberlain's campaign for Tariff Reform, launched in 1903, was another major break by him with Gladstonian Liberalism, it echoed, in some respects, Gladstone's campaign for Home Rule. Both were the impatient initiatives of old men in a hurry, who rashly embarked on a controversial policy without securing the united support of the Cabinet and their party. They also failed to 'educate' the general public, which led to the defeat of their policy at a general election. In both cases, however, their party was soon largely won over and the cause eventually succeeded, although in a different form and era.

Chamberlain not only admired and imitated Gladstone but also regarded him as in a class of his own. At Birmingham, in 1885, he declared,

It may be that we shall have to put between us and Mr Gladstone a space of time before we shall know how much greater he has been than any of his competitors for fame and power. I am certain that justice will be done to him in the future and ... there will be a signal condemnation of the men who, moved by motives of party spite, in their eagerness for office, have not hesitated to load with insult and indignity the greatest statesman of our time.[129]

Although the subsequent Irish Home Rule crisis created a lasting political breach between the two men, their mutual respect and admiration for each other remained largely undiminished. That was based on appreciation of each other's personal and political qualities, which transcended policy differences.

Notes

1. *Margot Asquith's Great War Diary 1914–1916: The View from Downing Street*, ed. M. Brock and E. Brock (Oxford University Press, 2014), p. 193, 18 September 1915.
2. J.L. Garvin, *The Life of Joseph Chamberlain, vol. I, 1836 – 1885* (London: Macmillan, 1932), p. 609.
3. C.H.D. Howard (ed.), *Joseph Chamberlain: A Political Memoir 1880–1892* (London: Batchworth Press, 1953), p. xv.
4. P. Magnus, *Gladstone, A Biography* (London: John Murray, 1954), p. 277.
5. R. Shannon, *Gladstone and the Bulgarian Agitation 1876* (Hassocks: Harvester, 1975), p. 273; R. Quinault, 'Joseph Chamberlain: A Re-assessment', in T.R. Gourvish and A. O' Day (eds), *Later Victorian Britain 1867–1900* (London: Macmillan, 1988), pp. 80–1.
6. R. Jay, *Joseph Chamberlain: A Political Study* (Oxford: Clarendon, 1981), p. 94.
7. P. Marsh, *Joseph Chamberlain, Entrepreneur in Politics* (London: Yale University Press, 1994), p. 274.
8. Garvin, *Life of Joseph Chamberlain*, vol. 1, p. 98.
9. Ibid., pp. 111–13.
10. Ibid., p. 132, Chamberlain to the Nonconformist Committee at Birmingham, 18 March 1872.
11. Ibid., p. 240, Chamberlain to Dilke, 10 Oct. 1876.
12. *Parliamentary Debates*, third series, vol. 234, cc. 449, 455.
13. British Library, Gladstone Papers, Add. MS 44125, f. 3, Chamberlain to Gladstone, 16 April 1877; f. 5, Chamberlain to Gladstone, 26 May 1877.
14. A. Ramm (ed.), *The Political Correspondence of Mr Gladstone and Lord Granville, 1876–1886*, vol. 1 (Oxford: Clarendon, 1962), p. 40, Gladstone to Granville, 19 May 1877.
15. *The Times*, 1 June 1877.
16. Joseph Chamberlain, 'The Caucus', in *Fortnightly Review*, 24, 143, November 1878, p. 741.
17. *The Times*, 2 June 1877.

18. Garvin, *Life of Joseph Chamberlain*, vol. 1, p. 261.
19. Ramm, *Political Correspondence of Mr Gladstone and Lord Granville*, vol. 1, p. 43, Gladstone to Granville, 1 June 1877.
20. Garvin, *Life of Joseph Chamberlain*, p. 247, Chamberlain to Jesse Collings, 18 Feb. 1878.
21. Ibid., p. 248, Chamberlain to Jesse Collings, 2 April 1878.
22. *Parl. Debates*, 3rd, vol. 243, c. 388; vol. 244, cc. 1906–16.
23. *Parl. Debates*, 3rd, vol. 246, cc. 1374–78.
24. Cf. Garvin, *Life of Joseph Chamberlain*, vol. 1, p. 536; Jay, *Joseph Chamberlain*, p. 68.
25. Garvin, *Life of Joseph Chamberlain*, vol. 1, p. 409.
26. Garvin, *Life of Joseph Chamberlain*, vol. 1, pp. 301–2, Gladstone to Chamberlain, 27 April 1880.
27. BL Gladstone Papers, Add. MS 44791, ff. 40–1, Gladstone's autobiographical memorandum, 1894.
28. H.C.G. Matthew (ed.), *The Gladstone Diaries*, vol. 10 (Oxford University Press, 1990), p. 381, Gladstone to Harcourt, 17 December 1882.
29. Chamberlain, *Memoir*, p. 3.
30. Chamberlain, *Memoir*, pp. 13–14.
31. Add. MS 44125, ff. 43–5, Chamberlain to Gladstone, 16 Nov. 1880.
32. Chamberlain, *Memoir*, pp. 103–4, Chamberlain to Gladstone, 9 March 1884.
33. S. Gwynn and G.M. Tuckwell, *The Life of the Rt. Hon. Sir Charles W. Dilke Bt.*, *M.P.*, vol. 2 (London: John Murray, 1917), p. 51.
34. Add. MS 44125, ff. 188–9, Gladstone to Chamberlain, 2 July 1883.
35. Add. MS 44125, f. 190, Chamberlain to Gladstone, 2 July 1883.
36. Chamberlain, *Memoir*, p. 90, Gladstone to Chamberlain, 3 Dec. 1883.
37. Ramm, *Political Correspondence of Mr Gladstone and Lord Granville*, vol. 2, p. 121, Gladstone to Granville, 8 Dec. 1883.
38. Add. MS 44125, ff. 216–18, Gladstone to Chamberlain, 11 Dec. 1883; Chamberlain to Gladstone, 11 Dec. 1883.
39. Add. MS 44126 f. 20, Gladstone to Chamberlain, 27 March 1884.
40. Chamberlain, *Memoir*, pp. 93–4, Chamberlain to Gladstone, 21 Dec. 1883; Gladstone to Chamberlain, 22 Dec. 1883.
41. G.E. Buckle (ed.), *The Letters of Queen Victoria*, second series, vol. 3 (London: John Murray, 1928), p. 522, Queen Victoria to Gladstone, 25 July 1884.
42. *Letters of Queen Victoria*, 2nd, vol. 3, p. 558, Queen Victoria to Gladstone, 27 Oct. 1884.
43. Chamberlain, *Memoir*, p. 99, Gladstone to Chamberlain, 8 Oct. 1884.
44. Add. MS 44126, f. 48, Chamberlain to Gladstone, 28 Dec. 1884.
45. D.W.R. Bahlman (ed.), *The Diary of Sir Edward Walter Hamilton 1880–1885*, vol. 2 (Oxford University Press), 1972, p. 776, 20 January 1885.
46. Chamberlain, *Memoir*, p. 111, Gladstone to Chamberlain, 31 Jan. 1885.
47. Add. MS 44126, ff. 56–9, Chamberlain to Gladstone, 3 Feb. 1885.
48. Add. MS 44126, f. 62, Gladstone to Chamberlain, 5 Feb. 1885.
49. Add. MS 44126, ff. 65–8, Chamberlain to Gladstone, 7 Feb. 1885.
50. Add. MS 44126, f. 74, Chamberlain to Gladstone, 7 May 1885.
51. A.B. Cooke and J.R. Vincent (eds), *Lord Carlingford's Journal, Reflections of a Cabinet Minister* (Oxford: Clarendon, 1971), p. 100, 9 May 1885.
52. Add. MS 44126, f. 79, Chamberlain to Gladstone, 20 May 1885.

53. Add. MS 44126, f. 82, Gladstone to Chamberlain, 20 May 1885.
54. Garvin, *Life of Joseph Chamberlain*, vol. 1, p. 613, Chamberlain to Gladstone, 22 May 1885.
55. *The Times*, 18 June 1885, Chamberlain's speech at Holloway Hall.
56. *Letters of Queen Victoria*, 2nd series, vol. 3, p. 653, Gladstone to the Queen, 23 May 1885.
57. J.L. Garvin, *The Life of Joseph Chamberlain, vol. II, 1885–1895* (London: Macmillan, 1933), pp. 15–16, Chamberlain to Dilke, 28 June 1885.
58. Chamberlain, *Memoir*, pp. 122–4, Chamberlain to Gladstone, 10 Sept. 1885.
59. Chamberlain, *Memoir*, p. 126, Chamberlain to Gladstone, 12 Sept. 1885.
60. Chamberlain, Memoir, pp. 130–1, Gladstone to Chamberlain, 22 Sept. 1885.
61. H.C.G. Matthew (ed.), *The Gladstone Diaries*, vol. 11 (Oxford University Press, 1990), p. 410, 8 October 1885.
62. Ramm, *Political Correspondence of Mr Gladstone and Lord Granville*, vol. 2, pp. 403–4, Gladstone to Granville, 8 Oct. 1885.
63. Chamberlain, *Memoir*, pp. 167–8, Gladstone to Chamberlain at Hawarden, 8 Oct. 1885.
64. Garvin, *Life of Joseph Chamberlain*, vol. 1, p. 623.
65. *Letters of Queen Victoria*, 2nd series, vol. 3, p. 701, Gladstone to Queen Victoria, 10 Oct. 1885.
66. *Gladstone Diaries*, 11, p. 417, Gladstone to Chamberlain, 25 Oct. 1885.
67. *Gladstone Diaries*, 11, p. 423, Gladstone to Lord Richard Grosvenor, 6 Nov. 1885.
68. *Gladstone Diaries*, 11, p. 452, Gladstone to Chamberlain 18 Dec. 1885.
69. Marsh, *Joseph Chamberlain*, pp. 223–4.
70. Chamberlain, *Memoir*, p. 188.
71. Add. MS 48642, ff. 113–14, E.W. Hamilton's account of the formation of Gladstone's third ministry, 1886.
72. Chamberlain, *Memoir*, p. 60, Chamberlain to John Morley, 16 Aug. 1888.
73. Chamberlain, *Memoir*, p. 189.
74. *Gladstone Diaries*, 11, p. 491, Gladstone to Chamberlain, 8 Feb. 1886.
75. *Gladstone Diaries*, 11, p. 525, Gladstone to Collings, 5 April 1886.
76. Chamberlain, *Memoir*, p. 187, Chamberlain to Gladstone, 30 Jan. 1886.
77. Add. MS 48642, ff. 119–23, E.W. Hamilton's account of the formation of Gladstone's third ministry, 1886.
78. *Gladstone Diaries*, 11, p. 491, Gladstone to Chamberlain, 8 Feb. 1886. Add. MS 44548, f. 58, Gladstone to Chamberlain, 25 Feb. 1886.
79. *Birmingham Daily Post*, 5 Feb. 1886.
80. Chamberlain, *Memoir*, p. 189, Gladstone to Chamberlain, 5 Feb. 1886.
81. Chamberlain, *Memoir*, pp. 195–6, Chamberlain to Gladstone, 15 March 1886.
82. Chamberlain, *Memoir*, p. 197, Gladstone to Chamberlain, 15 March 1886.
83. *Gladstone Diaries*, 11, p. 518, 26 March 1886.
84. *Diary of Sir Edward Hamilton*, p. 31, 28 March 1886. J. Morley, *Recollections*, 2 vols (London, 1917), vol. 1, p. 296.
85. Chamberlain, *Memoir*, p. 199, Gladstone to Chamberlain, 27 March 1886.
86. *Parl. Debates*, 3rd series, 304, cc. 1181–3, 1548, 1811.
87. Chamberlain, *Memoir*, p. 204, Gladstone to Chamberlain, 11 April 1886.
88. Chamberlain, *Memoir*, p. 206, Gladstone to Chamberlain, 15 April 1886.

89. R.C. Temple (ed.), Rt. Hon. *Sir Richard Temple, Letters & Character Sketches from the House of Commons* (London: John Murray, 1912), p. 59, 17 April 1886.

90. *Parl. Debates*, 3rd series, 304, cc. 1817–18.

91. *The Times*, 22 April 1886.

92. Chamberlain to Labouchere, 17 May 1886, copy Chamberlain Papers, JC 5/50/109, cited in Peter T. Marsh, 'Chamberlain's Separation from the Gladstonian Liberals, 1885–6', in Bruce L. Kinzer (ed.), *The Gladstonian Turn of Mind, Essays Presented to J.B. Conacher* (University of Toronto Press, 1985), p. 147.

93. *Gladstone Diaries*, 11, p. 534, Gladstone to E.R. Russell, 19 April 1886.

94. *Gladstone Diaries*, 11, p. 535, Gladstone to Arnold Morley, 20 April 1886.

95. *Gladstone Diaries*, 11, p. 536, Gladstone to John Morley, 20 April 1886.

96. *Gladstone Diaries*, 11, p. 547, Gladstone to Rosebery, 7 May 1886.

97. I. Cawood, *The Liberal Unionist Party, A History* (London: I.B. Tauris, 2012), pp. 36–9.

98. *Gladstone Diaries*, 11, p. 564, 31 May 1886.

99. *Letters of Queen Victoria*, 3rd series, 3 vols (London, 1930), vol. 1, p. 138, Gladstone to the Queen, 31 May 1886.

100. *Parl. Debates*, 3rd series, vol. 306, cc. 698–700.

101. *Gladstone Diaries*, 11, p. 602, Gladstone to Harcourt, 2 Aug. 1886.

102. J. Morley, *The Life of William Ewart Gladstone*, vol. 2 (London: Macmillan, 1908), p. 447, Gladstone to Acton, 13 Jan. 1887.

103. M. Hurst, *Joseph Chamberlain and Liberal Reunion* (Newton Abbott: David and Charles, 1970), pp. 380–3, Appendix II, Mrs Dilke's diary, 7 and 11 Feb. 1887.

104. H.C.G. Matthew (ed.), *The Gladstone Diaries*, vol. 12 (Oxford University Press, 1994), pp. 12–13, 21 Feb. 1887.

105. Garvin, *Life of Joseph Chamberlain*, vol. 2, p. 292.

106. Chamberlain, *Memoir*, pp. 264–5, Chamberlain to Gladstone, 4 April 1887.

107. *Gladstone Diaries*, 12, p. 23, 5 April 1887.

108. BL Add. MS 44773 ff. 35–8, Gladstone's memorandum of a conversation with Chamberlain on Irish policy, 5 April 1887.

109. Chamberlain, *Memoir*, p. 273, Chamberlain to Morley, 18 Sept. 1887.

110. *The Times*, 7 November 1888; 8 November 1888.

111. *Parl. Debates*, 3rd series, vol. 333, cc. 720–34.

112. Chamberlain, *Memoir*, p. 272, Morley to Chamberlain, 14 Aug. 1887.

113. Gwynn and Tuckwell, *Life of Charles Dilke*, vol. 2, pp. 269–70, 24 Oct. 1887.

114. *Gladstone Diaries*, 12, p. 99, 11 Feb. 1888.

115. Chamberlain, *Memoir*, pp. 305–6, Chamberlain to Morley, 30 Oct. 1891.

116. Chamberlain, *Memoir*, p. xv, Chamberlain to J. Collings, 23 Jan.1891.

117. *Diary of Sir Edward Hamilton*, p. 421, 31 July 1902.

118. *Letters of Queen Victoria*, 3rd series, vol. 2, p. 129, Sir Henry Ponsonby to Queen Victoria, 17 July 1892.

119. Garvin, *Life of Joseph Chamberlain*, vol. 2, p. 563.

120. Ibid., p. 593, Chamberlain's speech at the Birmingham Liberal Unionist Club, 7 March 1894.

121. Ibid., p. 594, Chamberlain's memorandum, 28 July 1894.

122. Ibid., p. 595, note 2.

123. Magnus, *Gladstone*, p. 347; Marsh, *Joseph Chamberlain*, p. 354.
124. W.E. Gladstone, *Midlothian Speeches 1879* (Leicester University Press, 1971), pp. 86–8, 26 November 1879.
125. Garvin, *Life of Joseph Chamberlain*, vol. 1, p. 579, Chamberlain to W.H. Duignam, 17 Dec. 1884.
126. *Gladstone Diaries*, 12, p. 25, 10 April 1887.
127. Jay, *Chamberlain*, p. 350.
128. Randolph S. Churchill, *Winston S. Churchill*, vol. 2, companion part 1 (London: Heinemann, 1969), pp. 219–20, Chamberlain to Churchill, 15 Aug. 1903.
129. *The Times*, 4 June 1885.

5

Joseph Chamberlain and Leonard Courtney: Freely Disagreeing Radicals?

Eleanor Tench

Certainly the most significant point of disagreement between Leonard Courtney and Chamberlain was their battle over the second Anglo–Boer War, when Courtney founded the pro-Boer South African Reconciliation Committee and Chamberlain was regarded as the chief architect of the war, due to his brinkmanship in negotiating the rights of the Uitlanders with the Transvaal President, Paul Kruger. In fact, it was simply the last in a long series of issues, both personal and political, where the two radical Liberals disagreed. Despite the two men both entering politics on the radical wing of the Liberal party and then becoming leading figures in the Liberal Unionist party, it is hard to find points where they agreed, beyond a dislike for state collectivism, aristocratic privilege and each other.[1] It is even harder to find places where they agreed for the same reason. Aside from the belief that reform was necessary, they were poles apart in personality, political style and priorities. The purpose of this chapter is to examine the differences between Courtney and then to focus on the few specific incidents that highlight this rivalry and Chamberlain's relationship with other political figures within the radical Unionists.

In contrast to the London-born Chamberlain, who left school at 16, Courtney was a Cornishman, born in Penzance, and educated at Cambridge, where he was second wrangler. His family, however, unlike the Chamberlains, was not wealthy. His father was a bank clerk who borrowed money from his employer to pay for Courtney's education. Despite his debt to his father, both moral and financial, Courtney somewhat drifted after his time at Cambridge. He had to earn to repay his father and to cover the costs of educating his younger siblings. But, he lacked the background and family connections to be successful as a barrister, even though he was academically brilliant enough to be made professor of political economy at University College London. He was to eventually accept a role as journalist for *The Times* after turning down an offer from his father's employer to become a bank manager in Melbourne. By this time, however, he had started to set his sights on a political career. He was interviewed for his home town of Penzance but was to accept the role of candidate for Liskeard. After one failed attempt, he won two years later in 1876 and, after the Redistribution Act, he was accepted to represent the combined county constituency. Although he swiftly attached himself to the radical section of the party, Chamberlain was unimpressed. Despite the fact that he and Courtney both rebelled against Gladstone in 1881 over the prospect of war with the Boers, Chamberlain did not believe Courtney was a proper radical and from his position that was a fair description. Courtney was very strongly opposed to many of Chamberlains interventionist proposals, for example he was the only one of the radicals to vote against the 'three acres and a cow' amendment that brought down the Tory ministry in early 1886. This move was infuriating to many radicals and not terribly popular in his agricultural-based consistency.[2] However, Courtney was able to mollify his electorate with an explanation that, although he supported the principle of allotments, he believed that any measure that had to be obtained by compulsion would result in far greater costs than benefits. It was, however, the beginning of a serious divide between himself and Chamberlain, made more bitter by the fact that the amendment had been introduced by Jesse Collings, Chamberlain's closest lieutenant in his Birmingham 'duchy'.

Chamberlain was also to complain that Courtney was insufficiently committed to the nonconformist cause. Courtney was an Anglican, but he represented a consistency that was significantly Wesleyan Methodist. However, Cornwall was an area where Methodism tended to constrict political radicalism. Courtney's commitment to the temperance movement and his very strong belief that disestablishment was necessary to strengthen the church was more than enough commitment for his nonconformist voters. His promotion of achievement through self-improvement rather than state intervention was also mirrored in local Methodist creeds. Courtney's relationship with Chamberlain was therefore hampered by their fundamental philosophical and political differences, with Chamberlain favouring interventionist policies (at least until 1895), and Courtney preferring to focus on political inclusion. Courtney believed that allowing people to have access to involvement in the political system would give them the chance to solve their own problems. He also believed that parliament should not be making the kind of significant changes that Chamberlain was proposing until it was representative of the entire populace (women included). He also publicly warned that to increase the electorate substantially without introducing fundamental electoral reform was to risk passing political power from the hands of the politicians and into the hands of 'wire-pullers'. As Chamberlain's 'duchy' of Birmingham was organised exactly in the form of an American style caucus, which Courtney disavowed, there were practical as well as philosophical grounds for their rivalry.[3] Courtney's preferred method of making parliaments more representative was through universal suffrage under an electoral system of proportional representation. He planned with Henry Fawcett to resign from his post as Financial Secretary to the Treasury, in protest at the failure to include proportional representation in the Third Reform Act. This gesture seemed somewhat futile, however, as Courtney took this stance alone after Henry's death in November 1884.[4] Chamberlain was to comment that Courtney was a fool who had thrown away his career on the worthless gesture. However, it was not entirely worthless. Courtney's loyalty to Fawcett and to campaigning for universal suffrage was rewarded when Henry's widow, Millicent Fawcett, joined Courtney's wife, Kate and the Ulster suffragist Isabella Tod in campaigning for Courtney in 1886. Both Fawcett and Tod remained staunch allies of Courtney and important leaders of the Women's Liberal Unionist Association, at least until the advent of Tariff Reform.[5]

Despite Courtney's opposition to the idea of separate parliament for Ireland, which he had made clear in his election address in December 1885, Gladstone had requested Courtney to take on the role of chairman of committees, also known as the role of the deputy Speaker.[6] Courtney was one of the group of Liberals around Sir John Lubbock and George Goschen who began to plot against the Home Rule Bill as soon as it became clear that the G.O.M. was determined to proceed with such a policy. They opposed the policy on the grounds that it was a surrender to the violence and intimidation of the Nationalists, which, they believed, lay behind Parnell's achievement of 86 parliamentary seats in the general election. Chamberlain, unable to persuade Gladstone to abandon the clauses of the Land Bill, which would have compensated the hated absentee landlords of Ireland, eventually resigned from Gladstone's short-lived government and formed a reluctant alliance with Courtney, Lord Hartington and Goschen. Together they contributed to defeat of the Home Rule Bill on 8 June 1886 by 30 votes, which significantly altered the course of British history.

In the election that Gladstone then called, somewhat unexpectedly, Courtney's position in Cornwall was soon revealed to be not at all secure; nor had it ever been, and not just because of the Liberal split. His role as deputy Speaker meant that he had to stay in London after many others had left to begin campaigning in the 1886 Home Rule election. He had also rejected some of Chamberlain's radical policies but there were also some extremely strong rivalries between the two former boroughs in his consistency. This meant that although one area, Liskeard, was loyal to him, a meeting in Bodmin had literally turned him away at the door earlier that year saying they would not hear him until they could hear him speak alongside a rival Home Rule candidate. At a meeting of the central committee of the South East Cornwall Liberal Association, only nine of the members supported him, in the face of opposition from the remaining 59.[7] Courtney was forced to set up his own rival Liberal Association, though his popularity with the electorate was such that he still won the seat with nearly double the vote for his Liberal rival.[8] Together with Bodmin, the Liberal Unionists held Totnes, St Ives, Truro, South Molton, Tavistock and Barnstaple. The recent history of the Liberal Unionist party asserts that, just as in the West Midlands, it did particularly well in Devon and Cornwall where the Free Church movement was strongest and where the middle-class voters were most free of landlord influence.[9] Devon and Cornwall were acknowledged as 'the next strongest redoubt' of the party after Birmingham.[10] Nonconformity in Devon and Cornwall was dominated by Wesleyan Methodism which, unlike Primitive Methodism, but like Unitarianism in Birmingham, seemed particularly susceptible to fears for the fate of Irish Protestants under a Catholic-dominated Home Rule Parliament.[11] In the 1887 St Austell by-election, George Chubb, later president of the Nonconformist Unionist Association, confidently assured Lord Salisbury of growing support for the Union among Wesleyans in Cornwall.[12]

Courtney's choice of women to lead his campaign at this time was not an experiment being performed by a man in a secure seat but a gesture of trust and support not in only those he was asking to campaign but also that his constituency would listen to them and support them. Courtney believed that if women received the vote, it would help to liberate them from excessive domestication and social subjugation: a position which Chamberlain rejected both politically and in his own personal life.[13] Courtney's belief in proportional representation also informed his views on Irish Home Rule. He believed the election result of 1885 was not an indicator of the true views of the Irish people but the outcome of an unfair electoral system. He believed proportional representation would allow a greater variety of candidates to stand and allow the Protestant minority proper representation. This would bring out a greater degree of inclusion in the political process, lead to a more stable Ireland and for Britain to become a true union of sister kingdoms, each helping the other with its own special expertise.

After the 1886 election, Courtney remained in his role as deputy Speaker and, although it was not strictly required of him, he took a neutral role in Westminster debates and was therefore not forced to decide whether or not to stay loyal to his liberal principles or to support the Union's policies, for example over the 1887 Coercion Act. Outside Parliament, however, he and Chamberlain were actively involved in establishing and improving the organisation of the Liberal Unionist party, which had been hastily set up after the 1886 election. Courtney and Chamberlain met with Lord Hartington, the accepted leader of the Liberal Unionists, at the house of Sir John Lubbock, Courtney's partner in the campaign for proportional representation. Here they agreed to form a separate party and to maintain the Conservatives in a minority government for as long as Gladstone remained committed to Home Rule for Ireland.[14] Courtney and Chamberlain also contributed to the creation of the Liberal Unionist Association, the professional organisation that would help the new party to survive for over 25 years. While Chamberlain ensured that the 'six hundred', the Liberal caucus in Birmingham, stayed loyal to him, Courtney recommended his own political agent, John Boraston, to be appointed as assistant secretary to the LUA, and he spoke frequently on behalf of the Liberal Unionists at meetings across the country, defending the party's support for the 1887 Coercion Bill.[15] He hoped, however, to be able to persuade Gladstone to shelve Home Rule and reunite the Liberal party as soon as possible. He was pleased, therefore, when Chamberlain and Charles Trevelyan entered into the 'Round Table' negotiations with Harcourt and Morley. He was soon disillusioned, however, coming to believe that the entire event was merely a charade to allow Chamberlain to paint Gladstone as the obstacle to reunion. Chamberlain, he believed, had no intention of swallowing his pride and returning to the Liberal fold.[16] Courtney did not approve of such games with the future of the Union and warned his friends, 'the ways of our Joseph were dark'.[17]

Courtney, probably the only radical unionist with a profile as high as that of Chamberlain between 1886 and 1892, soon became labelled in one of two ways. Either as a man of great integrity whose principles were strong and uncompromising or an obsessive whose inability to compromise made him impossible to work with. His opposition to Chamberlain's 1892 'social programme' of collectivist measures had soured relations between them further and the rivalry between Courtney and Chamberlain came to a head in 1895. In the final months of the Rosebery administration the speaker, George Peel, announced his impending resignation and there being no obvious Liberal candidate, Harcourt suggested Courtney. The Liberal *Westminster Gazette* commented that 'Mr Courtney's qualifications for the post are so universally admitted.'[18] Harcourt believed that Courtney would receive the support of the Liberal Unionists and enough of the Liberals to ensure he would win any contest. He also believed that the Tories would not oppose a Liberal Unionist candidate.[19] Harcourt was wrong. As expected, a great many radical liberals opposed Courtney. For example, Labouchere complained of his 'smug old almightyism'. Sir Walter Hamilton had concerns that Courtney could not retain his seat at Bodmin. He also lacked presence and 'has not too plentiful a supply of aitches'. Other complaints were voiced about his faddism, his inability to compromise, to consult others, and that he was not enough of a gentleman to sit in the Speaker's chair.[20]

The Conservatives, increasingly restive of allowing Liberals to sit in seats they were forbidden by the Unionist 'compact' to contest, believed it was time one of their own took the role and nominated Sir Matthew White Ridley. Lord Salisbury was apparently annoyed by Courtney's outspoken disestablishmentarian views and Balfour by his support for Rosebery's government in the debate on the Evicted Tenants Bill.[21] The Tories were also able to claim, more than a little disingenuously, that Courtney's outspoken hostility to any separate legislature for Ireland would mean that his nomination as Speaker might provoke the Nationalists to the return of the parliamentary obstruction that had plagued Gladstone in his second government.[22]

Claiming an apparent disinterest that became later obvious that he did not feel, Courtney put the matter in the hands of Chamberlain, the Liberal Unionist party leader in the Commons, and suggested a meeting be held to discuss the matter. However, as Ian Cawood has analysed, before that happened, the battle over the Speaker's seat in Warwick and Leamington became a huge contest, the last in a long line of battles between the Tories and the Liberal Unionists over who should stand as the representative for the Unionist coalition in parliamentary seats.[23] As these were seriously threatening the Unionist alliance, Chamberlain therefore instructed the Liberal Unionist meeting to vote overwhelmingly to support White Ridley. Their priority was to smooth over the cracks in the alliance and not cause further offence to the Tories.[24] Hartington wrote that Courtney would make a fine Speaker but circumstances ensured they could not afford him. Beatrice Chamberlain wrote only of the decision smoothing over Tory ruffled feathers.[25]

Beatrice Webb was the sister of Leonard Courtney's wife. Courtney some years earlier had advised Beatrice to follow her own political dreams, which would mean that she would have to end her relationship with Chamberlain. It is unclear whether or not Chamberlain knew about this and, with the level of animosity that was there already, it is by no means certain that it would have made much difference. Beatrice Webb had never been an uncritical admirer of Leonard Courtney, having written on first meeting him, 'he had no subtlety, no originality'.[26] As she got to know him, however, the then Beatrice Potter noted that 'his personality – perfect integrity and courage – stands out like a rock'.[27] Having famously broken with Chamberlain many years before, however, convinced that he wanted 'intelligent servility' from his womenfolk, by 1895 she very much took Courtney's side over Chamberlain's.[28] She believed Chamberlain's opposition to Leonard's promotion was a personal attack on the Bodmin MP simply because Courtney had never taken the position of being one of Chamberlain's followers.

To return to the Speakership debate, although Courtney had claimed he was not all that interested in the role, it is clear from his wife's diary that he was taking it personally. He had taken a lot of pride in his success as deputy Speaker and he did not disagree with Harcourt's assessment that he was well suited for the role. Harcourt was to resort to a blistering attack on Chamberlain in the Commons for his failure to support one of his own party and the *Daily News* commented that it showed up the 'boasted alliance of the "Unionist Party" as an idle mockery and a hollow sham'.[29] As Kate Courtney sadly noted in her diary, 'it seems that the L.U. Party in Parliament are not as independent as we thought', noting that Chamberlain had proved himself to be 'too clever a wire-puller for a small party to be at all free under his leadership'.[30] Leonard Courtney visited Harcourt's constituency and delivered a withering speech of his own, condemning the whole existence of political parties which he later wrote up into an article for the *National Review*. In it, he condemned the way political parties ensured that recipients of patronage were only those who had been 'clipped and pared and trimmed and stretched out of natural shape and likeness to slip along the grooves of supply'.[31]

He would have nothing to do with them; he would hence forth be an independent man beholden to no one. This brings about one of the most interesting responses to Courtney's career: that of T.B. Bolitho, who was the Liberal Unionist MP for Penzance. Courtney's father had been a bank clerk and Bolitho's father had been the owner of that bank and their family was one of the most influential in West Cornwall. Bolitho was also a major donor to the Liberal Unionist party and it is probably thanks to him that the Liberal Unionists developed a regional base in the southwest of England. Bolitho wrote about the meeting that rejected Courtney and offered his full support, writing off letters of complaint. He also offered to resign from his parliamentary seat alongside Courtney should he wish to take that response. There was also a suggestion that was going around in Cornwall, should Courtney's own consistency association reject him after his blistering attack on the party, that Bolitho would step aside and let Courtney take his exceedingly secure Liberal Unionist seat. This was a very wealthy and influential local man deferring to the son of a former employee because he believed in Courtney's principles and stance. And this shows that Courtney had been interested in building a personal following. He probably could have done so. It was not that people around Courtney did not like him, it was the fact that he had no real wish to build a following and to put himself into a position of leadership. However, both men were to stand again as independent Liberal Unionists in the 1895 election, Courtney to win with an increased majority and Bolitho again to face no contest. The local radical press that had been attacking Courtney regularly since 1886 – newspapers such as the *Western Daily Post* – was to offer support for his independence. Courtney also received support from other liberal sources including W.S. Caine, who stated his deep disappointment that Courtney had not been chosen, and he hoped Courtney's energies had been reserved to greater services.[32]

As it was, Courtney put his energies to the cause of embarrassing Chamberlain, now leader of the Liberal Unionists in the Commons, between 1895 and 1900. While many Liberal Unionists were able to swallow the party's growing ideological closeness to their Conservative partners, in issues such as imperialism, education, social reform (or rather the lack of it), Courtney continued to stick to his liberal principles . As 'Toby' (Henry Lucy) later described, there was only one true Liberal Unionist, 'it is Mr. Courtney's peculiarity that, on whichever side of the House he chances to sit, he is ever in a party of one'.[33] He continued to assert that the Liberal Unionists should retain an independent organisation and should be 'neither merged, fused nor absorbed'.[34] He was an outspoken critic of the Jameson Raid and began to draw a group of disaffected Unionists around his house in Cheyne Row in Chelsea.

The war between the two finally became open in 1899, when Salisbury proposed a Clerical Tithes Bill which would subsidise Anglican clergy and schools from the rates. It provoked a storm of nonconformist protest, which Courtney, as MP for a largely Methodist constituency felt much sympathy for. Most Liberal Unionists were able to swallow their principles for the sake of the coalition unity, but as an 'independent', Courtney was under no obligation to obey the Liberal Unionist whip. During the debate, he stood and declared, 'Why are the Liberal Unionists here?' He contrasted the high-minded behaviour of men who between 1886 and 1892 refused the easy course of submission to Gladstone and stood firm to their belief in the benefits of a reformed Union with Ireland, and those of the current parliament. To a chorus of laughter from the Liberal benches, he poured out his scorn for the way in which Chamberlain had distorted the purpose of the Liberal Unionist party for the sake of mere vote-grabbing, which was simply for the benefit of the Liberal Unionist leadership:

> Why do the astute mangers of party conflict go here and there, choose or select men who are Liberal Unionists instead of men called Conservatives [opposition cheers and laughter]. They don't do it if they can help it perhaps [laughter], but that only enforces the argument. The Liberal Unionists are necessary evils [renewed laughter] … They are selected because they can appeal to a certain number of electors who can turn the scale and elect them.

With the subsequent resignation of Lord Portsmouth and the Earl of Durham from the Liberal Unionists over the same issue in 1900 and the growing animosity of the Ulster Liberal Unionist leader, T.W. Russell, it seemed that Courtney was on the point of leading a rebellion against Chamberlain, in which the party's very modest record of reform since 1895 would be measured and found wanting against the bold promises on which so many Unionists were elected.

Luckily for Chamberlain, both personally and as party leader, the Boer War intervened. As mentioned earlier, Chamberlain and Courtney had found themselves as allies against imperialist ventures in South Africa in early 1881, but, although Courtney's views on the issue had barely changed, Chamberlain's most definitely had, not least because he was now Secretary of State for the Colonies. Wilfred

Lawson very strongly believed that Courtney's later efforts were a greater service to his country as one of the leaders in the movement that became known as the *Pro*-Boers. Courtney had a long-running interest in maintaining cordial relations with South Africa. It was believed by some that he advised delegations in the late 1870s on how to make their presentations more suitable for a British audience. However, while Chamberlain became the public face of the war, Courtney became one of the Pro-Boer leaders, speaking at a heated public meeting alongside his close friend John Morley in September 1899, when he described the press campaign against the Transvaal government as 'Lies! Lies! Lies!'[35] Although the Pro-Boers were still a minority group in Cornwall, there is some evidence that they were less a minority there than in other areas of the country. There were many Cornish among the outlanders working in the goldfields and it appears that they were less impressed with the war that was being fought on their behalf than was expected. Reports abound that mention British workers in the goldfields who used to wait for the British newspapers so as to find out what it was that they were supposed to be aggrieved about.

Demonstrating a willingness to leave aside his rivalry with Chamberlain for the sake of international peace, Courtney now wrote to the colonial secretary directly, for the first time since the tussle over the Speakership, four years earlier. He implored Chamberlain to consider 'is there no way out but through war?' and called on him to replace Milner as High Commissioner.[36] Chamberlain rejected Courtney's intervention, however, and commented that the loss of Milner 'would, I am convinced, be deplored and resented by the majority of Englishmen'.[37] Unfortunately for Courtney and fortunately for Chamberlain and the Liberal Unionist leadership, Bodmin, Courtney's constituency, was not among those prepared to question the war. Following the Boers' ultimatum to the British government, Courtney tried to convince them to follow him rather than Chamberlain. Despite a passionate 90-minute peroration in front of his electors on 12 October, Leonard lost a vote of confidence and a resolution in favour of the war was passed. This did nothing to abate Courtney's determination to stop the war though and he criticised Chamberlain directly from the government benches in the debate on supplies for the war on 19 October.

Two days before he sent the 'qualified acceptance' to the ultimatum, he had delivered an inflammatory harangue at Highbury. Finally Chamberlain had said that he would formulate fresh proposals, but instead of doing so he had hurried out troops.

All this backfired, however, as government won the vote and gained the support of the Liberal Imperialists and split the opposition. Courtney proceeded to found the South African Reconciliation Committee on 1 November 1899 and was duly elected president.[38] He continued to speak against the war and singled out Chamberlain for criticism, commenting that although he exonerated the Colonial Secretary for causing the war, 'it was his own fault if suspicion hung about him'.[39] He even visited Chamberlain's 'duchy' and spoke to a ticketed meeting of the S.A.R.C. in Birmingham on 10 February 1900, an event that Chamberlain must surely have read as a challenge.[40] Courtney received death threats and hate mail for his principled stance (which no doubt delighted him) and was eventually ousted by his constituency association by an overwhelming majority on 16 June 1900.[41] T.B. Bolitho promptly announced his retirement as MP for St Ives at the forthcoming election. Courtney continued to protest against the war in the area, however, holding a meeting at Liskeard in July 1900 with his friends including Wilfred Lawson, David Lloyd George and the locally born Emily Hobhouse, which turned into a near riot of which Courtney was later to write that it 'turned out better than expected'. Courtney then turned to full-time work for the S.A.R.C. In this capacity, he supported Emily Hobhouse, who by then, alongside her brother, was referring to him as her 'Uncle Hobney'. Her report from the concentration camps became the inspiration for Henry Campbell-Bannerman's 'methods of barbarism' speech. Shaken by the findings Hobhouse presented, Courtney wrote to John Hobson and commented that he had come to the conclusion that imperialism was 'a vain and costly delusion'.[42]

Even during his long, slow drift back towards the Liberal party, Courtney continued to plague Chamberlain. He wrote an article dismissing the Tariff Reform campaign on orthodox liberal grounds, almost as soon as it was announced.[43] Courtney then made a speech at Glasgow, where the Liberal Unionists held more seats than in any other city outside Birmingham. Unlike during the war, when he had been careful not to attack Chamberlain directly, he now focused on Chamberlain's character, in particular his consistency, noting that 'although Mr Chamberlain was now a red-hot protectionist, only last May he declared himself a free-trader'. He continued relentlessly, asserting that Tariff Reform would bring not only economic misery upon Britain 'but great dishonour'. He claimed that such a policy significantly cheapened the bonds of friendship between the colonies and 'he denounced as mischievous and impossible Mr Chamberlain's ideal'.[44]

Chamberlain replied, singling out Courtney in one of his speeches as an example of 'men who showed no trace of what the Empire really meant'.[45] Courtney eventually agreed to stand as a Liberal candidate against the long-serving Liberal Unionist Lewis McIver in Edinburgh West. He reduced McIver's majority by over 1,000 votes, but the extent of the swing needed was just too great and Courtney fell 306 votes short. Although he lost in Edinburgh and Chamberlain could boast that in Birmingham, 'we are seven', in reality, Courtney's hard work had paid off and Tariff Reform had been defeated. In the Liberal Unionists' other strongholds, the Unionists were finally ousted. In Glasgow, the only Liberal Unionists who won their seats both won as 'Liberal Unionist free traders'.[46] In Courtney's native Cornwall, the Unionists lost Truro, St Ives and even Bodmin, Courtney's old seat, with only the veteran F.B. Mildmay, holding Totnes (a seat he held until 1922).

Courtney was elevated in 1906 to the House of Lords as Baron Courtney of Penwith and, while he did not approve of Emily Hobhouse's continuing political swing to the left, he did approve of her continued pacifism and he was one of the few men that supported her when she went to Germany during the later stages of the Great War and tried to negotiate a peace treaty. It is a measure of his patience and tolerance that Courtney was able to maintain a friendship with Emily Hobhouse. One of the very few others who could manage that particular trick was Gandhi.[47]

Leonard Courtney and Joseph Chamberlain were never going to be friends. They came from two entirely different traditions of liberalism and their points of agreement were almost accidental rather than any kind of plan or any wish to collaborate. Chamberlain certainly did his best to damage Courtney's career in 1895, possibly because of his role in Joe's abortive romance with Beatrice Potter, but more probably because Chamberlain could not tolerate an independent-minded radical at loose within his own small parliamentary party. For his part Courtney disliked the modern machine politics which Chamberlain epitomised and he took every opportunity after 1895 to question publicly Chamberlain's leadership (over the Clerical Tithes Bill), his judgement (over the outbreak of the Boer War) and finally his character (over Tariff Reform). The relationship between the two demonstrates one of the fundamental weaknesses of Victorian radicalism (and left-wing politics in Britain in general) – the influence of individual personality on the unity of the movement. These two men could have been allies in modernising Britain by confronting privilege and vested interest and offering an alternative to state socialism, but they chose instead to come to blows over the methods by which they advanced their causes and, as a consequence, they reduced their politics to a vulgar game of score-settling that lasted nearly two decades and which left radical politics in Britain unable to move forwards until an election was held which rejected the parliamentary presence of Courtney and the parliamentary power of Chamberlain.

Notes

1. L. Courtney, 'The Difficulties of Socialism', *The Economic Journal*, 1.1 (1891), pp. 174–88; J. Chamberlain, 'The Labour Question', *The Nineteenth Century*, 189 (1892), pp. 677–701.
2. J. Dingle to L. Courtney, 2 February 1886, Courtney Papers, London School of Economics Special Collections, CP V/9.
3. L. Courtney, 'Political Machinery and Political Life', *Fortnightly Review*, 20 (1876), pp. 86–7.
4. See L. Goldman, 'Introduction: An "Advanced Liberal": Henry Fawcett, 1833–1884', in L. Goldman (ed.), *The Blind Victorian: Henry Fawcett and British Liberalism* (Cambridge University Press, 1989), p. 35.
5. See I. Cawood, *The Liberal Unionist Party: A History* (London: I.B. Tauris, 2012), pp. 148–53; 235–6.
6. Courtney held this position for the duration of the next parliament and was described as being 'impartially unfair to both sides'. H.C.G. Matthew, 'Leonard Courtney', *Oxford Dictionary of National Biography*.
7. *Western Daily Mercury*, 16 June 1886.
8. Courtney gained 64 per cent of the vote in the 1886 election in Bodmin.
9. F. Tillyard, 'The Distribution of the Free Churches in England', *Sociological Review*, 27 (1935), pp. 1–18; E. Jaggard, *Cornwall Politics in the Age of Reform* (Woodbridge: Boydell Press, 1999), pp. 184–5.
10. *Liberal Unionist*, 42, July 1889.
11. D.W. Bebbington, 'Nonconformity and Electoral Sociology 1867–1918', *Historical Journal*, 27 (1984), pp. 650–1.
12. G.H. Chubb to Salisbury, 19 May 1887, Salisbury Papers, Hatfield House, Hertfordshire.
13. B. Griffin, *The Politics of Gender in Victorian Britain: Masculinity, Political Culture and the Struggle for Women's Rights* (Cambridge University Press, 2012), pp. 266–75.
14. M. Patton, *Science, Politics and Business in the Work of Sir John Lubbock: A Man of Universal Mind* (Aldershot: Ashgate, 2007), p. 179.
15. Boraston went on to become the LUA secretary and eventually became the principal agent of the Conservative and Unionist party when the two parties finally coalesced in May 1912.
16. Kate Courtney's diary, 26 January 1887. CP XXIII.
17. Quoted in G.P. Gooch, *Life of Lord Courtney* (Basingstoke: Macmillan, 1920), p. 272.
18. *Westminster Gazette*, 11 March 1895.
19. P. Jackson, *Harcourt and Son: A Political Biography of Sir William Harcourt, 1827–1904* (Madison, NJ: Fairleigh Dickinson University Press), p. 264.

20. *The Diary of Sir Edward Hamilton vol. 3: 1886–1903*, ed. D. Bahlman (Kingston-Upon-Hull: University of Hull Press, 1993), pp. 289–91.
21. *Leeds Mercury*, 18 March 1895.
22. *The Times*, 12 March 1895.
23. I. Cawood, 'Joseph Chamberlain, the Conservative Party and the Leamington Spa Candidate Dispute of 1895', *Historical Research*, 79.206 (2006), pp. 554–77.
24. A decision described by the *Northern Echo* as 'one of the most pernicious and dishonourable political bargains made for many years'. *Northern Echo*, 27 March 1895.
25. Beatrice Chamberlain to Neville Chamberlain, 30 March 1895, Neville Chamberlain Papers, University of Birmingham Special Collections, NC1/13/2/61.
26. Quoted in J. Hart, *Proportional Representation: Critics of the British Electoral System, 1820–1945* (Oxford: Clarendon, 1992), p. 124.
27. *The Diary of Beatrice Webb, vol. 1: 'Glitter around and Darkness within'*, ed. N. MacKenzie and J. MacKenzie (Cambridge, MA: Harvard University Press, 1982), p. 190.
28. Ibid., p. 103.
29. *Reynold's Newspaper*, 14 April 1895, *Daily News*, 16 March 1895.
30. K. Courtney's diary, 8 April 1895, CP XXVIII.
31. L. Courtney, 'To my fellow disciples at Saratoga Springs', *The National Review* 26 (1895), pp. 21–6.
32. J. Newton, *W.S. Caine, MP* (London,: James Nisbet, 1907), p. 123.
33. H.W. Lucy, *A Diary of the Unionist Parliament, 1895–1900* (London, 1901), p. 301
34. *Standard*, 19 October 1895.
35. Gooch, *Life of Lord Courtney*, p. 372, Herbert Spencer, hitherto one of the leading intellectual supporters of Liberal Unionism wrote to Courtney to offer his support.
36. Courtney to Chamberlain, 18 September 1899, quoted in Gooch, *Life of Courtney*, pp. 373–4.
37. Chamberlain to Courtney, 21 September 1899, quoted in ibid., p. 375.
38. B.S. Seibold, *Emily Hobhouse and the Reports on the Concentration Camps during the Boer War, 1899–1902* (Stuttgart: Ibidem-Verlag, 2011), p. 41.
39. Courtney speaking at Liskeard, *The Times*, 24 January 1900.
40. *The Times*, 12 February 1900.
41. *The Times*, 17 June 1900.
42. Quoted in F. Trentmann, *Free Trade Nation: Commerce, Consumption and Civil Society in Modern Britain* (Oxford University Press, 2008), p. 174.
43. L. Courtney, 'Mr Chamberlain's Balloon', *Contemporary Review*, 84 (August 1903), pp. 265–79. This was despite his own earlier flirtation with bi-metallism.
44. *The Times*, 14 October 1903.
45. Chamberlain, speaking in Birmingham, 4 November 1903. *The Times*, 5 November 1903.
46. C. Burness, 'The Making of Scottish Unionism', in S. Ball and I. Halliday (eds), *Mass Conservatism: The Conservatives and the Public since the 1880s* (London: Frank Cass, 2002), p. 23.
47. J.H. Balme, *To Love One's Enemies: The Life and Work of Emily Hobhouse* (Cobble Hill, Canada: Hobhouse Trust, 1994), *passim*.

6

'The People's Bread': A Social History of Joseph Chamberlain and the Tariff Reform Campaign

Oliver Betts

As the election results of late January were declared, evening after evening, and the columns of small 'M's denoting elected members of the new 1906 Parliament that supported the Prime Minister, Henry Campbell-Bannerman, chased the opposing 'O's across the graph that topped each morning's issue of *The Times*, the paper itself became increasingly confident about the causes of the Liberal landslide. On the morning of 17 January, the day before the Birmingham polls were called and Joseph Chamberlain's own constituency result declared, *The Times* mused that for all the confidence Tariff Reform organisers had about the result, it would be, crucially, a limited one. 'The further they go afield the more difficult does their task become of getting "the man in the street" to realize that the "big loaf *versus* little loaf" cry is a meaningless shibboleth', the paper concluded.[1] As more results came in and the sheer scale of the Liberal victory became apparent, the more the press was willing to venture into analysis. Two days before, on the 15th, the *Manchester Guardian* had already passed judgement on the results in Lancashire. 'A candidate had only to be a Free Trader to get in', it argued, 'he had only to be a Protectionist to lose all chance.'[2] By the 20th the *Spectator* felt able to declare that the fact 'that the election was fought and won on the issue of free-trade is beyond dispute'.[3] By early February, as the final few constituency results trickled in, dissection of the result was in full swing, and this was by no means confined to journalists and editors. The verdict was clear: the crushing defeat of the Conservatives and Liberal Unionists hung on one issue, Tariff Reform, and on the shoulders of one man, Joseph Chamberlain. For, as an anonymous letter to the editor of *The Times* succinctly put it, 'it is upon Mr. Chamberlain's policy that the election has turned'.[4]

Historians have, on the whole, agreed with this summation. A.K. Russell's study of the *Liberal Landslide* pointed out that it was an election where the fiscal question of Chamberlain's proposed tariff reforms was dominant. Ninety-eight per cent of Liberal candidates mentioned free trade in their election addresses in 1906, the same percentage of Unionist candidates who discussed issues of Tariff Reform.[5] Tariff Reform has, moreover, consistently been seen as Chamberlain's product. Although pointing to the 'latent ... protectionism' bubbling within the Unionists in this period, Martin Pugh, for instance, has argued that the Tariff Reform movement was the first occasion this had been given impetus from above. 'The bulk of the party fell into Chamberlain's lap after 1903', he observes.[6] Biographers of the man himself have, depending on their consideration of Chamberlain, either seen the Tariff Reform movement as a misguided mistake or as the triumph of hubris and personal vanity. Denis Judd, for example, has argued that the concept was one that for Chamberlain 'had become the key ... which might open many doors' after the bruising political after-effects of the Boer War.[7] Chamberlain's most recent biographer, Travis Crosby, has argued that whatever the benefits of Tariff Reform may have been in his mind, any examination of the events of 1906 must reveal that this campaign lay partly in Chamberlain's 'own need to maintain and pursue additional avenues of power'.[8] Peter Marsh, in his seminal biography, was more sympathetic, but still labelled the campaign over Tariff Reform an 'all-consuming venture' and argued that Chamberlain's movements were, at best, impulsive.[9] There exists a clear correlation between the Tariff Reform movement, Chamberlain's personal impetus and the disastrous Unionist showing at the 1906 election that places the failure of the Unionist campaign squarely at Chamberlain's feet. Indeed, so strong is the criticism that it seems almost unbelievable that a politician of Chamberlain's calibre, with the experience of electioneering that Jon Lawrence has observed was so crucial to late Victorian politics, could make such a clear mistake.[10] Examined through this lens, Tariff Reform seems a terrible error of judgement.

Yet there is a danger in oversimplifying this vision of the 1906 election and the Tariff Reform movement that Chamberlain initiated. As Frank Trentmann has argued, it is important that, despite the clear ways in which the nation-state and free trade advanced 'hand-in-hand' in Britain, that they not been seen as 'some historical norm' from which deviation was impossible.[11] Many accounts of the 1906 election campaign suffer from hindsight and are cast, ultimately, with the historian's foreknowledge not only of the crushing defeat at the polls but also of

Chamberlain's debilitating stroke which followed.[12] Both Chamberlain and Tariff Reform are, in these configurations, doomed. This leaves, however, a crucial stumbling block: how could a political giant like Chamberlain, a man who 'made the weather' to borrow Churchill's phrase, launch a political movement that so badly missed its mark? Any historical account where the failure of Tariff Reform *in the polls* is given prime position cannot adequately answer this question. Instead, this study will instead draw upon different sources to offer a social history of Tariff Reform. For, as will become clear, examined from another angle, this 'doomed' campaign in fact touched upon a vital issue in national politics, but, at the same time, was one in which participants struggled to convince the public of the merits of their proposals. Seen in this light, Chamberlain's venture into Tariff Reform was not so much the error-strewn end of a career in Victorian politics, but a bold, yet slightly misplaced step into a more modern national politics of engagement with broader issues.

The end of the election campaign of 1906 was, undeniably, draining for Joseph Chamberlain, and while the returns may have left him 'more excited than exhausted' as Marsh claims, he had already planned a fortnight's holiday in the Riviera.[13] One only has to glance at his itinerary over the previous years to understand why. From the launch of his Tariff Reform programme in Birmingham in May 1903, Chamberlain had embarked on a frenetically paced speaking tour criss-crossing urban Britain in a bid to win over the electorate. Birmingham, Newcastle, Liverpool, Glasgow, London and others – Chamberlain was a man with his eye firmly set on conveying his message of fiscal reform to the population at large. It was, as Julian Amery argues, a 'direct appeal over the heads of Ministers to public opinion'.[14] Yet it was also one that, from the outset, was met by a sharp and widespread critique. It went far beyond, as Trentmann has shown, 'simplistic images of bad enthusiastic jingoists and good reasoning free traders'.[15] It was, in reality, a bitterly fought campaign. Both the adherents to Tariff Reform and their critics were more than capable of harnessing the newest forms of political interaction to get their points across. The Tariff Reform League, that Chamberlain established to support his campaign, published a *Short Handbook for Speakers* in which it listed 25 specific trades and industries that were under specific threat from abroad.[16] All over the country Chamberlain, his supporters, and their opponents did battle over this grand economic project.

One specific moment in the Tariff Reform campaign demonstrates the extent to which the exchange represents a distinct moment in British political history. Under attack for much of 1903 on the costs of Tariff Reform, particularly the notion that it would amount to nothing more than a price-hike on everyday foodstuffs, Chamberlain concluded a speech at Bingley Hall in Birmingham with a theatrical flourish. After a long speech discussing the tax on corn, and whether this would harm the food supply, he unwrapped and held aloft two loaves of bread, one made with a little less flour as the proposed tax would demand and the other a free-trade loaf. While admitting that the first loaf was a little lighter it was, he felt, still 'a sporting question which is the big one and which is the little one'.[17] It was a move which, the *Illustrated London News* pointed out, caused 'great diversion' among the audience, but was also one that shaped the political debate to come.[18] Even though Chamberlain had, as he mentioned in his speech, drawn inspiration from an opposition poster that featured two unevenly sized loaves as evidence of the follies of Tariff Reform, it was the Bingley Hall speech that really thrust bread onto the political landscape of Edwardian Britain in the 1900s.

While Chamberlain had never intended for the Tariff Reform campaign to revolve around the issue of food, this was what the central theme of the following years of political struggle became. The price of bread, very specifically, became a significant part of public political discourse. From the Bingley Hall speech onwards Chamberlain was routinely depicted with loaves of bread in satirical images. Juggling them, holding them, selling them, presenting them to a grateful nation or trying, as a shopkeeper, to offload them onto an unsuspecting public; the popular image of the campaign solidified around bread. A tiny model of Chamberlain, replete with trademark monocle and button-hole orchid, could even be made to pop, like a jack-in-the-box, from a toy loaf of bread.[19] Such a clearly defined motif for the campaign, drawn from Chamberlain's Bingley Hall flourish, captures the growing power of the popular press in encapsulating political moments at the start of the new century. As Matthew Roberts has emphasised in the case of urban conservatism from the 1880s onwards and as James Thompson has shown in his work on public opinion, this was 'an era characterised by widespread and significant political engagement' with issue-based politics.[20] Such a focus, regardless of intent or accident, is also evidence of how debates over Tariff Reform touched on wider anxieties over food that were swirling around the increasingly disturbed waters of Edwardian Britain. The relationship between the 1906 election campaign and both the wider Tariff Reform movement and the growing crisis over National Efficiency have been widely documented.[21] G.R. Searle has argued that

Chamberlain's political machinations destroyed 'for the best part of a decade whatever lingering possibilities still remained for creating a new alignment reflecting the ideal of national efficiency'.[22] Yet to treat the politics of this 1903–06 period as somehow distinguishable from the intellectual foment around the Condition of England question that was taking place throughout Edwardian Britain is a mistake. As the introduction to their 2007 edited collection on moral values and economic debates in modern British politics argued, Duncan Tanner and Ewen Green's observation that more attention needs to be paid to the *reception* of ideas and issues is a vital one. 'Political or cultural ideas leaders ideas credence' they point out, lending them significance.[23] Chamberlain, and by extension the Tariff Reform issue, came to be completely intertwined, not just with each other, but with the Condition of England question, and it was around food, especially, that such debates found popular purchase.

It had been the poverty experts, particularly Charles Booth and Seebohm Rowntree, who had thrust the cost-of-living debate into the public eye at the start of the twentieth century. They were not the first, by any means, to raise questions about the relationship between the state, trade and the price of food. Popular rhetoric around the time of the Corn Laws, and the attendant rural disturbances of the 1830s and 1840s, had drawn upon themes of hunger and need, and, as Anna Clark has pointed out, Chartist orators and writers drew heavily upon a conflicted but evocative image of the domestic.[24] Yet never before had the actual price of items been thrust into public view, so poured over and debated, and this was the direct legacy of the poverty experts. Booth had been circumspect about his classification of poverty, aware of the fluctuations of London life and the cries of exceptionalism that would greet his conclusions about the Imperial capital.[25] Rowntree, however, was more strident. Trained as a chemist and with a keen eye for figures he chose York as 'fairly representative of the average conditions … in other provincial towns' across England and dove into creating a statistically based model of poverty.[26] Much of this analysis was based, as with Booth's work, on obtaining actual shopping lists, averaged out over a number of weeks, from working-class families. Whereas these only formed a part of Booth's analysis, part of a three-volume study that ranged across not only poverty but trade, industry and moral and religious influences, they formed the centrepiece of Rowntree's *Poverty: A Study of Town Life* when it was published in 1901. Soon sample household budgets, listing everything from rent to sugar to fuel to boot-black, dotted surveys of poverty and were debated in statistical and social reform clubs and journals. Lady Florence Bell's study of Middlesbrough, published the year after the 1906 election, included a whole chapter dedicated to sample budgets and their discussion. They revealed, as she argued, that even the 'thrifty part of the population' existed 'very near the margin of the absolutely poor' in many cases.[27] It was a charged atmosphere that was particularly sensitive to the politicisation of food prices.

It is unclear whether Chamberlain actually studied these budgets in detail, but he would certainly have been aware of them; the poverty studies of men like Booth and Rowntree were widely discussed in the national press. Chamberlain himself had made use of surveys much earlier in his career during his work with Birmingham School Boards, but the new national prominence of such social investigations spurred on his conviction that controlling prices was the key to tackling poverty. It was a conviction he shared with Booth, whom, in 1903, Chamberlain persuaded to serve on his Tariff Reform commission.[28] Indeed in a speech in Liverpool in October 1903 he reminded his audience that there had been two guiding passions of his life, 'the union and the strengthening of the Empire' and 'the condition of the working classes'.[29] Regardless of whether he welcomed, or had even intended, this shift to domestic economics in the political dialogue surrounding Tariff Reform, Chamberlain threw himself into the new arena wholeheartedly. Tea, bacon, sugar and milk, as well as bread, all found their way into Chamberlain's speeches on a regular basis; some were responses to press attacks or Liberal denouncement, but others were of his own initiative, attempts to explain the benefits of his policy to ordinary people. 'I am not going to tax food', he insisted in Gainsborough in 1905. 'I tax one kind of food in order that I may be able to untax another kind of food.' And then he treated the audience to an example of tea and bread and butter in a coffee shop where one day the tea was more expensive, then, the second day, the bread and butter was the more costly item. 'You pay a penny either case', he explained.[30] Chamberlain, in a speech that ranged from basic analogies addressing the price of bread to the lofty ideals of his dream of a protectionist empire, was preaching a mixed message of price control and affordability that not only promised an escape from poverty but also the suppression of the heavy burden of poverty for ratepayers. Historians have often seen Chamberlain as on the defensive during the Tariff Reform campaign, lurching to recover from one Liberal blow after another. It was a campaign that was, as Richard Jay has argued, already 'beginning to falter' by its first year, and the success that Jay ascribes to

Arthur Balfour in fending off Chamberlain led the latter into increasing and furious quandary.[31] This is certainly true, but a closer examination of where Chamberlain spoke, and the topics on which he focused in his speeches, also reveals a politician struggling to get to grips with a new and confused political issue.

The context of the first decade of the Edwardian era is vital to this discussion because of the slowly rising standard of living. Recent work, particularly the statistical re-evaluation of the work of the poverty experts by Ian Gazeley and Andrew Newell, has challenged the picture of outright destitution presented by social investigators in this period. There was widespread poverty in the first years of the twentieth century, they have found, but 'relatively little depth of poverty' among wage-earning families.[32] Wages could and did keep families from dropping too far below the level of subsistence. From 1899 onwards both the cost of living and wages rose, yet, as Martin Pugh has shown, these were not always in exact tandem.[33] Some years families might feel the pinch on their purse-strings a little more harshly than others. There were also fluctuations on a local level across the nation. Bell, in 1907, was able to chart the rise of the tallyman among Middlesbrough's well-earning iron and steel workers. 'The tallymen ... come round to the doors of the workmen's houses offering all kinds of wares on the hire system', she wrote, 'wares of a motley and amazing description.' While Bell may have found it hard to disguise her distaste for these new and, to her eyes, random items, 'a china dog, a writing-case, a piano, a gramophone', they were for the new hire-purchasers markers of security and status.[34] Such items, as Rowntree found in York, could very easily be cashed in at the pawnbrokers when times got harder.[35] If working-class living standards were rising, it meant that, in years where real wages stuttered, they felt the pinch of price-points more profoundly. The 'big loaf little loaf' argument, when mobilised by both Chamberlain and his opponents, was, at its heart, a concerted attempt to tie the complex issues of Tariff Reform to a widespread concern over the relationship between wages and prices and, in doing so, target those across Britain for whom this particular interpretation of Tariff Reform would be most comprehensible.

A discussion of food prices, whether intentional or a by-product of public interest, was never Chamberlain's sole aim when pitching Tariff Reform throughout the run-up to the election. It had, from the first, been an issue of trade, commerce and industry. It would have been impossible for Chamberlain, with his background in a Birmingham dominated by a plethora of light industry and manufacture, to have

ignored the growing economic competition faced by British producers and workers. As Peter Marsh has pointed out, 'the more he dwelt
on the domestic danger, the more economic his message became'.[36] In
this Chamberlain was hardly a voice in the wilderness. From at least
the early 1890s questions of trade, of foreign competition and, more
generally, the Condition of England, as it was known at the time, were
on the lips of many.[37] Although there have been considerable studies
of the agonies and anxieties about the nation in reformist and intellectual circles, it is of vital importance to consider how the discussion
extended well beyond the polite arenas of the House of Commons,
the broadsheet press and the drawing room or club of the middle-class
intellectual. In the 1890s Charles Booth was concluding much of the
fieldwork that he would eventually publish in the multi-volume *Life
and Labour of the People in London*. Booth, as previously noted, is perhaps
most famous for his study of poverty, yet he was interested in a much
wider array of issues, and his investigators were charged with an extensive series of questionnaires that they put to men and women across
the late Victorian capital. Chief among these was what Booth would
finally draw together as the Industry Series, a selection of inquiries
into employment in London. While the finished material offers little
of interest in a political sense, the raw material of the survey, the notebooks housed at the LSE archive, provide fascinating snippets of dialogue and information on the ordinary men and women towards whom
Chamberlain's rhetoric of competition and protection was tailored.

One of the questions George Duckworth, one of Booth's researchers,
was primed to ask was about the impact of foreign competition on
trade. He was met with mixed responses depending largely upon the
industry in question. Coopers, for example, offered no comment on
foreign trade – they plied their trade exclusively in an English context
with local materials. Basket-makers, however, were more anxious.[38]
'There is very keen competition from Belgium and France in laun-
dry baskets', William Cook, a small employer in South East London,
told Duckworth. 'Nearly all of those you see hanging up in shops are
imported.' Although by no means as good as a London-made basket,
Cook hastened to add, he had to admit they were 'cutting up the
London trade altogether'.[39] Of course it varied from person to person.
The next entry in the notebook detailing the basket-making trade was
with a similar small-workshop owner in the Charing Cross Road. He
was fine, he confidently told Duckworth, largely due to a lucrative
government contract, but he was clearly an exception. 'In fact', he told
Duckworth proudly, 'we stand above competition in every respect.'[40]

It is tempting to simply see this as the working-class reluctance that Judd has argued pushed Chamberlain into more 'determined and unsavoury' measures over foreign immigration, but the reality is more complex.[41] The Booth notebooks contain a wealth of information that muddies the historical waters.

Three key, and interrelated, themes emerge from the industrial interviews conducted for Charles Booth, all of which have a bearing on the political and social landscape into which Chamberlain was to launch the Tariff Reform campaign. The first was that employers, union officers and workers all were more than aware of the importance of foreign trade, either as competition or as a source of profit. Thomas Okey, another basket-maker, was well aware of the French competition in the market and informed Duckworth sagely that it was down to the 'growing co-operative system' in the French workplace.[42] The workers at Heinrichs and Co., a bamboo furniture-maker in St Luke's, however, were ecstatic about their growing export market in Germany and were more worried about the current war between China and Japan which was disrupting their bamboo shipments.[43] The second significant aspect to these interviews was the keen awareness which men and women displayed about the political debates concerning their trade and the long memories they had of such exchanges. A Mr C. Olley, a cork manufacturer in Shadwell, recalled one particular exchange relating to an earlier attempt to tax foreign wine:

> There had been in the 70's a proposal to tax foreign wine ... which the cork merchants of London opposed. They sent a deputation and were received by Mr Gladstone who had surprised them all – 'not of course by his knowledge of the practical workings' – but of the theory of the trade and the names of the principal kinds of cork trees and the districts from which they came. Mr G's knowledge was still talked of with wonderment in the trade.[44]

While the domestic slant of the rhetoric was new and especially invigorating for a working class which was cutting its teeth on a higher, yet somewhat unstable, standard of living, individuals across Britain also drew upon older political memories when assessing the issue of Tariff Reform. There is much about Mr Olley's story, despite the slight difference in subject matter, which bears resemblance to the father of one prospective Conservative Tariff Reform candidate in Norwich that Barry Doyle has uncovered. Writing to the local party he observed that he could not 'face the "big and little loaf" question' again, having already been firmly 'on the side of the big loaf … from Sir Robert Peel's time onwards'.[45] Chamberlain traded on these political afterlives again and again in his rhetoric. Cobden, the Corn Laws, Gladstone and his 'great mistakes', instances of foreign preference and industrial collapse, he mentioned them all in his set pieces as he criss-crossed the country in a battle for public opinion.[46]

Of course, such reflections relied on established political knowledge and the third, and perhaps most significant aspect of the Booth interviews is that they reveal a working populous deeply divided over the issue at hand. Posing his questions in the 1890s, Booth was not directly interested in the issue of Tariff Reform at the time, so the responses of men and women across the industries and trades of London that he and his staff collected cannot be seen as direct comments on Chamberlain's electoral gambit. Booth instructed his researchers to ask, more vaguely, about the question of foreign competition in the economy. In many cases workers and employers misunderstood the question. Mr Johnson, a furniture-maker in Bethnal Green, pointed out very vociferously that the problem was about the 100,000 Jewish workmen already in London 'who work', he told Duckworth, 'for any number of hours and live on bread and water'.[47] Mrs Schneider, a cane-maker in Clerkenwell, agreed. 'Now the trade is almost entirely in the hands of foreigns', she claimed, who had 'cut prices lower and lower.'[48] Not only was there confusion over the nature of the 'foreign' competition but, as even the most cursory study of the notebooks reveals, men who worked within yards of each other had completely different opinions on the matter. Duckworth interviewed five furniture workers in Bethnal Green in one afternoon and got five different opinions on international trade, immigration, the general condition of the industry and whether government regulation was required.[49] A Mr Wood, whose chair workshop was at most a hundred yards from Mr Johnson's, was much more disinterested in the question. His men were working long hours, 'I found … [them] … at work on a Saturday afternoon', Duckworth noted, but this was not, he argued, anything to do with competition either at home or abroad. 'Jews cannot make chairs', he informed Duckworth simply.[50] There were as many voices as interviews; one master of a sawmill in Old Kent Road took Duckworth to task for a considerable time as he expounded on the threat posed to his trade not by foreign workers or tariffs but by 'General Booth' of the Salvation Army who had set up a workshop for the unemployed that was undercutting his prices.[51] When confronted with the question of foreign competition, tradesmen across London, the very workers and masters Chamberlain hoped to tempt on the issue by means of Tariff Reform, were unsure about whether the threat lay at home, abroad or even existed in the first place.

London, of course, was a hotbed of not just Jewish immigration in this period but also a mecca of small trades and industries, yet beyond the capital the same themes of uncertainty and confusion governed the responses of workers and tradespeople to the issue. In late 1903 the Trades Union Congress set its stance firmly against Tariff Reform, as Marsh has observed, yet this by no means represented a stranglehold on trade union opinion across the country.[52] The following years, however, did not see a groundswell of support or opposition to the issue of Tariff Reform. Instead there was more of an uncertain abstention. The pages of *The Women's Trades' Union Review*, for instance, a publication so punctilious in recording political developments that might affect the working man and woman that it featured a regular summary of events in Parliament in each month's issue, breathed not a word about the Tariff Reform campaign throughout its 1900s print run. Many trade unions were divided over the issue of government intervention in trade on any level. The Secretary to the Amalgamated Tin and Iron Plate workers, having heard rumours of Government intervention in both the international trade and the internal workings of the metal industry, pressed Duckworth to report back that the union was against any form of regulation. 'Don't let us have state pensions of any kind!', was his parting shot.[53] Despite speeches pitched at the heart of urban and commercial Britain, Chamberlain seemed unable to settle widespread hearts and minds on his grand plan.

Chamberlain's attempts to reach out and, as Ian Cawood has shown, 'promote the interests of the national above those particular classes or national groups' when it came to Tariff Reform was not always a successful approach.[54] Although initially there had been no specific class approach to this public airing of the issues, Chamberlain, as Marsh notes, soon began to tailor his material to different audiences, recognising, for example, 'that the value of a tariff on manufacturers would not be obvious to the working class' and therefore concluding a tour of Scotland in 1903 with a discussion of unemployment which, he felt, would play better to the crowds of working men that gathered to hear him.[55] Partly this was, as his biographers have observed, reactive, with Chamberlain forced to address the specific applicability of Tariff Reform following criticisms from different groups about the complexity of his overall vision.[56] Yet it is important to remember, as the above material gathered from Booth's interviews across late Victorian London demonstrates, that these men and women, employers and employees, producers and retailers, did not necessarily respond as classes to such arguments, no matter how tailored they were. Marc Brodie, whose close analysis of voting among the poor in the East End of London has done so much to dispel the 'Angels in Marble' model of a working-class jingoistic conservatism, has pointed out that there is 'little evidence' for a working class ready to jump at the mere mention of protectionism. This is not to say that such discourses did not move the working class in the capital; as Brodie observes, they could respond vociferously 'given the right circumstances'.[57] What they did not do, as is clear from the notes Booth's researchers took, is move as one monolithic political force. There were as many opinions on foreign competition, and as many definitions, as there were men and women in the capital in the 1890s and it was into this uncertain landscape that Chamberlain launched his campaign. The reality was that not only did voters politically elude targeted Tariff Reform discourses between 1903 and 1906 but, as this study will go on to illustrate, the vagaries of both the post-1867 Reform Act world of British politics and the human shifts of turn-of-the-century urban populations in the country meant that they could also physically elude electioneering focus.

The themes of confusion and uncertainty that surrounded Tariff Reform find most prominent display in the by-election battles that led up to the Unionist defeat in the general election. Between the start of the Tariff Reform campaign in May 1903 and the Liberal landslide in 1906 there were 39 by-elections across Britain, and at the time these were by no means seen as clear portents of Liberal victory. For political commentators at the time the results of these by-elections by no means forecast a Liberal triumph later on in the year. By-elections, often glossed over by necessity in more overtly political histories, offer the social historian a chance to measure the appeal of particular ideas or campaign slogans at the constituency, rather than the national, level. As Thomas Otte and Paul Readman have pointed out, they were 'energetic exertions' that have, nevertheless, 'rarely left their mark on scholarly literature'.[58] They are, as Jon Lawrence has observed, 'windows on to broader social and cultural phenomena'.[59] In this case examining four London by-elections in correlation with the social and economic material encompassed in Charles Booth's Life and *Labour of the People in London* study offers new perspectives on how Tariff Reform played out in the constituencies before the 1906 general election.

Of the four by-elections, three were Unionist victories: Dulwich and Lewisham, held on the same day in 1903, and Mile End in East London in January 1905. The fourth, the Finsbury East by-election held in June

1905, was a Unionist defeat. In all four constituencies Tariff Reform played a crucial part in the debates, candidates not shying away from identifying as for or against Chamberlain's scheme for Imperial preference. In the first two elections, which took place in December 1903, half a year after his 'bombshell' of a first speech on the issue was first drafted, there seemed no escape from the topic.[60] Major Edward Coates, the Unionist Candidate for Lewisham, spoke at the hustings of his firm belief in the 'rearrangement of our fiscal system' in a manner that would improve trade, the Empire and domestic finance. His opponent, meanwhile, stated simply that he was in favour of 'untaxed food'.[61] A little over a week later, with only a few days to go before the polls opened, Coates was again reported as giving a speech about the 'languishing' industries of the north of England and their need for protection.[62] Both Tariff Reform groups and free-food campaigners were active throughout both constituencies in the run-up to the voting, with leaflets and pamphlets distributed widely.[63] In the two 1905 by-elections the discussion of Tariff Reform had taken on an even sharper edge. In Mile End the Unionist candidate, Harry Levy-Lawson, told electors that 'in Tariff Reform and the exclusion of undesirable aliens they will have a better chance of getting work', yet the Liberal candidate, Bertram Strauss, was heavily supported by a slick Free Trade League campaign.[64] In Finsbury East, meanwhile, in June, it was the Liberal candidate, Joseph Baker, who was able to most clearly articulate a position on free trade, while the Unionist hopeful, Nathaniel Cohen, issued a long electoral address that echoed the Prime Minister's own lack of position on the topic in its evasive discussion of 'wider opportunities' for trade and 'closer consultative relations' with the colonies.[65] Candidates in all four by-elections positioned themselves, whether willingly or otherwise, in relation to the debate over Tariff Reform, and these discussions shaped the outcomes in each constituency. Even if *The Times* remained uncertain over the accuracy of such a yardstick, musing shortly before the 1903 results that 'by-elections are a very uncertain index to the opinion of the country on any single great political question', it did not stop them, nor other papers, musing over the results.[66] Other factors, of course, must be considered. All four constituencies had been held by Unionist candidates before the by-elections and in each case it had been the unexpected death of the sitting MP that had triggered the vote, which left local Liberal organisations suddenly scrabbling for candidates to oppose relatively buoyant Unionist party organisations. Yet the Liberal candidates in each constituency were by no means random no-hopers. In Dulwich the Liberal organisation selected Charles

Masterman, the well-known journalist, to fight the election, while in Lewisham James William Cleland came fresh from a 1901 victory over a Moderate candidate in the area for a London County Council seat.[67] With campaigners for both free trade and Tariff Reform descending upon London for the events, and the debate continually referenced, all four by-elections served, for the Edwardian press, as litmus tests of the Tariff Reform argument.

The only successful Liberal candidate of the four, Joseph Baker in Finsbury East, offers perhaps the most important insight into the relationship between Tariff Reform and by-election success. Baker, a Canadian, was able to present an informed and critical assault on the supposed Imperial benefit of the Tariff Reform scheme. Moreover his was the only clear voice on the issue in the by-election. Cohen, uncertain on the issue, hedged, leaving Baker the field. At a Liberal meeting on the evening of 22 June, Baker announced, to laughter, that he would not 'try to run with the hare and hunt with the hounds' as his opponent wanted, instead presenting himself as an 'out-and-out free trader'. Cohen, meanwhile, struggled to stay afloat. His own address that evening was well attended but poorly received. After shying away from the issue of Tariff Reform, emphasising his reluctance to support the idea of tariffs, a shout sounded out from the back of the room of 'Poor Old Joe!' and there was great disorder once the issue of Chinese labour was raised in the hall, with Cohen and his fellow speakers drowned out amid 'much shouting and booing'.[68] It is tempting to see Cohen as simply the victim of the violent upheaval of popular electioneering in the period which, as Lawrence has observed, 'took a new turn as it built on the vulgar parades' of popular issues such as Chinese slave labour, unemployment, and the question of 'differently sized loaves'.[69] All three of these issues were present at Cohen's disastrous evening meeting of the 22 June, and frequent charges of disruption and intimidation were levelled at the Liberal and Progressive groups in the constituency by Cohen and his supporters in the press.[70] Yet this particular by-election was more than just an unprepared candidate falling foul of the rough and tumble of late Victorian popular politics. The key difference between the Liberal victory in Finsbury East and the other three by-elections won by Unionist candidates, however, is the obvious absence in the case of the former of *two* clear and opposing positions on the issue of Tariff Reform. Baker made much of Cohen's 'shilly-shallying, milk and water address', and clearly much of the electorate was inclined to agree.[71] A clear position of Tariff Reform did not necessarily guarantee success for the other three Unionist candidates, but it did clarify a complicated issue in the minds of the local electorate. Furthermore such by-elections were not simply microcosms of national conflicts but were also, as the rough reception of Cohen indicates, still contests that hinged on the candidate, his presentation, and his party's position on local issues.[72]

A second factor also rendered the outcomes of these by-elections so uncertain for commentators at the time – the ever shifting nature of constituency composition. On the morning of 3 December 1903 *The Times* refused to call the result of the Lewisham by-election in advance, observing that it was simply 'impossible' to predict. Local Liberal Associations, however, seemed more confident for they had been pinning their hopes on 'the city clerks of small income' who dominated the area and, as the paper averred, 'have small salaries and are sensitive to an increase in the cost of living'. Electoral strategy based on such groupings, however, was crucially flawed in the hectic world of Edwardian London. The borough had doubled in size since the previous election, and it was not the only part of urban Britain to have done so.[73] The residential clustering that Richard Dennis has observed in the latter part of the Victorian period was occurring in urban centres nationwide, and between 20 and 30 per cent of the electorate are thought to have shifted constituency boundaries in elections since the 1867 Reform Act.[74] In London this was even more extreme and it is important that, when considering the more representative hue that electoral rolls took on in the capital after 1867, it was not just the poor who were shifting routinely.[75] While both parties might have counted on the support of certain sections, such as the Liberal courting of middle-class clerks in Dulwich and Lewisham or the Unionist assault on alien (here read Jewish) immigration in Mile End, such targeting strategies were built on feet of clay. In many cases the constituencies had shifted substantially between elections.

The notebooks of Booth's survey not only contain comments from residents of London but observations *on* residents by the researchers. Guided around the capital by police officers, thought to represent expert geographical knowledge, the hand-written notes capture a capital in flux. In Dulwich, for example, an area that Liberal candidates hoped would embody a solid middle class that would be terrified of the price fluctuations they claimed Tariff Reform would bring, Booth's observers found something quite different. Some areas, it was true, were becoming 'quieter and more orderly' with each passing year with 'shoals of silk-hatted people ... [leaving] ... every morning for the City'. If there was a 'marked tendency' in the area overall, however, Booth and his team were convinced that it was 'downwards'.[76] The expansion of schools like Dulwich College into cheaper day-boarding was encouraging a shift from yellow ('wealthy') to red ('middle class') on Booth's maps of the area.[77] Pockets of poverty and wealth shifted, both in relative and absolute terms, across the capital. Subdivisional Inspector Drew, the guide in Mile End, 'spoke of a general tendency of Central London to become poorer', but this, he added, was due to the rich moving out rather than the poor moving in, and the area remained a spectrum of blues and pinks (ranging from poverty to reasonable comfort and stability) throughout the period.[78] Deliberate policy, such as the clearing away of the Charterhouse slums in the Finsbury East constituency, coincided with more spontaneous fluctuations, such as the efforts of a police sergeant, residing in the Mercy Lane area of Lewisham, to encourage his neighbours to settle into a 'good and quiet order'.[79] The demographic landscape of London, in constant flux in this period, produced an uncertain electoral landscape.

It was this figurative political quicksand into which Unionist candidates and their Liberal opponents launched their Tariff Reform or free-trade campaigns. In all four cases, newspaper reports indicate that both parties expected that certain social groups would respond to particular arguments or proposals. 'We admit that the clerk has not the same direct interest in Tariff Reform as that which is unquestioningly felt by the working-man', *The Times* mused in 1903, 'but ... we do not suppose that he will show himself any more obtuse than the rest of the community in gauging the merits of the question'.[80] Not only were such assumptions about class or sectional support for free trade or Tariff Reform misguided, as this study has shown, but moreover electoral strategies that relied on targeting such groups often missed the mark. Middle-class clerks anxious about the price of food, established artisans concerned by trade depression and the difficulties of foreign competition, or xenophobic East End workers threatened by the sweating system were not just political but also geographical abstractions. The political map of not just London, as emphasised by these by-election case studies, but of Britain as a whole was by no means neatly settled into targetable classes. With a household qualification still governing the franchise, the movement of voters across Britain created uncertainty, with an average of 25 months' residence needed on a practical level to qualify to vote in one's new constituency.[81] It is clear that, in all four cases, both parties could only really hope to offer up a clear position on the political issue of the day and hope that their strategy ultimately hit home in the uncertain electoral landscape of Edwardian Britain.

There is a temptation, when concluding a history of a failed political movement such as Tariff Reform, to veer into the counter-factual. To consider whether, if his assessment of the political landscape had been more accurate, his prose more polished or his fiscal policies more robust to external scrutiny, Joseph Chamberlain might have carried the day with Tariff Reform in 1906. This would, however, not just ignore the findings of such a social history study but also mistake the initial critical intent behind it. This study began with a double objective: to offer a more nuanced and detailed picture of the electoral landscape into which Chamberlain launched his Tariff Reform campaign and, by extension, an examination of whether such a study might explain his motivation in launching into this last political venture. A speculative reimagining of the 1906 result would therefore be useless, for what this study has tried to emphasise is that, if it is studied with clarity, the land-scape that both encouraged and received the Tariff Reform campaign needs to be divorced from the general election result that followed it. For it was this landscape that, shifting in unseen and unimagined ways for contemporary politicians and pundits, was both the inspiration and the undoing of the Tariff Reform moment.

There are two clear and conjoined conclusions to draw from this social history. The first is that Tariff Reform touched on a political current in Edwardian Britain that turned out to be a live wire. What was generally referred to as the Condition of England question was a national source of anxiety, debate, argument and hope in the last decade of the nineteenth century and the first decade of the twentieth. Hopes for some sort of reform or sea change were high across the political spectrum.[82] The work of men such as Booth and Rowntree, while offering a valuable source basis for historians, were at the time merely reflective of wider anxieties over the state of the nation. A growing desire for intervention, of some sort, was shaping the political landscape of Britain at the time, and Chamberlain, attuned to the popular mood and experienced in civic and national reform movements, was aware of this gathering storm. His struggle with 'free-fooders' over the prices of everyday goods demonstrated that Chamberlain had grasped the political issue of the moment, and that Tariff Reform was his proposed solution.

Yet it was not one that the country was willing to embrace and therein lies the second crucial aspect of this study: that Tariff Reform was not the answer to the Condition of England question that the majority of the electorate wanted. As Barry Doyle has pointed out, Unionist defeat in Norwich 'owed a great deal' to the failure to convince 'either the leaders or workers in the city's leading industrial sectors that they would benefit from protection'.[83] Tariff Reform did not convince, but this should not see it labelled as a quixotic gamble or a wild and zealous crusade. For men and women across the country were clearly searching for solutions. Neither Rowntree nor Booth was convinced by Chamberlain's proposal, but both men went on to fight for their own visions of intervention. Booth campaigned vociferously for old-age pensions while Rowntree became increasingly drawn into the Liberal government's reforms after the 1906 election. The Edwardian period was a time of enormous agitation and political upheaval and a social history of the Tariff Reform movement in these years can offer a window onto this national debate. With such a plethora of opinions, a shifting electorate and striking changes in affluence and poverty, the combative politics of the early 1900s represent an anxious yet confused search for solutions to huge national issues. Trade, food, foreign competition, immigration and social reform, all factors tied to the Tariff Reform question by both Chamberlain and his opponents, were not merely the hollow cries of the popular ephemera surrounding politics as usual within the limited Victorian franchise. As the notes taken by Booth's researchers show, these were questions that touched on the lives of men and women across the country, of every position and status, and ones that they themselves were passionate about, but also make clear the myriad of opinions and positions on these issues. Faced with such a broad and uncertain electorate, especially within the swirling context of Britain's urban centres where Chamberlain pitched his most strident speeches on Tariff Reform, candidates on both sides could only, as the four by-elections emphasise, offer up a clearly defined position on the issue and hope that they had done enough to convince the electorate. Attempts to target particular social groups on a constituency level were mired in even more problems than Chamberlain himself found on the national scale. Tariff Reform fascinated but did not, ultimately, convince.

Notes

1. *The Times*, 17 January 1906.
2. *Manchester Guardian*, 15 January 1906.
3. *The Spectator*, 20 January 1906.
4. *The Times*, 7 February 1906.
5. A.K. Russell, *Liberal Landslide: The General Election of 1906* (Newton Abbot: David and Charles), 1973, pp. 65, 83.
6. M. Pugh, *The Making of Modern British Politics: 1867–1945* (Oxford: Blackwell, 2002), p. 102.

7. D. Judd, *Radical Joe: A Life of Joseph Chamberlain* (Cardiff: University of Wales Press, 1993), p. 242.
8. T.L. Crosby, *Joseph Chamberlain: A Most Radical Imperialist* (London: I.B. Taurus, 2011), p. 164.
9. P.T. Marsh, *Joseph Chamberlain: Entrepreneur in Politics* (New Haven: Yale University Press, 1994), p. 563
10. J. Lawrence, 'The Culture of Elections in Modern Britain', *History*, 96 (2011), pp. 461–2.
11. F. Trentmann, 'National Identity and Consumer Politics: Free Trade and Tariff Reform', in D. Winch and P. O'Brien (eds), *The Political Economy of British Historical Experience 1688–1914* (Oxford University Press, 2002), pp. 216–17.
12. Judd, *Radical Joe*, pp. 256–63; Crosby, *Joseph Chamberlain*, p. 182.
13. Marsh, *Joseph Chamberlain*, p. 632.
14. J. Amery, *The Life of Joseph Chamberlain*, vol. 4 (London: Macmillan, 1951), p. 452.
15. Trentmann, 'National Identity and Consumer Politics', pp. 233–4.
16. Russell, *Liberal Landslide*, p. 84.
17. C.W. Boyd (ed.), *Mr Chamberlain's Speeches*, vol. 2 (London: Constable and Company Ltd, 1914), Birmingham 4 November 1903, pp. 253–4.
18. *The Illustrated London News*, 14 November 1903.
19. This item is held in the collection of the Birmingham Museum and Art Gallery.
20. M. Roberts, *Political Movements in Urban England 1832–1914* (London: Palgrave Macmillan, 2009), pp. 118–27. J. Thompson, *British Political Culture and the Idea of 'Public Opinion' 1867–1914* (Cambridge University Press, 2013), pp. 243–4.
21. In particular see A. Sykes, *Tariff Reform in British Politics 1903–1913* (Oxford: Clarendon Press, 1979), pp. 55–74 and G.R. Searle, *The Quest for National Efficiency: A Study in British Politics and Politics Thought, 1899–1914* (Oxford: Basil Blackwell, 1971), pp. 142–70.
22. Searle, *The Quest for National Efficiency*, p. 145.
23. E.H.H. Green and D.M. Tanner (eds), *The Strange Survival of Liberal England: Political Leaders, Moral Values and the Reception of Economic Debate* (Cambridge University Press, 2007), pp. 1–36.
24. See, for instance, A. Clark, 'The Rhetoric of Chartist Domesticity: Gender, Language, and Class in the 1830s and 1840s', *Journal of British Studies*, 31.1 (1992), pp. 62–88.
25. R. O'Day and D. Englander, *Mr Charles Booth's Inquiry: Life and Labour of the People in London Reconsidered* (London: Continuum, 1993), pp. 42–5.
26. B.S. Rowntree, *Poverty: A Study of Town Life.* (York: Policy Press Edition, 2000), p. 12.
27. Lady F. Bell, *At the Works: A Study of a Manufacturing Town* (London: Virago Edition, 1985), p. 76.
28. Marsh, *Joseph Chamberlain*, pp. 92–8, 593.
29. Boyd, *Mr Chamberlain's Speeches*, Liverpool, 28 October 1903, p. 230.
30. Boyd, *Mr Chamberlain's Speeches*, Gainsborough, 1 February 1904, pp. 311–12.
31. R. Jay, *Joseph Chamberlain: A Political Study* (Oxford: Clarendon Press, 1981), pp. 293–300.

32. I. Gazeley and A. Newell, 'Poverty in Edwardian Britain', *Economic History Review*, 64.1 (2011), p. 69.
33. Pugh, *Making of Modern British Politics*, p. 122.
34. Bell, *At the Works*, p. 81.
35. Rowntree, *Poverty*, pp. 263–84.
36. Marsh, *Joseph Chamberlain*, p. 585.
37. Although the phrase itself was coined by Thomas Carlyle in 1839, the Condition of England question really came of age in the Edwardian era. See, for example, W. Booth, *In Darkest England and the Way Out* (London: McCorquodale and Co., 1890); C. Masterman (ed.), *The Heart of Empire: A Discussion of the Problems of Modern City Life in England* (London: T. Fisher Unwin, 1901) and, for a more everyday use, 'A National Emergency', *The British Medical Journal*, 1.2570 (2 April 1910), pp. 831–2.
38. See the distinct lack of interest in the question in the pages of notebook B83.
39. London School of Economics Archive, London, B82, Booth Notebooks, p. 30.
40. B82, p. 48.
41. Judd, *Radical Joe*, p. 254.
42. B82, pp. 44–6.
43. B82, pp. 84–6.
44. B82, p. 10.
45. B. Doyle, 'A Crisis of Urban Conservatism? Politics and Organisation in Edwardian Norwich', *Parliamentary History*, 31.3 (Oct. 2012), p. 430.
46. See, for example, Boyd, *Mr Chamberlain's Speeches*, Greenock, 7 October 1903, pp. 168–9, Liverpool, 23 October 1903, pp. 226–8, Birmingham, November 4 1903, pp. 232–55, Gainsborough, 1 February 1904, p. 282.
47. Booth Notebooks, A6, p. 22.
48. B82, p. 64.
49. A6, pp. 171–3; 224–30; 322–9.
50. A6, p. 229.
51. B82, pp. 88–9.
52. Marsh, *Joseph Chamberlain*, p. 587.
53. B88, p. 66.
54. I. Cawood, *The Liberal Unionist Party: A History* (London: I.B. Tauris, 2012), p. 230.
55. Marsh, *Joseph Chamberlain*, p. 585.
56. Judd, *Radical Joe*, pp. 254–61; Crosby, *Joseph Chamberlain*, pp. 167–77.
57. M. Brodie, *The Politics of the Poor: The East End of London 1885–1914* (Oxford: Clarendon Press, 2004), pp. 42–3.
58. T. Otte and P. Readman (eds), *By-Elections in British Politics, 1832–1914* (Oxford: Boydell Press, 2013), p. 1.
59. Lawrence, 'The Culture of Elections', p. 459.
60. Crosby, *Joseph Chamberlain*, p. 166.
61. *The Times*, 1 December 1903.
62. *The Times*, 9 December 1903.
63. *The Times*, 3 December 1903.
64. *The Times*, 11 January 1905.
65. *The Times*, 6 June 1905; 9 June 1905.

66. *The Times*, 7 December 1903; *Daily Mirror*, 22 December 1903; *Manchester Courier and Lancashire General Advertiser*, 16 December 1903; *Northampton Mercury*, 18 December 1903.
67. *The Times*, 7 December 1903.
68. *The Times*, 23 June 1905.
69. Lawrence, 'The Culture of Elections', p. 469.
70. *The Times*, 19 June 1905.
71. *The Times*, 23 June 1905.
72. Otte and Readman (eds), *By-Elections*, pp. 8–9.
73. *The Times*, 3 December 1903.
74. R. Dennis, *English Industrial Cities of the Nineteenth Century: A Social Geography* (Cambridge University Press, 1986), pp. 186–99; J. Dunbabin, 'Electoral Reforms and Their Outcome 1865–1914', in T. Gourvish and A. O'Day (eds), *Later Victorian Britain, 1867–1900* (Basingstoke: Palgrave Macmillan, 1988), p. 102.
75. Brodie, *Politics of the Poor*, p. 47; D. Englander, *Landlord and Tenant in Urban Britain 1838–1918* (Oxford University Press, 1983), pp. 8–9.
76. Booth Notebooks B369, p. 217.
77. B375, pp. 97–9.
78. B350, pp. 75–9.
79. B353, pp. 41–7; B374, p. 7.
80. *The Times*, 7 December 1903.
81. Dunbabin, 'Electoral Reforms', p. 102.
82. Pugh, *The Making of Modern British Politics*, p. 122.
83. Doyle, 'A Crisis of Urban Conservatism', p. 405.

Part III
Local Icon

7

George Dixon
and Joseph Chamberlain:
Friends, Rivals and Even Enemies

James Dixon

The Advanced Radicals George Dixon and Joseph Chamberlain knew each other for more than 40 years. It was not, however, the calm friendship that some have depicted. Despite the quite extraordinary number of features in their lives which they shared, they did fall out seriously in the 1870s, and to a very minor extent in the mid-1890s. On both occasions, in the 1870s and the mid-1890s, at the heart of the disagreements lay the role of religion in elementary education, most especially in Birmingham.

The earlier period of discord has until now never been explored in any great depth. The first volume of J.L. Garvin's authorised biography of Chamberlain only alludes to the 1878 dispute between Dixon and Chamberlain. Garvin notes that, by 1876, as Chamberlain recovered from the twin blows of the death of Florence and his mother, 'for some time relations between [Dixon's] supporters on the Executive [of the Education League] and Chamberlain's controlling group were more careful than harmonious'. When pressure was brought to bear on Dixon to resign, Garvin notes that 'the Mayor's friends felt that they were unfairly dealt with; Dixon's group considered that their hands were being forced; cordiality ceased'. In a footnote, Garvin adds, 'The two men drew more apart', going on to note Dixon's denial that 'Chamberlain is Birmingham or Birmingham, Chamberlain' and Chamberlain's angry note to Collings in May 1878 that 'Birmingham must choose between Dixon and me', without explaining the exact cause of the dispute. Garvin quickly dismisses the issue, writing that 'the trouble passed of itself. No test of Chamberlain's ascendancy was attempted.'[1]

D.H. Elletson, Richard Jay and Enoch Powell make no mention of the dispute in their biographies of Chamberlain, and Dennis Judd merely claims that Dixon resented being forced to resign in 1876.[2] Travis Crosby states that he was 'less than pleased', though the two were 'later reconciled'.[3] Peter Marsh is, of course, somewhat more thorough, but he claims that when Dixon threatened to resign in 1878 having 'attacked Chamberlain's tyranny', 'Chamberlain crushed the initiative' by threatening to resign himself and 'Birmingham duly bowed the knee'.[4] He does go on to record that in 1879 when Dixon and the School Board challenged his policy of employing volunteer teachers to deliver religious instruction outside normal school hours, 'Dixon's men won' but that Chamberlain and he had settled their differences in 1880.[5]

While Dixon and Chamberlain had very similar ideas in the 1860s as to how major progress could be made to reform elementary education in England and Wales, Dixon's ecumenical Anglicanism was at variance with Chamberlain's nonconformity and in the 1870s the tensions were exacerbated by differences of temperament. This served to split the Liberal ranks on the School Board over the key issue as to whether the Bible should be read in class, whether education should be unsectarian or secular. Notwithstanding such differences, it is worth stressing what they had in common. Chamberlain was born in July 1836, 16 years to the month after Dixon, and that figure of 16 years curiously repeats itself time and time again. Neither came from a poor background, and both received a not dissimilar type of education, with an emphasis on modern subjects. Indeed, Dixon attended Leeds Grammar School whose curriculum a few decades earlier had been under close scrutiny by the Lord Chancellor, Lord Eldon.[6] His epic judgement when it eventually came to be delivered did not materially advance the governors' calls for reform, but Dixon grew up in an environment where it had been demonstrated that change could be secured through action. At the age of 18, Chamberlain moved to Birmingham from London to join the family screw-making business, echoing Dixon's move 16 years previously to join his brother at the Rabone merchanting business. They were both 'immigrants'.

Both came to be wealthy through their own endeavours, each profiting to some extent from the troubles of others in wars overseas: Chamberlain benefited from Paris's inability to supply the French screw industry during the Franco–Prussian war of 1870–71, and Dixon supplied arms to the north in the American Civil War. Both displayed skills and interest in accounting, even though neither was a qualified accountant. For a time, they were near-neighbours in Augustus Road. They shared an interest in gardening, and for Chamberlain's love of orchids, substitute the Dixon family's love of lilies. There was, however, one interest which they did not share: music. Dixon was involved in the organisation of the Triennial Festival, which brought much joy, his wife Mary being an enthusiastic singer. There was little or no music in Chamberlain's life.

Their appearances were distinctive, Chamberlain being noted for his trademark monocle, and Dixon for his black coat, top hat and carrying an umbrella. It would be tempting to suggest that Chamberlain's choice of attire was an act of self-promotion, but Dixon's motivation is more difficult to discern: all the family records were destroyed in a German bombing raid in 1941. His family made fun of him in his later years, speaking of him in the manner of *Onward Christian Soldiers*:

Look at Mr Puddie
Walking as to War
With his umberella
Going on Before[7]

They both became involved in arbitration, Chamberlain most notably in a fisheries dispute with the USA, and Dixon in problems involving farm-workers and brassworkers.

They were both equally large shareholders in Lloyds Banking upon its incorporation in 1865, and active in its very early management. Likewise, they both featured in the annals of the local Chamber of Commerce, Dixon rather more so than Chamberlain, having also aspired to get involved in the national organisation. Dixon especially became involved in various campaigns for changes in partnership legislation which would have led to improvements in the lot of the ambitious working man.

Neither was especially skilled in oratory in their early days. Membership of a debating society was a partial remedy. Indeed Dixon was the last president of the Birmingham society before the merger with its Edgbaston counterpart, and both extended their circle of contacts thereby. But in more mature years their skills differed substantially, with Chamberlain displaying a cutting edge which Dixon lacked. It was clear as early as March 1870 when Dixon led a deputation to 10 Downing Street to make representations on Forster's recent Education Bill, that Chamberlain, nominally his lieutenant and then aged just 33, made more of an impression on Gladstone than did Dixon. Months later, Chamberlain as a member of the newly created Birmingham School Board, began to shine: 'It was on the school board ... that Chamberlain shook off his stilted, over-rehearsed uneasiness of speech and turned into an effective orator, by turns persuasive and denunciatory.'[8]

Both entered Parliament having previously been Mayor of Birmingham, and on entry neither was totally unknown to those who worked at Westminster. Chamberlain had been renowned for his reforming zeal in Birmingham itself in the fields of gas, water and slum clearance, while Dixon had attracted national acclaim for his handling of the Murphy Riots.[9] Both shared the same party allegiances throughout their lives, although Dixon became a little 'independent' in the very last years of his life, even voting with the Liberals once more in his final debate in Parliament rather than with the Liberal Unionists, of whom he was one by then. In their private lives, Chamberlain was widowed twice over, and Dixon once. However, by a stroke of irony, it was Mary Dixon's very serious illness in 1876 that was the occasion for Chamberlain succeeding Dixon as one of Birmingham's three MPs. This episode is described in more detail below.[10]

Chamberlain was highly regarded as a competent organiser, but Dixon was no slouch in this regard either. He was one of many who helped form the original Birmingham Liberal Association in 1865, and in the next few years established the Birmingham Education Society and from that, the National Education League. The League was to be the springboard from which Chamberlain launched his career in national politics.

They were both philanthropists and originators. Tombstone announcements on the front page of the *Birmingham Daily Post*, for example, recorded their financial contributions aplenty alongside the names of many other leading members of Birmingham society. Both the Birmingham Education Society and the National Education League were beneficiaries of their generosity. Their names endure in being associated with major educational establishments. At the age of 64, in 1900 Chamberlain and others were involved in the opening of Birmingham University. At its heart stands the Joseph Chamberlain Memorial Clock Tower. And what had Dixon been doing 16 years previously? In 1884, the Bridge Street Seventh Grade Technical School had been opened, in effect the country's first secondary school, largely out of Dixon's own pocket. Its lineal descendant, the George Dixon Academy, still prospers today.

They both travelled the world. Chamberlain travelled to North America in 1887 for mediation purposes, and visited South Africa in 1902 in the aftermath of the Boer War. In 1888 Dixon travelled to New Zealand for a variety of reasons: to inspect schools, ascertain how the Dixon Investment Company was assisting English emigrants, and to make contact with the Taylor family relatives. He also took frequent holidays in continental Europe. Finally, Chamberlain died in July 1914. It should come as no surprise therefore that Dixon had died 16 years previously, in 1898.

There was no time differential when the two joined forces with others in the formation of the Birmingham Education Society in 1867 and subsequently the National Education League in 1869, both under the overall chairmanship of Dixon. They shared a common belief in religious faith as a means to improve society, although they were to differ on matters of detail with the passage of time. Against the huge backdrop of shared practical experiences, why was there such a substantial breakdown in their relationship in the 1870s, and in the final two years of that decade in particular? I would like to suggest three factors.

First there was the question of Dixon's temperament, poles apart from Chamberlain's. In the summer of 1870, at the height of the Parliamentary battle to enact Forster's Education Bill, the *London Figaro* described him thus:

> Dixon was one of those quiet men with a purpose, who worked like warmth – noiseless, agreeable, and if so unusual a word is permissible – unbaffleable.
>
> Utterly unassailable in his own religious opinions – with a personal courtesy amounting to gentleness – and possessing a clear, generous, and honest quality of speech – he disarms hostility; or, better still, he does not awaken it. He excites neither suspicion nor distrust. The enemy must attack his proposals – they cannot the proposer. No invective on his part irritates them – no aspersion diverts public attention from the great principles to be fought out.[11]

Chamberlain, by contrast, was described thus by Lord Salisbury, the one man who tamed his restless 'push' in 1895:

> I never came across so sensitive a public man before. I have known one distinguished statesman who went half-mad whenever he was caricatured in *Punch*: and another who wished to resign his office, because he was never caricatured in *Punch* – which he looked upon as a slight on his public importance. But I never met anyone before who was disturbed by articles in the *Standard* except the foreign ambassadors.[12]

Second was the issue of Dixon's overall aims. Like Chamberlain, Dixon was reported as 'minded to slay National Ignorance'. But additionally,

> he [Dixon] votes for equity in all things – for the political equality of men – the civil equality of women – for the equality of the elector at the polling booth, as the Ballot would secure it – for the representation of labour, as costless elections would make it possible – and against accumulation of landed property, the oldest and most prolific inequality of all.[13]

There is a more left-wing flavour to this agenda than would have appealed to Chamberlain, even in the early 1870s when he briefly flirted with republicanism.[14]

Third was the question of religion, at the end of the day perhaps the most important factor that set them apart. Dixon was an ecumenical Anglican, but married to a Unitarian; Chamberlain was a Unitarian, a nonconformist, fully alert to the handicaps which in the past had ensued from dissenting, which would not as a matter of course have sprung to the forefront of Dixon's mind.

The origins of the tensions between the two men related almost exclusively to the issue of elementary education. Dixon's name appears in the *Hansard* index 194 times during his Parliamentary career, and of these entries, 132 related to educational matters.

The story begins in 1867, when Dixon was already mayor. It was a year of frenetic activity for him. In January he presided over the formation of the Birmingham Education Society, whose members were drawn from a wide range of religious beliefs. Jesse Collings was Secretary, and Chamberlain was on the Committee. Modelled on the older Manchester Education Aid Society, its role was to investigate the scale of educational deprivation, and to provide aid to the very considerable number of children not attending school.[15]

In the summer, Bright's fellow Birmingham MP, William Scholefield, died.[16] Riding on the crest of his new-found popularity stemming from his handling of the Murphy Riots, Dixon was returned to Parliament in the ensuing by-election.[17] Chamberlain's speech in support was his first political performance, according to one contemporary.[18]

Early 1869 saw Dixon presiding over the formation of the National Education League in parallel with the Birmingham Education Society, the latter enduring for at least another 12 months. The League drew upon research and writings by both Chamberlain and his close friend Collings. As its name implied, the National Education League sought to extend the education debate nationally, with a focus on campaigning. A circular distributed after the inaugural meeting 'invited adhesions to the League on the following basis':

OBJECT
The establishment of a system which shall secure the education of every child in the country.

MEANS
[1] Local authorities shall be compelled by law to see that sufficient school accommodation is provided for every child in their district.

[2] The cost of founding and maintaining such schools as may be required, shall be provided out of local rates, supplemented by Government grants.

[3] All schools aided by local rates shall be under the management of local authorities and subject to Government inspection.

[4] All schools aided by local rates shall be unsectarian.

[5] To all schools aided by local rates admission shall be free.

[6] School accommodation being provided, the State or the local authorities shall have power to compel the attendance of children of suitable age not otherwise receiving education'.[19]

Dixon was chairman of the Council, and Chamberlain was chairman of the Executive Committee. Dixon spent much of his time as MP in London, while the League's offices were in Birmingham. The perception was to grow rapidly that Chamberlain ran the organisation, and this was borne out by the reality of the geographical situation.

At the League's first major conference in the autumn of 1869, Dixon displayed his talents at securing compromises, not least the very awkward question of religion in education. Was it going to be secular or unsectarian? Definitions were mouth-wateringly difficult. The big fear of the nonconformists in particular was that they would have to pay taxes for compulsory education, and many of them would land up having their children educated at Anglican schools. At this stage it was thought that the proposed new Birmingham schools would be managed by the Town Council, rather than by separately elected School Boards, as was eventually enacted in Forster's legislation. Ambitious to be involved in the running of the new schools, Chamberlain sought election to the Town Council, his entrée into local politics.

It was Dixon's handling of the relationship between Birmingham and Manchester as to which town should lead the national campaign that showed the difference in temperament between him and Chamberlain.

Dixon was perfectly prepared to let Manchester take the lead given that it had been involved in campaigning for longer, a stance that Chamberlain with all his ambitions would never have countenanced. But eventually in December Dixon stood firm for his own town, and the name of Birmingham became forever associated with radical educational reform. There were, however, straws in the wind that change was afoot: in January 1870 he wrote a letter apologising for his inability to attend a meeting in Wolverhampton, and suggested that Chamberlain go instead. 'Mr Joseph Chamberlain, who is a better speaker than I am, will go.'[20]

All was then set for Forster's speech of 17 February 1870. Just days earlier John Bright had fallen ill, and had withdrawn from public life. Dixon thus became the senior Birmingham MP for the next three years, Muntz, the third MP, scarcely featuring on the stage.[21] It was an ideal opportunity for the young Chamberlain to fill the void in Birmingham life.

With a thud, the world changed. For the first few days after Forster's speech, there was almost universal relief that the state had at long last assumed responsibility for eventual compulsory and free elementary education. Just how much detail Dixon knew of Forster's proposals in advance will never be known, but he had to be grateful that the Rubicon had at long last been crossed. Like a present-day Leader of the Opposition forced to respond to a Chancellor's Budget Statement at a moment's notice, he was faced with a mass of detail which needed mature reflection. Forster's speech had impressed the House. Dixon could but proclaim that he 'felt persuaded that the country generally would support them in their endeavours to carry its provisions out'.[22]

Then came the message from Chamberlain: 'Strong exception was taken to the first paragraph in your speech.'[23] Chamberlain got busy and organised the biggest ever deputation to Downing Street to date, in March, comprising 46 MPs and 400 League members. Dixon nominally led the deputation, but the discerning Gladstone was heard to say of Chamberlain, 'who I may consider as in some sense being your chairman – the representative of you all'.[24]

A couple of years later, one of Dixon's colleagues on the School Board reflected on his relationship with his own supporters (including Chamberlain):

> Mr Dixon is a gentleman of moderate mind. He put himself into the hands of allies possessed of considerable ability and little discretion: of allies, friends to education but more friends to popular

agitation: liberals in politics; bigots in religion. Mr Dixon, left to himself, would not have run into extravagances. But he got together and undertook to drive a team far too lively for his gentle guidance: he gave his cattle their heads, and they fairly ran away with him. He now appears as the nominal chief of a masterful and bitter faction.[25]

Not only that, but there was a difference in outlook between the two men: Dixon was intent on educational reform above all else; Chamberlain saw education as part of a much larger political jigsaw, citing the disestablishment of the English church as an example. So the Bill reached the Statute Book in August 1870, and the first School Board elections took place a few months later. The Liberals were overconfident and failed to recognise the importance of tactical voting, thus allowing the Conservative Church party to win eight out of the fifteen available seats. In the complex voting system introduced, Dixon won the support of more voters than anyone else, but with each voter entitled to 15 votes apiece, it was the total number of votes that mattered. George Dawson got the most Liberal votes, with Dixon slightly behind. Chamberlain came fifth out of the six successful Liberal candidates.[26] Indeed, Chamberlain never secured more votes than Dixon in elections in which they stood in tandem, but given the substance of organisation subsequently, this counts for very little.

So far as Dixon's campaigning for compulsory and free education in the following six years was concerned, an annual pattern of events can be discerned. Every year the League's Executive Committee would propose a number of resolutions at its annual meetings, and these points would then be presented by Dixon in Parliament, invariably word for word. He had become more of a delegate than a representative. There was also a sniff in the air that Chamberlain might be wishing to replace Dixon in Parliament, for in November 1871 at a meeting of the United Kingdom Alliance, he 'expressed his belief in the truth, honour, loyalty and good faith in Mr Dixon ... yet he said that even he could not go into the House of Commons except by pushing his friend Mr Dixon out, [and] he would never go'.[27]

In 1873 the second triennial School Board elections took place. This time the Liberals organised themselves properly, and crucially secured a majority 8 out of 15 seats. The Liberal-inclined *Daily Telegraph* described Dixon as the 'veteran reformer', and the outcome overall as 'remarkable'.[28] Chamberlain was now chairman, and Dixon remained a member while continuing of course to be an MP. There would have been a great deal of train travel between Euston and New Street while Parliament was sitting.

Chamberlain almost immediately introduced a policy of secular education, against which he had argued back in 1869. In those early days of the National Education League he had backed Dixon's policy of striving for unsectarian rather than secular education, on the basis that the latter might offend those who were shocked at the omission of all religious instruction.[29] But now that Chamberlain was chairman of the School Board, he was emboldened. The secular policy involved representatives of the various denominations providing religious instruction in separate classes at the beginning and end of the school day. Dixon was far from supportive, and indeed had absented himself from a crucial meeting in 1872 when the new policy had been adopted by the Liberal minority, on the grounds that he had an important meeting in St Helens to attend.[30] Bright was to cast doubt on the wisdom of pursuing the secular policy, which was ultimately to fail on practical grounds: not all the denominations supported it; those that did could not provide enough teachers to cope with the ever-expanding school population; and such teachers as were provided often lacked the skill sets to maintain discipline.

Dixon's position within the League deteriorated. Chamberlain had decided on a policy in which the League should field its own candidates in Parliamentary elections, most notably in the Bath by-election. Mundella in Sheffield (to whom Forster had given credit for campaigning alongside Dixon in his speech of February 1870), always on the fringes of the League, wrote to a colleague, 'I appealed to Dixon to stop [the League candidate] Cox's proceedings at Bath, but he is weak and powerless. Chamberlain and the fanatics have the mastery, and mean to gratify their vanity and magnify their importance by showing their power to do mischief.'[31]

The general election of 1874 saw Dixon returned unopposed. Initially the Association had nominated Bright and Dixon unanimously, and Muntz by a large majority, for the three-member constituency. With the arrival of a potential fourth candidate, supported by working men, fears were aroused that the Conservatives would contest the seat after all. There was thus the possibility that either Bright or Dixon might lose their seats. Dixon decided to test the waters by threatening to withdraw his candidature, but Dr Dale spoke strongly for Bright and Dixon, and the fourth potential candidate withdrew.[32] It was the first of several episodes in his life when Dixon continued in public office through the strength of popular acclaim.[33]

Meantime Chamberlain was having much less success in Sheffield, where he was attempting to gain a Parliamentary seat for the first time. Saddled with the problem of serving as Mayor of Birmingham at the same time as fighting the election campaign, while seemingly failing to fully understand the dynamics of local politics in Sheffield, eventually 'beer and the Bible' beat him. Thereafter he no longer attempted to put himself forward primarily as a working man's representative.[34]

Fault-lines now began to develop between Dixon and Chamberlain. The resignation of Gladstone saw Chamberlain supporting Hartington, and Dixon supporting Forster. But ultimately much more inflammatory was the issue of the governance of the Grammar School. Dixon had made his position abundantly clear a decade earlier, when he had played a leading role in the Free Grammar School Association.[35] He strongly objected to the effective hijacking of the provision of free education, originally intended for the poor, by the middle classes, and wanted radical change. The Town Council with Chamberlain as mayor wanted the whole power of electing Governors to be in the hands of the Town Council itself. At the other end of the spectrum was the view of the existing governors who wanted to self-select, filling vacancies in their own body. Dixon adopted a typical position of compromise, seeking to have the majority to be representative men, who would select the remainder.[36] There the debate temporarily stalled.

The year 1875 saw Dixon in Parliament go through his annual exercise of seeking to introduce legislation for universal compulsory education, an issue on which he and Chamberlain were united. The majority against him had been 164 in 1874, and now it was down to just 91. Public opinion was swinging in his favour, not least from the established schools: in an era when free education was still a distant prospect, all that additional income ensuing from compulsion was a considerable attraction. But Dixon had personal problems ahead. As his brother-in-law James Stansfeld opined, 'There is no doubt that he [Chamberlain] is King in Birmingham but whether there will be a vacant seat [as MP] is another matter.'[37]

And there was a problem with the state of his wife's health. Ultimately Mary Dixon lived on until the spring of 1885, dying eventually of a cancerous growth, but there were considerable problems at the end of 1875. While there were public discussions in early 1876 about Dixon's standing down in favour of Chamberlain, in December 1875 he had sought to open a new school, a High School for Girls in Edgbaston, to which he would send his offspring.[38] This did seem to indicate that he was mindful of making Birmingham his main family base, instead of dividing his time between London and the Midlands. Many other leading Liberals were involved in the plans, including Chamberlain, who inevitably raised the issue of religious instruction at the school.[39]

The events of the first six months of 1876 were very murky, with Dixon's application for the Chiltern Hundreds being postponed much longer than Chamberlain wanted.[40] There was scope for misunderstanding between the parties as to timing, but in Dixon's defence it has to be said that many Birmingham people did not want to be represented by a man such as Chamberlain in his current state of health: his friends worried that he was overburdening himself, and his doctor ordered him away to recuperate.[41] Eventually it was the *Birmingham Daily Post* under the editorship of Chamberlain's friend, Bunce, which set the timetable for the transition.[42]

Dixon remained dignified throughout, writing courteously but firmly immediately after Chamberlain's election:

> So much enthusiasm & unanimity has seldom been displayed in a large constituency; and I do most heartily congratulate you on your brilliant entrance into Parliamentary life. You have richly deserved your splendid success, and I am one of those who firmly believe that you will gain the highest positions in the House of Commons – and that your popularity in the country will be even greater than in the House.
>
> I do not hide from myself that you will have some difficulties to overcome, as for instance your facility of invective, & your too low estimate of the position & character of your opponents. But who has not difficulties to overcome? & yours require only to be felt to be discarded at once.
>
> After having so frequently heralded your approach to the House of Commons, with a very loud trumpet, I shall watch your career there with interest. My best wishes accompany you, and it will always be a pleasure to me to hear of your successes.[43]

There had been no overwhelming need for Chamberlain to enter Parliament at the very moment he did, other than to satisfy his own personal ambition to become an MP before the age of 40. Dixon had fought tirelessly for many a long year in the cause of compulsory education, and he was just weeks away from seeing his hopes fulfilled in the shape of Sandon's Act.

Chamberlain by contrast seriously misbehaved. Suffering from gout, he snapped at a School Board meeting, denouncing Disraeli 'as a man who went down to the House of Commons and flung at the British Parliament the first lie that entered his head'. There was a general outcry, and Chamberlain was forced to apologise, pleading overwork, but not before Disraeli had described this attack as what 'you might expect from the cad of an omnibus'.[44]

The press was far from enthusiastic about Birmingham's change of representation in Parliament. The then-Liberal *Daily Telegraph*, in the short gap after Dixon's departure had been publicised but before Chamberlain had been elected, opined, 'while we regret Mr Dixon's secession from public life, we shall have more calls for sorrow if his probable successor, Mr Chamberlain, reproduces in the House of Commons the tone, temper and verbiage he thinks good enough for the Birmingham School Board'.[45] The *Globe*, by this time supporting the Tory party, suggested

> that the change is to be regretted. Dixon's political opinions may be of far too advanced a school to receive a general acceptance. Nevertheless, we heartily wish that he would remain member of Birmingham for many years, sooner than see that important borough represented by its present mayor. Of these two enthusiastic Radicals, Mr Chamberlain is apparently somewhat the cleverer. There, however, his superiority seems to stop.[46]

The *Birmingham Daily Post* had a great deal to say about the change:

> The announcement we make in another column ... will be received with general and sincere regret, and also with surprise by those who have not hitherto been acquainted with Mr Dixon's strong desire to return, at least for a time, to the private life which his friends know to be so congenial to his tastes.
>
> It is a great thing to say of a public man that he has no enemies; but as regards Mr Dixon we may go further, and say with truth that in public and private, in his representative and personal character, he has none but friends.

With Dixon now standing down, 'the town instinctively turned to Mr Chamberlain as his successor ... In choosing a successor to Mr Dixon we are performing what is in reality a national task.' It concluded,

> we rejoice that to Birmingham has fallen the good fortune of sending him [Chamberlain] to Westminster as the fittest successor to

Mr Dixon, as a worthy colleague to Mr Bright, and as one who is destined to take high rank amongst the future leaders of the Liberal party.[47]

Dixon himself, having 'let it be known that he had been harried to make the change', went on holiday with some of his former parliamentary colleagues, including Mundella, John Gorst, and Lord Edmund Fitzmaurice.[48] The latter prophetically said that Chamberlain was 'full of overweening ambition, destined to a considerable degree of disappointment, but so clever and intriguing withal, that he will sacrifice party interests to his own'.[49]

The relationship between Dixon and Chamberlain now took a serious turn for the worse. The deal between the two was that while Dixon applied for the Chiltern Hundreds, to be succeeded immediately by Chamberlain, the latter would surrender the chairmanship of the School Board in November to the former. Chamberlain was also obliged to stand down as mayor, a job he loved. Chamberlain progressed to the formation of the National Liberal Federation. Dixon did attend its 1877 conference, but his participation in those early days was minimal. He had lots of other things to do to keep himself busy: his wife Mary's health improved, and it was not until 1885 that she passed away, while there were still the younger members of the family of six children to bring up; there was the Edgbaston High School for Girls to develop; but above all there was the Birmingham School Board to chair.

Then, in the late spring of 1878, war broke out between the two. The battleground was the governance of the King Edward's Foundation. The Town Council, of which Dixon was not then a member, was in a position to nominate a number of Governors, but Dixon's name was passed over. Indeed, Chamberlain was pursuing a policy whereby all the Council-nominated governors should only be drawn from among the ranks of the councillors.[50] The voting was 9 for Chamberlain's proposals, 44 abstentions, and none against.[51] That could scarcely be called an overwhelming majority. Dixon was absolutely furious. At the School Board he ranted,

Mr Joseph Chamberlain is a remarkably clever man, but he is undertaking a great work; he is undertaking to create the public opinion of the Town Council and of Birmingham and also to be its public exponent. In fact, it seems as if the terms of Mr Joseph Chamberlain and Birmingham were becoming synonymous. Mr Joseph Chamberlain is Birmingham, Birmingham is Mr Joseph Chamberlain. He represents himself in the Town Council and he also represents himself in the House of Commons.[52]

Such was his fury that the proceedings were temporarily suspended.[53] The local press suggested that he got rather emotional. The local Tory satirical publication, the *Dart and Midland Figaro*, reported, somewhat gleefully, that 'Mr Dixon was greatly moved in making his long personal statement. So deeply affected was he that at times he almost broke down, and he appeared to have been wounded to the quick by the cavalier treatment of the Council.'[54] In fact, he threatened to resign. The School Board fully supported its chairman. The reason for wanting to forge stronger links with the Foundation was to facilitate a system of graded schools, a principle which Dixon had floated as long ago as 1867.[55] Chamberlain's policy on the face of it did nothing to strengthen such links and no case has ever been put forward to justify his stance.

The local press had a field day and there even appeared a cartoon depicting Chamberlain riding a coach to Birmingham's eastern neighbour: in effect, he had been sent to Coventry.[56] For several weeks the correspondence columns of the *Birmingham Daily Post* featured a lively debate on the merits of the situation, with the majority of the letters in support of Dixon. There was some regret that he had introduced a personal element into his outburst against Chamberlain, but there was much support for the principles for which he stood.[57]

Dixon had his friends, most notably among the working classes, a point which has been missed by all previous Chamberlain biographers. A petition bearing 12,000 signatures was organised by W.J. Davis, General Secretary of the National Society of Amalgamated Brassworkers, whereupon Dixon withdrew his resignation threat.[58] Chamberlain sulked, and in private correspondence with Collings had implied that he saw the episode as a personal attack on his position. Hearing about the petition to Dixon asking him to stay in office as Chairman of the School Board, he wrote:

> Now once for all I am not going to stand this. A requisition to Dixon is inferentially a vote of censure on me, and if this is to go on I see only one course open viz. to summon the 600 [the Birmingham Liberal Association] & challenge a decision between Dixon and me. If it is for Dixon, I will either resign at once, or hold my seat till the General Election for the convenience of the Party, but I am not going to pretend to be a representative of Birmingham, if there is the least

colour for the statement that an unprovoked and gratuitous attack on me is approved and sustained by my constituents.[59]

As it happened, Chamberlain never did summon a meeting of the Birmingham Liberal Association, for Dixon was emboldened. It was time to sort out the question of religious teaching in Birmingham schools once and for all. Chamberlain's policy of having teachers from the various denominations do the job was described as 'about the most melancholy farce ever perpetrated in political annals ... amiable individuals, who undertook a task like that of mopping up the Atlantic'.[60]

But the stage was not yet set for restoring the reading of the Bible, and explaining its meanings. Instead, Dixon came up with his own compromise solution: moral lessons would be put in the school timetable. These lessons comprised the teaching of good manners, punctuality, order, neatness, obedience, perseverance, courage, temperance, truthfulness, honesty, industry, kindness, consideration for others and the idea of duty. The *Dart* portrayed this as the 'Gospel according to St George'.[61]

The situation moved on rapidly. Dixon's friend on the School Board, John Skirrow Wright (a rival to Chamberlain but lacking his political weight), proposed a motion that the Bible should be read daily in Board schools. He was supported by Dixon and the Conservatives, with all the other Liberals and the solitary Catholic abstaining.[62] So it was that until Dixon's retirement as Board Chairman in 1896, Board policy was the reading of the Bible without note or explanation, and religious teaching would take place outside school hours.[63]

Chamberlain's educational policies were in tatters, and in the spring of 1880 he sought to mend his fences with Dixon. The timing is interesting: as the *Dart* was lamenting that 'George Dixon had effectively retreated into private life', in February the School Board minutes reveal that his doctor had advised him to go abroad for a while.[64] And Chamberlain might well have been mindful of the *Dart's* edition of 20 March:

Forward! Sons of Birmingham
Liberty and Right
Love and honour vote for
Dixon, Muntz and Bright
Bear our standard proudly
As in days of yore
O'er the host assailant
Onward to the war.

Calm was restored for the next 15 or so years. Dixon was elected Treasurer of the Birmingham Liberal Association; Chamberlain allowed Dixon to reign supreme over the School Board world; and Dr Dale of Carrs Lane Church observed that Dixon had

> reigned over a Board which had had its rough and stormy times, but which was now as calm and peaceful as an Italian lake under a July sun … It was possible the tranquilising influence of Mr Dixon's own gentle and kindly spirit might be seen in the better manners and conduct of his colleagues.[65]

In 1884, however, Dixon's name came to the forefront following riots at Aston Park, when Liberals sought to break up a Conservative meeting being addressed by Lord Randolph Churchill. Chamberlain subsequently made various allegations which were based on false evidence, and there was some adverse comment about Chamberlain's behaviour in asking Dixon to apologise rather than do it himself.[66] But that was no more than one facet of the perception that Dixon was becoming one of Chamberlain's henchmen in the turbulent world of the 1880s. Dixon became a leading light in the Birmingham Liberal Association, succeeding Harris as president when the latter stood down due to ill health. This position was no doubt of great assistance in his procuring Edgbaston as his constituency in 1885 after the boundary changes associated with the Third Reform Act.

This was not before another significant achievement in the educational world, for in 1884, largely out of his own resources, he had established the Bridge Street Seventh Grade Technical School, the first of its kind in the country. Although the word had a different meaning at that time, it was effectively the nation's first secondary school. People came from far and wide to view it. He pushed the boundaries of the word 'elementary' as in Forster's *Elementary* Education Act, and he played one government department against another in order to obtain maximum funding. Perhaps therein lay the roots of his conduct in 1896, when he came to oppose Chamberlain over proposed changes to national education legislation.

The *Dart* praised his achievements, proclaiming that 'the school at Bridge Street is worth attention, and is one of the most satisfactory blossoms on the big Board School tree'.[67] Dixon was 'the amiable gentleman whom Mr Joseph Chamberlain shifts about as he wants him'.[68] Later it commented that 'if Birmingham Liberalism were synonymous with George Dixon, it would be better for all of us'.[69] Given the *Dart's* antipathy towards Chamberlain, it was clear that Joe's enemy was the Birmingham Tories' friend.

A week might have been a long time in politics in later twentieth-century Britain, but a few months in early 1886 must have seemed an eternity. Gladstone's stance on Irish Home Rule served to change the face of Birmingham politics for ever. The same publication now described Dixon as a jellyfish, knuckling under to his old rival, Chamberlain. A cartoon appeared bearing the caption 'A political beauty show'. All the leading lights featured, clad in dresses, and sitting on a bench. Chamberlain was described as 'Uncertain temper, just divorced'; Bright as 'Aged, grumpy'; while Dixon was 'Very easy natured. Do anything for a quiet life.'[70] They were united in their opposition to Home Rule, but not necessarily for the same reasons, a point which Dixon himself made in conversation with Henry Sidgwick, co-founder of Newnham College, Cambridge. Sidgwick recorded,

> spent three pleasant days with Mr George Dixon (MP) a thoroughly <u>nice</u> man. (This is not an adjective I often use, nor did I expect to apply it to a leading BRUMMAGEM politician, but it is the word for Dixon; he is not brilliant nor exactly impressive, and though he is able, it is not his ability that strikes one so much as a gentle thoughtfulness, sustained, alert, mildly humorous.) Asked George Dixon why the Unionist phalanx in Birmingham appeared to be united, and George Dixon thought 'it was half an accident; the party was really divided here as elsewhere just below the top, but that Bright and Chamberlain and himself – no one of the three ordinarily in the habit of taking his opinions from either of the other two – happened to coincide on this question'; and they, I gathered, were the three recognized leaders. Bright being the old time-honoured political chief, Chamberlain the established 'boss' in the industrial action of the municipality, and Dixon the educational boss.[71]

Soon after, John Bright died. The *Daily News* observed, 'Mr Dixon was perhaps the man most universally respected in Birmingham. He had none of Mr Chamberlain's showy qualifications. But he had "character", and in England character always counts.'[72] Indeed, with the new compact with the Conservatives, Dixon never had to contest his Parliamentary seat again before his death in 1898. The passage of the free-school legislation in 1891 no doubt enhanced his reputation still further, with a cartoon describing him as 'The Father of Free Education' having already appeared the previous year;[73] but for the record Dixon did not do too much to secure its final enactment. He was also able to bask in the glory of an American article which described Birmingham as the best-governed city in the world.[74]

In the 1890s major concerns were being expressed about the finances of the so-called voluntary sector of education. The 1896 Education Bill presented Dixon with particular problems as he was seemingly locked in a time-warp, craving as always a national system in which the voluntary schools would be eliminated through the competitive force of their young upstarts, the School Board schools. The latter had had a relatively easy time financially since the 1870 Act, funded as they were through a combination of national and local resources. The quality of their buildings, especially in Birmingham, was ample testimony to this.

Chamberlain was now a member of a coalition government, albeit one with a Conservative majority. He publicly claimed to have changed his mind since Forster's Act some 20 years previously.[75] The *School Board Chronicle*, invariably a strong supporter of Dixon's position, protested strongly against this reversal: 'The utterly indefensible faults of the denominational system as it stands, more particularly in the rural districts, have not undergone any modification since the days of Mr Chamberlain's fierce rhetoric in condemnation.'[76] Four out of seven children nationally were taught in voluntary schools and the cost to the rates would be totally unaffordable unless help were provided immediately. But this offended against Dixon's principle that public money should not be handed over to authorities unless there was some measure of public control.

There were mutterings of the resuscitation of a pressure group akin to the former National Education League amidst open hostility from a large number of Midlands radicals who now looked to Dixon to bring Chamberlain to heel.[77] W. Ansell, a member of the Birmingham School Board, wrote a letter of protest to the *Liberal Unionist Association Memoranda*, which Chamberlain responded to with a typically robust defence of the government's policy.[78] As it happened, the 1896 draft legislation was eventually withdrawn for a variety of reasons and the embarrassment of a further split between Dixon and Chamberlain was avoided.

Dixon appeared in Parliament for the last time in January 1897, and died a year later. Had he lived four years more, he would have seen the educational world as he had known it turned upside down, as the 1902 Education Act abolished the School Boards completely. It seems entirely possible to suggest that Chamberlain would not have attempted this had Dixon still been alive, or at the very least that Dixon could have persuaded him that it would be a serious obstacle to retaining nonconformist support for the Unionist parties. As it was, protest against the Bill resulted in some very awkward encounters for the Colonial Secretary in Birmingham and he admitted to the Duke of Devonshire that 'our best friends are leaving us by scores and hundreds, never to return'.[79] The contemporary political commentator Edward Porritt believed that 'much of the disappearance of Liberal Unionism is traceable to the Education Act of 1902'.[80] The nonconformist unionists began gravitating back to the Liberals, which may have influenced Chamberlain's reckless and politically disastrous (outside Birmingham) decision to advocate Tariff Reform between 1903 and his debilitating stroke in 1906.

Chamberlain did not attend Dixon's funeral, having an important meeting to attend. Instead, he was represented by Austen and Neville. But he was ultimately generous in his tribute to his former colleague: 'He now leaves behind him to his children – as a priceless legacy – the reputation of an English gentleman, honourable, simple-minded, straight-forward and disinterested.'[81] Chamberlain himself died 16 years later, a few days short of his 78th birthday. His lifespan was just a tiny bit longer than that of his former colleague, sometime friend, sometime rival and sadly for a time, enemy, by just a few weeks. His obituary in the *Times* on 4 July 1914 ran to over 17,000 words. Rather more succinctly, the leader column of that day described a very different character to that of Dixon: 'He was directness itself, with courage and resource to match his power of thought. No man could misunderstand his language: he said precisely what he meant ... Men might question his judgement: they could not question his force.'[82]

Today the name of George Dixon lives on in Edgbaston in the form of the George Dixon Academy, well respected in the local community and embodying the spirit of the very words that he spoke so characteristically in 1867:

> It was most important that they should seek in all educational work that they took in hand, to make the ultimate end of that work a gradation of schools – schools that is, not uniform, not of the same character, but so diverse that they should be adapted to the wants of every class of the community, from the richest down to the very lowest, and that they should be so easy of access from the lower schools to the higher that they should feel that there was not one boy in Birmingham, however low in the school, or however indifferent his

parents might be to his education, if he had really those natural powers which would enable him to profit in an extraordinary degree by the advantages offered, who would have anything in the shape of a barrier put in the way of his progress upwards, even to the highest honours of the University.[83]

The manner in which this message was delivered says much as to why Dixon did not make a wider mark on late nineteenth-century political life. But has Joseph Chamberlain bequeathed any similar message of such stature?

Notes

1. J.L. Garvin, *The Life of Joseph Chamberlain, Vol. 1: 1836–1885* (London: Macmillan, 1935), p. 225.
2. D. Judd, *Radical Joe: A Life of Joseph Chamberlain* (London: Hamilton, 1977), p. 75.
3. T. Crosby, *Joseph Chamberlain: A Most Radical Imperialist* (London: I.B. Tauris, 2011), p. 21.
4. P. Marsh, *Joseph Chamberlain: Entrepreneur in Politics* (New Haven, CT: Yale University Press, 1994), p. 123.
5. Ibid., pp. 128, 140.
6. J.W. Dixon, *Out of Birmingham: George Dixon (1820–98), 'Father of Free Education'* (Studley: Brewin, 2013), p. 18.
7. K. Rathbone, *The Dales: Growing Up in a Victorian Family*, ed. B. Walker and H. Walker (Ledbury: Northstep, 1989), p. 121.
8. P. Marsh, *Joseph Chamberlain*, p. 51.
9. Murphy was a fanatical Protestant rabble-rouser. Dixon displayed considerable personal bravery in riding into the midst of an angry rioting crowd in the Bull Ring, and there reading the Riot Act. The matter was subsequently discussed in Parliament on 23 July 1869. See *Hansard*, Third Series, vol. CXCVIII, pp. 592–633.
10. See p. 163.
11. Reproduced in the *Birmingham Daily Post*, 22 June 1870.
12. Quoted in A. Roberts, *Salisbury: Victorian Titan* (London: Phoenix, 1999), p. 597.
13. Reproduced in the *Birmingham Daily Post*, 22 June 1870.
14. R. Jay, *Joseph Chamberlain: A Political Study* (Oxford: Clarendon, 1981), p. 20.
15. While the two education societies had very similar objectives, the Birmingham-based National Education League was opposed by the Manchester-based National Education Union.
16. Prior to the 1868 general election, Birmingham was a two-member constituency. John Bright had been one of its two members since 1857.
17. The claim is made by G.H. Kenrick in 'George Dixon: A Lecture', in J.H. Muirhead (ed.), *Nine Famous Birmingham Men* (Birmingham: Cornish Brothers, 1909), p. 53.

18. J.M. Davidson, *Eminent Radicals In and Out of Parliament* (London: W. Stewart & Co., 1880), p. 86.
19. F. Adams, *History of the Elementary School Contest in England* (London: Chapman and Hall, 1882; in new ed. Hassocks: Harvester, 1973), p. 197.
20. *Birmingham Daily Post*, 11 January 1870.
21. P.H. Muntz (1811–88) was a former mayor of Birmingham with radical credentials from a previous era.
22. *Hansard Third Series*, vol. CXCIX, col. 475, 17 Feb. 1870.
23. A. Briggs, 'Introduction', Adams, *History of Elementary School Contest*, p. lvii, fn.
24. Institute of Education, National Education League pamphlets vol. 1, pamphlet 18, *Verbatim Report of the Proceedings of a Deputation* (Birmingham: National Education League, 1870), p. 26.
25. W.L. Sargant, *Essays of a Birmingham Manufacturer*, vol. 4 (London: Williams and Norgate, 1872), p. 4. Sargant was a member of the Conservative Church Party on the School Board. Intemperate language such as 'bigots' flourished at this time. It is recorded that the radical grouping was also 'branded as sectarians, revolutionists, irreconcilables, sciolists, infidels and communists' (Adams, *History of Elementary School Contest*, p. 204).
26. Dixon, *Out of Birmingham*, p. 140.
27. *Birmingham Daily Post*, 22 November 1871.
28. As reported in the *Birmingham Daily Post*, 21 November 1873.
29. See Dixon, *Out of Birmingham*, p. 94.
30. Institute of Education, National Education League pamphlets vol. 2, pamphlet 32, *Religious Instruction in Board Schools* (Birmingham: National Education League, 1872), p. 77.
31. W.H.G. Armytage, *A.J. Mundella, 1825–97: The Liberal Background to the Labour Movement* (London: Benn, 1951), p. 130.
32. *Birmingham Daily Post*, 30 January 1874.
33. The intervention by W.J. Davis in organising a petition in Dixon's support in 1878 is described in more detail below. A second occasion was the School Board election of 1888, at which time Dixon was absent in New Zealand, and not a word was heard from throughout the contest. He was nominated by both the major parties, securing the second highest number of votes out of a total of 15 candidates. See A.F. Taylor, 'The History of the Birmingham School Board, 1870–1903' (MA thesis, University of Birmingham, 1955), p. 70.
34. Marsh, *Joseph Chamberlain*, p. 74.
35. Dixon, *Out of Birmingham*, p. 51.
36. *Hansard*, vol. 221, col. 519, 20 July 1874.
37. Ibid., p. 67.
38. J. Whitcut, *Edgbaston High School, 1876–1976* (Warwick: Roundwood Press, 1976), p. 30.
39. Ibid., p. 36.
40. Marsh, *Chamberlain*, p. 110.
41. Ibid.
42. Dixon, *Out of Birmingham*, p. 169.
43. Dixon to Chamberlain, 28 June 1876, University of Birmingham Special Collections, Joseph Chamberlain Papers, JC5/27/3.
44. Marsh, *Joseph Chamberlain*, p. 111.
45. As reported in the *Birmingham Daily Gazette*, 19 June 1876.

46. As reported in the *Birmingham Daily Gazette*, 20 June 1876.
47. *Birmingham Daily Post*, 17 June, 1876.
48. Marsh, *Chamberlain*, p. 111.
49. Armytage, *A.J. Mundella*, p. 179.
50. *Birmingham Daily Post*, 1 May 1878.
51. *School Board Chronicle*, vol. 19, 11 May 1878, p. 445.
52. Ibid.
53. Birmingham School Board Minutes, Library of Birmingham Archives and Heritage Service, SB/B1/1/3, p. 399.
54. The *Dart*, 11 May 1878.
55. Dixon, *Out of Birmingham*, p. 67.
56. The *Dart*, 18 May 1878.
57. See, for example, letter dated 13 May 1878 from 'a Liberal'. *Birmingham Daily Post*, 14 May 1878.
58. *Birmingham Daily Post*, 6 June 1878. See also W.A. Dalley, *The Life Story of W.J. Davis, J.P.* (Birmingham Printers, 1914), p. 50.
59. Chamberlain to Collings, 7 May 1878, Joseph Chamberlain Papers, JC5/16/85.
60. *The Dart and Midland Figaro*, 27 July 1888.
61. The *Dart*, 10 May 1879.
62. SB/B1/1/4, p. 64.
63. *Hansard Fourth Series*, vol. XV, col. 968, 31 July 1893.
64. SB/B1/1/4, p. 93.
65. *Birmingham Daily Post*, 10 November 1880.
66. Dixon, *Out of Birmingham*, p. 196.
67. The *Dart*, 13 March 1885.
68. The *Dart*, 23 October 1885.
69. The *Dart*, 27 November 1885.
70. The *Dart*, 2 July 1886.
71. A. Sidgwick and E.M. Sidgwick, *Henry Sidgwick: A Memoir* (London: Macmillan, 1906), p. 456.
72. Reproduced in the *Birmingham Daily Post*, 25 January 1898.
73. The *Town Crier*, 10 May 1890.
74. J. Ralph, 'The Best-Governed City in the World', *Harper's New Monthly Magazine*, 81 (New York, 1890), p. 101.
75. *Birmingham Daily Post*, 25 April 1891.
76. *School Board Chronicle*, vol. 45, 2 May 1891, p. 465.
77. S. Maccoby, *English Radicalism, 1886–1914* (London: Routledge, 1953), p. 228.
78. *Liberal Unionist Association Memoranda*, 4.5 (May 1896).
79. Chamberlain to Devonshire, 22 September 1902, Devonshire Papers, Chatsworth House, 340.2998.
80. E. Porritt, 'Party Conditions in England', *Political Science Quarterly*, 21 (1906), p. 213.
81. G. Hayward, 'The Dixon Family of Cherkley Court, Leatherhead', *Proceedings of the Leatherhead and District Local History Society*, part 2 (1976), p. 356.
82. *The Times*, 4 July 1914.
83. Kenrick, 'George Dixon', p. 55. See also Dixon, *Out of Birmingham*, p. 67.

8
Joseph Chamberlain and the Birmingham Satirical Journals, 1876–1911

Ian Cawood and Chris Upton

Joseph Chamberlain came to prominence in the second great age of political caricature, which was also the first age of mass-circulation political satirical periodicals.[1] Although historians of journalism have been preoccupied with the concept of the 'new journalism' in the late nineteenth century, recent studies have demonstrated that there was as much continuity across the media of the second half of the nineteenth century (after the abolition of stamp duty in 1855) as there was change.[2] Chamberlain was in many ways the first modern politician to manipulate the media effectively, cultivating a visual image, using a range of printed propaganda to promote his causes and making careful allegiances with journalists such as J.L. Garvin, John St Loe Strachey and John Jaffray. Consequently, one might expect the Birmingham satirical press to have been part of this effective media-management and to have been as acerbic towards his enemies as Chamberlain himself famously was. But, in reality, for the majority of Chamberlain's career, the Birmingham satirical press was vehemently opposed to Chamberlain, constituting a thorn in his side in the very heart of his 'duchy' of the West Midlands. This article will explore the long-term reasons why the satirical press in Birmingham was so prolific and so enduring, in contrast to most provincial cities, and also so independently minded that it was prepared to defy the wishes of 'King Joe' for so long. In doing so, the article will demonstrate the astonishing political culture of the Birmingham press, hitherto ignored by almost all historians, in the age when Birmingham, for the only time in its history, set the tone for the politics of Britain.[3]

The illustrated periodical press was 'read by peers, politicians and the proletariat alike'.[4] It is, however, striking how limited a range of journals are offered for examination in most historical studies of the media.

The predominance of *Punch* as the chief example of Victorian satire, which, on examination of the contemporary media, seems hardly as common as scholars suggest, appears to derive largely from the easy availability of the journal to modern academics.[5] Even today, national journals such as *Moonshine* or *Judy* barely feature in studies of the political culture of the period.[6] Unsurprisingly, therefore, there has been a distinct lack of attention given to the regional satirical press by historians hitherto. Even the accepted scholarly gazetteer of the Victorian satirical press, Vann and Van Arsdel's *Victorian Periodicals and Victorian Society*, includes no references to any of the non-London journals of the periods.

Alan Lee estimates that the number of newspapers and periodicals increased from 109 in 1853 to 230 by 1913. The number of *provincial* magazines trebled between the 1860s and the 1890s. One of the more successful forms was the urban satirical weekly, popular from the 1860s into the twentieth century.[7] They included at least seven *Figaros*, such as the *Thanet Figaro* and the *Tunbridge Wells Figaro*. Many were named after small, bothersome animals, such as the *Chorley Weasel* (1881–83) or Cambridge's *Wasp* (1891). As early as 1887 the *Journalist* noted that there were several long-lived provincial journals that rivalled the London press. Among these were singled out Glasgow's *Bailie*, Liverpool's *Porcupine* (1860–1915) and Manchester's *City Lantern* (later the *City Jackdaw*) (1874–84). In Birmingham, it noted that there were, unusually, two journals, both of which were over ten years old at the time of writing.[8] These magazines went on sale each Friday, offering 16 pages (almost half of them filled with advertisements) for one penny. Aimed at the provincial flâneur, they included poetry and illustration but their mainstay was satire and comment on local politics and public affairs in a knowing tone of voice, and treated the city as 'an arena of pleasure'.[9] Making use of the increasingly cheap means of reproducing line illustrations and, by the turn of the century, photographs, the provincial satirical press was able to appeal both to middle-class audiences, with their reports of respectable pastimes and prominent personalities, but also to the lower classes with their disrespectful tone, abundance of visual images and doggerel verses.[10] Keen to promote themselves as the most popular satirical magazine in the town and thereby to impress potential advertisers, they often boasted about the numbers they sold, relating stories about disappointed people not being able to buy their copies. The *Dart*, in 1880, claimed to have 20,000 readers, and in March told of a crowd at New Street Station 'who called for "the Dart", "the Dart" and, when they were told there was "no Dart", they would not be comforted'.[11] The comic tone of the publication meant that such a claim did not have to be defended literally.

In the article on 'Provincial Humorous and Satirical Journals' in 1887, the *Journalist* noted that 'nearly every large town in the kingdom has a record of brilliant but evanescent journals of this kind which have died rapid deaths, not without the regrets both of contributors and of the reading public'.[12] In common with Manchester journals such as the *Sphinx* and the *Shadow*, several other satirical journals were published in Birmingham from the mid-1860s onwards, but they were all short-lived. The *Third Member*, enlivened by cartoons by G.H. Bernasconi, Birmingham's finest cartoonist, was an election publication and ran for 16 issues in 1867–68. The following year *Brum*, also featuring cartoons by Bernasconi, also ran for 16 issues. The *Lion* appeared in the first half of 1877 and Harry Furniss had his first illustrations published in it before moving to London to work for *Punch*. Though it announced that it was committed to no party, affiliations of the *Lion* were Conservative.[13] It was uncomplimentary about 'the Republican Chamberlain' and referred to the preparations for Gladstone's visit to the town in May 1877 as 'fuss and tomfoolery'.[14] It, too, employed Bernasconi as its cartoonist. Declaring that it would switch from a weekly to a monthly in autumn 1877, the *Lion* in fact ceased publication altogether. The *Magpie* lasted about as long in 1880, and in 1885–86 the *Cracker*, owned by W.B. Vince, a solicitor, and illustrated again by Bernasconi, did its bit to raise the political temperature during the period between the two fiercely fought elections of December 1885 and July 1886. There was also, in 1886–87, the *Freelance*, with cartoons by E.C. Mountford, who later found work on the *Dart*, which managed 12 months of existence. There were also the *Speaker*, the *Midland Parliamentary* and the *Grasshopper* in this period. The Black Country produced the *Lantern* and Bernasconi published his own illustrated journal, the *Camera*.

These magazines are rare (only a few individual copies of the *Owl* and the *Dart* are held at the British Library), difficult to interpret without a detailed knowledge of local politics and personalities, and they changed ownership frequently. Writers came and went, some jumping from one magazine to another. 'Old Sarbot', for example, contributed at different times to both the *Gridiron* and the *Owl*. Our knowledge of those who owned and wrote for the satirical journals of nineteenth-century Birmingham is highly incomplete. The various editors and journalists who worked for these magazines never identified themselves in their own pages, and most proprietors preferred to remain in the shadows. A small ad in an early issue of the *Town Crier* in 1861 declared, 'Wanted by everybody – the name of the editors of the *Town Crier*.'[15] Nevertheless, it seems likely that the main contributors were experienced journalists who had worked for either the *Birmingham Daily Post* or the *Birmingham Daily Gazette*. Though the owners and writers preferred to conceal their true identities, they were known within journalistic circles in Birmingham and occasionally identities were leaked by rival magazines.

Inevitably, then, such periodicals were deeply rooted in their own journalistic milieu, sharing stories, writers, readers and even editors between them. In many cases they cannot be read except in the context of their rivals in the wider Birmingham press. In 1870 the *Town Crier* poked fun at the proliferation of local newspapers – 'Sunday Syringe, Tuesday Twopenny (out on Wednesday), Saturday Stirrup, Sixpenny Scorpion and Halfpenny Gazette (out every five minutes)'.[16] Yet the journals' parodies of newspaper conventions – archaeological excursions, medical conferences, notes and queries, court circulars and so on – could not be appreciated without prior knowledge of the format. They illustrate the complexities of the ever-changing politics, culture and daily life of Birmingham and its 'multiple centres' at the time when the city reached its peak in national influence and reforming zeal, not least by the fact that three of the Birmingham journals lasted far longer than the average lifespan of these publications: the *Town Crier* (1861–1903); the *Dart* (1876–1911) and the *Owl* (1879–1911).[17] They also reveal a surprisingly ambivalent attitude towards the most successful politician to emerge from Birmingham, Joseph Chamberlain, and depicted the former three-time mayor in such a manner, which, we believe, contributed to his consistently negative portrayal in almost all the national satirical periodicals; a remarkable fact given his leadership of one part of the Unionist alliance and the Unionist affiliations of most of the national press.

Birmingham had established a strong and vibrant press by the later eighteenth century, even if it was one sharply divided on religious and political grounds.[18] Asa Briggs has shown how in the 1820s periodicals such as the *Birmingham Review* and the *Birmingham Reporter* asserted that Birmingham's political and cultural life was as rich and full as anything in London.[19] Birmingham's satirical press goes back at least to the *Monthly Argus and Public Censor*, edited by Joseph Allday, which, according to Briggs, 'anticipated the popular appeal of late-nineteenth century sensationalism within a framework of local scandal and gossip'.[20] Briggs might well be right about the strength of Birmingham's political culture, but that was not necessarily the perception, either locally or nationally. In its first edition in August 1829 (which ran to no less than 48 pages), Allday's editorial was keen to challenge 'the universal charge preferred against [Birmingham] of being the Boeotia of England', that is, a place of low intelligence and little culture.[21]

The driving force of Allday's publication were Juvenal's lines from *Satires* I:

> Difficile est saturam non scribere, nam quis iniquae
> Tam patiens urbis, tam ferreus, ut teneat se ...
> (It is hard not to write satire, for who is so tolerant of the unjust city, so steeled, that he can restrain himself ...)[22]

That is, so full is the town of corruption and hypocrisy, pauperism and newfangledness, that the observer cannot refrain from putting pen to paper, even if he is more inclined to righteous indignation than to humour. Later periodicals would learn to use humour and parody more adeptly to lobby for reform.

The *Argus* was a Peelite Tory publication, giving voice to Birmingham Anglicans worried by the growing power of the Birmingham Political Union. Volume 5 number 3, which appeared in April 1833, for example, refers to the 'virulent lying of [BPU] supporters', complains that Thomas 'Attwood [was] again at his dirty work' and described the BPU's newspaper as a 'lying one-eyed Journal'.[23] The same number also carried the first political cartoon (entitled 'Argus sketches') to appear in Birmingham (Fig. 8.1). The *Argus* began the tradition of failing to name

Figure 8.1 Anti-BPU cartoon, *Monthly Argus and Censor*, vol. 5 no. 3, April 1833

its editors and authors and using nicknames, initials and innuendo in order to spread its views of the great and the good in Birmingham and the Black Country. It was less adept at concealing its victims. The *Argus* eventually folded under a series of libel cases, brought when physical violence and imprisonment had failed to silence its editor.[24]

There is an evident gulf between the embittered, rejectionist rhetoric of Joseph Allday's *Argus* and the cheerier entertainment offered by the mid-century journals. Yet the *Argus* did help to set many of the ground rules for its successors. What we might call the 'gossip column' was introduced here, a collection of short, speculative statements, prefaced by 'We hear that ...' or 'It is not true that ...' Second, the *Argus* established the importance of the pronoun 'we' in the editorial. Satire of this kind, and particularly when it seeks a political goal, does so by recruiting its readers into the endeavour, by persuading them to endorse its opinions. The enterprise becomes collective by such means. Third, Allday's Juvenalian approach underlined the urban nature of the satirical periodical. The city, with its constant innovation and teeming life, was itself the most eye-catching character in the genre.

The eventual successor to the *Argus* was the *Town Crier*, which appeared monthly from 1861 until 1889, and then weekly until its demise in 1911 (Fig. 8.2). Named in honour of Jacob Wilson, Birmingham's last and well-loved town crier, the journal cost two pence at first for eight pages (which was prohibitively expensive), but increased to 12 pages in its second edition. By issue 9 in September 1861 it had grown to 16 pages with a full-page cartoon, but the cost had risen to an eye-watering 3d. Like the *Argus*, the *Town Crier* had to work hard to carve out a niche. It ceased publication in December 1861 and then relaunched in May 1862 as an occasional publication, albeit reduced to 12 pages and without a cartoon.

With its Vergilian quote (in Latin) on the front cover and its range of literary and classical reference within, the *Town Crier* was pitched at an educated and well-read audience, perhaps even an intellectual one. If anything in Birmingham could be said to counter the charge of Boeotian, it was the *Town Crier*. It sought, in the words of Wolff and Fox, to tell 'the city-dweller about himself' but to do so with a certain disdainful *hauteur*.[25] The journal was launched at the instigation of the town's most prominent minister-politician, the prophet of the Civic Gospel, George Dawson, with a full-page report of his lectures in the first issue.[26] The journal was highly critical of the Birmingham Corporation and the other elements of the local establishment, and their resistance to root-and-branch reform. It advocated (as did Joseph Chamberlain himself)

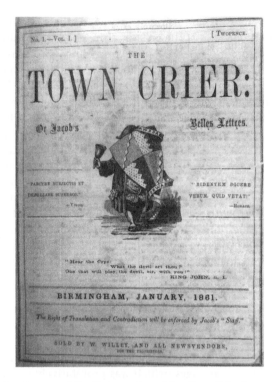

Figure 8.2   Front cover of the first number of the *Town Crier*, January 1861

a wider, more ambitious model of local government than the penny-pinching of the current administration, known as the 'economists'. As early as the second number, the *Town Crier* was promising to 'cleanse the Town Council and polish the Board of Guardians'. It parodied the Tory *Birmingham Gazette* and referred to the eminent Birmingham and Midland Institute as the 'Midland Destitute'.[27]

Typical of its acerbic and insulting style was this response to criticism from the Council: 'The sixty-four communications which, from their indifferent grammar and defective orthography, seem to have emanated from the members of the Town Council, have been cut up into narrow strips, neatly folded and placed in receptacles on Jacob's mantelpiece.'[28] The knowing reader would recognise here a parody of the old 'recommended candidates' lists, which were cut up by electors in just this way.

The *Town Crier* could be seen as the voice of Birmingham Liberalism. Four of the seven men who combined to found the journal – the

Shakespearean scholar Samuel Timmins, the architect John Henry Chamberlain, the Queen's College professor G.J. Johnson and the surveyor William Harris – were members of Dawson's church. The three other men who put money into the venture were Thomas Anderton, who was possibly its first editor, 'Jacob', J.T. Bunce, editor of the *Birmingham Daily Post* and Sebastian Evans, editor of the Tory-supporting *Gazette*, but a friend of Dawson's.

The *Town Crier* epitomised the gleeful anarchy of mid-Victorian periodicals, happily offending all. Having guyed Dawson over his lecturing style and having cheekily written of the glee that publication of its own epitaph would bring, the journal was even unafraid of attacking Joseph Chamberlain himself, when it printed a mock election address from the radical leader:

Fellow men: My heart bleeds for my fellow creatures. It always did bleed; and it will keep on bleeding, I fear, until I'm Prime Minister. I will never rest until every man, woman and child has a vote and then I shall never rest until they vote as they are told i.e. for me.[29]

The *Town Crier* had developed that tone of 'teasing loyalty' as early as March 1874, just as Chamberlain embarked on his mayoralty. Chamberlain's search for a parliamentary seat having been rejected by the voters of Sheffield, the *Town Crier* welcomed their hero back to Birmingham with affection, mixed with gentle censure:

Joe Chamberlain, my Joe, Josh,
Of the School-Board keep the chair.
Be humble and contented,
In the parlour of the Mayor.
You've now learnt how to cut, Sir,
You're very sharp, I know.
But Sheffield's blades are sharper,
Joe Chamberlain, my Joe.[30]

In 1886, when the Liberal party was fractured by the issue of Irish Home Rule, the *Town Crier* unhesitatingly supported Chamberlain and became the Liberal Unionist periodical, alongside the *Birmingham Post*, Chamberlain's most loyal ally in the press. 'Of Mr Chamberlain's conduct during this, the gravest crisis of modern times ...' it pronounced, 'Jacob cannot speak too highly.'[31] Unfortunately this declaration of partisan support led to a significant decrease in reporting of political issues.

The journal began printing portraits of Unionist statesmen and covering pantomimes and local events. Full-page political cartoons began to appear but these were frequently defensive or obscure in their references. One wonders at how the magazine retained a readership, but, as Henry Miller has recently observed, 'the longevity of later [periodicals] ... suggests that the reduction of costs, resulting from improvements in printing technology, the abolition of the last of the taxes on knowledge, and the long-term fall in the paper prices, were crucial in making cheaper comic periodicals commercially viable'.[32]

A change of ownership in 1889 led to the relaunch of the magazine as a weekly from January 1890. The editorial announced,

> To the Public:
> The moment has arrived when it is deemed desirable to convert the *Town Crier* from a monthly into a weekly paper. Humorous journals, or journals which pretend to be humorous, are no longer acceptable in monthly form. Their wit and humour (if they have any) have been bottled up too long, and, however well corked, they are apt to become a little flat when produced for consumption. *The Town Crier* has had a fairly long life, considering how brief is the career of some newspapers. It was started some twenty eight years ago... it has never had to sustain an action for libel, and, although, no doubt, it has sometimes trod on people's corns, it has done so gingerly.[33]

The relaunch was also marked by the appointment of G.H. Bernasconi as 'cartoonist-in-chief'. The new owner, who has not been identified, soon sold up. In January 1892, the *Dart*, which took a keen interest in the fortunes of its rival, announced that, after passing through the hands of a number of owners, the main proprietor was J. Moore Bayley, a solicitor and long-standing champion of the Conservative cause in Birmingham. It added that Moore Bayley was joined in this enterprise by seven other shareholders, among them the publisher, Fred Mundy, the advertising agent, Alfred Gilbert, Bernasconi and a journalist, Lewis James (both of whom contributed). The *Dart* declared that the *Town Crier* was Moore Bayley's 'toy newspaper', which had 'got him into no end of hot water – more than he would ever need for a shave'.[34] In August 1892 the *Dart* took great pleasure in making public that its rival had had five editors in two years and enquired, 'Why don't they stay with you, Mr Bayley?'[35] It seems that a few years later Mundy took control and, in 1902, sold the magazine, but it is unclear who owned the magazine in its final years.

Along with Chamberlain and the Birmingham Liberal Unionists themselves, the *Town Crier* gradually evolved into a supporter of imperialism and Lord Salisbury's administrations, a vocal critic of increased expenditure by the council and a critic of budding Labour politicians such as Eli Bloor and W.J. Davis. By the turn of the century the *Town Crier* was unrecognisable as the progressive publication it had once been. It became critical of what it perceived as excessive council spending, such as the building of a workhouse infirmary.[36] In short, it ended up inhabiting the very position, that of the 'economists', that it had been established to discredit in 1861. When it closed in October 1903, the *Dart* noted that 'it ought not to have been started as a weekly' and that 'it had no support'.[37]

The *Dart* was launched on 28 October 1876 as a weekly, competitively priced at one penny, and owned for the first two years of its existence by Bernard Hackney, a barrister and the son-in-law of the Liberal organiser Francis Schnadhorst. Under Hackney, the *Dart* featured a masthead on which the figures of John Bright, Phillip Muntz and Joseph Chamberlain supported a crest, engraved by John Swain, on which was emblazoned the Birmingham motto 'Forward' (Fig. 8.3). It described

Figure 8.3 Masthead of the *Dart*, 4 November 1876

itself as 'a journal of sense and satire' and addressed its first editorial 'To Our Readers': 'Our natural modesty prevents us boasting or even insinuating that this weeks' *Dart* is by any means superior to any previous number of the same publication ... we shall not shrink from throwing "darts" at existing evils.'[38]

The magazine was the first Birmingham periodical to feature a regular cartoon (with a double-spread at Christmas), drawn by the up-and-coming Bernasconi, and, as Matthew Roberts has described late Victorian cartooning, these focused 'just as much, if not more on politicians and their shortcomings'.[39] The *Dart's* editorial tone was mainly critical of public officials, with gossip about bankruptcies, squibs and puns, even ones aimed against the recently retired mayor:

> Nursery Rhymes – Joseph Chamberlain MP (when young)
> How did the little busy C.
> Improve each shining hour
> And gather money all the day
> Till it came all in a shower.[40]

Yet its political preferences were clear enough in images such as that of the famous Christmas Special in December 1876, showing Chamberlain's achievement in transforming Birmingham over the past three years as the equivalent of the transfiguration scene which concluded every Victorian Christmas pantomime (Fig. 8.4).[41]

The classified columns frequently carried adverts for meetings of the Birmingham Liberal Association and a black-bordered page was given over to an 'In Memoriam' for George Dawson on 6 December 1876. Most venom in its early years was aimed at the Conservative *Birmingham Gazette*, shown in cartoons as 'Mrs Aris', a generic old lady in a bonnet. In January 1877, under a column entitled 'Advice Gratis', it reported a fictional conversation between 'Mrs Aris' and an elderly interviewer in which 'Mrs Aris' claimed, 'I'm a-going to start a comic paper', but she refused to divulge the title.[42]

Birmingham's longest-lived weekly newspaper, *Aris's Birmingham Gazette*, founded in 1741, was an inevitable target for the satirists for its conservatism, longevity and its popularity (both with readers and advertisers). Joseph Allday had earlier referred to the paper as 'my grandmother', and berated her double standards: 'She exclaims against the sin of prize-fighting, and the next hour copies from a ballad-monger's catch-penny "the full and true account of the fight".'[43]

Figure 8.4 'Grand Transformation Scene: A Vision of the Future', the *Dart*, 23 December 1876

On 30 December 1876, the *Dart* increased in size, stating that 'we had not intended making the change until the beginning of the year, but the favours of our subscribers and advertisers, unexampled so far as Birmingham is concerned, have necessitated an immediate alteration'. It was therefore after some success that in October 1877 the *Dart* was bought for £75 by Robert Simpson Kirk, a journalist of Scottish origins who had for a time worked on the *Birmingham Evening Mail*.[44] At first Simpson Kirk employed R.H. Sadler as editor, but it seems likely that he later took on this role himself. Unable to make the paper pay, in May 1879 Simpson Kirk accepted £50 for the copyright from Joseph Rowlands, another of the town's solicitors, who was also a prominent figure in the Birmingham Conservative Association. The response of the Birmingham Liberals to this troubling development was the launch, at the beginning of 1879, of the *Owl*, which declared in August that the *Dart* was 'practically under the control of the Conservatives'.[45] The *Gridiron* was soon describing its rival magazine as 'the Dirt'.[46] Rowlands was wise enough not to allow his new acquisition to come out for the Conservatives immediately in the great Liberal stronghold of Birmingham, but instead allowed it to proclaim itself an independent Liberal publication. It was also expanded to 16 pages from 7 June 1879. In 1879 it responded to criticism of its treatment of Chamberlain's election to the Commons with the disingenuous rebuttal, 'it is because we love Mr Chamberlain that we chide him so much' and attempted to distract attention with a slur on its main rival: 'The editor of the *Owl* is at heart a Tory. He was for some years the London correspondent of the *Daily Gazette* and, in his time, took delight in making fun of Birmingham Liberalism and its leaders.'[47] In August 1879, however, the *Dart* published the first outright attack on Chamberlain and the Liberal Council: 'The town finds itself burdened with a costly street improvement scheme which is so far a financial failure.'[48] The Liberal *Gridiron* responded immediately: 'So Sandy has at last like – very like – the ass in the lion's skin in the old fable, thrown off the mask of independent Liberalism and come out in his true colours of blatant Toryism' , claiming four weeks later that 'the fact is, the Tory "Truthful" has been a Tory in disguise from the commencement'.[49]

The consequences of this defection were soon seen. The *Gridiron* gleefully reported that Simpson Kirk, who was also the Birmingham correspondent of the liberal *Daily News*, had been excluded from a Liberal meeting in North Warwickshire because 'Mr Schnadhorst had a political grudge against him'.[50] Kirk was then sacked as correspondent for the *Daily News*, having apparently broken a pledge to the *Daily News* that the *Dart* would continue to support the Liberal party and its local leaders in Birmingham, and the job was given instead to a brother of Bernard Hackney. The *Owl* reported that 'it would appear from an article in last week's *Dart* that ... something has been done to disestablish the Scotch *Kirk*'.[51]

After this drama, the *Dart* became the scourge of Chamberlain who, together with his close supporters Schnadhorst, Bunce, Timmins, J.H. Chamberlain, Jesse Collings, William Kenrick and the minister Henry Crosskey, it accused of running the town like a private fiefdom. It lamented the lack of a following for Chamberlain's Liberal rival Skirrow Wright and that George Dixon had effectively retired into private life. The magazine frequently made use of phrases such as 'a ruling clique', 'this modern star chamber', 'Communistic Liberalism', 'Mr Chamberlain's self-glorification', 'Joseph the Great' and so forth. The cartoons became increasingly aggressive, culminating on 17 October 1884, when E.C. Mountford depicted 'King Joseph' welcoming 'King Mob', while a crowd stormed a walled enclosure in

Figure 8.5 Anti-Chamberlain cartoon from the *Dart*, 17 October 1884

the background: a clear reference to the Aston riots earlier that month (Fig. 8.5).[52]

The *Dart*, now subtitled the *Birmingham Pictorial*, continued to claim that it was non-partisan ('the only organ of the middle party in the town') and promoted the 'Municipal Reform Association' rather than the Conservatives directly.[53] The *Owl* dismissed the MRA in 1879 as 'an association that isn't likely to exist for long'.[54] It was quite right – no more was heard of the MRA after that year.

By the late 1880s Simpson Kirk was offering payments for ideas for cartoons and annual subscriptions to the magazine for a supply of local items. The *Dart* finally became an overtly Conservative publication in the 1890s, but one that still criticised Chamberlain, even as he grew closer to the Tories. It condemned old-age pensions as 'tommy rot' and called for a reduction in income tax, paid jury service and, curiously, 'a Conservative government conceding reasonable home rule'. With the decline of popular passion for politics in the later 1890s, the *Dart* managed to struggle on, its dull pages enlivened only by lively reports of the progress of Aston Villa and the Warwickshire cricket team.

In its declining years the *Dart* embraced Tariff Reform after 1903, subjecting its readers to articles and cartoons on the subject for two years in the run up to the general election. Having experienced damascene conversion, the *Dart* warmed towards Chamberlain. In July 1903 it announced that 'Mr Chamberlain should be thanked for the stimulus his ideas have given'.[55] By September it printed a full-page article praising 'Mr Chamberlain's scheme'[56] and the following month it portrayed Chamberlain as a masterful 'modern St. George' slaying the dragon of 'foreign tariffs'.[57] By the time of the 1906 election, it openly stated that 'The *Dart* wishes Mr Chamberlain and his party success.'[58] The electoral rout of Tariff Reform (outside Birmingham, at least) did little to stem the stream of cartoons by E. Huskisson, bemoaning the fate of the British workman and/or John Bull in the hands of 'the dumper', 'free imports', faithless 'C.B' (Campbell-Bannerman) and 'Cobdenism'. Chamberlain's 70th birthday celebrations were reported in enormous detail and in the gossip column 'what we hear' it reported, without the slightest degree of shame for its previous treatment of the MP for West Birmingham, 'not even Mr Chamberlain knew that Birmingham thought so much of him'.[59] It refused to speculate on Chamberlain's health after his withdrawal from society in July 1906, blandly stating that 'his recovery continues to progress satisfactorily'.[60]

The *Dart*, by now increasingly concerned with reporting weddings in a regular 'Ladies' column' and printing photographs of the Birmingham YMCA, unsurprisingly opposed Lloyd George's 'People's Budget' (but seemed to enjoy ribbing the Lords as well), but did not live out the year of crisis in 1911. The last edition appeared on 1 September 1911 (complete with a photographic portrait of the Lord Mayor's Secretary), with a simple notice that 'The *Dart* will not be published after this date.'[61]

If Chamberlain did not like what was said about him in the *Dart*, then he could be more than satisfied (at least until 1886) with the *Owl*, which proudly proclaimed that 'there shall be no mistake from the first as regards one thing – the *Owl* is a Liberal bird' set up by his own supporters.[62] The *Owl* began life on 30 January 1879, subtitled 'A Journal of Wit and Wisdom', and priced at one penny (Fig. 8.6). It also poached Bernasconi (whom the *Gridiron* called 'the only cartoonist that Birmingham yet turned out') from the *Dart* by offering to double his salary.[63] Towards the end of its first year the magazine had changed hands, but not political affiliation. Its new editor was the Liberal loyalist Bernard Hackney. According to the *Dart*, he employed H.J. Jennings and Frank Heath as writers. The new journal had 16 pages, and two full-page cartoons, in direct competition with the *Dart*, which only had 12 pages and a single cartoon for the same price.

The *Owl* was aimed at a slightly more highbrow audience with a promise to devote 'considerable attention to Literature and the Arts',

Figure 8.6   Front cover of the *Owl*, 25 February 1886

with frequent theatrical profiles of figures such as Sarah Bernhardt and a series of spoofs entitled 'Brummagem Shakespeare'. A regular column entitled 'Stage Whispers' featured (mainly London) theatrical gossip. The *Owl* was not afraid to be critical of Gladstone, especially during the Egyptian war of 1882, when it openly supported John Bright's resignation on moral grounds.[64]

The *Owl* was no mere mouthpiece for the Birmingham Liberal Association, however, and began to express concerns over the undemocratic nature and excessive power of the 'Six Hundred' on the BLA's committee. On 11 February 1881, it published an editorial decrying the Coercion Bill, which had Chamberlain's support. On 7 July 1882 the *Owl* carried an opinion piece entitled 'The Caucus', in which it opined that

It is to be feared that the earnest, free thinking Liberal has fallen upon evil days. Only in a very recent chapter for history he was compelled to take 'a pig in a poke' – to vote for a candidate whose name he may never have heard, but who was invited by 'a large and influential body of voters' nobody knew whom, to 'stand in the Liberal interest'.[65]

The *Owl* complained that the Liberal voter was invited to become enthusiastic about some person whose only recommendation was a 'long purse, not closed':

> If the continuance of power in the hands of his party is the object of a Liberal, then he should indeed be thankful for the caucus, but if he think that liberty of thought and expression is above this, then even clever Mr Schnadhorst's admirable defence will hardly satisfy him that the system of which Mr Schnadhorst is the centre, is quite an unmixed blessing.

All this was accompanied, as was usual, with a satirical song entitled 'The Caw Cuss' Cuss':

> All hail to our great Secret-ary!
> All hail to our chief, chick-a-leary!
> When King Joseph requires
> He touches the wires
> And no hand is raised to 'contrary'[66]

This was followed by a reference to 'Birmingham's Tammanny' (a reference to the corrupt New York political system run by William 'Boss' Tweed) on 4 August 1882. In December 1883, a familiar theme emerged. There had already been criticism of Chamberlain's failure to address the needs of the working classes during the eviction of the slum-dwellers in the Improvement Scheme area. The lack of social reform in the Liberal programme for 1884 was reflected in a cartoon showing Chamberlain, Bright and Dilke proudly presenting their 'measures for the next session' while a working family pointed to their empty hearth (Fig. 8.7).[67]

The independent position of the *Owl* was demonstrated by the editorial attitude to the press. It referred to the *Birmingham Gazette* as 'our frothy friend' and the *Birmingham Post* was frequently criticised for printing private correspondence.[68] On 15 September 1882, the *Owl* noted that 'In Birmingham the Democratic, there are two powers that

Figure 8.7 'While the grass grows, the steed starves', the *Owl*, 28 December 1883

rule the roost – the Caucus and the Press.' It was careful not to criticise Chamberlain directly, however, but, as he was now at Whitehall as President of the Board of Trade, it was possible to blame the poor state of Liberal politics in the city on his successors in the Council and the Birmingham Liberal Association. Nonetheless, it was a style of 'machine politics' or 'wire-pulling' closely associated with Chamberlain himself.

Although we cannot be certain about the original owners, by 1880 the *Owl* was owned by Houghton and Hammond, who sold it to J. Hardy Summers, who took over the editorship from Hackney. By 1884, the new proprietor was William Byron Smith. By the time of Chamberlain's resignation from the third Gladstone administration over the issue of Irish Home Rule, the *Owl* argued that Gladstone's treatment of Chamberlain had been 'pitiful and ungenerous in the extreme'.[69] In the previous December, the *Owl* had depicted him as coming to the rescue of Gladstone and the moderate Liberals, as they were beset by the wolves of 'Parnellism' and 'Tory Democracy'.[70] During the debate on the Home Rule Bill, however, it, like most of the Liberal press, was faced with an agonising choice.

The Liberal split of 1886 marked a dramatic shift in the allegiances of much of the political press across the country. As Edward Porritt noted 20 years later, 'after the Home Rule split, the Liberal sustained disastrous losses in the newspaper world'.[71] *Sell's Dictionary of the World's Press* commented in 1893 that 'no political question which ever agitated the country brought more changes in the press world than the controversy in regard to Home Rule for Ireland'.[72] Stephen Koss has stated that, in 1886, 'the weight of newspaper opinion had indeed abruptly shifted'.[73] *The Times'* fearsome denunciation of Home Rule, which it described as 'disastrous' as soon as it was announced, was part of a wider revolt against Gladstone's new policy by the London print media.[74] This 'shift', together with the advent of the 'new journalism' at around the same time, marked a significant change in the political allegiances and character of the British publishing industry.[75]

On 8 April 1886 many parts of the print media, previously Liberal, announced their resistance to Home Rule. Joseph Chamberlain was clearly concerned about the attitude of the press, as he had clearly taken a canvass of opinion, before he met Arthur Balfour to discuss Liberal–Conservative cooperation in March. As he reported, perhaps optimistically in order to convince the Conservatives of the Unionist Liberals' strength, 'the great bulk of the London newspapers – of course, I am talking of the Liberal newspapers, including *Reynolds's* and *Lloyd's*, are going against Home Rule, but the majority of the country newspapers are evidently preparing to support Gladstone'.[76] This opinion appeared to be confirmed next month when W.S. Caine informed Chamberlain that 'all the London working men's weekly papers are with you strongly'.[77] Chamberlain corresponded with John Jaffray to ensure that the *Birmingham Post* stayed loyal, but there is no evidence in his papers of any concerns about the allegiances of the satirical press.

The *Owl*, like so much of the Liberal press, attempted to avoid making a definite choice between Chamberlain and Gladstone, at least for the time being. It printed a provocative cartoon by R. Hill showing Chamberlain throttling Gladstone during the Westminster manoeuvres against the Home Rule Bill, but made no other comment (Fig. 8.8).[78] The following week, under the title 'Mr Gladstone and Mr Chamberlain', it deplored Gladstone's willingness to listen to Parnell and John Morley, but not Chamberlain and the other 'Liberal seceders'.[79] After the Bill's defeat, it commented that 'we must most cordially approve of the conduct of Mr Chamberlain and his friends' and showed Chamberlain bowling out Gladstone with a ball marked '30'.[80] The calling of the general election, however, changed their opinion significantly. On 2 July, under the title 'The Duty of the Hour', the *Owl* opined that 'the Chamberlain party are planning an unfair game: helping the Tories ... for purposes which are neither honourable or sincere'. Later in the same edition, in one of the regular 'Hoots of the week', it commented that 'really Mr Chamberlain is testing the respect of his friends to snapping point'.[81] The following week, the *Owl* described Chamberlain's election speeches as 'vitriolic, vicious, vulgar and wholly contemptible'.[82] By the end of the year, Chamberlain's character itself was the target for speculation, as the *Owl* asked the loaded question, 'is Mr Chamberlain an "honest" statesman or is he the veritable Artful Dodger of modern politics?'[83]

Lynda Nead, Peter Bailey and Peter Burke have recently established that the consumption of visual culture was at the heart of all aspects of Victorian life.[84] Politics, especially local politics, was no exception, and James Thompson has demonstrated how visual images became increasingly significant in the electoral campaigns of the late nineteenth century.[85] Chamberlain was frequently depicted by the

Figure 8.8 Cartoon from the *Owl*, 21 May 1886

Owl's cartoonists with the same vitriol hitherto employed by the *Dart* (Fig. 8.9). While John Tenniel, Linley Sambourne and Harry Furniss of *Punch* may have introduced a more respectful approach to their depiction of politicians, to suit their increasingly 'respectable' readership, the Birmingham satirical press retained the instincts of Gillray and Rowlandson, at least as far as Chamberlain was concerned.[86]

In Birmingham by 1886 therefore, two of the three illustrated satirical periodicals, for different reasons, were lining up to attack Chamberlain's integrity, his motives and, most of all, his consistency. We believe that these thorns in Chamberlain's side had a direct impact on the national media's visual depiction of Chamberlain. In the first instance, the *Dart* was the first periodical to regularly depict Chamberlain wearing a monocle, and later, an orchid in his buttonhole.[87] In this way, Chamberlain used props to create an 'immediate physical recognisability'.[88] Harry Furniss, chief cartoonist for *Punch*, commented on how 'it was impossible to make Mr Chamberlain heroic' and relied on the visual signifiers provided by the Birmingham periodicals.[89] It

Figure 8.9 Chamberlain depicted as 'the Demon' from the opera of the same name by Rubinstein, the *Owl*, 27 July 1888

is also striking how frequently the visual metaphors used to criticise Chamberlain by *Punch* and other leading satirical journals, such as *Judy*, *Fun* and *Moonshine*, were based on original cartoons in the *Dart* and *Owl*: Chamberlain as autocrat commanding other Chamberlains (Fig. 8.10); Chamberlain as a puppet-master (Fig. 8.11); Chamberlain as an unflattering Shakespearean character (Fig. 8.12); Chamberlain as Don Quixote (and his lieutenant, Jesse Collings, as Sancho Panza) (Fig. 8.13); Chamberlain wearing 'a coat of many colours' and 'playing many parts' (both attacks on his inconstancy of political orientation) (Fig. 8.14 and Fig. 8.15). All these visual tropes (and many others), commonly used by the national satirical press after 1886, originated in the pages of the *Town Crier*, the *Dart* and the *Owl*.

Punch, a once radical, but now solidly Unionist publication by this time (just like *The Times* and the *Daily Telegraph*), at first depicted Chamberlain in a relatively uncritical fashion. But when it became clear that Chamberlain was contemplating reunion with the Gladstonian Liberals, they, together with other Tory journals such as *St Stephen's Review*, also began to borrow the visual idioms employed by local critics of the Radical Unionist leader.

Figure 8.10 The *Owl*, 18 March 1887 (left) and *Punch*, 13 January 1904 (right)

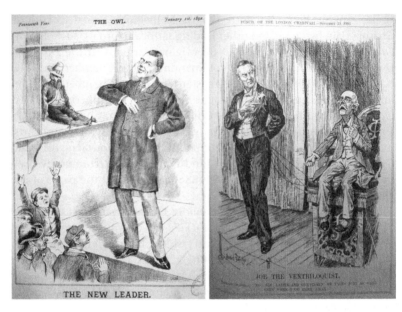

Figure 8.11   The *Owl*, 1 January 1892 (left) and *Punch*, 30 September 1903 (right)

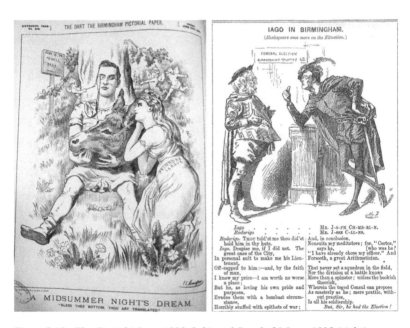

Figure 8.12   The *Dart*, 24 June 1892 (left) and *Punch*, 30 June 1892 (right)

Figure 8.13   The *Dart*, 6 May 1887 (left) and *Punch*, 29 October 1887 (right)

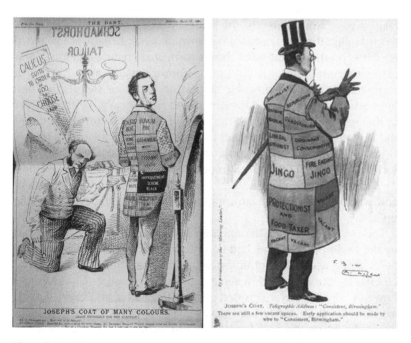

Figure 8.14   The *Dart*, 27 March 1880 (left) and postcard reproduction of cartoon from the *Morning Leader*, 1906 (right)

Figure 8.15 The *Owl*, 13 September 1889 (left) and postcard reproduction of cartoon from the *Morning Leader*, 1906 (right)

Phillipe Vervaecke has recently noted that *Punch*, 'a journal whose readers were almost exactly the same as the Conservative electorate, tended to use the same caustic irony towards Chamberlain' as his harshest critics on the Liberal side.[90] It was particularly telling that *Punch* was extremely hostile towards the Tariff Reform campaign after 1903, with cartoons vilifying Chamberlain appearing far more frequently than ones attacking Campbell-Bannerman and the Liberals. To this chorus of disapproval was also added the voice of Francis Carruthers Gould of the *Westminster Gazette*, founded by George Newnes in January 1893.[91] Gould's determination to expose what he saw as the false promises of social reforms in 1895 led him to pursue Chamberlain with an animosity that was noted by journalists of all shades of the political spectrum and which did the politician long-term damage in the eyes of public opinion.

The *Owl*'s attacks on Chamberlain became ever more scathing, but by the 1890s the magazine had become despondent about Liberal prospects, being decidedly unimpressed by Rosebery and referring to local Liberals as 'the Remnant'. It remained highly critical of Chamberlain, however. The Boer War was described as 'mistaken' and Tariff Reform as 'absurd'. Even Carruthers Gould had shown Chamberlain in a positive light on the occasion of his 70th birthday in July 1906, being congratulated by John Ball. The *Owl* was not prepared to show such magnanimity, however. A series of three scathing articles entitled 'The

Real Mr Chamberlain' appeared throughout July, not even ceasing when news of Chamberlain's illness (in truth his debilitating stroke) seeped out. In them, the *Owl*, discussed 'What has made him famous?' In the first piece, Chamberlain's reputation in his adopted town was discussed and the conclusion reached that 'there are in Birmingham today men who are superior to Mr. C. in any phase of ability', but that they lacked Chamberlain's 'unshakeable belief in his own infallibility'.[92] The second article, a week later, asserted that Chamberlain's reputation in the city was maintained chiefly by nostalgia (something that Chamberlain had exploited on the hustings at both the 1900 and 1906 general elections):

> Today the municipal achievements of Mr Chamberlain are lifted up to a pedestal and all imperfections are obscured by the halo of romance which a quarter of a century has created. This is what we mean by the 'unearned increment' which Mr Chamberlain is now enjoying to the full.[93]

The final article summarised Chamberlain's attributes: 'a pleasant, though by no means overwhelming, share of ability, assurance, fortune, good health, energy and nerve, self-reliance, and glibness of ... speech'. The editorial concluded that 'the support of the Press' (especially the local press) 'disguised [his] defects' and 'accorded verbatim reports to some of the stalest piffle ever heard from a platform and labelled it a "Great Speech"'. It concluded by summarising the attitude of many Liberals towards Chamberlain by the end of his career: 'Luck – down right luck, had done more for Mr Chamberlain than sound judgement.'[94]

It was the *Owl* that finally broke the respectful silence that followed Chamberlain's retreat from the political stage and questioned the official version of an attack of gout, which had been used to deflect attention from his incapacity.[95] In an article titled 'Is Mr Chamberlain ill?' it concluded that 'we fear he must be, seeing the pains some people have taken to convince that he isn't'.[96] Perhaps the removal of Joseph Chamberlain from public life after July 1906 deprived the *Owl* of their chief target, and the leader column was soon reduced to a three-part reflection on 'Sunday morning attire in Birmingham' and endless editorial articles promoting the services of their advertisers.[97] This naturally affected sales, already weakened by the decline in public taste for the satirical press after 1906. Whatever the reason, the *Owl* ceased publication on exactly the same day as the *Dart*, 1 September 1911.

Perhaps the most scurrilous of all the Birmingham periodicals was the *Gridiron* (1879–81; Fig. 8.16). Bernard Hackney, having sold the *Dart* to Simpson Kirk when it was 'fast declining in public favour', shared the duty of ownership with John Skirrow Wright, the wealthy button manufacturer and president of the Birmingham Liberal Association.[98] The *Gridiron* claimed that its first issue cut sales of the *Dart* by 500 and, in 1881, was boasting 5000 readers and relating how its editor had taken pity on a boy selling the *Owl* in New Street and bought up his unsold copies. Referring to Simpson Kirk as 'Sandy' or 'the Truthful' and the *Owl* as 'the Howl', the *Gridiron* had something unfavourable to say about its rivals in every issue. That they were 'dull' and 'dreary', lifted material from other magazines and their cartoons were often unfathomable. The *Dart* ignored its new rival and concentrated its fire on the *Owl*: it was 'the Caucus comic' and made up of 'dreary drivel'.

Hackney was determined to confront the *Dart* (which it sometimes referred to as the 'weekly refuse box') as it sought to attack Schnadhorst's control of the City Council's politics, and, by association, Chamberlain himself. Of Chamberlain, the *Gridiron* took great pride in the impact that he made at Westminster. He was reported as being 'to the fore again' in the Commons, as having 'deservedly attained' a 'high position in municipal and public life'.[99] Shortly after he was appointed President of the Board of Trade in May 1880, it printed a three-column profile of 'Our Junior Member', describing Chamberlain's career as 'one of almost unparalleled brilliancy and unparalleled rapidity'. The piece concluded with a retort to Chamberlain's critics in the Tory press:

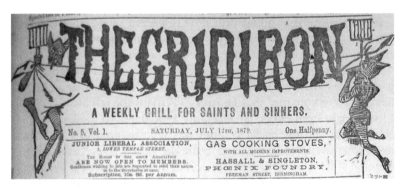

Figure 8.16 Original masthead of the *Gridiron*, 17 July 1879

Probably no living politician has been more persistently and recklessly abused by his opponents than Mr Chamberlain ... Its bitterness, its virulence and vindictive malignity have only served to increase the admiration, to intensify the zeal, and more firmly to unite in his behalf the good opinion of the Party of which he is so distinguished a member, and so competent a leader. May his years be many and his usefulness increase with his years.[100]

Certainly there was much speculation about who actually wrote copy for the *Gridiron*; in August 1879 its editor mischievously announced that a photograph of its staff had been placed in a window in New Street, and that 'we have taken out an insurance policy on the shop window'.[101] *Gridiron* no. 1 appeared on 14 June 1879, sold at one half-penny every Saturday. Its political affiliation was made clear by the appearance of an advert for the Junior Liberal Association. It was subtitled 'A weekly grill for saints and sinners'. The *Dart* took little time in pouring scorn on its new rival, claiming that 'our lively contemporary, the Griller, had a large sale the first day it came out. But the second week the sales had fallen by one half.'[102] The *Gridiron* responded with an article entitled 'The Poison and the Antidote':

It used to give us great pain to see political poison in the shape of the Dirt sold in quantities about the street, but now that the Arabs sell the antidote i.e. the Gridiron, at the same time as the poison and in much greater quantities than the poison we are satisfied.[103]

Perusal of the only surviving volume of the *Gridiron*, in the Birmingham Midland Institute, confirms the judgement of Fraser, Green and Johnston that 'journalism of the periodical press was a fundamentally provocative and reactive medium, initiating dialogue on topics of the day, and demanding a response'.[104] The *Gridiron* was keen in attacking all of its rivals, referring to 'the marvellous propensity of the *Owl* for lying',[105] criticising the Tory *Birmingham Gazette* as 'Mrs Aris, the Old Lady of High Street'[106] and finally rebutting the accusations of swift decline. It claimed that it had achieved success in its first month, 'never before exampled' in Birmingham, 'except in the early days of the *Dart*, when it was under other and better management'.[107] The *Gridiron's* direct approach did not go uncriticised, and in July 1879 it was forced to defend 'the strength of language' that the new journal used.[108]

Hackney and Wright were undeterred. The following issue contained verses headed 'What became of the *Dart* and the *Owl*?':

> We poked our fire with that *dart*
> Which blunted well its point
> We put that *owl* upon our Grid
> And pulled him joint from joint.[109]

A week later, it commented that 'It seems as though we should have to set apart a space every week for the purpose of correcting Sandy's errors',[110] and in the next issue, 'the *Dirt* describes itself as a journal of sense and satire. It should be called a satire on sense and then it would be nearer the truth.'

> *A pen'orth of 'Dirt'*
> Filled with nonsense sixteen pages
> Twisted facts and praise of self
> Liberal boobies, Tories sages –
> Anything to rake in pelf.
> Spice it well with Latin grammar
> Pilfered thoughts and notes inert.
> Schoolboy French and Celtic stammer
> That's a pennyworth of *Dirt*
> Notes and news so old and musty
> That they scarce keep one awake;
> Ancient jokes, time-worn and dusty
> San'd for old acquaintance sake
> Wretched, tasteless illustrations –
> Vulgar, silly, false or pert;
> General air of strong libations –
> That's a pennyworth of *Dirt*.[111]

The *Gridiron* was clearly successful at first, as it enlarged to 12 pages from 3 July 1880, began to feature occasional cartoons and doubled its cover price to a penny. Although difficult to be sure, there is no evidence of the *Gridiron* surviving after 1882. Either Hackney was unable to sustain two journals, or perhaps the venomous tone and aggressive media battles in its pages were not to the taste of Birmingham's periodical buyers, or too much to the taste of Birmingham's lawyers. It is a pity, for to the modern reader it is an astonishing insight into the ferocity of Victorian provincial satire.

Francis Gould once wrote that there was 'a large portion of the public which is more susceptible to impressions conveyed in pictorial form than to more subtle appeals to the intellect involved in reading and digesting statements, statistics and arguments'.[112] Cordery and Meisel agree, to some extent, seeing the cartoons as a 'visual cognate to verbal communication'.[113] The popularity and the longevity of the three main Birmingham satirical journals indicates an enduring regionalism in the British political culture in the era before the First World War, contrary to the views of those such as Luke Blaxhill, James Vernon and Matthew Roberts, who assert that that British political culture was 'nationalised' after the early 1880s.[114] And the *Dart*, the *Town Crier*, the *Owl* and the *Gridiron* did not merely reflect popular attitudes. In the Birmingham satirical periodicals of the late Victorian period, there is much evidence to support James Thompson's recent observation that 'the development of the press was integral to accounts of "public opinion"'.[115] As Asa Briggs commented in his study of the *Argus*, 'the press influenced the public, but it also mirrored the public'.[116]

The constant vilification of Joseph Chamberlain's career and character in the satirical press of Birmingham created an impression of inconstancy and unreliability that was further developed by cartoonists such as Francis Partridge in *Punch* and Carruthers Gould in the *Westminster Gazette*. By 1906, across the country and even to some extent inside Birmingham, a large portion of the public had lost faith in 'Pushful Joe' and his promises. Of course, the presence of Chamberlain on the national stage probably helps to explain the unique fecundity of the Birmingham satirical periodicals and their equally unique longevity (and their eventual decline mirrors that of Chamberlain himself). Ultimately, however, the unremittingly negative depiction of Chamberlain in two of the Birmingham periodicals was such that the national satirical press, including some Unionist journals, followed their lead in questioning Chamberlain's character, in particular his trustworthiness and constancy. Many explanations have been advanced to explain why Chamberlain's national career ended in such failure, in marked contrast to his career in Birmingham, where he is still revered to this day. It is possible to argue that the vibrant local political culture that Chamberlain's prestige helped to create in Birmingham in the 1870s set such a tone in their later treatment of the former mayor that, by 1903, in Beatrice Potter's words, 'no one trusts him, no one likes him, no one really believes in him'.[117]

Notes

1. Our particular thanks for his invaluable help in identifying the ownership of the Birmingham periodicals is due to Stephen Roberts, honorary research fellow in history at Newman University. Thanks also to Andrew Hobbs of the University of Central Lancashire for identifying many of the non-Birmingham periodicals and to Professor Peter Marsh for his excellent advice and cheerful assistance.
2. M. Conboy, *The Language of Newspapers: Socio-historical Perspectives* (London: Continuum, 2010); J.D. Startt, 'Good Journalism in the Era of New Journalism: The British Press 1902–1914', in J.H. Wiener (ed.), *Papers for the Millions: The New Journalism in Britain, 1850s to 1914* (Westport, CT: Greenwood Press, 1988), pp. 275–303; P. Waller, *Writers, Readers and Reputations* (Oxford University Press, 2006), pp. 83–5.
3. A. Briggs, 'Birmingham: The Making of a Civic Gospel', *Victorian Cities* (London: Penguin, 1965), pp. 239–40.
4. M. Huggins, 'Cartoons and Comic Periodicals, 1841–1901: A Satirical Sociology of Victorian Sporting Life', in M. Huggins and J.A. Mangan (eds), *Disreputable Pleasures: Less Virtuous Victorians at Play* (London: Frank Cass, 2004), p. 124.
5. In her recent article on journalistic networks, Laurel Brake admits that she has relied on the nineteenth-century journals digitised by ProQuest, none of which was published outside London. L. Brake, '"Time's Turbulence": Mapping Journalism Networks', *Victorian Periodicals Review*, 44.2 (2011), pp. 115–27. See also R.D. *Altick, Punch: The Lively Youth of a British Institution, 1841–1856* (Columbus: Ohio State University Press, 1997); P. Leary, *The Punch Brotherhood: Table Talk and Print Culture in Mid-Victorian London* (London: British Library, 2010).
6. The first serious study of *Judy* only appeared in 2013: R. Scully, 'William Henry Boucher (1837–1906): Illustrator and Judy Cartoonist', *Victorian Periodical Review*, 46.4 (2013), pp. 441–74.
7. See for example S. Gunn, *The Public Culture of the Victorian Middle Class: Ritual and Authority in the English Industrial City, 1840–1914* (Manchester University Press, 2000); H. Miller, 'The Problem with *Punch*', *Historical Research*, 82.216 (2009); A.G. Jones, 'The *Dart* and the Damning of the Sylvan Stream: Journalism and Political Culture in the Late-Victorian City', *Victorian Periodicals Review*, 35.1 (2002); J.K. Walton, 'Porcupine', *Dictionary of Nineteenth Century Journalism*, online edition, http://c19index.chadwyck.co.uk/home.do.
8. R.R. Dodds, 'Provincial Humorous and Satirical Journals', *The Journalist*, 20 May 1887, pp. 93–4.
9. P. Joyce, *The Rule of Freedom: Liberalism and the Modern City* (London: Verso, 2003), p. 204.
10. See E. Jacobs, 'Disvaluing the Popular: London Street Culture, "Industrial Literacy" and the Emergence of Mass Culture in Victorian England', in D.N. Mancoff and D.J. Trela (eds), *Victorian Urban Settings: Essays on the Nineteenth Century and Its Contexts* (London: Routledge, 2011), pp. 89–113; B. Reay, 'The Context and Meaning of Popular Literacy: Some Evidence from Nineteenth Century Rural England', *Past and Present*, 131 (1991), pp. 89–129.

11. *Dart*, 19 March 1880. The figure is unlikely as Ellegard estimates that, in 1870, *Fun* sold 20,000 copies nationally and even *Punch* only sold 40,000. A. Ellegard, 'The Readership of the Periodical Press in Mid-Victorian Britain', *Victorian Periodicals Newsletter*, 3 (1971), p. 20.

12. Dodds, 'Provincial Humorous and Satirical Journals', p. 93.

13. It was a frequent ploy of the new periodical or newspaper to declare political neutrality in its first issues, as a means to garner a wider initial readership. Such independence rarely continued for long.

14. *Lion*, 23 May 1877.

15. *Town Crier*, vol. 1 no. 3, March 1861. In 1879, for example, the *Owl* announced that its new editor was Mr John Smith of 491 and a half, Hagley Road. The *Owl*, 30 October 1879.

16. *Town Crier*, October 1870.

17. L.K. Hughes, 'Sideways! Navigating the Material(ity) of Print Culture', *Victorian Periodicals Review*, 47.1 (2014), p. 2.

18. J. Money, *Experience and Identity: Birmingham and the West Midlands, 1760–1800* (Manchester University Press, 1977), ch. 3, 'The Newspapers of the West Midlands', pp. 52–79.

19. A. Briggs, *Press and Public in Early Nineteenth-Century Birmingham* (Oxford: Dugdale Society, 1949).

20. Briggs, *Victorian Cities*, p. 210.

21. *Monthly Argus & Public Censor*, August 1829, p. 1.

22. Juvenal, *Satires*, I.30–1.

23. Unsurprisingly, Briggs notes that the *Argus* 'acquired a considerable notoriety in libel actions'. Briggs, 'Press and Public in Early Nineteenth-Century Birmingham', p. 13.

24. Anon., *The Birmingham Monthly Argus exposed by a person fully acquainted with the whole machinery (public and private) of that base publication* (Birmingham, 1834).

25. M. Wolff and C. Fox, 'Pictures from the Magazines', in H.J. Dyos and M. Wolff (eds), *The Victorian City: Images and Realities*, vol. 2 (London: Routledge and Kegan Paul, 1973), p. 559.

26. Briggs, *Victorian Cities*, pp. 297–8; *Town Crier*, vol. 1, no. 1, January 1861.

27. *Town Crier*, vol. 1, no. 2, February 1861.

28. *Town Crier*, vol. 1, no. 4, April 1861.

29. *Town Crier*, vol. 24 no. 25, November 1885.

30. *Town Crier*, vol. 13, no. 3, March 1874.

31. See the two-page editorial 'The Crisis', *Town Crier*, vol. 25, no. 12, July 1886.

32. H. Miller, 'John Leech and the Shaping of the Victorian Cartoon: The Context of Respectability', *Victorian Periodicals Review*, 42.3 (2009), p. 280.

33. *Town Crier*, vol. 29, no. 6, 3 January 1890.

34. *Dart*, 15 January 1892.

35. *Dart*, 12 August 1892.

36. See *Town Crier*, 19 April 1890.

37. *Dart*, 26 October 1903.

38. *Dart*, 28 October 1876.

39. M. Roberts, 'Election Cartoons and Political Communication in Victorian England', *Cultural and Social History*, 10.3 (2013), pp. 371.

40. *Dart*, 22 June 1877.

41. *Dart,* 'Double Christmas number', 23 December 1876.
42. *Dart,* 6 January 1877.
43. *Monthly Argus & Public Censor,* August 1829.
44. Aled Jones incorrectly states that the *Dart* was 'started by Robert Simpson Kirk in October 1876' and that the early editions were 16 pages long. In fact the *Dart* was only eight pages long until 23 December 1876, when it expanded to 16 pages for the 'Double Christmas number', before shrinking to 12. Jones, 'The *Dart* and the Damning of the Sylan Stream', pp. 177–8.
45. *Owl,* 14 August 1879.
46. *Gridiron,* 12 July 1879.
47. *Dart,* 20 July 1879.
48. *Dart,* 2 August 1879.
49. *Gridiron,* 2 August 1879; *Gridiron,* 30 August 1879.
50. *Gridiron,* 9 August 1879.
51. *Owl,* 16 August 1879.
52. *Dart,* 17 October 1884. For detail on the Aston Riots see P. Marsh, *Joseph Chamberlain: An Entrepreneur in Politics* (New Haven: Yale University Press, 1994), pp. 174–6. The *Dart* took great pleasure in illustrating the subsequent court case, showing Chamberlain giving evidence in a manner that made him appear to be on trial, *Dart,* 28 November 1884.
53. *Dart,* 23 August 1879.
54. *Owl,* 14 August 1879.
55. *Dart,* 10 July 1903.
56. *Dart,* 4 September, 1903
57. *Dart* 26 October 1903.
58. *Dart,* 12 January 1906.
59. *Dart,* 13 July 1906.
60. *Dart,* 17 August 1906.
61. *Dart,* 1 September 1911.
62. *Owl,* 30 January, 1879.
63. *Gridiron,* no. 7, 26 July 1879.
64. *Owl,* 21 July 1882.
65. *Owl,* 7 July 1882.
66. Ibid.
67. *Owl,* 28 December 1883.
68. *Owl,* 18 August 1882.
69. *Owl,* 16 April 1886.
70. *Owl,* 11 December 1885.
71. E. Porritt, 'Party Conditions in England', *Political Science Quarterly,* 21 (1906), p. 215.
72. *Sell's Dictionary of the World's Press* (London, 1893), quoted in S. Koss, *The Rise and Fall of the Political Press in Britain. Volume 1: The Nineteenth Century* (London: University of North Carolina Press, 1981), p. 286.
73. Koss, *The Rise and Fall of the Political Press in Britain. Volume 1,* p. 286.
74. *The Times,* 9 April 1886.
75. Analysed most recently in: K. Jackson, *George Newnes and the New Journalism in Britain, 1880–1910: Culture and Profit* (Aldershot: Ashgate, 2001); M. Hampton, *Visions of the Press in Britain, 1850–1950* (Chicago: University of Illinois Press, 2004); Waller, *Writers, Readers and Reputations*; Conboy,

The Language of Newspapers; J.H. Wiener, *The Americanisation of the British Press, 1830s–1914: Speed in the Age of Transatlantic Journalism* (Basingstoke: Macmillan, 2012).

76. Balfour to Salisbury, 24 March 1886, in R. Harcourt-Williams (ed.), *Salisbury–Balfour Correspondence*, 1869–1892 (Hertford: Hertfordshire Records Society, 1988), p. 138.

77. Caine to Chamberlain, 17 April 1886, Joseph Chamberlain Papers, Cadbury Research Room, University of Birmingham, JC5/10/4.

78. *Owl*, 21 May 1886.

79. *Owl*, 28 May 1886.

80. *Owl*, 11 June 1886.

81. *Owl*, 2 July 1886.

82. *Owl*, 9 July 1886.

83. *Owl*, 31 December 1886.

84. L. Nead, *Victorian Babylon: People Streets and Images in Nineteenth Century London* (New Haven: Yale University Press, 2000); P. Bailey, *Popular Culture and Performance in the Victorian City* (Cambridge University Press, 1998); P. Burke, *Eyewitnessing: The Use of Images as Historical Evidence* (London: Reaktion, 2001).

85. J. Thompson, '"Pictorial Lies?" – Posters and Politics in Britain c.1880–1914', *Past and Present*, 197 (2007), pp. 177–210.

86. G. Cordery and J.S. Meisel (eds), *The Humours of Parliament: Harry Furniss's View of Late Victorian Political Culture* (Columbus: Ohio State University Press, 2014), pp. 4–11; Miller, 'The Problem with *Punch*', pp. 283–302; Roberts, 'Election Cartoons and Political Communication', p. 374.

87. *Dart*, 25 November 1876; *Dart*, 28 December 1883.

88. L. Hamilton, 'The Importance of Recognizing Oscar: The Dandy and the Culture of Celebrity', *The Center & Clark Newsletter*, 33 (1999), p. 4.

89. H. Furniss, *Some Victorian Men* (London: Jon Lane, 1924), p. 203.

90. P. Vervaecke, 'La "caricature au vinaigre": Francis Carruthers Gould et Joseph Chamberlain, 1895–1907', *Revue Française de Civilisation Britannique*, 16.2 (2011), pp. 27–42.

91. Jackson, *George Newnes and the New Journalism in Britain*, p. 129.

92. *Owl*, 6 July 1906.

93. *Owl*, 13 July 1906.

94. *Owl*, 20 July 1906.

95. See Marsh, *Joseph Chamberlain*, pp. 647–9.

96. *Owl*, 28 September 1906.

97. *Owl*, 31 August, 7 September, 14 September 1906.

98. *Gridiron*, 23 August 1879.

99. *Gridiron*, 16 August 1879.

100. *Gridiron*, 3 July 1880.

101. *Gridiron*, 30 August 1879.

102. *Dart*, 28 June 1879.

103. *Gridiron*, 2 August 1879; 6 March 1880.

104. H. Fraser, S. Green and J. Johnston, *Gender and the Victorian Periodical* (Cambridge University Press, 2003), p. 1.

105. *Gridiron*, 21 June 1879.

106. *Gridiron*, 28 June 1879.

107. *Gridiron*, 12 July 1879.
108. *Gridiron*, 26 July 1879.
109. *Gridiron*, 2 August 1879.
110. *Gridiron*, 9 August 1879.
111. *Gridiron*, 16 August 1879.
112. F.C. Gould, *Manuscript Autobiography*, vol. 16, f. 386, House of Lords Record Office.
113. Cordery and Meisel (eds), *The Humours of Parliament*, p. 35.
114. L. Blaxhill, 'Electioneering, the Third Reform Act and Political Change', *Parliamentary History*, 30.3 (2011), pp. 343–73; J. Vernon, *Politics and the People: A Study in English Political Culture, c.1815–1867* (Cambridge University Press, 1993), p. 337; M. Roberts, 'Election Cartoons and Political Communication', p. 390.
115. J. Thompson, *British Political Culture and the Idea of 'Public Opinion', 1867–1914* (Cambridge University Press, 2013), p. 245.
116. Briggs, 'Press and Public in Early Nineteenth Century Birmingham', p. 6.
117. *The Diary of Beatrice Webb*, reprinted in B. Webb, *Our Partnership*, ed. Barbara Drake and Margaret I. Cole (London: Longmans and Green, 1948), p. 125.

9
Birmingham's Protestant Nonconformity in the Late Nineteenth and Early Twentieth Centuries: The Theological Context for the 'Civic Gospel'

Andy Vail

This chapter considers the strength and significance of Protestant nonconformity in the city of Birmingham in the late nineteenth and early twentieth centuries, during the height of Joseph Chamberlain's influence.[1] The key issues usually identified by students of faith communities in nineteenth-century Birmingham tend to centre around Birmingham's role in the national debate over education, the significance of nonconformists such as George Dawson, R.W. Dale and the Chamberlains in the development of the 'Civic Gospel' or 'Municipal Gospel' and the influence of key Quaker families such as the Sturges and the Cadburys. This chapter will seek to identify the general strength and significance of nonconformity in Birmingham during this period, and the impact of the Chamberlains on nonconformity in Birmingham.

By the 1870s the most significant dissenting ministers in Birmingham were Dr R.W. Dale (Carrs Lane Congregational), George Dawson (Church of the Saviour, Unitarian) and Dr H.W. Crosskey (Church of the Messiah, Unitarian). Also of significance in the city were John Jenkin Brown, minister of Wycliffe Baptist Church, Charles Vince, who succeeded George Dawson at Mount Zion Baptist Church, the Chartist turned Baptist minister Arthur O'Neill (d. 1896) and John Skirrow Wright, a teaching elder at the Chartist-influenced Baptist Church in Hockley, the People's Chapel.[2] Birmingham was not unique in having prominent nonconformists in positions of civic power and responsibility in the late nineteenth and early twentieth centuries – other examples include the Rowntrees in York, and the Gurneys and Colmans in Norwich.

George Dawson was one of Birmingham's best-known nineteenth-century nonconformists. He originally came to Birmingham in 1844 as pastor of the Mount Zion Baptist chapel, Graham Street, but in 1847, having been ejected from there for preaching Unitarianism, he went on to found the Church of the Saviour, in Edward Street, which became famous as the home of the 'Civic Gospel', under Dawson and his successors, by whom it was conducted as a 'free Christian' or Unitarian chapel. In 1851, at the height of Dawson's popularity, there were sittings for 1400, and an estimated average congregation of 1300, but it declined following his death in 1876, and the main Sunday congregation had fallen to 483 by 1892. The chapel continued to decline and closed at the end of 1895.

The Baptist turned Unitarian Dawson has largely been credited with the concept of the 'Civic Gospel' or 'Municipal Gospel' which actively supported and encouraged the municipal reforms of Chamberlain and his colleagues in Birmingham. What was significant here was not an attempt to put Christian ethics into action in wider society, examples of which can be found through much of church history, but rather an organised attempt to use the powers of a local authority to implement the social implications of Christianity, particularly in respect to providing for the poorer in society. Vince, Dale, Crosskey, Jenkin Brown and Skirrow Wright were also enthusiastic advocates of the doctrine, and Dale and the Baptists were able to reframe it in a format more acceptable to the evangelicals. The Quaker and Adult-School pioneer Alderman William White was also an enthusiastic supporter of Chamberlain's reforms. It should be stressed, however, that this ideal, although always associated with Birmingham, had been previously seen in Glasgow where, following lobbying by Liberal and United Presbyterian town councillors, municipal control of the water supply was achieved in 1855 and of the gas supply in 1869, following on from their previous success in restricting alcohol licences from 1850.[3] As control of the water supply had been debated in Glasgow as early as 1819, it is interesting to speculate whether this had come to Dawson's attention during his time as a student at Glasgow University.[4]

Arguably the most significant free church in Birmingham in the nineteenth century was Carrs Lane Congregational Church, a thriving city centre church from which many other churches in the Birmingham area were successfully planted. Its pastors had a national as well as local prominence. John Angel James, minister of Carrs Lane from 1805 to 1859, played a key role in the movement which resulted in the foundation of the Congregational Union of England and Wales in 1832, which he served as Chairman in 1838, and also of the Evangelical Alliance, founded in 1846. James's co-pastor and then successor, R.W.

Dale, minister from 1854 to 1895, had an even higher profile. In 1869 he was appointed chairman of the Congregational Union of England and Wales. He also edited *The Congregationalist* from 1871 to 1878 and served as moderator of the first International Congregational Council, held in London in 1891.

A *Birmingham Daily Mail* report recalled an 1872 school board meeting with Charles Vince, George Dawson and John Skirrow Wright. It described how 'the three men who sat side-by-side on that summer day in 1872 are those only in Birmingham whose loss has occasioned great demonstrations of public grief since the death of John Angel James in 1859'.[5] However, all three of these prominent figures in local and national life had died by the end of the nineteenth century: Vince in 1874, Dawson in 1876 and John Skirrow Wright in 1880, leaving the way open for new leaders for a new century.

Birmingham had played a significant role in the debates surrounding the faith element in proposals to introduce universal primary education. In 1867 an Education Aid Society was established in Birmingham. The leading Anglican (and future archbishop) Dr Temple spoke at the inaugural meeting and leading local nonconformists such as Chamberlain and Dale were prominent members. Their focus was on raising awareness and fundraising.[6] Many leading figures in the Society went on to be part of the National Education League founded in Birmingham in 1869 under the leadership of George Dixon. This was, however, the outworking of a split in opinion as the Education League advocated a national system of rate-aided non-denominational or 'unsectarian' schools.[7] In response, the local Anglicans formed a 'Birmingham Education Union' in 1869, which advocated an extended denominational system.[8] This was not, however, a simple Anglican/Tory versus nonconformist/ Liberal debate. Some leading nonconformists, such as Dale, were not happy with the approach of the National Education League, which they saw as too secular: they advocated a non-denominational Christian basis to education instead.[9] This view was also maintained by the evangelical Quakers, George and Elizabeth Cadbury, who, in the early twentieth century, donated Bournville Infant and Junior Schools to the Birmingham School Board on the understanding that they would provide education on a non-denominational Christian basis.

The Education Bill presented to parliament by W.E. Forster in 1870 was a compromise which appeared to anger all parties. It left much of the decision-making as to whether to raise rates for denominational schools, and whether to charge for schooling, to the local school boards.[10] In April 1870 a protest signed by 5173 nonconformist ministers was handed to the government by the honorary secretaries of Central Nonconformist Committee: Birmingham ministers Dale (Congregationalist) and Crosskey (Unitarian).[11] As a consequence of the national education debates and new powers being granted to school boards, school board elections became more significant. In 1870 in Birmingham, the denominational representatives were successful, resulting in grants to denominational schools, but in 1873 the Liberals and nonconformists were triumphant.[12] However, despite the strength of their political influence, the Quakers and Unitarians remained numerically small minorities, and the Unitarians were excluded locally and nationally from many significant organisations (such as the Evangelical Free Church Councils) for reasons of theology. As Unitarians denied the Trinity, one of the basic tenets of the Christian faith, the Chamberlains would always have been viewed as outside of the theological mainstream by other nonconformists. Birmingham Quakers during this period, due to the Cadbury influence, were still predominantly evangelical and therefore still part of mainstream nonconformity, despite the theologically liberal drift of their movement nationally.

An immediate problem faced by any historian of faith communities is how to effectively measure their size and influence. Different types of faith community left different types of records. Records of rites of passage such as baptisms, weddings, funerals and confirmations can be helpful indicators, but comparison between denominations can be difficult; for example it is not helpful to compare Anglican and Baptist baptismal numbers, when one baptises children and the other practises believers' baptism. Neither is an Anglican electoral roll really the equivalent of free-church membership as it is theoretically open to anyone who lives in the parish to sign up, while free-church membership requires both a profession of faith and commitment to the local church.

Religious belief is almost impossible to quantify, but for nineteenth-century Birmingham and Aston there are the results of both the *Census of Religious Worship* of 1851 and the *Birmingham News* Religious Census of 1892, which give two valuable snapshots of religious observance. The former was held across Great Britain on Mothering Sunday (30 March) 1851. It was the first serious modern attempt to discover levels of British attendance at places of worship. Its aim was to assess the amount of available space in churches and chapels across the country and the numbers actually attending. Numbers attending Sunday Schools were also counted. A separate education survey also enumerated the numbers attending schools, including Church of England National Schools, nonconformist British Schools and other denominational schools.

The census was not a measure of church affiliation, nor of the nature of personal religious belief. A major purpose was to discover 'how far the means of Religious Instruction provided in Great Britain during the last fifty years have kept pace with the population during the same period, and to what extent those means are adequate [for] the increased population of 1851'.[13] For this reason the census also sought to identify changes in provision since 1801. It was an attempt to discover whether the various denominational church extension programmes had kept pace with the doubling of the population in this period, and to highlight any inadequacies or over-provision.

No attempt was made to quantify the number of 'twicers', that is, those attending more than one service on the same day, whether the second service be in the same church or chapel or elsewhere. There was, however, space on the returns to give average figures as well as those for the census Sunday. In producing his report that accompanied the census returns, Horace Mann's approach to this problem was to assume that half the afternoon congregation had previously attended in the morning and that two thirds of the evening congregations had already attended worship that day. He did, however, concede that this had brought complaints of bias from the Wesleyans that their best-attended services were being reduced by two-thirds as compared to the least well-attended Anglican services.[14]

Including estimates for 'defective returns', it revealed nearly 11 million attendances in England and Wales, 48.6 per cent of which were in Anglican churches and 51.4 per cent in other places of worship.[15] This was the first clear evidence that the Church of England no longer held a dominant position – a result that was hotly contested by some Anglicans. The Anglicans had over 5,000,000 attendances, the only other denominations with more than 1,000,000 were the Wesleyan Methodists and the Independents. Next came the Particular Baptists[16] and the Primitive Methodists. The Roman Catholics were down in seventh position with 383,630 attendances at 570 places of worship. It also showed noticeable regional variations in the levels of attendance and in the levels of support for each of the major denominations.

Hugh McLeod has noted local factors such as many in the West Midlands blaming Mothering Sunday for low attendances.[17] He, however, went on to argue that the figures for major towns, including the West Midlands, were largely confirmed by broad similarities with what he calls the 'miniature religious census' of 1881, when local newspapers organised enquiries in about 80 English and Scottish towns and cities.[18] However, in Birmingham, the *Birmingham News* census was not conducted until 1892. In Birmingham there were some noticeable differences between the two censuses, particularly significant was the fact that the 1892 census showed more people attending nonconformist places of worship than Anglican, a reversal of the situation in 1851.[19]

McLeod's study of the 1851 census reveals the West Midlands as having a lower percentage of the population attending worship, as compared with the East Midlands which reported one of the highest. Birmingham and Coventry had attendances 30 per cent lower than the surrounding countryside, but the Black Country returns varied from town to town. He also compared the attendances across 19 English towns and cities in 1851 with the results of the various local censuses in the 1880s and 1890s: Birmingham was 18th out of 19 in 1851, and 19th in the later censuses (although the Birmingham census was later than the others). By contrast, Wolverhampton remained in ninth place on both occasions. The census returns for the Birmingham area have been studied in detail by Robson, who helpfully compared the published census report with the original returns. He identified that the Birmingham census figures may be abnormally low in 1851 due the decline of over 1100 in Wesleyan Methodist membership since 1847 as a consequence of local dissention, presumably related to the Wesleyan Reform agitation.[20] Where the reformers were now attending, if anywhere, and if such gatherings were counted, is not clear. Aitken reveals other errors, such as the Birmingham Bull Street Quaker Meeting being counted twice and a rural Roman Catholic Church that ended up among the Birmingham returns.[21] Nevertheless the results appear to be broadly consistent with other sources.

The 1892 census was organised by the *Birmingham News*, with the costs being met by the evangelical Quaker philanthropist George Cadbury.[22] It was held on 30 November 1892, this time deliberately avoiding church festivals. It appears to have been professionally organised, with the numbers not being counted by clergy or church secretaries but by over 500 assistants recruited for the task.[23] Undenominational services, informal Sunday afternoon meetings and even an open-air service at Aston Hall were all counted. Although precise comparison is not possible as the boundaries were not identical, the 1892 survey appears to show a success story for the churches in that in a period in which the city's population had more than doubled, there was an increase of about 6 per cent of the population attending worship compared to 1851. Once estimates had been made for the number of 'twicers', it appears that about a third of the population were attending at least one act of worship, and more than half of school-age children were attending Sunday School.

However, there were some interesting denominational variations compared with 1851. The biggest surprise was for the Anglicans who no longer had the majority of attenders. If the total attendances for Birmingham, Aston and Kings Norton in 1851 are compared with those for the enlarged Birmingham with Aston Manor in 1892, the Anglicans' accommodation for worshippers had doubled, but their attendance 'market share' was down from 49.7 per cent in 1851 to 38.6 per cent. Roman Catholic attendance had increased, presumably as a consequence of Irish immigration, but had only reached five per cent. Among old dissenters, Presbyterian, Baptist and Congregationalist attendances had more than doubled, thus maintaining their percentage of attenders. The Quakers had more than tripled their attendance; largely a reflection of the success of the Adult-School movement promoted by the Sturges and Cadburys across the city. But even that increase gave them only three per cent of attendances. All three Methodist connections had managed to maintain their position too. Among the more theologically liberal Unitarians there had been a decrease to just 1.7 per cent. The 1851 census recorded five Unitarian congregations with 1852 attendants at the largest services. The 1892 *Birmingham News* religious census also showed five congregations but a reduction to 1313 attending. Based on these figures, they dropped from the seventh largest denomination to the thirteenth, falling behind the Methodist New Connection, Primitive Methodists, United Methodists, Presbyterians, Quakers and Salvation Army.

Other non-trinitarian groups established in Birmingham included Mormons, Swedenborgians, Spiritualists and both factions of Christadelphians, overall the non-trinitarian worshippers had reduced from 5.5 per cent to 3 per cent. The largest percentage rise in attendances came in newer trinitarian movements such as the Churches of Christ, the Christian Brethren and the Salvation Army, and the growth in the number of non-denominational missions, such as the Birmingham City Mission, the Boatmen's Mission, the Railway Mission and the Medical Mission. Added together they represented over 12 per cent of attendances compared to 3 per cent in 1851. This means that the attendances of the churches of Old and New dissent had grown at the same speed as the population and thus maintained their share of attendances; the only major changes were the drop in Anglican attendance and increase in attendance at non-denominational missions and churches from the newer movements of around 10 per cent.

There are some puzzling aspects to these statistics: Why had the predominantly evangelical Anglicans failed to keep up with the rate of population growth, as the evangelical free churches had done? Some have blamed it on the poor leadership of the octogenarian Bishop of Worcester, or on the absence of clear local leadership: the Bishop was in Worcester, the Archdeacons in Coventry: the highest local office was the rural dean of Birmingham, which was combined with a parish role as vicar or rector.[24] There appeared to have been a fair amount of mission effort: a Birmingham Church Extension Society had been founded in 1865, and the number of Anglican churches and missions doubled since 1851. Theological divisions within the Church of England may have been a factor; however, Anglo-Catholicism had made few inroads into Birmingham Anglicanism as yet, with only about six high church incumbents in place, so the churches remained predominantly evangelical. Pew rents may have had an impact as only 7 of the 57 Anglican churches had completely free sittings.[25]

Another possibility is that it was more difficult for a centrally organised denomination to respond quickly to population growth than a congregationally organised one such as Baptists or Congregationalists, but then the more centrally organised Roman Catholics and Wesleyan Methodists appear to have managed it.

Although the nineteenth century was largely an era of cooperation and growth among Birmingham's churches, there was some conflict. Wrottesley Street Protestant Chapel, in connection with the 'Protestant evangelical mission and electoral union' of London, was purchased and opened by the anti-Catholic preacher William Murphy in September 1867, a few months after his preaching had occasioned the Birmingham 'Murphy riots'.[26] The establishment of Roman Catholic Bishops in England in 1850, including a Bishop of Birmingham, had provoked some anti-Catholic hostility, but that was nothing compared to the activities of William Murphy. In 1867 he came to national attention after a series of anti-Catholic lectures in Wolverhampton led to such disturbances that the Lord Mayor had to ask the Government for protection and advice. After he delivered an anti-Catholic lecture in Birmingham, during which he called the Pope 'a rag and bone gatherer in the universe', there was a riot, led by Irish immigrant labourers, and the crowds which gathered in the streets the next day were estimated at between 50,000 and 100,000. After considerable property damage, the mayor was forced to supplement his police force with some 400 soldiers (including 100 cavalry) and a force of some 600 special constables. Murphy only acted more defiantly and provocatively by saying that he was willing to risk his life for the cause of truth and liberty and that 'Popish stones would let him see what Popery was'. Murphy's supporters went on to attack a Catholic chapel and loot houses. In 1869, Murphy was arrested to prevent him attending a meeting in Birmingham Town Hall on Irish Disestablishment, addressed by Joseph Chamberlain.[27] More typical of this period was the interdenominational cooperation among most of the Protestant churches in nineteenth-century Birmingham such as in support of short-term non-denominational missions. These included Dwight Moody and Ira Sankey's mission in Bingley Hall in 1875 for a fortnight which claimed 4400 converts. R.T. Booth's 'gospel temperance' mission of 1882 combined evangelism and temperance, with its organisers claiming 50,184 new pledges for the period May–June 1882.[28] In 1888 they conducted a further mission in Summer Hill from which many conversions, restorations and 1000 temperance pledges were claimed, and a new successful adult Bible class launched.[29] They remained active in the city for some years with Cadbury family patronage, conducting 11 'Tent Missions' in Birmingham in 1900.[30] 1904 saw the Torrey/Alexander mission in the Bingley Hall, which also claimed thousands of converts.[31] This mission also had Cadbury support: Helen Cadbury went on to marry Alexander after meeting him while she was counselling new converts at the mission.[32]

One particular reason why the Birmingham church attendance figures had remained strong were national movements which were particularly strong in Birmingham: the Adult School movement and the Brotherhood and Sisterhood or Pleasant Sunday Afternoon Movement. The significance of both movements numerically can be lost in the statistics where they tend to be treated as additional early morning or afternoon services. However, both the fact that afternoon service attendance had more than doubled from 1841 to 1892, and the large attendances at many of the meetings shows the effectiveness of the Brotherhood/PSA movement in the period.

As Birmingham grew in size and significance it began to host national church conferences. In 1839 Birmingham hosted the Congregational Union's Autumn Meetings, which was the first time they had been held outside of London. Birmingham hosted them again in 1861 and 1897. Birmingham went on to host the Baptist Assembly for the first time in 1876, the Free Church Congress in 1895 and 1906 and the National Brotherhood Conference in 1913. Birmingham was also significant for publishing: the pastor of Frederick Street Strict Baptist chapel, J.T. Dennett, was editor of the *Gospel Standard* from 1884 to 1891.[33] Similarly, the Churches of Christ *Ecclesiastical Observer* (later the *Bible Advocate*) was edited by David King in Birmingham from 1876. The Churches of Christ opened their book room in Birmingham in

1903, which developed into their publishing house, the Berean Press. Birmingham was the home of the *Christadelphian* magazine from 1868, edited by J. Roberts, and the city went on to become the main British centre of Christadelphian printing.

Of greater significance, perhaps, was the founding in the city of theological and missionary training colleges: Spring Hill Congregational College was opened in 1830, and remained in Birmingham until 1885, when it relocated to Oxford as Mansfield College. Handsworth Wesleyan Theological College, in Friary Road, was opened in 1880. In 1903 George Cadbury donated one of his homes, 'Woodbrooke', to become a Quaker settlement and training college in Selly Oak. Selly Oak soon became a national centre for missionary training as each of the major free churches, as well as the Anglicans, opened training colleges there.

The 1890s saw a noticeable increase in free-church cooperation, nationally and locally. The Free Church Council Movement grew out of an invitation to the Congregationalist, Guinness Rogers, to write an article for the *Methodist Times* in 1890 advocating a free-church congress. The proposal was well received by representatives of Old and New Dissent alike and the First free-church congress was held in Manchester in November 1892. One of the key speakers at the Congress was the Wolverhampton Congregationalist Dr Charles Berry. On the occasion of the visit of the Evangelical Free Church Council Conference to Birmingham in 1906, the origins of the national movement were described as follows:

> In consequence of the Home Rule split in 1886 Free Churchmen were compelled to find some other basis for united action remote from the debatable ground of politics. But it was not until seven years later that any definite step was taken to reorganize the forces of the Churches.[34]

This therefore implies that the Liberals Home Rule split in which Chamberlain played a significant role was responsible for the breaching of the relationship between political Liberalism and nonconformity, causing the free churches to have to establish new forms of collective representation.

The 1906 article went on to explain that in Birmingham, following the 1892 religious census, George Cadbury invited all evangelical free churches to cooperate in house-to-house visitation: an act which led to the formation of a Birmingham and District Evangelical Free Church Council in November 1893.[35] This had come about following a February

1893 conference of free churchmen in Birmingham: George Cadbury served as president, and other key local participants included Dale and Revd F. Luke Wiseman of the Wesleyan Central Hall. At the meeting Cadbury had proposed a house-to-house visitation scheme which was unanimously agreed. However, when Wiseman proposed a Birmingham Free Church Council, Dale opposed the move, fearing social and political concerns would outweigh spiritual ones. Cadbury and Wiseman's view proved victorious. Cadbury went on to become the first president.

By March 1895, the Birmingham Free Church Council was strong enough to host the Third Free Church Congress. Dr Charles Berry of Wolverhampton presided. At the Congress, Revd Thomas Law was invited to become resident in Birmingham as the organising secretary, with J. Rutherford of the Birmingham Sunday School Union as his assistant. George Cadbury was appointed one of the treasurers. George and Richard Cadbury made available 'a considerable sum of money annually' for the benefit of the movement. Later in that year the name of the movement became the National Council of the Evangelical Free Churches. The following year Law and the central offices relocated to London, again with the Cadburys' financial assistance. On 7 May 1896 a West Midlands Federation of EFCCs was founded at a meeting at the Temperance Hall in Birmingham, bringing together 21 free-church councils across Warwickshire, Worcestershire and South Staffordshire. George Cadbury remained a driving force as treasurer of both the National and West Midlands Evangelical Free Church Councils.

The Birmingham and District Council by 1901 had a total of 140 churches affiliated, representing Baptists, Congregationalists, Presbyterians, Quakers, all the Methodist connections, the Salvation Army and a number of non-denominational missions. Thus by the turn of the century the Free Church Councils, which Chamberlain and his colleagues had inadvertently provoked and from which the Unitarians were excluded by reasons of theology, were firmly established as the representative body of the free churches locally and nationally.

The Labour Church Movement which had been founded in Manchester by the Unitarian minister John Trevor, and sought to combine elements of Christianity and socialism, reached Birmingham in the 1890s. The Birmingham Labour Church was founded in September 1892.[36] They were less than impressed by Chamberlain's political manoeuvres. *The Pioneer* (published by Birmingham Labour Church and Socialist Centre) in 1899 reported that the Revd L.P. Jacks, minister of the Chamberlain's Church of the Messiah in Broad Street, hoped that the new university would train men 'conversant not only with the inner technicalities of business, but with its wider bearings on moral and economic questions', that it would lead citizens to demand

'houses comfortable, streets pleasant, factories slightly, and all their buildings beautiful'. These are beautiful ideals, but when it comes to bold plans for carrying them out, what are the Unitarian leaders of the day doing? This body is, unhappily, like the Liberal party, muzzled by its Whig plutocrats, and by endowed old women ... In this, as in many churches, there is an evil law, the survival of the sheepish.[37]

There was also criticism of Chamberlain's support for the Boer War, as in early 1900 the *Pioneer* reported, 'The Birmingham newspapers have been doing all they can in the last few weeks to increase the war fever, and to fawn at the feet of Chamberlain and the infallible Tories.'[38]

In 1903 the Birmingham Labour Church was joined by another in Bordesley.[39] The hosting of the National Conference of Labour Churches in Birmingham in 1906 appeared to act as a catalyst to further growth, so that by the end of the year there were also Labour Churches in Selly Oak and Aston, plus another in Stirchley by 1911.[40] Earlier scholarship has suggested that nationally 'only a few of the churches survived the First World War'.[41] This was clearly not the case in Birmingham, however, as not only did the Birmingham and Stirchley Labour Churches survive the conflict, but new ones were opened in Erdington and East Birmingham. Barnsby's analysis of reports in the Birmingham Labour paper *Town Crier* from 1919 onwards reveals that the number of Labour Churches in Birmingham grew from these four in 1919 to 16 in 1926.[42]

Unique to Birmingham was the belt of Friends' Institutes across the south of the city, largely financed by the wealth of the Cadbury family. The first day-Adult-School movement the Sturges and Cadburys had helped to establish across the city from 1845 onwards by 1914 had 127 meetings and was therefore attracting far more attenders than the Friends' own meetings for worship.[43] The Adult-School movement was numerically very significant: the city had more Adult Schools than Anglican churches.

After the Unitarians, the strongest of the non-trinitarian groups were the Christadelphians with five ecclesia. Christian Science, Swedenborgianism, Spiritualism and International Bible Students (later known as Jehovah's Witnesses) were also in evidence. The Christadelphians British headquarters was in Birmingham, although by this period they were in two separate factions.

The strength and influence of late nineteenth-century Birmingham nonconformity was also demonstrated in the city's statuary. Royalty predominated in Victoria Square, but Chamberlain Square was dominated by statues of local nonconformists: there was a memorial fountain and spire commemorating Joseph Chamberlain (1880),[44] statues of fellow Unitarians, George Dawson and Joseph Priestley (1874) and a statue of John Skirrow Wright (1883). There was also a statue of Joseph Sturge (1862) at Five Ways, one of his fellow Quaker, John Bright and one of the Congregationalist R.W. Dale in the art gallery and a bust of Dawson in the reference library.[45] It is, however, possibly significant that they all appear to have been erected before the demise of Birmingham's (political) Liberalism following the division over Home Rule in 1886.

The Unitarians and Quakers remained numerically weak but politically significant. In the 20 years of its existence, Dawson's Church of the Saviour had provided Birmingham with 12 local councillors (1847–67), six of whom became mayors. Four members of Dawson's congregation, Samuel Timmins, G.J. Johnson, William Harris and J.H. Chamberlain, were involved in the 1860s in the production of a radical satirical local paper, the *Town Crier*, which actively promoted the ideals of the 'Civic Gospel'.[46] The Unitarian 'old meeting' had also been a source of Liberal councillors.[47] However, the Chamberlain family were active in the Unitarian 'New Meeting' which in 1862 relocated to Broad Street as the Church of the Messiah. Joseph Chamberlain served the church as treasurer for a time and as a trustee, even when, after the death of his second wife his faith and his church attendance decreased. Through the influence of key families such as the Chamberlains, Kenricks, Martineaus, Nettlefolds, Beales and Rylands the Unitarians although numerically weak had a strong civic influence. In the period 1851 to 1908, 16 Quakers had sat on the City Council, of whom seven had been elected mayor.[48] Among the Quakers, the Cadburys, Sturges, Lloyds and Brights had been particularly active in civic life. The People's Chapel (Baptist) in Hockley had provided one Liberal MP (Skirrow Wright) and at least three local councillors in the late nineteenth century.[49] The strength of the 'nonconformist conscience' was demonstrated in the fact that from 1832 to 1886 Birmingham had been represented entirely by Liberal MPs. However, the split in Liberalism over Home Rule resulted in the defection of six of Birmingham's seven MPs to the Liberal Unionists, including prominent nonconformists John Bright, William Kenrick and Joseph Chamberlain, which meant that since 1886 Birmingham had been entirely represented by Conservatives or Unionists. This terminally damaged the Liberal-nonconformist power base by dividing them into opposing camps.

Added to this, after the turn of the century, the Labour party had begun to make inroads on the City Council: by 1911 there were five Labour councillors including the ILP activist and Primitive Methodist local preacher John Kneeshaw, representing Chamberlain's Rotton Park Ward. In the 1911 city council election at least eight Protestant nonconformists were elected: four as Liberal Unionists, one Liberal, two Independent Liberals and one Labour.[50] In a 1913 by-election for the first time a member of a prominent nonconformist family, Clara Martineau, was elected to the city council as a Conservative. By 1915 there were still many prominent nonconformist families represented among the City Councillors and Aldermen including two Cadburys, two Chamberlains, two Martineaus, two Kenricks and a Lloyd, as well as the Quaker, Harrison Barrow and the Baptist, James Homer.[51] However, there was now a clear political division between them. Analysis of the nonconformists elected between 1911 and 1919 (see Appendix) reveals all of the Unitarians now aligned to the Liberal Unionists or Conservatives, the Quakers mostly remaining Liberal (although one Quaker was elected for Labour and the Conservatives respectively). The Methodist representatives were all elected as Labour councillors. Therefore the nonconformist representation on the council was now irrevocably divided across the political parties. The Quaker, Harrison Barrow, was appointed to succeed the Unitarian, Ernest Martineau, as mayor of the city in 1914, but relinquished the role on the outbreak of the war, due to the incompatibility with his faith regarding what he would be asked to do in wartime. Another Unitarian, Neville Chamberlain, went on to serve as mayor of the city from 1915 to 1917.

Numerically, the Baptists, Congregationalists and Methodists had remained the strongest nonconformist communities in Birmingham throughout the late nineteenth and early twentieth centuries. Through the influence of the Chamberlains, alongside other key Unitarian families such as the Kenricks, Martineaus, Nettlefolds and Rylands and Quaker families such as the Sturges, Cadburys and Lloyds, the Unitarians and Quakers, although never numerically strong had made the major contribution to Birmingham's civic life. However, the split in Liberalism, with Chamberlain and his supporters shifting to Liberal Unionism, alongside the rise of Labour, had irrevocably broken the nonconformist–Liberal partnership upon which the Chamberlains and their allies had previously relied for support. It would also appear that by their actions (in dividing Liberalism) the Chamberlains and their allies had inadvertently inspired the creation of the Evangelical Free Church Council movement which was to effectively unite the mainstream trinitarian free churches (but exclude the Unitarians) in future generations.

Appendix – Protestant Nonconformists elected to Birmingham City Council between 1911 and 1919*

James Frederick Homer (LU) Cllr Sandwell 1911–19	Baptist
J.W. Kneeshaw (Lab.) Cllr Rotton Park 1911–19	Primitive Methodist
Tom Hackett (Lab.) Cllr Rotton Park 1913–20	United Free Methodist
Harrison Barrow (Lib.) Cllr St Martins and Deritend 1911–18, Cllr All Saints 1922–25, Cllr Duddeston and Nechells 1926–32	Quaker
George Cadbury Jr. (Ind. Lib./Lab.) Cllr Selly Oak 1911–21	Quaker
William Adlington Cadbury (Lib.) Cllr Kings Norton 1911–19	Quaker
Elizabeth Mary Cadbury (Ind. Prog./Lib.) Cllr Kings Norton 1919–24	Quaker
Adelaide Jane Lloyd (Con.) Cllr Sparkbrook 1919–20	Quaker
Eldred Hallas (Lab.) Cllr Duddeston and Nechells 1911–19, MP 1918–22	Spiritualist
Hubert Kenrick Beale (LU/Con.) Cllr Market Hall 1914–32	Unitarian
Arthur Neville Chamberlain (LU/Con.) Cllr All Saints 1911–20, MP 1918–40	Unitarian
Norman Gwynne Chamberlain (LU) Cllr Small Heath 1911–17	Unitarian
William Byng Kenrick (Con.) Cllr Harborne 1914–30	Unitarian
Ernest Martineau (LU) Cllr St Martins and Deritend 1911–20	Unitarian
Clara Martineau (Con.) Cllr Edgbaston 1913–34	Unitarian

* This list does not reflect political service on Birmingham City Council or the neighbouring UDCs prior to the Greater Birmingham Act of 1911.
Source: C. Phillips, *Birmingham Votes, 1911–2000* (Plymouth: Local Government Chronicle Elections Centre, 2000).

Notes

1. This essay incorporates material extracted from my forthcoming University of Birmingham PhD thesis on 'Birmingham's Evangelical Free Churches and the First World War'.
2. A.S. Langley, *Birmingham Baptists Past and Present* (London: Kingsgate Press, 1939), p. 11; D.M. Thompson, 'R.W. Dale and the "Civic Gospel"', in A. Sell (ed.), *Protestant Nonconformists and the West Midlands of England* (Keele University Press, 1986), pp. 100–3.
3. T.M. Devine and G. Jackson (eds), *Glasgow Vol. 1: Beginnings to 1830* (Manchester University Press, 1995), p. 248; W.H. Fraser and I. Maver (eds), *Glasgow Vol. 2:1830–1912* (Manchester University Press, 1996), pp. 456–8.
4. Fraser and Maver (eds), *Glasgow Vol. 2*, p. 454.
5. E. Edwards, *John Skirrow Wright MP, A Memorial Tribute* (Birmingham: Cornish Bros, 1880), pp. 36–8.
6. A.W.W. Dale, *The Life of RW Dale of Birmingham* (London: Hodder & Stoughton, 1902), pp. 269–71.
7. G.I.T. Machin, *Politics and the Churches in Great Britain* (Oxford: Clarendon Press, 1987), pp. 31–2.
8. Machin, *Politics and the Churches*, p. 32.
9. Dale, *R.W. Dale*, p. 271; Machin, *Politics and the Churches*, p. 32.
10. Machin, *Politics and the Churches*, p. 33.
11. Ibid., p. 35.
12. Ibid., p. 38.
13. Registrar-general to Anglican clergy 13 March 1851: Census of Great Britain, Instructions to Enumerators, Parliamentary Papers XLIII (1851), quoted in J. Aitken (ed.), *Census of Religious Worship, 1851: The Returns for Worcestershire* (Worcester: Worcestershire Historical Society, 2000), p. xi.
14. H. Mann, 'On the Statistical Position of Religious Bodies in England and Wales', *Journal of the Statistical Society of London*, 18.2 (1855), p. 147. Mann's statistics on p. 152 show that the Calvinistic Methodists could also have raised a similar concern.
15. *British Parliamentary Papers*, Session 1852–53, Population 10, 1851 Census of Great Britain (Shannon: Irish University Press, 1970), p. clxxxxii.
16. The survey predated the coming together of (most of) the Particular Baptists and the General Baptists into the Baptist Union in 1891.
17. H. McLeod, 'Class, Community and Region: The Religious Geography of Nineteenth Century England', in M. Hill (ed.), *A Sociological Yearbook of Religion in Britain 6* (London: SCM Canterbury Press, 1973), pp. 60–1.
18. Ibid., p. 43.
19. J. Aitken, 'Never Before, Yet Never Again: Birmingham in the 1851 Religious Census', *Birmingham Historian*, 22 (2002), p. 28.
20. G. Robson, *Dark Satanic Mills? Religion and Irreligion in Birmingham and the Black Country* (Carlisle: Paternoster Press, 2002), p. 235.
21. Aitken, 'Never Before, Yet Never Again', p. 24.
22. R. Peacock, 'The 1892 Birmingham Religious Census', in A. Bryman (ed.), *Religion in the Birmingham Area, Essays in the Sociology of Religion* (University

of Birmingham Institute for the Study of Worship and Religious Architecture, 1975), p. 12.
23. Ibid., p. 13.
24. Ibid., p. 12.
25. Ibid., pp. 22–4.
26. 'Religious History: Places of Worship', *A History of the County of Warwick: Volume 7: The City of Birmingham* (London: Victoria County History, 1964), pp. 434–82.
27. Machin, *Politics and the Churches*, p. 25.
28. 'Religious History: Protestant Nonconformity', *A History of the County of Warwick: Volume 7*, pp. 411–34.
29. *'Summer Hill' Magazine*, 1 (March 1897).
30. *Midland Temperance Witness*, 3 (27 April 1901).
31. 'Religious History: Protestant Nonconformity', pp. 411–34.
32. H. Cadbury, *Charles M. Alexander: A Romance of Song and Soul Winning* (London: Marshall Bros, *c*.1921).
33. B.A. Ramsbottom, *The History of the Gospel Standard Magazine*, 2nd edn (Harpenden: Gospel Standard Trust, 2010), p. 4.
34. *The Free Church Chronicle*, 8.87 (March 1906), p. 75.
35. Ibid., and *Birmingham & District Evangelical Free Church Council Annual Report* (February 1912–13).
36. Birmingham Labour Church, Minute Book No. 5 (November 1903–November 1906). Library of Birmingham, Archives and Heritage Service, ZZ72a 53806.
37. *The Pioneer*, No.3, 8/1899, p. 1, Library of Birmingham, Archives and Heritage Service, Store B76.22 No. 3.
38. *The Pioneer*, No.8, 1/1900, p. 57, Library of Birmingham, Archives and Heritage Service, Store B76.22 No. 8.
39. Birmingham Labour Church, Minute Book No.4 (August 1898–October 1903), report of meeting, 4 January 1903. Library of Birmingham, Archives and Heritage Service, ZZ72a, 538061.
40. Syllabus of lectures for the season 1 October 1911 to 3 March 1912, Stirchley Labour Church, Library of Birmingham, Archives and Heritage Service, Lp19.9 245850.
41. Machin, *Politics and the Churches*, p. 282, citing H. Pelling, *Origins of the Labour Party 1880–1900* (Oxford University Press, 1966), pp. 132–42; D.F. Summers, 'The Labour Church and Allied Movements of the Late Nineteenth and Early Twentieth Centuries' (PhD thesis, University of Edinburgh, 1958), pp. 311–20.
42. G.J. Barnsby, *Socialism in Birmingham and the Black Country, 1850–1939* (Wolverhampton: Integrated Publishing Services, 1998), pp. 353–6.
43. *Handbook of the Yearly Meeting of the Society of Friends* (Birmingham: Society of Friends, 1908), p. 100; *Cornish's Birmingham Yearbook 1914* (Birmingham: Cornish Bros, 1914), pp. 205–7.
44. The architect J.H. Chamberlain, although unrelated to Joseph, was also a Unitarian; see G.C. Boase, 'Chamberlain, John Henry (1831–1883)', rev. Michael W. Brooks, *Oxford Dictionary of National Biography* (Oxford University Press, 2004), http://www.oxforddnb.com/view/article/5047, accessed 11 April 2015.

45. *Birmingham Illustrated: Cornish's Stranger's Guide through Birmingham* (Birmingham: Cornish Bros, 1913), pp. 48–53.
46. E.P. Hennock, *Fit and Proper Persons: Ideal and Reality in Nineteenth-Century Urban Government* (London: Edward Arnold, 1973), pp. 77–9.
47. Ibid., pp. 93–7.
48. *Handbook of the Yearly Meeting of the Society of Friends*, p. 153.
49. A.S. Langley, *Birmingham Baptists Past and Present* (London: Kingsgate Press, 1939), p. 110.
50. See Appendix of this essay.
51. *Cornish's Birmingham Yearbook 1915–16*, pp. 18–22.

Conclusion
Joseph Chamberlain:
His Reputation and Legacy

Ian Cawood

Chamberlain's story, as the first self-made businessman to enter the Cabinet, the founder of a political dynasty and, arguably, the first truly modern politician, is perhaps unique in British political history. Unsurprisingly, his life was frequently celebrated while he was still alive, mainly by his adopted city of Birmingham. In a lavish civic publication marking the beginning of the twentieth century, Chamberlain's biography is presented second, only preceded by the current Lord Mayor, and notes that as the current Colonial Secretary he was 'more than ever prominent among British statesmen'.[1] Given the length of his career, and his undoubted influence in local, national and international politics, his life has largely been studied by political biographers, beginning before he had even died. Often overlooked, Alexander Mackintosh wrote the first full biography of Chamberlain in 1906 and produced a second edition shortly after his death in 1914. He tried to remain impartial, but noted how difficult this was, as for many, 'he [Chamberlain] was either saint or devil'.[2] He revealed his own position when he commented that Chamberlain's changes of political view 'were unusually numerous and violent' and that they did not merely happen 'in the judgement of his youth, but in those of his ripe and mature manhood'.[3]

Since Mackintosh, biographers have had access to the extensive Chamberlain papers, now superbly catalogued in the Cadbury Research Library of the University of Birmingham, and the passions provoked by Tariff Reform and Irish Home Rule have gradually subsided. James Louis Garvin, the long-serving editor of *The Observer*, was contracted by the Chamberlain family in 1915 to write the official biography and the first three volumes appeared between 1932 and 1934, when it seemed, in the face of 'the Slump', that Chamberlain's advocacy of Imperial tariff protection had finally been proved correct.[4] Although written from a strongly supportive position and largely avoiding his flirtation with republicanism in the early 1870s, Garvin does engage with many of the criticisms that were made of Chamberlain's character and political consistency and is unafraid to quote passages of correspondence which seem to at least partly confirm some of these in Chamberlain's own words.[5] Given the initial closeness of relations between Garvin and the Chamberlain family and the excellent documentary materials in the volumes, drawn from the whole of Joseph's correspondence, Garvin's work is still widely used, despite its age. It is thus unfortunate that, distracted firstly by an illness in his family in the early 1930s, and then by duties of his editorship of *The Observer* during the international crises from 1931 to 1939, Garvin never completed the work.[6] As a result, Garvin was unable to offer a synoptic overview of Chamberlain's career. It was left to Julian Amery (son of the last Liberal Unionist MP for Birmingham South) to write the final volumes after Garvin's death.[7]

Following the appearance of Garvin's biography, interest in Chamberlain peaked on the anniversary of Chamberlain's birth in July 1836, just before his son became prime minister. Most of the right-wing press depicted Chamberlain as a political prophet, sadly ignored in his own age. *The Times* printed a leader column dedicated to his career on 8 July which used his memory to comment on the state of international affairs and noted that 'he saw that the day of [Britain's] effortless supremacy was passing'.[8] The Birmingham Unionist journal *Straight Forward* printed a 'Commemoration Number' of 12 pages, with a feature entitled 'Tariffs Vindicated'. The edition concentrated on his contribution to Birmingham and the Tariff Reform campaign, largely overlooking the cause of Unionism, which was largely downplayed by the Unionist party in the interwar years, following the granting of nationhood to the Irish Free State.[9] Birmingham City Council held a distinctly secular memorial to the former mayor at the Town Hall, at which it was claimed by the Vice-Chancellor of Birmingham University that Chamberlain belonged in the pantheon of great Victorian statesmen, alongside Peel, Palmerston, Disraeli and Gladstone.[10] With even King Edward VIII taking time from the racetracks of England to send a message of tribute, one can date the somewhat disproportionate attention that Chamberlain has subsequently received from historians to the effects of these centenary events.

Between 1952 and 1968, Julian Amery chose to devote a further three volumes to the remaining 13 years of Chamberlain's life, the first of which was admired by some for its thoroughness of detail in its study of domestic issues, but rather lacking depth on foreign affairs and very difficult to negotiate.[11] Sadly, Amery's own political career in the Tory party delayed the final two volumes until 1969 and clearly inhibited their quality.[12] M.C. Hurst described them as 'downright bad', listing factual errors, criticising Amery's research methodology and mocking his decision to title the final volume '1903–1968'.[13] Amery's preoccupation with Tariff Reform certainly distorted the final volumes and it is to be regretted that he chose to ignore Garvin's draft chapters and instead included a highly ahistoric 129-page section in volume 5 entitled 'the origins of Tariff Reform' which seemed to offer more insights into Amery's contemporary enthusiasm for the European Economic Community than Chamberlain's thinking 65 years earlier.

Possibly it was this failure to complete satisfactorily the heroic narrative which Garvin had begun over half a century before, which led to the explosion of biographies of Chamberlain in the next 15 years, with no fewer than three full-length biographical studies published,[14] two short studies for popular audiences[15] and two advanced studies textbooks, including an edition of Longman's celebrated textbook 'Seminar Studies' series devoted to 'Brummagem Joe' (the only volume in the original series devoted to an individual modern politician – even though Chamberlain failed to reach any of the highest political offices).[16] Perhaps the best political biography of this period was Richard Jay's short 1981 study, which was the first to identify the huge gulf between Chamberlain's influence and his legislative achievements. It was also unafraid of criticising Chamberlain directly, noting that 'Chamberlain's unorthodox policies might have been tolerated more readily had he not proved so unpredictable and unreliable.'[17]

Of the modern biographies, Peter Marsh has come the closest to producing a definitive one-volume study, having already written one of the most penetrating studies of the politics of late Victorian Britain.[18] He attempted to measure Chamberlain by the standards of business, which, unlike politics, does not automatically criticise reinvention or sudden changes of direction. Even he had to conclude, however, that once he had left Birmingham, Chamberlain's career may have increased in prestige both nationally and internationally, but that he failed to find solutions to the pressing issues of what contemporaries referred to as 'the condition of England' question and that he became increasingly fixated with the desire to control. First, the politicians of Birmingham were expected to fall behind his enthusiastic adoption of Unionism in 1886. Second, the Liberal Unionists themselves were required to sign up to Chamberlain's ambitious 'social programme' after he became leader of the party in the Commons in 1892. Finally, he attempted to convert both Unionist factions, and the Prime Minister Arthur Balfour to the cause of Tariff Reform. Such efforts left behind three divided parties (Liberals, Liberal Unionist and Conservative) and actually achieved little, apart from a Conservative hegemony for 20 years. Marsh's work, a third of million words long, made the best use yet of the Chamberlain archives and revealed the private man behind the famous monocle. It did receive some criticism for failing to engage more thoroughly with Chamberlain's activities as a minister or in examining the influence of Unitarianism on his attitude towards social reform, but was recognised as the definitive political study, confirming and correcting Jay's work where needed.[19]

Although the weakest, by far, of the modern biographies of Joseph Chamberlain, Enoch Powell's 1977 study is perhaps the most remembered, because of its famous aphorism that 'all political lives ... end in failure'.[20] The choice for all biographers of Chamberlain is whether to follow the path laid down by Dennis Judd and to examine Chamberlain's career as a series of failed political experiments, or to attempt to find elements of consistency in his varied political positions, which only Peter Marsh has ever succeeded in doing. The most recent biography by the American scholar Travis Crosby also found it difficult to feel much sympathy for his subject. This is probably because, although he was notorious for treating colleagues in a cavalier fashion, Chamberlain himself was intensely conscious of his own feelings. Lord Salisbury, the only man to tame Chamberlain's restless ambition (temporarily), once wrote that 'I never came across so sensitive a public man before.' Yet he constantly used and exploited those around him and then ruthlessly discarded them as soon as they ceased to be of political value to him. He worked his loyal lieutenant, Joseph Powell Williams, to death; he treated former allies who refused to support him on his crusade for Tariff Reform as his bitterest opponents; and he even seriously considered withdrawing his support for his own son Austen in 1892 when his candidature was blocked by his Tory rivals.

Crosby, co-editor of a collection entitled *Psycho/History: Readings in the Method of Psychology, Psychoanalysis, and History*, might have been the ideal biographer to get to grips with Chamberlain's personality, but regrettably there were few insights into what caused his relentless, borderline sociopathic behaviour and his bizarre relationship with his sons – with one (Neville) banished to the Andros plantation in the 1890s and the other (Austen) who appeared in public in an imitation of his father's distinctive dress with a frock coat, orchid and monocle (which hindered his own career as it did nothing to alleviate his myopia). The best psychological judgement in the book, that the death of Chamberlain's wives drove him to abandon friendship and to pursue political success at all costs, was borrowed from Beatrice Webb (née Potter) whom Chamberlain briefly wooed.[21] Although he was right to point out the immense loyalty that Chamberlain's hard work and departmental leadership engendered, Crosby neglected other judgements, such as that of the lawyer Sir Henry James, who, after over 20 years of working alongside Chamberlain, seriously wondered if he was mentally stable during the Tariff Reform campaign.[22]

Although Crosby's biography was subtitled *A Most Radical Imperialist*, there was little attempt to address the contradictions and ambiguities that resulted as Chamberlain attempted to satisfy both his nonconformist and his nationalist supporters. After 1895 any serious analysis of Chamberlain's ongoing radicalism swiftly faded in favour of a rather plodding account of the colonial escapades into which Chamberlain plunged the country. The 1985 study of Chamberlain's foreign policy by Michael Balfour, recently reissued by Faber and Faber, managed, by contrast, to demonstrate that Chamberlain's temperament, ideal for municipal politics and effective in the Commons, was almost disastrous in his dealings with the other great powers of Europe.[23] As the late John Ramsden put it in his review of Balfour's book, 'Chamberlain was a poor hand at combining ideas and actions.'[24]

Recently, political biography has been transformed by the work of Philip Williamson, who, in his biography of Stanley Baldwin, demonstrated the importance of analysing a politician's worldview, yet among Chamberlain's biographers, with the honourable exception of Peter Marsh, there seems to be little to say about Chamberlain's historic significance beyond Richard Jay's judgement that Chamberlain was an ambitious man and 'not a very nice one'. Peter Marsh himself, like D.H. Elletson before him, has gone on to interpret Chamberlain as the founder of a political dynasty, an approach which allowed him to address the contradictions of a wealthy radical Unitarian family who sought entry into the aristocratic milieu most associated with distinctly nonconformist-unfriendly activities such as gambling, horse racing and fancy-dress balls.[25]

It has long been understood that the traditional political biography is a very unsatisfactory form of history. As Lord Lexden recently commented, 'the main current biographies provide a large amount of information about [Chamberlain], but leave the great paradoxes of his extraordinary career unexplained'.[26] Some of the best recent studies of Chamberlain have been in texts on the political philosophies that suddenly sprung up with the advent of mass politics in the late nineteenth century. Jules Gehrke argues convincingly that Chamberlain's advocacy of municipal social reform was a continuation of mid-Victorian campaigns against 'jobbery' and inefficiency. Chamberlain 'rejected the idea that municipal socialism should alter the principles of ... laissez-faire economics and minimal government'.[27] Peter Fraser described Chamberlain as the first 'professional' politician, but he was accused of failing to substantiate that judgement.[28] It was not until recent interest in the 'new political history' that the true nature of Chamberlain's work in the Birmingham caucus, the nascent National Liberal Federation, the Radical Unionist Association and finally the Tariff Reform League had been analysed and understood.[29] The attempt to use a cultural approach to analyse Conservative politics, championed by those such as Jon Lawrence and Michael Bentley, has recently resulted in Frank Trentmann's fascinating cultural overview of the later years of Chamberlain's career.[30] One hopes that this will, eventually, lead to an attempt by at least one proponent of the 'New Political History' to explain Chamberlain's earlier career by closer reference to the wider intellectual and popular cultural influences of his age.

In her study of the civic culture of Victorian Birmingham, Anne Roderick attempted to explain the self-educating, self-improving, high-minded, provincial milieu from which Chamberlain emerged in the 1860s in her excellent study of urban mentalities.[31] In many ways, of course, this built on some of the classic first urban histories of the 1970s, in particular E.P. Hennock's comparison of the social composition of municipal government in Leeds and Birmingham from the 1830s to the First World War. Hennock identified the significance of the contribution of religious thinkers such as George Dawson and R.W. Dale far more effectively than the contemporary political biographers did, and it is a pity that Hennock did not return to study Chamberlain's Birmingham later in his career.[32] Chamberlain scholars are, however, fortunate that Professor Roger Ward, of what was the University of Central England (now Birmingham City University) has, since his retirement, completed a series of excellent studies of Victorian Birmingham, chief among them his study of its political history between 1830 and 1940, in which Chamberlain figures prominently. Ward tries hard to bring others such as Jesse Collings, George Dixon and Joseph Sturge from under Chamberlain's shadow, but he is forced to devote 100 of the book's 258 pages to the period of Chamberlain's ascendancy. Although it is debateable to what extent Birmingham's political 'exceptionalism' was a result of the city's long-standing unique social and economic class relations, rather than, as Ward claims, Chamberlain's successful repositioning of the city on the political right of the spectrum after 1886, this remains one of the few successful recent texts that manages to integrate local and national history and to offer a contextualised view of Chamberlain's political impact on the city.[33]

The most damning of all Amery's critics, M.C. Hurst, never wrote a full study of Chamberlain's career. His first study, now very hard to find, was an insightful account of Chamberlain's relationship with his 'duchy' in the period after his break with Gladstone.[34] Although it did not fully explore the decisive impact of the months before the 1895 general election that led Chamberlain to realise that his only possible future lay as the junior partner in a Conservative administration, it demonstrated an exemplary appreciation of the politics of the West Midlands region in the last quarter of the nineteenth century.[35] This was followed by a forensic examination of the Round Table discussions of early 1887, which nearly reunited the Radicals and the Liberals, but which collapsed at the last minute, never to be resurrected.[36] Hurst was the only historian before Marsh to fully appreciate the delicacy of Chamberlain's hold over Birmingham. Encouraging a radical city to support coercive methods against the oppressed and exploited Irish people was a masterful sleight of hand by its leading politician and the Round Table was the central strategy in this legerdemain. It is only recently that similar studies of regional politics have confirmed much of Hurst's thesis – that Birmingham was, and remains, a frequent exception to British political trends.[37] It is to be greatly mourned that Hurst was never able to write something more substantial than this micro-study, as the Chamberlain that emerges from its pages, the master tactician and manipulator of both mass electors and political elites, is far more convincing than the paragon of Garvin's volumes, or the sinister cipher of many other biographies.[38]

So how radical a politician was Joseph Chamberlain and what sort of legacy did he leave behind? As Winston Churchill demonstrated in his review of the first volume of Garvin's biography, Chamberlain's remarkable career can appear an achievement in itself.[39] It is true that he put a number of issues on to the political agenda for the first time, but, as Peter Marsh comments, 'he failed to find answers to the great questions', such as state education, land reform and welfare provision, and, in particular, old-age pensions.[40] Not only did Joe fail to produce any meaningful solutions to these issues, or to the Irish question of course, but any legislation with which he *was* involved was soon swept away by the changed circumstances of the First World War and the mass democracy that followed it. His radical credentials as the man who refused to share a carriage with the Prince of Wales when the latter visited Birmingham in 1874, was soon forgotten once he entered politics at Westminster in 1876. He flirted with the idea of forming a new, centre party with Lord Randolph Churchill after the defeat of Home Rule in 1886, but he fell out with 'Randy' when the latter dared to challenge Chamberlain's dominance of the City of Birmingham, following the death of John Bright in 1889. Instead he had to make the best of the weak hand that he had to play as the leader of the radical wing of a Unionist faction, dominated by the passive Lord Hartington and tied to a reactionary Conservative leadership. As he put it, he would support 'the Tories, as long as they behave themselves and pass liberal measures'.[41] Hardly 'the British Robespierre' that some had accused him of being in the 1870s.

Chamberlain famously broke two political parties, the Liberals in 1886 and the Conservatives in 1903, but both of these had managed to reconstruct themselves by the time of his death, and his last great crusade for a reform of British import tariffs had been repudiated by the newly united Unionist parties in the previous year. He never rose above the middle rank of Cabinet positions, having only held the posts of President of the Board of Trade, President of the Local Government Board and Colonial Secretary (though he arguably raised the importance of the last post far beyond its usual status by his actions following the 1897 Diamond Jubilee which he helped to turn into a celebration of Britain's imperial power). He had turned down Salisbury's offer to be Chancellor of the Exchequer or Home Secretary in 1895 and, in 1902, when Salisbury's resignation was widely anticipated, he made a point of refusing demands from back-bench Tories that he should offer himself as an alternative candidate to Arthur Balfour as Prime Minister.[42] His major business venture, developing a sisal plantation on the island of Andros in the Bahamas, was a catastrophic failure and he was only saved from bankruptcy by his ministerial salary in 1895.[43] Unsurprisingly therefore, Richard Jay described 'an aura of failure' that surrounds him.

Some Conservative politicians such as David Willetts and Greg Clark have recently tried to claim Chamberlain as the epitome of regional English identity, a figurehead for the challenge to metropolitan-centred politics, but the truth is that Chamberlain left regional issues far behind him when he entered Westminster in 1876 and soon became the champion of *national* radical politics.[44] Chamberlain did claim that he found the Conservatives far more conducive to ideas of social reform than he had found Gladstone. While Gladstone's new zeal for Home Rule meant that Chamberlain's 'unauthorised programme' of radical reform had been shelved (although, in reality, it had proved to be a very ineffective electoral weapon in 1885), Chamberlain hoped that some Tories, such as Randolph Churchill and Arthur Balfour, might be more amenable to reform. In the period when the Liberal Unionists supported a minority Conservative administration after 1886, Chamberlain successfully pressurised the Tory leadership for elected county councils, free elementary education and a Small Holdings Act. Once the two parties formed a coalition government in 1895, however, the Liberal Unionists' bargaining power (and Chamberlain's interest in social reform once he became Colonial Secretary) dramatically declined. The next eight years of Unionist government only produced a highly compromised Workmen's Compensation Act, which left Chamberlain open to much justified criticism, when he had made bold promises of old-age pensions, housing reform and shorter working hours in 1895. Any constructive legislation that Salisbury would allow such as education reform and the Clerical Tithes Bill were largely designed to benefit the established church and this led to heightened accusations that Chamberlain had sold his principles for the sake of high office. The greatest achievements of the ministry in these years were in fact in Ireland, where the renegade Unionist T.W. Russell successfully persuaded Gerald Balfour and George Wyndham to introduce local government and land reform in the teeth of opposition from the Ulster Unionists, Conservative backbenchers and Chamberlain himself.[45]

Towards the end of his career, Chamberlain seemed increasingly desperate to set the agenda, but repeatedly blundered. His attempt to escape Britain's 'splendid isolation' by forming an alliance with the Kaiser's Germany was hampered by his indiscreet speeches and the war in South Africa. His desire to reassure Conservatives of his changed attitude towards the Established church merely alienated his own supporters in the controversy surrounding the 1902 Education Act, and his final crusade for Tariff Reform was so strident that it failed to convince the bulk of Unionists to support it and the promises of social reform funded by tariffs were never properly articulated and failed to convince the working classes, at least outside Birmingham. As a result of his intervention the Unionists presented the public with a disunited and divided appearance which suffered the usual fate that the electorate reserves for publically warring political parties (expect in Birmingham). As a result therefore, Chamberlain bears the lion's share of blame for one of the worst defeats in the Conservative party's history. Britain turned from Chamberlain's offer of protection for British industry and chose, in effect, to adopt Lloyd George's model of a centrally controlled, state welfare system, funded by graduated taxes. Chamberlain, exhausted from his efforts, suffered a massive stroke shortly after the celebrations for his 70th birthday and retreated into an enforced retirement. Perhaps Chamberlain's greatest legacy lies not in legislative achievement and certainly not in his racialist vision of an Anglo-Saxon Imperial Federation, but in the method and style of politics that he championed. Peter Clarke describes him as the first truly modern politician. As a self-made man with a limited fortune and a relatively modest education, he adopted a system of organisation, based on the American 'caucus', in which he ensured his followers dominated all the Liberal party's elected bodies, from the local ward to the National Liberal Federation. In this way, although his views were not shared by the bulk of Liberals (and after 1886 not even the bulk of radicals), it allowed him to claim a democratic mandate for his opinions, and gave him an electoral machine which made his opponents tremble. No wonder, then, that all politicians wishing to force their views on democratic parties, from Bevanites through to Thatcherites, Militant Tendency and Orange-Book Liberal Democrats, have adopted his model of manipulation and control. It is a very questionable legacy and one that has, increasingly in recent years, forced frustrated voters outside the political spectrum.

Chamberlain's ruthless use of the caucus, the Birmingham 'six hundred', his exploitation of his local, denominational and seemingly classless background and his engagement with modern media, especially the use of systematic canvassing, the employment of paid political agents and the production of electoral propaganda, mark him out as a crucial figure in the transition to modern political culture. Nick Timothy, a special advisor to the Home Office has described Chamberlain as 'the Conservative Party's forgotten hero'.[46] Lord Carrington of Fulham gives Chamberlain the credit for paving the way 'for Andrew Bonar Law, Stanley Baldwin, F.E. Smith, Neville Chamberlain and Leo Amery to lead the party into becoming the mass party it became in the 1930s'.[47] He goes onto to offer a view of Chamberlain as 'a campaigning, conviction politician, a populist who used the media to further his argument', but he questions whether Chamberlain had a decisive impact on the emergence of a more democratic Conservative politics.[48]

In Birmingham, where real legislative achievement meant that his style of politics won popular favour, Chamberlain may still be remembered as 'Our Joe'. George Dawson, Chamberlain's spiritual mentor, saw the city as 'a solemn organism through which should flow, and in which should be shaped all the highest, loftiest and truest ends of man's intellectual and moral nature' and Chamberlain and his colleagues on the City Council attempted to put the idea of a unified local government as opposed to a collection of local service agencies into practice.[49] The former leader of Birmingham City Council, Sir Albert Bore, speaking at the Chamberlain centenary conference in July 2014, argued that Chamberlain pioneered an approach towards local government that is more accurately described as 'municipal capitalism', whereby the council took over the monopolies of gas and water supply and created 'a joint stock or cooperative enterprise' in which every citizen was a shareholder'. Not only did this result in Birmingham becoming known as 'the best-governed city in the industrial world' but it also became a centre of a flourishing civic culture, with new libraries, its first university, three daily newspapers, and at one point in the early 1880s, four weekly illustrated satirical periodicals.

Sir Albert also highlighted that, under Chamberlain, provincial cities had the powers to raise and spend revenue as they saw fit. The demands of the world wars in the first half of the twentieth century led to the erosion of this independence and then the inherent logic of the welfare state and the centralising impulses of the Thatcher governments saw councils rate-capped, surcharged and roundly dismissed as incompetent, and, in the words of Tristram Hunt, 'local government became a client state of Westminster'.[50] Greg Clark, Cabinet Minister for Cities at the time of the conference, agreed with the other political speakers at the centenary conference that there was much to be said for restoring the autonomy that Birmingham had enjoyed under Chamberlain and his successors, in order to rebalance the British economy away from its unhealthy dependence on London and the financial sector.

Certainly Conservatives, Liberal Democrats and Labour politicians have come to recognise that the regional legacy of Chamberlain has been in the enduring and surprising 'exceptionalism' of Birmingham's politics, which was first decisively signalled by Chamberlain's clean sweep of the city's seven constituencies for Unionism, in the face of the Liberal landslide across the rest of the country in 1906. Birmingham continued to defy national political movements, with the city returning three Conservatives in the face of the Labour electoral landslide of 1945 and remaining largely Labour in 1983, at the height of Margaret Thatcher's ascendancy. As the *Birmingham Post* noted in 1974, 'Birmingham has always had its peculiar electoral factors.' Some have argued that this unique political behaviour was the product of the unique labour relations in the city, owing to the number of small independent craftsmen, but students of politics have learned that traditions are a lot more influential than sociological theorising.[51]

Elsewhere in Britain, however, Chamberlain came to epitomise the new political class, supporting themselves largely from their Parliamentary salaries, playing 'the game of politics' in their Westminster bubble. He pioneered electoral sound bites such as 'three acres and a cow' and 'Tariff Reform means work for all' and adopted the wearing of a monocle and orchid to allow the caricaturists of *Punch, Fun* and all the other satirical periodicals a visual shorthand with which to identify his otherwise rather undistinguished features.[52] Increasingly distant from their constituencies and relying on the expensive apparatus of a professional political party, with a mass communications strategy to carry the electorate with them, this new class of MP came to dominate British politics in the twentieth century. The negative consequences of this pattern of modern politics that Chamberlain pioneered have undergone a far more critical scrutiny in recent years by voters and commentators alike. Some have recently blamed Margaret Thatcher for all this, but it is Joseph Chamberlain who should be seen as the progenitor of this very mixed blessing for the British Parliamentary system. He may have 'made the weather' in British politics for over 20 years, as Winston Churchill famously claimed, but he made it so intemperate that little of lasting value was achieved while he whipped up the storms that ravaged both of the dominant political parties of the age.[53]

Notes

1. W.T. Pike (ed.), *Birmingham at the Opening of the 20th Century: Contemporary Biographies* (Brighton: W.T. Pike, 1900), p. 52.
2. A. Mackintosh, *Joseph Chamberlain: An Honest Biography*, 2nd edn (London: Hodder and Stoughton, 1914), p. ix. Mackintosh capitalised on the interest in Chamberlain's life by writing a second book, *The Story of Mr Chamberlain's Life* (London, 1914) in the same year.
3. Mackintosh, *Joseph Chamberlain*, p. x.
4. See the papers in the Cadbury Research Library, University of Birmingham, JC23/4/1–14; JC23/5/1–22; JC24/3/1–43.
5. A. Mackintosh, 'Review of *The Life of Joseph Chamberlain*, vol. 1', the *British Weekly*, 1 December 1932. Garvin was particularly pleased that the first volume received positive reviews in both *The Times* and the *Manchester Guardian*. J.L. Garvin to A. Chamberlain, 30 November 1932, Austen Chamberlain Papers, Cadbury Research Library, University of Birmingham, AC 42/6/39.
6. See the correspondence between Garvin and Austen and Neville Chamberlain between 1926 and 1936: AC/42/6/1–53; ACLAdd/220–225; NC1/7/1.

7. Garvin had completed a draft plan for volumes IV and V, the first of which would have covered the years of the Boer War and Chamberlain's subsequent tour of South Africa and the final volume was to be largely given over to the Tariff Reform Campaign. The plan and initial notes for these volumes (largely handwritten on brown foolscap envelopes) survive: JC 24/3/7–11.

8. *The Times*, 8 July 1936.

9. *Straight Forward*, 58, July 1936. When I wrote the supplement for the centenary supplement of the *Birmingham Post* to mark Chamberlain's death, although it was possible to take a less positive view of Chamberlain's trenchant imperialism, I did receive complaints that I had failed to pay enough respect to the memory of one of Birmingham's most famous statesmen.

10. *Birmingham Daily Post*, 9 July 1936.

11. C.H.D. Howard, 'Review of *The Life of Joseph Chamberlain*, vol 4', *English Historical Review*, 263 (April 1952), pp. 278–80; R.D. Challener, 'Review of *The Life of Joseph Chamberlain*, vol 4', *American Historical Review*, 57.2 (Jan. 1952), pp. 432–4.

12. Peter Fraser actually managed to produce the first single-volume biography of Chamberlain since Mackintosh in the years between volume IV and the final two volumes of the official biography. P. Fraser, *Joseph Chamberlain: Radicalism and Empire, 1868–1914* (London: Cassell, 1966).

13. M.C. Hurst, 'Review of *The Life of Joseph Chamberlain*, vols. 5 & 6', *English Historical Review*, 341 (October 1971), pp. 816–22.

14. D. Judd, *Radical Joe: Life of Joseph Chamberlain* (London: H Hamilton, 1977); R. Jay, *Joseph Chamberlain: A Political Study* (Oxford University Press, 1981); J.E. Powell, *Joseph Chamberlain* (London: Thames and Hudson, 1977).

15. C.W. Hill, *An Illustrated Life of Joseph Chamberlain, 1836–1914* (Aylesbury: Shire, 1973); J. Tann, *Joseph's Dream: Joseph Chamberlain and Birmingham's Improvement* (University of Birmingham Press, 1978).

16. H. Browne, *Joseph Chamberlain: Radical and Imperialist* (London: Longman, 1974); R. Grinter, *Joseph Chamberlain: Democrat, Unionist and Imperialist* (London: Arnold, 1971).

17. R. Jay, *Joseph Chamberlain: A Political Study* (Oxford: Clarendon, 1981), p. 348.

18. P. Marsh, *The Discipline of Popular Government: Lord Salisbury's Domestic Statecraft: 1881–1902* (Hassocks: Harvester, 1978).

19. D. Nicholls, 'Review of Joseph Chamberlain: Entrepreneur in Politics', *Social History*, 20.2 (May 1995), pp. 257–60; J. Harris, 'Review of Joseph Chamberlain: Entrepreneur in Politics', *Independent*, 21 August 1994; J. Parry, 'Review of Joseph Chamberlain: Entrepreneur in Politics', *London Review of Books*, 16.12 (23 June 1994).

20. J.E. Powell, *Joseph Chamberlain* (London: Weidenfeld and Nicholson, 1977), p. 151.

21. *The Diary of Beatrice Webb, Vol. 1: 'Glitter around and Darkness within'*, ed. N. MacKenzie and J. MacKenzie (Cambridge, MA: Harvard University Press, 1982), pp. 266–7.

22. Sir Thomas Farrar, Permanent Under-Secretary of State at the Board of Trade in the early 1880s, when asked in 1895 by the Permanent Under-Secretary of the Colonial Office as to Chamberlain's abilities, replied, 'Chamberlain was

the best chief I ever had.' Austen Chamberlain to J.L. Garvin, 14 December 1932, AC/42/6/42.

23. M. Balfour, *Britain and Joseph Chamberlain* (London: Allen and Unwin, 1985).

24. J. Ramsden, 'Review of *Britain and Joseph Chamberlain'*, *Journal of Modern History*, 60.2 (1988), p. 377.

25. P. Marsh, *The Chamberlain Litany: Letters within a Governing Family from Empire to Appeasement* (London: Haus, 2010).

26. A. Lexden, 'Review of *Our Joe: Joseph Chamberlain's Conservative Legacy'*, *The House Magazine*, 18 April 2013.

27. J.P. Gehrke, 'Municipal Anti-Socialism and the Growth of the Anti-socialist Critique in Britain, 1873–1914' (PhD thesis, University of Minnesota, 2005), p. 69.

28. C.L. Mowat, 'Review of *Joseph Chamberlain: Radicalism and Empire, 1868–1914'*, *English Historical Review*, 327 (April 1968), p. 364.

29. See I. Cawood, *The Liberal Unionist Party, 1886–1912: A History* (London: I.B. Tauris, 2102).

30. M. Bentley, *Lord Salisbury's World: Conservative Environments in Late Victorian Britain* (New York: Cambridge University Press, 2001); J.M. Lawrence, 'Class and Gender in the Making of Urban Toryism, 1880–1914', *English Historical Review*, 108 (1993), pp. 629–52; F. Trentmann, *Free Trade Nation: Commerce, Consumption and Civil Society in Modern Britain* (Oxford University Press, 2008).

31. A.B. Rodrick, *Self-Help and Civic Culture: Citizenship in Victorian Birmingham* (Aldershot: Ashgate, 2004).

32. E.P. Hennock, *Fit and Proper Persons: Ideal and Reality in Nineteenth Century Urban Government* (London: Arnold, 1973).

33. R. Ward, *City State and Nation: Birmingham's Political History, 1830–1940* (Chichester: Phillimore, 2005).

34. M.C. Hurst, *Joseph Chamberlain and West Midland Politics, 1886–1895: Dugdale Society Occasional Papers No. 15* (Oxford: Dugdale Society, 1962).

35. See also I. Cawood, 'The Unionist "Compact" in West Midland Politics 1891–1895', *Midland History*, 30 (2005), pp. 92–111; I. Cawood, 'Joseph Chamberlain, the Conservative Party and the Leamington Spa Candidature Dispute of 1895', *Historical Research*, 79 (2006), pp. 554–77.

36. M.C. Hurst, *Joseph Chamberlain and Liberal Reunion: The Round Table Conference 1887* (London: Routledge Kegan Paul, 1967).

37. See, for example, J.R. Moore, 'Liberal Unionism and the Home Rule Crisis in Leicester, 1885–1892', *Midland History*, 26 (2001), pp. 177–97; J.R. Moore, 'Manchester Liberalism and the Unionist Secession, 1886–1895', *Manchester Regional History Review*, 15 (2001), pp. 31–40; C. Burness, *'Strange Associations': The Irish Question and the Making of Scottish Unionism, 1886–1918* (East Linton: Tuckwell Press, 2003); M. Roberts, '"Villa Toryism" and Popular Conservatism in Leeds, 1885–1902', *Historical Journal*, 49 (2006), pp. 217–46; A. Windscheffel, *Popular Conservatism in Imperial London, 1868–1906* (Woodbridge: Boydell & Brewer, 2007); I. Cawood, 'The Persistence of Liberal Unionism, 1886–1912', in G. Doherty (ed.), *The Home Rule Crisis, 1912–1914* (Cork: Mercier Press, 2014).

38. J. Howarth, 'Review of *Joseph Chamberlain and Liberal Reunion'*, *Historical Journal*, 11.2 (June 1968), pp. 394–7.

39. W.S. Churchill, 'Joseph Chamberlain: This Robust, Virile, Aggressive Champion of Change', *Daily Mail*, 1 December 1932.
40. P. Marsh, *Joseph Chamberlain: Entrepreneur in Politics* (New Haven: Yale University Press, 1994), p. 668.
41. Quoted in A.B. Cooke and J.R. Vincent, *The Governing Passion: Cabinet Government and Party Politics in Britain, 1885–86* (Hassocks: Harvester, 1974), p. 43.
42. See Cawood, 'Joseph Chamberlain, the Conservative Party', p. 575; Recollections of a conversation between Chamberlain and Balfour's private secretary, J.S. Sandars, 25 February 1902, AC 42/6/26.
43. D. Dilks, *Neville Chamberlain 1896–1929* (Cambridge University Press, 1984), p. 72.
44. D. Willetts, *The Conservatives in Birmingham* (Molesey: Centre for Policy Studies, 2008); Greg Clark, speaking in the House of Commons, 7 July 2014.
45. See I. Cawood, 'The Persistence of Liberal Unionism in Irish Politics, 1886–1912', in Doherty (ed.), *The Irish Home Rule Crisis*, pp. 333–52.
46. N. Timothy, 'It is Time for the Conservative Party to Remember Its Historical Debt to Radical Joe', *Conservative History Journal*, 2.3 (2014), p. 61.
47. Lord Carrington of Fulham, 'Joseph Chamberlain's Political Legacy to the Conservative Party', *Conservative History Journal*, 2.3 (2014), p. 57.
48. Ibid., p. 59.
49. G. Dawson, speech at the opening of the Birmingham Central Library and Art Gallery, 6 September 1865.
50. T. Hunt, 'Freedom of the City', *The Guardian*, 29 July 2002.
51. See, for example, G.J. Barnsby, *Socialism in Birmingham and the Black Country 1850–1939* (Wolverhampton: Integrated Publishing Services, 1998); E. Hopkins, 'Working Class Life in Birmingham between the Wars 1918–1939', *Midland History*, 15 (1990), pp. 129–50.
52. Chamberlain had a vast number of greenhouses at Highbury to grow these, but historians cannot agree on an exact number, with estimates varying from 24 to 37.
53. W.S. Churchill, *Great Contemporaries* (London: Thornton Butterworth, 1937), p. 57.

Bibliography

Printed Primary Sources

J. Aitken (ed.), *Census of Religious Worship, 1851, The Returns for Worcestershire*, Worcester: Worcestershire Historical Society, 2000.

D.W.R. Bahlman (ed.), *The Diary of Sir Edward Walter Hamilton 1880–1885*, vols 2–3, Oxford University Press, 1972.

F. Bell, *At the Works: A Study of a Manufacturing Town*, London: Virago, 1985.

W. Booth, *In Darkest England and the Way Out*, London: McCorquodale and Co., 1890.

C.W. Boyd (ed.), *Mr Chamberlain's Speeches*, 2 vols, London: Constable and Company Ltd, 1914.

M.V. Brett (ed.), *Journals and Letters of Reginald, Viscount Esher* Vol. 1, London: Nicholson and Watson, 1934.

M. Brock and E. Brock (eds), *Margot Asquith's Great War Diary 1914–1916: The View from Downing Street*, Oxford University Press, 2014.

G.E. Buckle (ed.), *The Letters of Queen Victoria*, second series, vol. 3, London: John Murray, 1928.

A. Chamberlain, *Down the Years* (2nd edn), London: Cassell, 1935.

A. Chamberlain, *Politics from the Inside: An Epistolary Chronicle, 1906–1914*, London: Cassell, 1936.

J. Chamberlain, 'Manufacture of Iron Wood Screws', in S. Timmins, (ed.), *The Resources, Products, and Industrial History of Birmingham and the Midland Hardware District*, London: Robert Hardwicke, 1866.

J. Chamberlain, 'The Labour Question', *The Nineteenth Century*, 189 (1892), pp. 677–701.

J. Chamberlain, *Patriotism: Address Delivered to the Students of the University of Glasgow on November 3rd, 1897, on the Occasion of His Installation as Lord Rector*, London: Constable, 1897.

J. Chamberlain, *Imperial Union and Tariff Reform: Speeches Delivered from May 15 to Nov. 4, 1903*, London: G. Richards, 1903.

P.W. Clayden, *England under the Coalition: The Political History of Great Britain and Ireland from the General Election of 1885 to May 1892*, London: T.F. Unwin, 1892.

A.B. Cooke and J.R. Vincent (eds), *Lord Carlingford's Journal, Reflections of a Cabinet Minister*, Oxford: Clarendon, 1971.

G. Cordery and J.S. Meisel (eds), *The Humours of Parliament: Harry Furniss's View of Late Victorian Political Culture*, Columbus: Ohio State University Press, 2014.

L. Courtney, 'Political Machinery and Political Life', *Fortnightly Review*, 20 (1876), pp. 74–92.

L. Courtney, 'The Difficulties of Socialism', *The Economic Journal*, 1.1 (1891), pp. 174–88.

L. Courtney, 'To My Fellow Disciples at Saratoga Springs', *The National Review*, 26 (1895), pp. 21–6.

L. Courtney, 'Mr Chamberlain's Balloon', *Contemporary Review*, 84 (August 1903), pp. 265–79.

J.M. Davidson, *Eminent Radicals in and out of Parliament*, London: W. Stewart & Co., 1880.

G. Dawson, *Inaugural Address* at the Opening of the Free Reference Library, October 26, 1866, Birmingham: Borough of Birmingham, 1866.

R.R. Dodds, 'Provincial Humorous and Satirical Journals', *The Journalist*, 20 May 1887, pp. 93–4.

E. Edwards, *John Skirrow Wright MP, A Memorial Tribute*, Birmingham: Cornish Bros, 1880.

W.E. Gladstone, *Midlothian Speeches 1879*, Leicester University Press, 1971.

G. Hamilton, *Parliamentary Reminiscences and Reflections, 1886–1906*, London: John Murray, 1922.

W.K. Hancock and J. van der Poel (eds), *Selections from the Smuts Papers, Vols I & II*, Cambridge University Press, 1966.

R. Harcourt-Williams (ed.), *Salisbury–Balfour Correspondence, 1869–1892*, Hertford: Hertfordshire Records Society, 1988.

C.H.D. Howard (ed.), *A Political Memoir: 1880–1892 by Joseph Chamberlain*, London: Batchworth, 1953.

S.J.P. Kruger, *The Memoirs of Paul Kruger, Four Times President of the South African Republic, Told by Himself*, London, T. Fisher Unwin, 1902.

P. Lewsen (ed.), *Selections from the Correspondence of John X. Merriman 1890–1898*, Cape Town: The Van Riebeeck Society, 1963.

H.W. Lucy, *A Diary of the Unionist Parliament, 1895–1900*, Bristol: J. Arrowsmith, 1901.

N. MacKenzie and J. MacKenzie (eds), *The Diary of Beatrice Webb, vol. 1: 1873–1892: 'Glitter Around and Darkness Within'*, Cambridge, MA, 1983.

P.T. Marsh, *The Chamberlain Litany: Letters within a Governing Family from Empire to Appeasement*, London: Haus, 2010.

C. Masterman (ed.), *The Heart of Empire: A Discussion of the Problems of Modern City Life in England*, London: T. Fisher Unwin, 1901.

H.C.G. Matthew (ed.), *The Gladstone Diaries, with Cabinet Minutes and Prime-Ministerial Correspondence Vols 11–13, 1883–1896*, Oxford: Clarendon Press, 1990–94.

W. Maycock, *With Mr Chamberlain in the United States and America, 1887–88*, London: Chatto & Windus, 1914.

W.T. Pike (ed.), *Birmingham at the Opening of the 20th Century: Contemporary Biographies*, Brighton: W.T. Pike, 1900.

J. Ralph, 'The Best-Governed City in the World', *Harper's New Monthly Magazine*, 81, New York, 1890.

A. Ramm (ed.), *The Political Correspondence of Mr Gladstone and Lord Granville, 1876–1886*, vol. 1, Oxford: Clarendon, 1962.

K. Rathbone, *The Dales: Growing Up in a Victorian Family*, ed. B. Walker and H. Walker, Ledbury: Northstep, 1989.

W.P. Reeves, *The Long White Cloud: Aotearoa*, London: Horace Marshall and Sons, 1898.

B.S. Rowntree, *Poverty: A Study of Town Life*, York: Policy Press Edition, 2000.

J. St. Loe Strachey, *The Adventure of Living: A Subjective Autobiography*, London: Hodder and Stoughton, 1922.

W.L. Sargant, *Essays of a Birmingham Manufacturer*, Vol. 4, London: Williams and Norgate, 1872.

J.R. Seeley, *The Expansion of England*, Basingstoke: Macmillan, 1883.

B.S. Seibold, *Emily Hobhouse and the Reports on the Concentration Camps during the Boer War, 1899–1902*, Stuttgart: Ibidem-Verlag, 2011.

R.C. Self (ed.), *The Austen Chamberlain Diary Letters*, Cambridge: Royal Historical Society, 1995.

V. Solomon (ed.), *Selections from the Correspondence of Percy Alport Molteno 1892–1914*, Cape Town: The Van Riebeeck Society, 1981.

E.C.M. Stewart and E. Satterthwaite, *Cornish Granite: Extracts from the Writings and Speeches of Lord Courtney of Penwith*, London: L. Parsons, 1925.

M.T. Steyn, *'n Bittereinder aan die Woord, Geskrifte en Toesprake van Marthinus Theunis Steyn*, M.C.E. van Schoor (ed.), Bloemfontein: Oorlogsmuseum van die Boererepublieke, 1997.

R.C. Temple (ed.), *Rt. Hon. Sir Richard Temple, Letters & Character Sketches from the House of Commons*, London: John Murray, 1912.

B. Webb, *My Apprenticeship*, Harmondsworth: Penguin, 1938.

Secondary Sources

Biographies

R.L.Q. Adams, *Balfour: The Last Grandee*, London: John Murray, 2007.

B. Alderson, *Arthur James Balfour: The Man and His Work*, London: G. Richards, 1903.

E. Alexander, 3rd Viscount Chilston, *Chief Whip: The Political Life and Times of Aretas Akers-Douglas 1st Viscount Chilston*, London: Routledge and Kegan Paul, 1961.

J. Amery, *The Life of Joseph Chamberlain*, vols 4–6, London: Macmillan, 1951–69.

W.H.G. Armytage, *A.J. Mundella, 1825–97: The Liberal Background to the Labour Movement*, London: Benn, 1951.

Lord Askwith, *Lord James of Hereford*, London: Ernest Benn, 1930.

A.J. Balfour, *Chapters of Autobiography*, ed. by B.E.C. Dugdale, London: Cassell, 1930.

J.H. Balme, *To Love One's Enemies: The Life and Work of Emily Hobhouse*, Cobble Hill, Canada: Hobhouse Trust.

M. Bassett, *Sir Joseph Ward: A Political Biography*, Auckland: Auckland University Press, 1993.

T. Brooking, *Richard Seddon, King of God's Own: The Life and Times of New Zealand's Longest Serving Prime Minister*, Auckland: Penguin, 2014.

H. Browne, *Joseph Chamberlain: Radical and Imperialist*, London: Longman, 1974.

H. Cadbury, *Charles M. Alexander, A Romance of Song and Soul Winning*, London: Marshall Bros, c.1921.

G. Cecil, *Life of Robert, Marquis of Salisbury Vol. III, 1880–1886*, London: Hodder and Stoughton, 1931.

R.S. Churchill, *Winston S. Churchill, Volume II*, London: Heinemann, 1969.

W.S. Churchill, *Great Contemporaries*, London: Thomas Butterworth, 1937.

R.A. Cosgrove, *The Rule of Law: Alfred Venn Dicey, Victorian Jurist*, Basingstoke: Macmillan, 1980.

T.L. Crosby, *Joseph Chamberlain: A Most Radical Imperialist*, London: I.B. Tauris, 2011.

A.W.W. Dale, *Life of R.W. Dale of Birmingham*, London: Hodder and Stoughton, 1898.

W.A. Dalley, *The Life Story of W.J. Davis, J.P.*, Birmingham Printers, 1914.

D. Dilks, *Neville Chamberlain Vol. I, 1869–1929*, Cambridge University Press, 2002.

J. Dixon, *Out of Birmingham: George Dixon (1820–98), 'Father of Free Education'*, Studley: Brewin, 2013.

W.H. Dunn, *James Anthony Froude: A Biography, 1818–1894 Vol. 2*, Oxford: Clarendon, 1963.

D. Dutton, *Austen Chamberlain: Gentleman in Politics*, Bolton: Ross Anderson, 1985.

A.R.D. Elliot, *The Life of Lord Goschen*, 2 vols, London: Longman, 1911.

F.V. Engelenburg, *General Louis Botha*, London: George G. Harrap & Co., 1929.

E. Fitzmaurice, *The Life of Granville George Leveson Gower, Second Earl Granville, 1815–1891*, 2 vols, London: Longmans, Green & Co., 1905.

T.H. Ford, *Alfred Venn Dicey: The Man and his Times*, Chichester: Barry Rose, 1985.

R.F. Foster, *Lord Randolph Churchill: A Political Life*, Oxford University Press, 1981.

H. Furniss, *Some Victorian Men*, London: Jon Lane, 1924.

P. Fraser, *Joseph Chamberlain: Radicalism and Empire, 1868–1914*, London: Cassell, 1966.

A.G. Gardiner, *The Life of Sir William Harcourt*, New York: G.H. Doran, 1914.

J.L. Garvin, *The Life of Joseph Chamberlain Vols 1–3*, Basingstoke: Macmillan, 1932–34.

D. Gilmour, *Lord Curzon*, Cambridge University Press, 1994.

G.P. Gooch, *Life of Lord Courtney*, Basingstoke: Macmillan, 1920.

A. Grant Duff (ed.), *The Life-Work of Lord Avebury (Sir John Lubbock), 1834–1901*, 2 vols, London: Watts & Co., 1924.

E.H.H. Green, *Balfour*, London: Haus, 2006.

R. Grinter, *Joseph Chamberlain: Democrat, Unionist and Imperialist*, London: Arnold, 1971.

S. Gwynn and G. Tuckwell, *The Life of the Rt. Hon. Charles Dilke, MP*, 2 vols, London: John Murray, 1917.

W.K. Hancock, *Smuts, The Sanguine Years 1870–1919*, Cambridge University Press, 1962.

B. Holland, *Life of Spencer Compton, 8th Duke of Devonshire*, 2 vols, London: Longman, 1911.

C.W. Hill, *An Illustrated Life of Joseph Chamberlain, 1836–1914*, Aylesbury: Shire, 1973.

H.G. Hutchinson, *Life of Sir John Lubbock, Lord Avebury*, 2 vols, Basingstoke: Macmillan, 1914.

P. Jackson, *The Last of the Whigs: A Political Biography of Lord Hartington*, London: Associated University Presses, 1994.

P. Jackson, *Harcourt and Son*, Madison, NJ: Fairleigh Dickinson University Press, 2004.

R. Jay, *Joseph Chamberlain: A Political Study*, Oxford: Clarendon, 1981.

R. Jenkins, *Gladstone*, Basingstoke: Macmillan, 1995.

D. Judd, *Radical Joe*, London: Hamilton, 1977.

S. Lee, *Queen Victoria: A Biography*, London: Smith, Elder & Co., 1904.
A. Mackintosh *Joseph Chamberlain, An Honest Biography*, 2nd ed., London: Hodder and Stoughton, 1914.
A. Mackintosh, *The Story of Mr Chamberlain's Life*, London: Hodder and Stoughton, 1914.
P. Magnus, *Gladstone, A Biography*, London: John Murray, 1954.
P. Marsh, *Joseph Chamberlain: Entrepreneur in Politics*, London: Yale, 1994.
H.C.G. Matthew, *Gladstone, 1875–1898*, Oxford: Clarendon Press, 1995.
W.F. Monypenny and G.E. Buckle, *The Life of Benjamin Disraeli, Earl of Beaconsfield Vol. 6*, London: John Murray, 1920.
J. Morley, *Life of W.E. Gladstone Vols 2 & 3*, Basingstoke: Macmillan, 1911.
J. Newton, *W.S. Caine, M.P.*, London: James Nisbet & Co., 1907.
M. Patton, *Science, Politics and Business in the Work of Sir John Lubbock: A Man of Universal Mind*, Farnham: Ashgate, 2007.
H. Paul, *The Life of Froude*, London: Pitman, 1905.
J.E. Powell, *Joseph Chamberlain*, London: Thames and Hudson, 1977.
A. Roberts, *Salisbury: Victorian Titan*, London: Weidenfeld and Nicholson, 1999.
R. Self, *Neville Chamberlain: A Biography*, London: Ashgate, 2007.
R. Shannon, *Gladstone Vol. 2: Heroic Minister, 1865–98*, Harmondsworth: Penguin, 2000.
A. Sidgwick and E.M. Sidgwick, *Henry Sidgwick: A Memoir*, London: Macmillan, 1906.
T.J. Spinner, *George Joachim Goschen: The Transformation of a Victorian Liberal*, Cambridge University Press, 1973.
D. Steele, *Lord Salisbury: A Political Biography*, University College London Press, 1999.
A. Strachey, *St. Loe Strachey: His Life and His Paper*, London: Gollancz, 1930.
J. Tann, *Joseph's Dream: Joseph Chamberlain and Birmingham's Improvement*, University of Birmingham, 1978.
A.L. Thorold, *The Life of Henry Labouchere*, London: G.P. Putnam, 1913.
L.E. van Niekerk, *Kruger se Regterhand, 'n Biografie van dr W.J. Leyds*, Pretoria: J.L. van Schaik, 1985.
M.C.E. van Schoor, *Christiaan Rudolph de Wet, Krygsman en volksman*, Pretoria: Protea Boekhuis, 2007.
B. Williams, *Cecil Rhodes*, New York: Greenwood Press, 1968.
J. Wilson, *C.B.: A Life of Sir Henry Campbell-Bannerman*, London: Constable, 1973.
D. Wormell, *Sir John Robert Seeley and the Uses of History*, Cambridge University Press, 1980.
J.E. Wrench, *Alfred Lord Milner: The Man of No Illusions, 1854–1925*, London: Eyre & Spotiswood, 1958.

Edited Collections

S. Ball and I. Holliday (eds), *Mass Conservatism: The Conservatives and the Public since the 1880s*, London: Frank Cass, 2002.
E.F. Biagini and A.J. Reid (eds), *Currents of Radicalism: Popular Radicalism, Organised Labour and Party Politics in Britain, 1850–1914*, Cambridge University Press, 1991.
R. Blake and H. Cecil (eds), *Salisbury: The Man and His Policies*, Basingstoke: Macmillan, 1987.

R. Colls and P. Dodd (eds), *Englishness: Politics and Culture, 1880–1920*, London: Routledge, 1986.

M.E. Daly and K.T. Hoppen (eds), *Gladstone: Ireland and Beyond*, Dublin: Four Courts Press, 2011.

T.M. Devine and G. Jackson (eds), *Glasgow Vol. 1: Beginnings to 1830*, Manchester University Press, 1995.

M. Francis and I. Zweiniger-Bargielowska (eds), *The Conservatives and British Society, 1880–1990*, Cardiff: University of Wales Press, 1996.

W.H. Fraser and I. Maver (eds), *Glasgow vol. 2: 1830–1912*, Manchester University Press, 1996.

P. Ghosh and L. Goldman (eds), *Politics and Culture in Victorian Britain: Essays in Memory of Colin Matthew*, Oxford University Press, 2006.

L. Goldman (ed.), *The Blind Victorian: Henry Fawcett and British Liberalism*, Cambridge University Press, 1989.

E.H.H. Green and D.M. Tanner (eds), *The Strange Survival of Liberal England: Political Leaders, Moral Values and the Reception of Economic Debate*, Cambridge University Press, 2007.

D. Hamer, (ed.), *The Webbs in New Zealand*, Wellington: Price Milburn for University of Victoria Press, 1974.

C. Holmes (ed.), *Immigrants and Minorities in British Society*, London: Allen and Unwin, 1978.

J.M. Lawrence and M. Taylor (eds), *Party, State and Society: Electoral Behaviour in Britain since 1820*, Aldershot: Scholar Press, 1997.

P. Mandler (ed.), *Liberty and Authority in Victorian Britain*, Oxford University Press, 2006.

M. McCormack (ed.), *Public Men: Masculinity and Politics in Modern Britain*, Basingstoke: Palgrave Macmillan, 2007.

A. Milner, J.A. Spender, Sir H. Lucy, J.R. Macdonald, H. Cox and L.S. Amery (eds), *Life of Joseph Chamberlain*, London: Associated Newspapers, 1914.

T.G. Otte (ed.), *The Makers of British Foreign Policy: From Pitt to Thatcher*, Basingstoke and New York: Palgrave, 2002.

T.G. Otte and P. Readman (eds), *By-Elections in British Politics, 1832–1914*, Oxford: Boydell Press, 2013.

A. Seldon and S. Ball (eds), *Conservative Century: The Conservative Party since 1900*, Oxford University Press, 1994.

J. Vernon (ed.), *Re-reading the Constitution: New Narratives in the Political History of England's Long Nineteenth Century*, Cambridge University Press, 1996.

R. Windscheffel, R. Swift and R. Quinault (eds), *William Gladstone: New Studies and Perspectives*, Aldershot: Ashgate, 2012.

Monographs

F. Adams, *History of the Elementary School Contest in England*, London: Chapman and Hall, 1882.

R.D. Altick, *Punch: The Lively Youth of a British Institution, 1841–1856*, Columbus: Ohio State University Press, 1997.

S. Anderson, *Race and Rapprochement: Anglo-Saxonism and Anglo–American Relations, 1895–1904*, London and Toronto: Fairleigh Dickinson University Press, 1981.

P. Bailey, *Popular Culture and Performance in the Victorian City*, Cambridge University Press, 1998.

M. Balfour, *Britain and Joseph Chamberlain*, London: Allen and Unwin, 1985.

P. Ballard, *'Rus in urbe': Joseph Chamberlain's Gardens at Highbury, Moor Green, Birmingham, 1876–1914*, Birmingham Museum and Art Gallery, 1987.

M. Barker, *Gladstone and Radicalism: The Reconstruction of Liberal Policy in Britain, 1885–94*, Hassocks: Harvester, 1975.

G.J. Barnsby, *Socialism in Birmingham and the Black Country, 1850–1939*, Wolverhampton: Integrated Publishing Services, 1998.

D.W. Bebbington, *The Nonconformist Conscience: Chapel and Politics, 1870–1914*, London: Harper Collins, 1982.

J. Belich, *Paradise Reforged: A History of the New Zealanders from the 1880s to the Year 2000*, Auckland: Penguin, 2001.

D. Bell, *The Idea of Greater Britain: Empire and the Future of the World Order, 1860–1900*, New York: Princeton University Press, 2007.

P.M.H. Bell, *Disestablishment in Ireland and Wales* London: SPCK, 1969.

M. Bentley, *Politics without Democracy, 1815–1914*, 2nd edn, Oxford: Blackwell, 1996.

M. Bentley, *Lord Salisbury's World: Conservative Environments in Late Victorian Britain*, Cambridge University Press, 2001.

E.F. Biagini, *Liberty, Retrenchment and Reform: Popular Liberalism in the Age of Gladstone, 1860–1880*, Cambridge University Press, 1992.

E.F. Biagini, *British Democracy and Irish Nationalism 1876–1906*, Cambridge University Press, 2007.

C.A. Bodelsen, *Studies in Mid-Victorian Imperialism*, Copenhagen and London: Gyldendalske, 1924.

D.G. Boyce, *The Irish Question and British Politics 1868–1986*, 2nd edn, Basingstoke: Palgrave Macmillan, 1996.

A. Briggs, *Press and Public in Early Nineteenth-Century Birmingham*, Oxford: Dugdale Society, 1949.

A. Briggs, *The Age of Improvement, 1783–1867*, London: Longman, 1959.

A. Briggs, *Victorian Cities*, London: Penguin, 1965.

M. Brodie, *The Politics of the Poor: The East End of London, 1885–1914*, Oxford University Press, 2004.

T. Brooking, *Lands for the People? The Highland Clearances and the Colonisation of New Zealand. A Biography of John McKenzie*, Dunedin: University of Otago Press, 1996.

J.T. Bunce, *History of the Corporation of Birmingham Vol. II*, Birmingham: Cornish Brothers, 1885.

M. Burgess, *The British Tradition of Federalism*, Leicester University Press, 1990.

P. Burke, *Eyewitnessing: The Use of Images as Historical Evidence*, London: Reaktion, 2001.

C. Burness, *'Strange Associations': The Irish Question and the Making of Scottish Unionism, 1886–1918*, East Linton: Tuckwell Press, 2003.

J. Butler, *The Liberal Party and the Jameson Raid*, Oxford: Clarendon, 1968.

F. Cammarano, *'To Save England from Decline': The National Party of Common Sense: British Conservatism and the Challenge of Democracy (1885–1892)*, Lanham: University Press of America, 2001.

D. Cannadine, *The Decline and Fall of the British Aristocracy*, Basingstoke: Macmillan, 1992.

D. Cannadine, *Class in Britain*, London: Yale, 1998.

I. Cawood, *The Liberal Unionist Party: A History*, London, I.B. Tauris, 2012.

R. Colls, *Identity of England*, Oxford University Press, 2002.

M. Conboy, *The Language of Newspapers: Socio-historical Perspectives*, London: Continuum, 2010.

A.B. Cooke and J. Vincent, *The Governing Passion: Cabinet Government and Party Politics in Britain 1885–6*, Hassocks: Harvester, 1974.

J. Crawford W.E. Ellis, *To Fight for the Empire: An Illustrated History of New Zealand and the South African War, 1899–1902*, Auckland: Reed/Historical Branch of the Department of Internal Affairs, 1999.

L.P. Curtis, *Coercion and Conciliation in Ireland 1880–1892: A Study in Conservative Unionism*, Princeton University Press, 1963.

R. Dalziel, *Origins of New Zealand Diplomacy: The Agent-General in London, 1870–1905*, Wellington: Victoria University Press/Price Milburn, 1975.

J. Darwin, *The Empire Project: The Rise and Fall of the British World System, 1830–1970*, Cambridge University Press, 2009.

T.R.H. Davenport, *The Afrikaner Bond, The History of a South African Political Party, 1880–1911*, Oxford University Press, 1966.

R. Dennis, *English Industrial Cities of the Nineteenth Century: A Social Geography*, University of Cambridge Press, 1986.

E. Ellis, *Teachers for South Africa: New Zealand Women and the South African War Concentration Camps*, Paekakariki: Hanorah Press, 2010.

H.V. Emy, *Liberals, Radicals and Social Politics, 1892–1914*, Cambridge University Press, 1973.

D. Englander, *Landlord and Tenant in Urban Britain 1838–1918*, Oxford University Press, 1983.

N. Ferguson, *The House of Rothschild, Vol. 2: The World's Banker, 1849–1999*, London: Viking, 1999.

M. Fforde, *Conservatism and Collectivism, 1886–1914*, Edinburgh University Press, 1990.

S. Fielding, *Class and Ethnicity: Irish Catholics in England, 1880–1939*, Buckingham: Open University Press, 1993.

B. Forster, *A Conjunction of Interests: Business, Politics and Tariffs, 1825–1879*, University of Toronto Press, 1986.

H. Fraser, S. Green and J. Johnston, *Gender and the Victorian Periodical*, Cambridge University Press, 2003.

J.A. Garrard, *Democratisation in Britain: Elites, Civil Society and Reform since 1800*, Basingstoke: Macmillan, 2002.

H. Giliomee, *The Afrikaners: Biography of a People*, Cape Town: Tafelberg, 2003.

E.H.H. Green, *The Crisis of Conservatism: The Politics, Economics and Ideology of British Conservatism, 1880–1914*, London: Routledge, 1995.

B. Griffin, *The Politics of Gender in Victorian Britain: Masculinity, Political Culture and the Struggle for Women's Rights*, Cambridge University Press, 2012.

S.Gunn, *The Public Culture of the Victorian Middle Class: Ritual and Authority in the English Industrial City, 1840–1914*, Manchester University Press, 2000.

R.F. Haggard, *The Persistence of Victorian Liberalism*, London: Greenwood Press, 2001.

D.A. Hamer, *Liberal Politics in the Age of Gladstone and Rosebery: A Study in Leadership and Policy*, Oxford: Clarendon Press, 1972.

D. Hamer, *The New Zealand Liberals: The Years of Power, 1891–1912*, Auckland University Press, 1988.

M. Hampton, *Visions of the Press in Britain, 1850–1950*, Chicago: University of Illinois Press, 2004.

H.J. Hanham, *Elections and Party Management: Politics in the Time of Disraeli and Gladstone*, London: Longman, 1959.

B. Harrison, *Drink and the Victorians: The Temperance Question in England, 1815–1872*, London: Faber, 1972.

J. Hart, *Proportional Representation: Critics of the British Electoral System, 1820–1945*, Oxford: Clarendon, 1992.

M. Hart, *A Trading Nation*, Vancouver: University of British Columbia Press, 2002.

R. Hattersley, *The Edwardians*, London: Little, Brown, 2004.

A. Hawkins, *British Party Politics, 1852–1886*, Basingstoke: Macmillan, 1998.

E.P. Hennock, *Fit and Proper Persons: Ideal and Reality in Nineteenth-Century Urban Government*, London: Edward Arnold, 1973.

R.V. Holt, *The Unitarian Contribution to Social Progress in England*, London: Allen and Unwin, 1938.

M.C. Hurst, *Joseph Chamberlain and West Midlands Politics, 1886–1895*, Dugdale Society Occasional Papers 15, Oxford: Printed for the Dugdale Society by V. Ridler, 1962.

M.C. Hurst, *Joseph Chamberlain and Liberal Reunion: The Round Table Conference of 1887*, Newton Abbot: David & Charles, 1970.

K.S. Inglis, *Churches and the Working Classes in Victorian England*, London: Routledge and Kegan Paul, 1963.

A. Jackson, *Home Rule: A History, 1800–2000*, Oxford University Press, 2003.

A. Jackson, *Ireland 1798–1998: War Peace and Beyond*, 2nd edn, Chichester: Wiley-Blackwell, 2010.

K. Jackson, *George Newnes and the New Journalism in Britain, 1880–1910: Culture and Profit*, Aldershot: Ashgate, 2001.

E. Jaggard, *Cornwall Politics in the Age of Reform*, Woodbridge: Boydell Press, 1999.

P. Jalland, *The Liberals and Ireland: The Ulster Question in British Politics to 1914*, Brighton: Harvester, 1980.

T.A. Jenkins, *Gladstone, Whiggery and the Liberal Party, 1874–1886*, Oxford University Press, 1988.

P. Joyce, *Visions of the People: Industrial England and the Question of Class, 1840–1914*, Cambridge University Press, 1991.

P. Joyce, *Democratic Subjects: The Self and the Social in Nineteenth Century England*, Cambridge University Press, 1994.

P. Joyce, *The Rule of Freedom: Liberalism and the Modern City*, London: Verso, 2003.

J.C.G. Kemp, *Vir Vryheid en vir Reg*, Cape Town: Nasionale Pers, 1941.

J.C.G. Kemp, *Die Pad van die Veroweraar*, Cape Town: Nasionale Pers, 1942.

G. Kitson Clark, *The Making of Victorian Britain*, London: Methuen, 1962.

S.E. Koss, *Nonconformity in Modern British Politics*, London: Batsford, 1975.

S E. Koss, *The Rise and Fall of the Political Press in Britain, Vol. 1: The Nineteenth Century*, London: Hamish Hamilton, 1981.

S.E. Koss, *The Rise and Fall of the Political Press in Britain Vol. 2: The Twentieth Century*, London: Hamish Hamilton, 1984.

R.V. Kubicek, *The Administration of Imperialism: Joseph Chamberlain at the Colonial Office*, Durham, NC: Duke University Press, 1969.

A.S. Langley, *Birmingham Baptists Past and Present*, London: Kingsgate Press, 1939.

J.M. Lawrence, *Speaking for the People: Party, Language and Popular Politics in England, 1867–1914*, Cambridge University Press, 1998.

P. Leary, *The Punch Brotherhood: Table Talk and Print Culture in Mid-Victorian London*, London: British Library, 2010.

J. Loughlin, *Gladstone, Home Rule and the Ulster Question, 1882–1893*, Dublin: Gill and Macmillan, 1986.

W.C. Lubenow, *Parliamentary Politics and the Home Rule Crisis: The British House of Commons in 1886*, Oxford: Clarendon Press, 1988.

P. Lynch, *The Liberal Party in Rural England, 1885–1910: Radicalism and Community*, Oxford: Clarendon Press, 2003.

G.I.T. Machin, *Politics and the Churches in Great Britain*, Oxford: Clarendon Press, 1987.

S. Maccoby, *English Radicalism, Vol. 5: 1886–1914*, London: Routledge, 1953.

J.S. Marais, *The Fall of Kruger's Republic*, Oxford University Press, 1961.

P. Marsh, *The Discipline of Popular Government: Lord Salisbury's Domestic Statecraft 1881–1902*, Hassocks: Harvester, 1978.

R. McWilliam, *Popular Politics in Nineteenth Century England*, London: Routledge, 1998.

J.S. Meisel, *Public Speech and the Culture of Public Life in the Age of Gladstone*, New York: Columbia University Press, 2001.

J. Money, *Experience and Identity: Birmingham and the West Midlands, 1760–1800*, Manchester University Press, 1977.

J.R. Moore, *The Transformation of Urban Liberalism: Party Politics and Urban Governance in Late Nineteenth Century England*, Aldershot: Ashgate, 2006.

L. Nead, *Victorian Babylon: People Streets and Images in Nineteenth Century London*, New Haven: Yale University Press, 2000.

A. O'Day, *Parnell and the First Home Rule Episode, 1884–1887*, Dublin: Gill & Macmillan, 1986.

R. O'Day and D. Englander, *Mr Charles Booth's Inquiry: Life and Labour of the People in London Reconsidered*, London: Continuum, 1993.

T.G. Otte, *The China Question: Great Power Rivalry and British Isolation, 1894–1905*, Oxford University Press, 2007.

A. Panebianco, *Political Parties: Their Organisation and Activity in the Modern State*, Cambridge University Press, 1988.

J.P. Parry, *The Rise and Fall of Liberal Government in Victorian Britain*, New Haven and London: Yale, 1993.

J.P. Parry, *The Politics of Patriotism: English Liberalism, National Identity and Europe, 1830–1886*, Cambridge University Press, 2006.

A. Peel, *These Hundred Years: A History of the Congregational Union of England and Wales 1831–1931*, London: Congregational Union of England and Wales, 1931.

H. Pelling, *Origins of the Labour Party 1880–1900*, Oxford University Press, 1966.

H. Pelling, *Popular Politics and Society in late Victorian Britain*, London: St Martin's Press, 1968.

H. Pelling, *Social Geography of British Elections, 1885–1910*, new edn, Aldershot: Gregg Revivals, 1994.

C. Petrie, *The Chamberlain Tradition*, London: Right Book Club, 1938.

J. Phillips, *A Man's Country? The Image of the Pakeha Male – A History*, Auckland: Penguin, 1987.

J. Phillips and T. Hearn, *Settlers: New Zealand Immigrants from England, Ireland and Scotland 1800–1945*, Auckland Univeristy Press, 2008.

A.N. Porter, *The origins of the South Africa War: Joseph Chamberlain and the Diplomacy of Imperialism*, Manchester University Press, 1980.

B. Porter, *The Absent-Minded Imperialists: Empire, Society and Culture in Britain*, Oxford University Press, 2004.

F. Pretorius, *Die Anglo–Boereoorlog 1899–1902*, Cape Town: Struik Uitgewers, 1998.

R. Price, *An Imperial War and the British Working Class: Working Class Attitudes and Reactions to the Boer War, 1899–1902*, London: Routledge and Kegan Paul, 1972.

M. Pugh, *The Making of Modern British Politics*, 3rd edn, Oxford: Blackwell, 2002.

M. Pugh, *The Tories and the People*, Oxford: Blackwell, 1985.

B.A. Ramsbottom, *The History of the Gospel Standard Magazine*, 2nd edn, Harpenden: Gospel Standard Trust, 2010.

J. Ramsden, *An Appetite for Power: A History of the Conservative Party since 1830*, London: Harper Collins, 1998.

P. Readman, *Land and Nation in England: Patriotism, National Identity and the Politics of Land*, London, RHS, 2008.

R.A. Rempel, *Unionists Divided: Arthur Balfour, Joseph Chamberlain and the Unionist Free Traders*, Newton Abbot: David and Charles, 1972.

M. Roberts, *Political Movements in Urban England 1832–1914*, London: Palgrave Macmillan, 2009.

G. Robson, *Dark Satanic Mills? Religion and Irreligion in Birmingham and the Black Country*, Carlisle: Paternoster Press, 2002.

A.B. Rodrick, *Self-Help and Civic Culture: Citizenship in Victorian Birmingham*, Aldershot: Ashgate, 2004.

A. Rogers, *While You're Away: New Zealand Nurses at War*, Auckland University Press, 2003.

A.K. Russell, *Liberal Landslide: The General Election of 1906*, Newton Abbot: David and Charles, 1973.

G.D. Scholtz, *Die Ontwikkeling van die Politieke Denke van die Afrikaner, Deel V, 1899–1910*, Johannesburg: Perskor-Uitgewery, 1978.

B. Schrader, *We Call It Home: A History of State Housing in New Zealand*, Auckland: Reed, 2005.

G.R. Searle, *The Quest for National Efficiency: A Study in British Politics and Politics Thought, 1899–1914*, Oxford: Basil Blackwell, 1971.

G.R. Searle, *The Liberal Party: Triumph and Disintegration, 1886–1929*, Basingstoke: Macmillan, 1992.

G.R. Searle, *Country before Party: Coalition and the Idea of 'National Government' in Modern Britain, 1885–1987*, London: Longman, 1995.

G.R. Searle, *A New England? Peace and War 1886–1918*, Oxford: Clarendon Press, 2004.

B. Semmel, *Imperialism and Social Reform: English Social-Political Thought, 1895–1914*, London: Allen & Unwin, 1960.

R. Shannon, *Gladstone and the Bulgarian Agitation 1876*, Hassocks: Harvester, 1975.

R. Shannon, *The Age of Salisbury, 1881–1902: Unionism and Empire*, London: Longman, 1996.

K. Sinclair, *Imperial Federation: A Study of New Zealand Policy and Opinion, 1880–1914*, London: Athlone Press, 1955.

K. Sinclair, *A Destiny Apart: New Zealand's Search for National Identity*, Wellington: Allen and Unwin/Port Nicholson Press, 1986.

D.C. Somervell, *British Politics since 1900*, London: Andrew Dakers, 1950.

D. Southgate, *The Passing of the Whigs, 1832–1886*, Basingstoke: Macmillan, 1962.

A. Sykes, *Tariff Reform in British Politics, 1903–1913*, Oxford University Press, 1979.

D. Tanner, *Political Change and the Labour Party 1900–1918*, Cambridge University Press, 1990.

C.C. Tansill, *Canadian–American Relations, 1875–1911*, New Haven, CT: Yale University Press, 1943.

A.S. Thompson, *Imperial Britain: The Empire in British Politics, c. 1880–1932*, London: Longman, 2000.

F.M.L. Thompson, *The Rise of Respectable Society*, London: Fontana, 1988.

J. Thompson, *British Political Culture and the Idea of 'Public Opinion' 1867–1914*, Cambridge University Press, 2013.

J.L. Thompson, *A Wider Patriotism: Alfred Milner and the British Empire*, London: Pickering and Chatto, 2007.

J. Tosh, *Manliness and Masculinities in Nineteenth Century Britain*, London: Pearson, 2005.

F. Trentmann, *Free Trade Nation: Commerce, Consumption and Civil Society in Modern Britain*, Oxford University Press, 2008.

B. Turner, *Free Trade and Protection*, London: Longman, 1971.

F.A. van Jaarsveld, *Van Van Riebeck tot P.W. Botha, 'n Inleiding tot die Geskiedenis van die Republiek van Suid-Afrika*, Johannesburg: Perskor, 1982.

M.C.E. van Schoor, *Spotprente van die Anglo-Boereoorlog*, Cape Town: Tafelberg, 1981.

J. Vernon, *Politics and the People: A Study in English Political Culture, c.1815–1867*, Cambridge University Press, 1993.

P. Waller, *Writers, Readers and Reputations*, Oxford University Press, 2006.

R. Ward, *City-state and Nation: Birmingham's Political History, c.1830–1940*, Chichester: Philimore, 2005.

E.S. Wellhofer, *Democracy, Capitalism and Empire in Late Victorian Britain, 1885–1910*, Basingstoke: Macmillan, 1996.

A. West, *Contemporary Portraits*, London: Thomas Nelson and Sons, 1920.

J. Whitcut, *Edgbaston High School, 1876–1976*, Warwick: Roundwood Press, 1976.

J.H. Wiener, *The Americanisation of the British Press, 1830s–1914: Speed in the Age of Transatlantic Journalism*, Basingstoke: Macmillan, 2012.

P. Williamson, *Stanley Baldwin: Conservative Leadership and National Values*, Cambridge University Press, 1998.

A. Windscheffel, *Popular Conservatism in Imperial London 1868–1906*, London: RHS, 2007.

Articles

J. Aitken, 'Never Before, Yet Never Again: Birmingham in the 1851 Religious Census', *Birmingham Historian*, 22 (2002), pp. 24–9.

D.W. Bebbington, 'Nonconformity and Electoral Sociology 1867–1918', *Historical Journal*, 27 (1984), pp. 633–56.

M. Bentley, 'Victorian Politics and the Linguistic Turn: Historiographical Review', *Historical Journal*, 42 (1999), pp. 894–902.

H. Berrington, 'Partisanship and Dissidence in the Nineteenth Century House of Commons', *Parliamentary Affairs*, 21 (1968), pp. 338–74.

L. Blaxhill, 'Electioneering, the Third Reform Act and Political Change', *Parliamentary History*, 30.3 (2011), pp. 343–73.

N. Blewett, 'Free Fooders, Balfourites, Whole Hoggers: Factionalism within the Unionist Party, 1906–1910', *Historical Journal*, 11 (1968), pp. 95–124.

L. Brake, '"Time's Turbulence": Mapping Journalism Networks', *Victorian Periodicals Review*, 44.2 (2011), pp. 115–27.

T. Brooking, '"Playing 'em like a Piana": Richard John Seddon and the Mastery of Public Performance', *Journal of New Zealand Studies*, 15 (2013), pp. 50–62.

E.A. Cameron, '"A far cry to London": Joseph Chamberlain in Inverness, September 1885', *Innes Review*, 57.1 (2006), pp. 36–53.

I. Cawood, 'The Unionist "Compact" in West Midland Politics, 1891–1895', *Midland History*, 30 (2005), pp. 92–111.

I. Cawood, 'Joseph Chamberlain, the Conservative Party and the Leamington Spa Candidature Dispute of 1895', *Historical Research*, 79.206 (2006), pp. 554–77.

I. Cawood, 'The 1892 General Election and the Eclipse of the Liberal Unionists', *Parliamentary History*, 29.3 (October, 2010), pp. 331–357.

A. Clark, 'The Rhetoric of Chartist Domesticity: Gender, Language, and Class in the 1830s and 1840s', *Journal of British Studies*, 31.1 (1992), pp. 62–88.

S. Collini, 'The Idea of "Character" in Victorian Political Thought', *Transactions of the Royal Historical Society*, 5th ser., 35 (1985), pp. 29–50.

J. Cornford, 'The Transformation of Conservatism in the Late Nineteenth Century', *Victorian Studies*, 7 (1963), pp. 35–77.

P. Davis, 'The Liberal Unionist Party and the Irish Policy of Lord Salisbury's Government, 1886–1992', *Historical Journal*, 18 (1975), pp. 85–104.

M. Dawson, 'Liberalism in Devon and Cornwall, 1910–1931: "the old time religion"', *Historical Journal*, 38 (1995), pp. 425–37.

M. Dawson, 'Party Politics and the Provincial Press in Early Twentieth Century England: The Case of the South-West', *Twentieth Century British History*, 9 (1998), pp. 201–18.

M. Diamond, 'Political Heroes of the Victorian Music Hall', *History Today*, 40.1 (1990), pp. 33–9.

B. Doyle, 'A Crisis of Urban Conservatism? Politics and Organisation in Edwardian Norwich', *Parliamentary History*, 31.3 (2012), pp. 396–418.

J.P.D. Dunbabin, 'British Elections in the Nineteenth and Twentieth Centuries: A Regional Approach', *English Historical Review*, 375 (1980), pp. 241–67.

R.E. Dumett, 'Joseph Chamberlain, Imperial Finance and Railway Policy in British West Africa in the Late Nineteenth Century', *English Historical Review*, 355 (1975), pp. 287–321.

A. Ellegard, 'The Readership of the Periodical Press in Mid-Victorian Britain', *Victorian Periodicals Newsletter*, 3 (1971), pp. 3–22.

J.D. Fair, 'From Liberal to Conservative: The Flight of the Liberal Unionists after 1886', *Victorian Studies*, 29 (1986), pp. 291–314.

D. Fraser, 'Joseph Chamberlain's Municipal Ideal', *History Today*, 37.4 (1987), pp. 33–9.

P. Fraser, 'The Liberal Unionist Alliance: Chamberlain, Hartington and the Conservatives, 1886–1904', *English Historical Review*, 77 (1962), pp. 53–78.

I. Gazeley and A. Newell, 'Poverty in Edwardian Britain', *Economic History Review*, 64.1 (2011), pp. 52–71.

G.D. Goodlad, 'The Liberal Party and Gladstone's Land Purchase Bill of 1886', *Historical Journal*, 32 (1989), pp. 627–41.

G.L. Goodman, 'Liberal Unionism: The Revolt of the Whigs', *Victorian Studies*, 3 (1959), pp. 173–89.

C. Green, 'Birmingham's Politics 1873–1891: The Local Basis of Change', *Midland History*, 2 (1973), pp. 84–98.

E.H.H. Green, 'Radical Conservatism: The Electoral Genesis of Tariff Reform', *Historical Journal*, 28.3 (1985), pp. 667–92.

E.H.H. Green, 'The Strange Death of Tory England', *Twentieth Century British History*, 2 (1991), pp. 67–88.

P.C. Griffiths, 'The Caucus and the Liberal Party in 1886', *History*, 61 (1976), pp. 183–97.

L. Hamilton, 'The Importance of Recognizing Oscar: The Dandy and the Culture of Celebrity', *The Center & Clark Newsletter*, 33 (1999), pp. 3–5.

M. Hampton, 'Rethinking the "New Journalism" 1850s–1930s', *Journal of British Studies*, 43 (2004), pp. 278–90.

E. Hopkins, 'Working Class Life in Birmingham between the Wars 1918–1939', *Midland History*, 15 (1990), pp. 129–50.

L.K. Hughes, 'Sideways! Navigating the Material(ity) of Print Culture', *Victorian Periodicals Review*, 47.1 (2014), pp. 1–30.

T.A. Jenkins, 'The Funding of the Liberal Unionist Party and the Honours System', *English Historical Review*, 105 (1990), pp. 920–38.

T.A. Jenkins, 'Hartington, Chamberlain and the Unionist Alliance', *Parliamentary History*, 11 (1992), pp. 108–38.

A.G. Jones, 'The *Dart* and the Damning of the Sylvan Stream: Journalism and Political Culture in the Late-Victorian City', *Victorian Periodicals Review*, 35.1 (2002), pp. 2–17.

S. Koss, 'Wesleyanism and Empire', *Historical Journal*, 18 (1975), pp. 105–18.

J.M. Lawrence, 'Class and Gender in the Making of Urban Toryism, 1880–1914', *English Historical Review*, 108 (1993), pp. 629–52.

J.M. Lawrence, 'The Decline of Popular Politics?', *Parliamentary History*, 13 (1994), pp. 333–7.

J.M. Lawrence, 'The Culture of Elections in Modern Britain', *History*, 96, (2011), pp. 459–76.

D.P. Leighton, 'Municipal Progress, Democracy and Radical Identity in Birmingham, 1838–1886', *Midland History*, 25 (2000), pp. 115–42.

J. Loughlin, 'Joseph Chamberlain, English Nationalism and the Ulster Question', *History*, 77 (1992), pp. 202–19.

W.C. Lubenow, 'Irish Home Rule and the Social Basis of the Great Separation in the Liberal Party in 1886', *Historical Journal*, 28 (1985), pp. 125–42.

G. Martin, 'Empire Federation and Imperial Parliamentary Union, 1820–1870', *Historical Journal*, 15 (1973), pp. 65–93.

H. Miller, 'John Leech and the Shaping of the Victorian Cartoon: The Context of Respectability', *Victorian Periodicals Review*, 42.3 (2009), pp. 267–91.

H. Miller, 'The Problem with *Punch*', *Historical Research*, 82.216 (2009), pp. 285–302.

J.R. Moore, 'Liberal Unionism and the Home Rule Crisis in Leicester, 1885–1892', *Midland History*, 26 (2001), pp. 177–97.

J.R. Moore, 'Manchester Liberalism and the Unionist Secession, 1886–1895', *Manchester Regional History Review*, 15 (2001), pp. 31–40.

T.G. Otte, '"Avenge England's Dishonour": By-elections, Parliament and the Politics of Foreign Policy in 1898', *English Historical Review*, 491 (2006), pp. 385–428.

J.P. Parry, 'Gladstone and the Disintegration of the Liberal Party', *Parliamentary History*, 20 (1991), pp. 392–404.

J.P. Parry, 'The Quest for Leadership in Unionist Politics', *Parliamentary History*, 12 (1993), pp. 296–311.

E. Porritt, 'Party Conditions in England', *Political Science Quarterly*, 21 (1906), pp. 206–36.

M. Pugh, 'Working-class Experience and State Social Welfare, 1908–1914: Old Age Pensions Reconsidered', *Historical Journal*, 45 (2002), pp. 775–96.

P.A. Readman, 'The 1895 General Election and Political Change in Late Victorian England', *Historical Journal*, 42 (1999), pp. 467–93.

P.A. Readman, 'The Conservative Party, Patriotism and British Politics: The Case of the General Election of 1900', *Journal of British Studies*, 40 (2001), pp. 107–45.

B. Reay, 'The Context and Meaning of Popular Literacy: Some Evidence from Nineteenth Century Rural England', *Past and Present*, 131 (1991), pp. 89–129.

M. Roberts, '"Villa Toryism" and Popular Conservatism in Leeds, 1885–1902', *Historical Journal*, 49 (2006), pp. 217–46.

M. Roberts, 'Election Cartoons and Political Communication in Victorian England', *Cultural and Social History*, 10.3 (2013), pp. 369–95.

S. Roberts, 'Politics and the Birmingham Working Class: The General Elections of 1900 and 1906 in East Birmingham', *West Midland Studies*, 15 (1982), pp. 12–21.

R. Scully, 'William Henry Boucher (1837–1906): Illustrator and *Judy* Cartoonist', *Victorian Periodical Review*, 46.4 (2013), pp. 441–74.

A.S. Thompson, 'Tariff Reform: An Imperial Strategy, 1903–1913', *Historical Journal*, 40 (1997), pp. 1033–54.

J. Thompson, '"Pictorial Lies?" – Posters and Politics in Britain c.1880–1914', *Past and Present*, 197 (2007), pp. 177–210.

F. Tillyard, 'The Distribution of the Free Churches in England', *Sociological Review*, 27 (1935), pp. 1–18.

R.C. Trebilcock, 'A "Special Relationship" – Government, Re-armament and the Cordite Firms', *Economic History Review*, 19.2 (1966), pp. 364–79.

P. Vervaecke, 'La "caricature au vinaigre": Francis Carruthers Gould et Joseph Chamberlain, 1895–1907', *Revue Française de Civilisation Britannique*, 16.2 (2011), pp. 27–42.

S.H. Zebel, 'Joseph Chamberlain and the Genesis of Tariff Reform', *Journal of British Studies*, 7.1 (1967), pp. 131–57.

Chapters in Edited Collections

H. Bradford, 'The Defiance of the *Bittereinder* Women', in B. Nasson and A. Grundlingh (eds), *The War at Home, Women and Families in the Anglo–Boer War*, Cape Town: Tafelberg, 2013.

C. Burness, 'The Making of Scottish Unionism', in S. Ball and I. Halliday (eds), *Mass Conservatism: The Conservatives and the Public since the 1880s*, London: Frank Cass, 2002.

I. Cawood, 'The Persistence of Liberal Unionism in Irish Politics, 1886–1912', in G. Doherty (ed.), *The Home Rule Crisis, 1912–1914*, Cork: Mercier Press, 2014, pp. 333–52.

R. Colls, 'Englishness and the Political Culture', in R. Colls and P. Dodd (eds), *Englishness: Politics and Culture, 1880–1920*, London: Routledge, 1986.

J. Cornford, 'The Parliamentary Foundations of the "Hôtel Cecil"', in R. Robins (ed.), *Ideas and Institutions of Victorian Britain: Essays in Honour of George Kitson Clarke*, London: G. Bell and Sons, 1967.

J. Cornford, 'Aggregate Election Data and British Party Alignments, 1885–1910', in E. Allardt and S. Rokkan (eds), *Mass Politics: Studies in Political Sociology*, New York: Free Press, 1970.

M. Crouzet, 'Joseph Chamberlain', in P. Renouvin (ed.), *Les Politiques d'Expansion Impérialiste*, Paris: Presses Universitaires de France, 1949.

H. Cunningham, 'The Conservative Party and Patriotism', in R. Colls and P. Dodd (eds), *Englishness: Politics and Culture, 1880–1920*, London: Routledge, 1986.

J. Dunbabin, 'Electoral Reforms and Their Outcome 1865–1914', in T. Gourvish and A. O'Day (eds), *Later Victorian Britain, 1867–1900*, Basingstoke: Palgrave Macmillan, 1988.

E. Ellis, 'New Zealand Women and the War', in J. Crawford and I. McGibbon (eds), *One Flag, One Queen, One Tongue: New Zealand, the British Empire and the South African War, 1899–1902*, Auckland University Press, 2003.

J. France, 'Salisbury and the Unionist Alliance', in R. Blake and H. Cecil (eds), *Salisbury: The Man and His Policies*, Basingstoke: Macmillan, 1987.

H. Giliomee, 'Afrikaner Nationalism, 1875–1899', in F. Pretorius (ed.), *A History of South Africa, from the Distant Past to the Present Day*, Pretoria: Protea Book House, 2014.

M. Harper, '"Everything is English": Expectations, Experiences and Impacts of English Migrants to New Zealand, 1840–1970', in L. Fraser and A. McCarthy (eds), *Far from 'Home': The English in New Zealand*, Dunedin: University of Otago Press, 2012.

M. Huggins, 'Cartoons and Comic Periodicals, 1841–1901: A Satirical Sociology of Victorian Sporting Life', in M. Huggins and J.A. Mangan (eds), *Disreputable Pleasures: Less Virtuous Victorians at Play*, London: Frank Cass, 2004.

E. Jacobs, 'Disvaluing the Popular: London Street Culture, "Industrial Literacy" and the Emergence of Mass Culture in Victorian England', in D.N. Mancoff and D.J. Trela (eds), *Victorian Urban Settings: Essays on the Nineteenth Century and Its Contexts*, London: Routledge, 2011.

G.H. Kenrick, 'George Dixon: A Lecture', in J.H. Muirhead (ed.), *Nine Famous Birmingham Men*, Birmingham: Cornish Brothers, 1909.

J.M. Lawrence, 'Popular Politics and the Limitations of Party: Wolverhampton, 1867–1900', in E.F. Biagini and A.J. Reid (eds), *Currents of Radicalism*, Cambridge University Press, 1991.

J.M. Lawrence, 'The Dynamic of Urban Politics, 1867–1914', in J.M .Lawrence and M. Taylor (eds), *Party, State and Society: Electoral Behaviour in Britain since 1920*, Aldershot: Scholar Press, 1997.

H. McLeod, 'Class, Community and Region: The Religious Geography of Nineteenth Century England', in M. Hill (ed), *A Sociological Yearbook of Religion in Britain 6*, London: SCM Canterbury Press, 1973.

P.T. Marsh, 'Chamberlain's Separation from the Gladstonian Liberals, 1885–6', in B.L. Kinzer (ed.), *The Gladstonian Turn of Mind, Essays Presented to J.B. Conacher*, University of Toronto Press, 1985.

P.T. Marsh, '"A Working Man's Representative": Joseph Chamberlain and the 1874 Election in Sheffield', in J.M.W. Bean (ed.), *The Political Culture of Modern Britain: Studies in Memory of Stephen Koss*, London: Hamilton, 1987.

C. McGeorge, 'The Social and Geographical Composition of New Zealand Contingents', in J. Crawford and I. McGibbon (eds), *One Flag, One Queen, One Tongue: New Zealand, the British Empire and the South African War, 1899–1902*, Auckland University Press, 2003.

W. Mock, 'The Function of "Race" in Imperialist Ideologies: The Example of Joseph Chamberlain', in P.M. Kennedy and A.J. Nicholls (eds), *Nationalist and Racialist Movements in Britain and Germany before the First World War*, London: Macmillan, 1981.

K.O. Morgan, 'The Liberal Unionists in Wales', in K.O. Morgan (ed.), *Modern Wales: Politics, Places and People*, Cardiff: University of Wales Press, 1995.

T.G. Otte, '"The Swing of the Pendulum at Home": By-elections and Foreign Policy, 1865–1914', in T.G. Otte and P. Readman (eds), *By-elections in British Politics, 1832–1914*, Woodbridge: Boydell and Brewer, 2013.

T.G. Otte, '"We are part of the community of Europe": The Tories, Empire and Foreign Policy, 1874–1914', in J. Black (ed.), *The Tory World: Deep History and the Tory Theme in British Foreign Policy, 1679–2014*, Farnham: Ashgate, 2015.

R. Peacock, 'The 1892 Birmingham Religious Census', in A. Bryman (ed.), *Religion in the Birmingham Area: Essays in the Sociology of Religion*, University of Birmingham Institute for the Study of Worship and Religious Architecture, 1975.

R. Quinault, 'Joseph Chamberlain: A Re-assessment', in T.R. Gourvish and A. O' Day (eds), *Later Victorian Britain 1867–1900*, London: Macmillan, 1988.

S.B. Spies, 'Chamberlain, Joseph', in D.W. Krüger and C.J. Beyers (eds), *Suid-Afrikaanse Biografiese Woordeboek*, Part III, Cape Town: Tafelberg Publishers for the Human Sciences Research, 1977.

J.D. Startt, 'Good Journalism in the Era of New Journalism: The British Press 1902–1914', in J.H. Wiener (ed.), *Papers for the Millions: The New Journalism in Britain, 1850s to 1914*, Westport: Greenwood Press, 1988.

D.M. Thompson, 'R.W. Dale and the "Civic Gospel"', in A. Sell (ed.), *Protestant Nonconformists and the West Midlands of England*, Keele University Press, 1986.

F. Trentmann, 'National Identity and Consumer Politics: Free Trade and Tariff Reform', in D. Winch and P. O'Brien (eds), *The Political Economy of British Historical Experience 1688–1914*, Oxford University Press, 2002.

M. Wolff and C. Fox, 'Pictures from the Magazines', in H.J. Dyos and M. Wolff (eds), *The Victorian City: Images and Realities*, vol. 2, London: Routledge and Kegan Paul, 1973.

Unpublished Theses

J.P. Gehrke, 'Municipal Anti-Socialism and the Growth of the Anti-socialist Critique in Britain, 1873–1914', PhD thesis, University of Minnesota, 2005.

N.S. Johnson, 'The Role of the Cabinet in the Making of Foreign Policy, 1885–1895', DPhil thesis, Oxford, 1970.

P.M.B. Schutte, 'Die verhouding tussen Boer en Brit in Transvaal, 1902–1910', MA dissertation, University of Pretoria, 1979.

D.F. Summers, 'The Labour Church and Allied Movements of the Late Nineteenth and Early Twentieth Centuries', PhD thesis, University of Edinburgh, 1958.

A.F. Taylor, 'The History of the Birmingham School Board, 1870–1903', MA dissertation, University of Birmingham, 1955.

Index

Macaulay, Thomas Babington   74
Mackenzie, Tom   83
Mackintosh, Alexander   229, 241
Mafeking   61
Magnus, Philip   97, 109
Magpie, the   178
Mahdist War (1881–99)   25
Majuba Hill, battle of (1881)   49
Manchester   3, 159–60, 177–8, 221
Manchester Education Aid Society   158
Manchester Guardian, the   130
Manchurian crisis (1901)   38
Mann, Horace   215
Mansfield College, Oxford   220
Maori   71, 73, 77, 78
Marais, J.S.   57
Marsh, Peter   52, 97, 109, 131, 137, 140, 154, 231, 233, 235
Martineau, Clara   224–5
Martineau, Ernest   224–5
Martineau family   viii, 223–4
Massey, William Ferguson   85
Masterman, Charles   142–3
McIver, Lewis   127
McKenzie, John   72
McLeod, Hugh   215
Medical Mission   217
Melbourne   117
Merchant Shipping Bill (1882)   9, 100
Merriman, John   53, 56, 58, 63
Methodism   69, 117, 119, 124, 215–18, 221, 224
Methodist New Connection   217
Methodist Times, the   220
Middlesborough   135–6
Midland Parliamentary, the   178
Mildmay, Francis Bingham   127
Mile End   141–2, 144–5
Miller, Henry   184
Milner, Alfred   11, 54, 56–60, 62–3, 125
Molteno, John   53
Molteno, John Tenannt   54
Molteno, Percy   54, 56–7
Monthly Argus and Public Censor, the   179–81, 205, 207
Moody, Dwight   219
Moonshine   177, 197
Moore Bayley, J.   184

Morley, John   106, 108–9, 120, 125, 194
Mormon Church   217
Morning Leader, the   199–200
Mount Zion Baptist Church, Birmingham   212
Mountford, E.C.   178, 188–9
Mundella, Anthony   162, 166
Mundy, Fred   184
Municipal Reform Association   189
Muntz, Philip   160, 162, 185
'Murphy Riots' (1867–68)   156, 158, 173, 218–19
Murphy, William   173, 218–19

Natal   51
National Brotherhood Conference   219
National Council of the Evangelical Free Churches, see Free Church Council
National Education League   ix, 4, 98, 153, 156–62, 171, 173, 213
National Education Union   173
National Liberal Federation   ix, 12, 99, 166, 234, 238
National Review, the   122
National Schools   214
National Scouts   60–2
National Society of Amalgamated Brassworkers   167
Nead, Lynda   195
Nelson Evening Mail, the   76
Nettlefold, John Sutton   3
Nettlefold, Joseph   3
Nettlefold and Chamberlain   3–5, 8
Nettlefold family   3, 223–4
New South Wales   74, 78, 84
New Street, Birmingham   203
New Vagabond Club   80–1
New Zealand   67–95, 156–7, 174
New Zealand Observer, the   76–7
New Zealand Press Association   78
New Zealand Times, the   77
Newcastle   132
Newell, Andrew   136
Newnes, George   200
Newnham College, Cambridge   170
Nonconformist Unionist Association   119